STUDY GUIDE

for

Aaron Jackson

Bentley University

Edward Gamber

Lafayette College

David Hakes

University of Northern Iowa

PEARSON

Boston Columbus Indianapolis New York San Francisco Upper Saddle River
Amsterdam Cape Town Dubai London Madrid Milan Munich Paris Montreal Toronto
Delhi Mexico City Sao Paulo Sydney Hong Kong Seoul Singapore Taipei Tokyo

Acquisitions Editor: Noel Kamm Seibert
Editorial Project Manager: Carolyn Terbush
Senior Production Project Manager: Kathryn Dinovo
Senior Manufacturing Buyer: Carol Melville

10 9 8 7 6 5 4 3 2 1

www.pearsonhighered.com

ISBN-10:   0-13-276942-5
ISBN-13: 978-0-13-276942-6

CONTENTS

Below are the 10th edition chapter numbers, with renumbered 3rd edition chapter numbers in parenthesis where applicable:

HOW TO USE THIS STUDY GUIDE

This *Study Guide* will help you learn the concepts in *The Economics of Money, Banking, and Financial Markets*. As you work your way through each chapter, you will actively review the important definitions, details of financial institutions, and economic principles from your textbook. You will also actively apply the economic models to graphical and numerical problems. This reinforcement of the important textbook ideas will allow you to more quickly master the concepts and will better prepare you for exams.

Each chapter corresponds with your textbook and contains the following learning tools.

- **Chapter Review:** Each chapter begins with a summary of the chapter. The chapter review is divided into sections based on the section headings provided in the text.

- **Helpful Hints:** This section provides some additional suggestions and examples to help clarify the more difficult material.

- **Terms and Definitions:** Students match key terms from the text to their definitions. This section is particularly important because a working economic and financial vocabulary is necessary in order for the student to advance through the material.

- **Problems and Short-Answer Questions:** We provide a number of multi-step problems that require numerical, graphical, or written solutions. The problems are based on the larger issues developed in the chapter. Smaller issues are addressed with approximately ten short-answer questions.

- **Critical Thinking:** This section provides a single multi-step problem that is an application of one of the major issues developed in the chapter.

- **Self-Test:** The self-test section provides fifteen true/false and twenty multiple-choice questions to validate areas of successful learning and to highlight areas needing improvement.

- **Solutions:** Detailed solutions for all problems and questions are provided at the end of each chapter.

You should experiment with different ways to use this *Study Guide* to better help you learn. Most students should work through each section of the *Study Guide* in order. However, if you feel very comfortable with the text material, then you might want to proceed directly to the Self-Test section. If you are happy with your performance, then you can begin the next chapter.

Note: This *Study Guide* includes material for both the 10th edition of *The Economics of Money, Banking, and Financial Markets* and the unique chapters of the 3rd edition of *The Economics of Money, Banking, and Financial Markets, Business School Edition*. The 10th edition material is provided first, followed by the material for the unique chapters of the 3rd edition. For those chapters that are common between the two volumes, we provide both applicable chapter numbers for reference.

1 Why Study Money, Banking, and Financial Markets?*

Chapter Review

PREVIEW

The study of money, banking, and financial markets is of value because it provides answers to everyday financial questions such as: How will an increase in interest rates affect my purchase of a new car or my decision to save for retirement? This chapter establishes the importance of learning about money, banking, and financial markets. Events in the financial markets will have direct effects on your financial well-being. Financial institutions in the economy have an impact on how efficiently funds are moved from savers to borrowers. Money and monetary policy influence inflation, interest rates, and national output.

WHY STUDY FINANCIAL MARKETS?

Financial markets allow funds to move from people with an excess of funds to those with a shortage. In the bond market, firms borrow by issuing securities (claims on the issuer's income or assets) called bonds. Bonds require the issuer to make periodic payments to the purchaser. These payments are known as interest. The interest rate is the cost of borrowing expressed as a percent per year. The interest rate is determined in the bond market. Since different interest rates tend to move together, economists often simply refer to "the" interest rate. In the stock market, firms issue securities called common stock. Stock represents a share of ownership of the company.

---

*This is also Chapter 1 in the 3rd ed.

WHY STUDY FINANCIAL INSTITUTIONS AND BANKING?

Financial institutions are necessary in order for financial markets to function efficiently. Financial intermediaries borrow from one group and lend to another. Banks are financial intermediaries that accept deposits and make loans. Financial crises are major disruptions in financial markets characterized by sharp declines in asset prices and the failure of many firms. Other related financial institutions are insurance companies, mutual funds, finance companies, and investment banks. Banks are still the largest group of financial intermediaries, but the other financial institutions are growing in importance. Financial innovation, such as the delivery of financial services electronically (known as e-finance), can make financial markets more efficient but can also sometimes lead to financial disasters.

WHY STUDY MONEY AND MONETARY POLICY?

Money, or the money supply, is defined as anything that is generally accepted in payment for goods and services or the repayment of debt. Changes in the money supply have an impact on many economic variables. Money affects the business cycle, the upward and downward movements in aggregate output. Output is usually measured by GDP. Reductions in the growth rate of the money supply have preceded almost every period of declining output, known as recessions, since the beginning of the twentieth century. Not every reduction in the money supply, however, is followed by a recession. The unemployment rate usually rises during recessions. The money supply also has an effect on the price level and the inflation rate. There is a positive relationship between inflation and the growth rate of the money supply. Generally, high growth rates of the money supply are associated with high interest rates on long-term bonds, and low growth rates of the money supply with low long-term bond rates, but this relationship is too complex to address here. Monetary policy is the management of money and interest rates. Monetary policy is conducted by a country's central bank, which in the United States is known as the Federal Reserve System (or the Fed for short). Fiscal deficits may result in a financial crisis, an increase in the growth rate of the money supply, a higher rate of inflation, and higher interest rates.

WHY STUDY INTERNATIONAL FINANCE?

Financial markets have become increasingly integrated throughout the world. In the foreign exchange market, currencies of one country are exchanged for currencies of another. The price of one country's currency in terms of another's is known as the foreign exchange rate, and can significantly affect the flows of goods, services, and capital across countries.

HOW WE WILL STUDY MONEY, BANKING, AND FINANCIAL MARKETS

This textbook stresses the economic way of thinking by developing a unifying framework for the study of money, banking, and financial markets. The text emphasizes the following basic concepts:

- A simplified approach to the demand for assets

- The concept of equilibrium

- Basic supply and demand to explain behavior in financial markets

- The search for profits

- An approach to financial structure based on transaction costs and asymmetric information

- Aggregate supply and demand analysis

This text focuses on tools rather than simple facts, so your knowledge will not become obsolete. The analytical framework focuses on changes in one variable at a time, holding all other variables constant.

Helpful Hints

1. Be prepared to rely on the model of supply and demand. This text, along with most economics texts, uses the model of supply and demand where applicable to illuminate the workings of the market. If you have forgotten the basics of supply and demand analysis, it might be to your advantage to improve your understanding of the model by reading the supply and demand chapter in the introduction of any principles of economics text.

2. Throughout the text, when dealing with supply and demand in the financial markets, always identify each side of the market as either the borrow or the lender of the funds. For example, in the bond market, the supplier of the bond is the borrower, and the demander of the bond is the lender. Then, after you have solved the analytical problem at hand, you can ask yourself, does this result make sense in term of the borrowers and lenders?

3. Aggregate income and aggregate output are considered equal because the purchase of final goods and services (output) generates an equivalent value of payments to the factors of production that produced the output (income).

4. The term "business cycle" mistakenly suggests that the movements in output are smooth and predictable. In reality, business cycles are irregular, unpredictable, and of varying duration. For this reason, business cycles are sometimes referred to as "economic fluctuations," which highlights their unpredictable nature.

Terms and Definitions

Choose a definition for each key term.

Key Terms:

_____ aggregate output
_____ aggregate price level
_____ asset
_____ banks
_____ bond
_____ budget deficit
_____ budget surplus
_____ business cycles
_____ central bank
_____ common stock
_____ e-finance

_____ Federal Reserve System (the Fed)
_____ financial crises
_____ financial innovation
_____ financial intermediaries
_____ financial markets
_____ fiscal policy
_____ foreign exchange market
_____ foreign exchange rate
_____ gross domestic product
_____ inflation

_____ inflation rate
_____ interest rate
_____ monetary policy
_____ monetary theory
_____ money (money supply)
_____ recession
_____ security
_____ stock
_____ unemployment rate

Definitions:

1. the market in which one currency is exchanged for another
2. a debt security that promises to make periodic payments for a specified period of time.
3. the upward and downward movements of aggregate output in the economy
4. a claim on the borrower's future income that is sold by the borrower to the lender
5. the management of the money supply and interest rates
6. institutions that borrow from people who have saved and then lend to others
7. the percentage of the labor force not working
8. the total production of final goods and services in the economy
9. the U.S. central bank responsible for monetary policy
10. an excess of government expenditure over tax revenues
11. the condition of a continuously rising price level
12. a security that is a claim on the earnings and assets of a company
13. the rate of change of the price level
14. markets in which funds are transferred from people who have a surplus of funds to those who have a shortage of funds.
15. the average price of goods and services in an economy

16. anything that is generally accepted in payment for goods and services or in the repayment of debt
17. the cost of borrowing or the price paid for the rental of funds expressed as a percent per year
18. the price of one currency in terms of another
19. the market value of all final goods and services produced within a country over a year
20. any financial claim or piece of property subject to ownership
21. the theory that relates monetary policy to changes in economic activity and inflation
22. major disruptions in financial markets characterized by sharp declines in asset prices or failure of many financial firms
23. making decisions on government spending and taxation
24. periods of declining aggregate output
25. financial institutions that accept deposits and make loans
26. delivery of financial products electronically
27. organization that conducts a nation's monetary policy
28. when tax revenues exceed government expenditures
29. the development of new financial products and services
30. a share of ownership of a corporation

Problems and Short-Answer Questions

PRACTICE PROBLEMS

1. Suppose you are the Chief Financial Officer (CFO) of a large corporation. For each of the following situations, which of the following financial markets would your company use: the bond market, the stock market, or the foreign exchange market? Explain.
    a. Your company has $100 million that it would like to use to construct a factory in Germany.

        _____

        _____

    b. Your company wishes to borrow $100 million to construct a factory in the United States.

        _____

        _____

    c. Your company wishes to raise $100 million to construct a factory by selling additional shares of ownership in the company. That is, your company wishes to take on new partners.

        _____

        _____

2. Suppose that you are the head of the central bank of the United States.
    a. What is the name of the organization that you direct?

        _____

        _____

    b. Suppose the United States is experiencing a high rate of inflation. Is the money supply likely to be growing slowly or quickly? Explain.

        _____

        _____

    c. If you wished to reduce the rate of inflation, what would you do to the growth rate of the money supply? Explain.

        _____

        _____

d. What is the likely effect of your anti-inflationary monetary policy on aggregate output and unemployment? Explain.

_____

_____

_____

SHORT-ANSWER QUESTIONS

1. Suppose that Ford Motor Company imports very little steel from foreign countries but exports a great number of cars to foreigners. Would Ford prefer that the dollar be strong on the foreign exchange markets (the dollar buys much foreign currency) or weak? Explain.

_____

_____

2. Suppose that you are going to travel in Europe for the summer after you graduate from college. Would you prefer that the dollar be strong on the foreign exchange markets or weak? Explain.

_____

_____

3. In which of the following markets is the interest rate determined—the bond market, stock market, or the foreign exchange market?

_____

4. Look at the graph in Chapter 1 of your text that shows the exchange rate of the U.S. dollar since 1970. During which year would you think that exporters would have had the greatest difficulty selling their goods overseas? Why?

_____

_____

5. What are financial intermediaries? Why is a bank considered a financial intermediary? Why do you think an insurance company is also considered a financial intermediary?

_____

_____

_____

_____

6. In addition to commercial banks, what other institutions are considered to be banks?

_____

_____

7. Suppose that the economy is in a recession. Just prior to the recession, what likely happened to the growth rate of money? In what direction is aggregate output likely to be moving? Unemployment? Inflation? Long–term bond interest rates?

_____

_____

_____

8. Monetary policy is the management of which two monetary variables? What institution is responsible for monetary policy in the United States?

_____

_____

Critical Thinking

You are watching a business news report on television with your roommate. The news reporter states that the Fed is raising interest rates and reducing the growth rate of the money supply in order to reduce the risk of future inflation. Your roommate says, "We need to take a bigger course load next semester and graduate early, because there is always a recession following a reduction in the growth rate of money. If we wait too long, it will be much harder to find a job."

1. Is it true that a recession always follows a reduction in the growth rate of the money supply? Explain.

_____

_____

2. If there is a recession, will it be more difficult to find a job when you graduate? Explain.

_____

_____

3. If the Fed reduces the growth rate of money, what will likely happen to the inflation rate? Explain.

_____

_____

Self-Test

TRUE/FALSE QUESTIONS

_____1. The interest rate is determined in the stock market.

_____2. An increase in the value of the dollar relative to foreign currency (a strong dollar) means that foreign goods have become less expensive to U.S. residents, and U.S. goods have become more expensive to foreigners.

_____3. Insurance companies are financial intermediaries because they borrow from their depositors and loan those funds to others.

_____4. A financial intermediary is an institution that borrows from people who have saved and then loans those funds to others.

_____5. Banks are the largest financial intermediaries in the U.S. economy.

_____6. Since different interest rates tend to move together, economists often refer to "the" interest rate.

_____7. An increase in the growth rate of money has preceded every recession in the United States since the beginning of the twentieth century.

_____8. A recession is a sudden expansion in Gross Domestic Product.

_____9. An increase in the growth rate of the money supply is associated with an increase in the rate of inflation.

_____10. Monetary policy is the management of fiscal deficits and surpluses.

MULTIPLE-CHOICE QUESTIONS

1. The foreign exchange market is where
    a. the interest rate is determined.
    b. the price of one country's currency in terms of another's is determined.
    c. the inflation rate is determined.
    d. bonds are sold.

2. Stock prices, as measured by the Dow Jones Industrial Average,
   a. have not changed much over time.
   b. have risen smoothly over time.
   c. have been extremely volatile over time.
   d. have declined substantially since they peeked in the mid 1980s.

3. Which of the following is an example of a debt security that promises to make payments periodically for a specified period of time?
   a. bond
   b. stock
   c. financial intermediary
   d. foreign exchange

4. Which of the following is likely to occur if the stock market has been rising quickly?
   a. Consumers are willing to spend more on goods and services.
   b. Firms will increase their investment spending on new equipment.
   c. Firms will sell newly issued stock to raise funds for investment spending.
   d. all of the above

5. If the dollar becomes weaker on the foreign exchange market (the value of the dollar falls relative to the value of foreign currency), which of the following is true?
   a. A trip to Europe is going to be less expensive in terms of dollars.
   b. Ford will export more cars to Mexico.
   c. A BMW automobile produced in Germany will cost less to import into the United States.
   d. U.S. citizens will import more goods and services from abroad.

6. When a firm issues stock, it
   a. has borrowed from the public.
   b. has taken on additional partners that own part of the assets of the firm and share in the firm's earnings.
   c. has purchased foreign currency.
   d. has agreed to make periodic payments for a specific period of time to the owner of the security.

7. Which of the following is an example of financial intermediation?
   a. A saver makes a deposit in a credit union, and the credit union makes a loan to a member for a new car.
   b. IBM issues a bond that is sold to a retired person.
   c. IBM issues common stock that is sold to a college student.
   d. All of the above are examples of financial intermediation.

8. Which of the following are the largest financial intermediaries in the U.S. economy?
   a. insurance companies
   b. finance companies
   c. banks
   d. mutual funds

9. The term "bank" generally includes all of the following institutions except
   a. commercial banks.
   b. credit unions.
   c. savings and loan associations.
   d. finance companies.

10. A decrease in the growth rate of the money supply is most likely to be associated with
    a. a decrease in both aggregate output and the inflation rate.
    b. an increase in both aggregate output and the inflation rate.
    c. a decrease in aggregate output and an increase in the inflation rate.
    d. an increase in aggregate output and a decrease in the inflation rate.

11. If inflation is higher in Canada than in the United States, it is likely that
    a. aggregate output is larger in Canada than in the United States.
    b. the Canadian money supply is growing faster than in the U.S. money supply.
    c. the United States has a larger fiscal deficit.
    d. the United States has higher interest rates.
    e. all of the above are true.

12. Monetary policy is the management of
    a. budget surpluses and deficits.
    b. government spending and taxation.
    c. the money supply and interest rates.
    d. unemployment and aggregate output.

13. Fiscal policy involves decisions about
    a. the money supply and interest rates.
    b. unemployment and inflation.
    c. government spending and taxation.
    d. central banking and the Federal Reserve System.

14. Low growth rates in the money supply are most likely to be associated with
    a. a high rate of inflation and high long-term bond rates.
    b. a high rate of inflation and low long-term bond rates.
    c. a low rate of inflation and high long-term bond rates.
    d. a low rate of inflation and low long-term bond rates.

15. An increase in the growth rate of the money supply is most likely to be followed by
    a. a low point in the business cycle.
    b. a recession.
    c. a reduction in inflation.
    d. an increase in inflation.

Solutions

Terms and Definitions

_8_	aggregate output
_15_	aggregate price level
_20_	asset
_25_	banks
_2_	bond
_10_	budget deficit
_28_	budget surplus
_3_	business cycles
_27_	central bank
_30_	common stock
_26_	e-finance
_9_	Federal Reserve System (the Fed)
_22_	financial crises
_29_	financial innovation
_6_	financial intermediaries
_14_	financial markets
_23_	fiscal policy
_1_	foreign exchange market
_18_	foreign exchange rate
_19_	gross domestic product
_11_	inflation
_13_	inflation rate
_17_	interest rate
_5_	monetary policy
_21_	monetary theory
_16_	money (money supply)
_24_	recession
_4_	security
_12_	stock
_7_	unemployment rate

Practice Problems

1. a. The foreign exchange market, because that is where dollars can be exchanged for euros.
   b. The bond market, because that is where firms sell debt securities, known as bonds, to borrow large sums of money for capital construction.
   c. The stock market, because that is where firms sell ownership shares of the company, known as common stock.
2. a. Federal Reserve System
   b. Quickly, because the growth rate of the money supply and the rate of inflation have a positive association.
   c. Reduce the growth rate of the money supply, because a lower growth rate of the money supply is associated with a lower inflation rate.
   d. Often, but not always, a reduction in the growth rate of money is leads to a reduction in aggregate output (recession) and a corresponding increase in the unemployment rate.

Short-Answer Questions

1. Ford would like a weak dollar (the dollar buys less foreign currency or foreign currency buys more dollars). This makes Fords appear cheap to foreigners, and they buy more.
2. You would like a strong dollar (the dollar buys a large amount of foreign currency). This makes your European trip cost less in terms of dollars.
3. The bond market.
4. Around 1985, because the value of the dollar hit its peak. Thus, U.S. goods were very expensive in terms of foreign currencies.
5. Institutions that borrow from one group and lend to another. Banks accept deposits (borrow from depositors) and lend those funds to loan customers. Insurance companies collect premiums (borrow from their insured customers) and lend those funds to loan customers (usually corporations).
6. Savings and loan associations, mutual savings banks, and credit unions.
7. Money growth decreased, output is decreasing, and it is likely that unemployment is rising, inflation is decreasing, and long-term bond rates are falling.
8. Money and interest rates. Federal Reserve System (or simply the Fed).

Critical Thinking

1. No. It is true that almost all recessions since the beginning of the twentieth century have been preceded by a reduction in the growth rate of money. However, sometimes a reduction in the growth rate of money is not followed by a recession, making recessions hard to predict.

2. Yes. When output falls, unemployment usually rises, making it more difficult to find a job.

3. Inflation will go down in the future because inflation rates and growth rates of the money supply have a positive association.

True/False Questions

1. F
2. T
3. F
4. T
5. T
6. T
7. F
8. F
9. T
10. F

Multiple-Choice Questions

1. b
2. c
3. a
4. d
5. b
6. b
7. a
8. c
9. d
10. a
11. b
12. c
13. c
14. d
15. d

2 An Overview of the Financial System*

Chapter Review

PREVIEW

Financial markets (bond and stock markets) and financial intermediaries (banks, insurance companies, pension funds) move funds from lender-savers to borrower-spenders. Well-functioning financial markets and financial intermediaries are crucial to an economy's health.

FUNCTION OF FINANCIAL MARKETS

Financial markets channel funds from those who have saved to those who wish to spend more than their income. This movement of funds can be accomplished by direct finance, where borrowers borrow directly from lenders by selling lenders securities. Securities are also known as financial instruments. This movement of funds improves efficiency by channeling funds to those with productive uses for the funds from those with no investment opportunities, producing an efficient allocation of capital (wealth that is used to produce more wealth). It also allows consumers to better time their purchases.

STRUCTURE OF FINANCIAL MARKETS

Financial markets can be categorized as debt and equity markets, primary and secondary markets, exchanges and over-the-counter markets, and money and capital markets. In a debt market, the borrower issues a debt instrument in which the borrower agrees to pay interest and principal payments until maturity. Alternatively, in an equity market, firms issue stock, which are claims to share the net income and assets of the firm. The owner may also receive dividends. Primary markets are where new issues of a security are sold, often to investment banks that underwrite

---

*This is also Chapter 2 in the 3rd ed.

the securities. Secondary markets are where existing issues are resold. Secondary markets can be exchanges, where buyers and sellers meet in a central location, or over-the-counter where dealers at different locations have an inventory of securities. The money market is where short-term securities (maturity of less than one year) are traded. The capital market is where longer-term debt and equity instruments are traded.

FINANCIAL MARKET INSTRUMENTS

The main money market instruments are U.S. Treasury bills, negotiable bank certificates of deposit, commercial paper, repurchase agreements, federal funds, and Eurodollars. U.S. Treasury bills are the most liquid instruments because they are most actively traded and have essentially no default risk. Federal funds are loans from one bank to another, usually overnight. The interest rate in this market, the federal funds rate, is important because it is a measure of the stance of monetary policy. The main capital market instruments are stocks, mortgages and mortgage-backed securities, corporate bonds, U.S. government securities, U.S. government agency securities, state and local government bonds (municipal bonds), and consumer and commercial loans. For corporate finance, the value of stocks outstanding exceeds the value of corporate bonds outstanding, but each year the volume of new issues of bonds exceeds the volume of new issues of stock. Interest payments on municipal bonds are exempt from federal income taxation.

INTERNATIONALIZATION OF FINANCIAL MARKETS

Foreign bonds are sold in a foreign country and are denominated in the currency of the country in which the bonds are sold. Eurobonds are bonds denominated in a currency other than the country in which it is sold. Eurodollars are dollar denominated deposits in foreign banks outside the United States or in foreign branches of U.S. banks. Eurodollars are an important source of funds to U.S. banks. Foreign stock markets have also grown in importance.

FUNCTION OF FINANCIAL INTERMEDIARIES: INDIRECT FINANCE

A second route by which funds can move from lenders to borrowers is known as indirect finance because an intermediary is between the lenders and the borrowers. A financial intermediary borrows funds from one group and lends to another in a process known as financial intermediation. Financial intermediaries reduce transactions costs, allow for risk sharing, solve problems caused by adverse selection and moral hazard, and provide economies of scope in the production of information.

- Transaction costs associated with borrowing and lending are reduced because banks exploit economies of scale when writing loan contracts. This gain in efficiency allows intermediaries to provide liquidity services to their customers.

- Risk sharing allows intermediaries to sell assets with less risk than the risk of the assets they purchase, which is known as asset transformation. Risk sharing also allows individuals to diversify their assets.

- Financial transactions suffer from asymmetric information because the borrower knows more about the probability of repayment than the lender. Before the transaction, adverse selection may occur because borrowers most unlikely to repay are most eager to borrow. After the transaction, moral hazard may occur if the borrower engages in immoral behavior by using the loan in a way that reduces the probability of repayment. Financial intermediaries screen out bad credit risks to reduce adverse selection, and monitor borrowers to reduce moral hazard.

- Economies of scope occurs when financial intermediaries can lower the cost of information production for any given service by applying one information resource to many different services, which increases efficiency of financial markets. Economies of scope can also lead to conflicts of interest and increase moral hazard, which reduces the quality of information production and reduces financial market efficiency.

TYPES OF FINANCIAL INTERMEDIARIES

The primary financial intermediaries are:

- *Depository institutions, or banks:* Commercial banks, savings and loan associations, mutual savings banks, and credit unions. The primary liabilities of these institutions are deposits. Their primary assets are mortgages, business and consumer loans, U.S. government securities, and municipal bonds.

- *Contractual savings institutions:* Life insurance companies, fire and casualty insurance companies, and pension funds. The primary liabilities of these institutions are premiums from policyholders or employee/employer contributions. Their primary assets are corporate bonds, municipal bonds, stocks, mortgages, and U.S. government securities.

- *Investment intermediaries:* Finance companies, mutual funds, money market mutual funds, and investment banks. The primary liabilities of these institutions are commercial paper, stocks, bonds, and shares. Their primary assets are consumer and business loans, stocks, bonds, and money market instruments.

REGULATION OF THE FINANCIAL SYSTEM

The government regulates financial markets for two main reasons: to increase the information available to investors and to ensure the soundness of the financial system. To avoid the problems of asymmetric information, the Securities and Exchange Commission (SEC) requires corporations that issue securities to disclose information about their sales, assets, and earnings, and restricts insider trading. To avoid a financial panic that could lead to a collapse of financial intermediaries, the government restricts who can enter into the financial intermediary industry, sets reporting requirements for financial intermediaries, restricts the activities of banks (banks could not be involved in the securities industry—repealed in 1999), and restricts the assets that financial intermediaries can hold (banks in the United States cannot hold common stock, although this is common in other countries). It also provides deposit insurance. In the past, the government has limited competition by limiting branching (which was recently repealed) and by setting the maximum interest rates that could be paid on checking and savings deposits, known as Regulation Q (repealed in 1986).

Helpful Hints

1. A financial instrument, such as a corporate bond, is a liability to the firm that issued it and an asset to the person who buys it. Therefore, if the question is asked, "Is a corporate bond an asset or a liability?" the response must be, "to whom?" That is, the same instrument will appear on different sides of the balance sheet for the issuer and the buyer.

2. When a security is traded in a secondary market, the firm receives no funds. Yet the secondary market is important to the firm because it makes their securities more liquid, making the securities more desirable and raising their price. In addition, the secondary market also sets the price of the security that the issuing firm receives in the primary market should the firm issue additional securities.

3. The problems of asymmetric information affect a loan transaction both before and after the loan is made. *Before* the loan is made, adverse selection may occur because risky borrowers have the greatest incentive to borrow. *After* the loan has been made, moral hazard occurs if borrowers use the borrowed money in a riskier fashion that was agreed to in the loan contract. To avoid this problem, banks screen and monitor borrowers.

Terms and Definitions

Choose a definition for each key term.

Key Terms:

7	adverse selection	3	economies of scale	29	maturity
20	asset transformation	19	economies of scope	1	money market
4	asymmetric information	13	equities	11	moral hazard
31	brokers	23	Eurobond	2	over-the-counter (OTC) market
24	capital	5	Eurodollars		
9	capital market	12	exchanges	21	portfolio
28	conflicts of interest	18	federal funds rate	15	primary market
35	currency	10	financial intermediation	30	risk sharing
33	dealers			17	secondary market
27	default	22	financial panic	26	thrift institutions (thrifts)
8	diversification	16	investment bank		
34	dividends	25	liabilities	14	transaction costs
		32	liquid	6	underwriting

Definitions:

1. a financial market in which only short-term debt instruments are traded

2. a secondary market in which dealers at different locations who have an inventory of securities stand ready to buy and sell securities to anyone who comes to them and is willing to accept their prices

3. the reduction in transaction costs per dollar of transaction as the scale of transactions increases

4. the unequal knowledge that each party to a transaction has about the other party

5. U.S. dollars deposited in foreign banks outside the United States or in foreign branches of U.S. banks

6. guaranteeing prices on securities to corporations and then selling the securities to the public

7. the problem created by asymmetric information before a transaction occurs when the people who are most undesirable from the other party's point of view are the ones who are most likely to want to engage in the financial transaction

8. investing in a portfolio whose returns do not always move together, with the result that overall risk is lower than for individual assets

9. a financial market in which longer-term debt and equity instruments are traded

10. the process of indirect finance whereby financial intermediaries link lender-savers and borrower-spenders

11. the risk that one party to a transaction will engage in behavior that is undesirable from the other party's point of view

12. secondary markets in which buyers and sellers of securities meet in one central location to conduct trades

13. claims to share in the net income and assets of a corporation, such as common stock

14. the time and money spent trying to exchange financial assets, goods, or services

15. a financial market in which new issues of a security are sold to initial buyers

16. firms that assist in the initial sale of securities in the primary market

17. a financial market in which securities that have previously been issued can be resold

18. the interest rate banks charge other banks on overnight loans

19. the ability to use one resource to provide many different products and services

20. turning risky assets into safer assets

21. a collection or group of assets

22. a widespread collapse of financial markets and intermediaries

23. bonds denominated in a currency other than that of the country where they were sold

24. wealth that is used to produce more wealth

25. debts or financial obligations that must be repaid

26. savings and loans, mutual savings banks, and credit unions

27. occurs when an institution is unable to make interest payments or pay off the amount owed on a debt instrument at maturity

28. can arise when a financial institution provides multiple services, leading to misleading or concealing of some information

29. the expiration date of a debt instrument

30. occurs when firms create and sell assets that are less risky and use proceeds to buy riskier assets

31. agents for investors who help match buyers and sellers

32. easily converted into cash

33. those who buy and sell securities at a specified price for buyers and sellers

34. periodic payments made to shareholders

35. paper money or coins

Problems and Short-Answer Questions

PRACTICE PROBLEMS

1. For each of the following financial transactions, determine whether the transaction represents a case of *direct finance* or a case of *indirect finance.*

    a. You deposit $10,000 in your savings account at Wells Fargo Bank, and Mary Smith borrows $10,000 from Wells Fargo Bank to buy a car.

    _____

    b. You purchase stock in IBM through your Merrill Lynch stockbroker.

    _____

    c. You pay your life insurance premiums, and your life insurance company makes a mortgage to a homebuyer.

    ____ _____

    d. You buy shares in a Fidelity mutual fund, and Fidelity buys stock in General Motors.

    _____

    e. You purchase bonds issued by General Electric through your Piper Jaffray broker.

    _____

    f. You borrow $10,000 from your parents to help pay for college tuition.

    _____

    g. You purchase a U.S. government bond in an over-the-counter market.

    _____

    h. You pay $1,000 per month into your pension fund. The pension fund purchases stock in Pearson Addison-Wesley Publishing Company.

    _____

2. For each of the following financial transactions, determine whether the transaction involves debt or equity markets, primary or secondary markets, exchanges or over-the-counter markets, and money or capital markets.

    a. You buy a U.S. Government Treasury Bill that matures in six months from your Morgan Stanley broker.

    _____

    _____

b. You buy stock in Microsoft from your UBS broker.

_____

c. The investment banking division of Edward Jones underwrites Microsoft's new issue of stock.

_____

_____

d. You buy a bond issued by Hewlett Packard that matures in 20 years from your local bond dealer.

_____

_____

e. You buy stock in Ford Motor Company through discount broker Charles Schwab.

_____

3. For each of the following financial intermediaries, identify the primary liabilities (sources of funds) and assets (uses of funds) from the following lists.

Sources of funds (assets): _____

a. commercial paper, stocks, and bonds
b. employer and employee contributions
c. premiums from policies
d. shares
e. deposits

Uses of funds (liabilities): _____

f. mortgages
g. corporate bonds and mortgages
h. stocks, bonds
i. business and consumer loans, mortgages, U.S. government securities, and municipal bonds
j. corporate bonds and stocks
k. consumer loans
l. consumer and business loans

	Sources	Uses
Commercial banks	_e_	_____
Savings and loan associations	_____	_____
Credit unions	_____	_____
Life insurance companies	_____	_____
Pension funds, government retirement funds	_____	_____
Finance companies	_____	_____
Mutual funds	_____	_____

4. The following questions address the soundness of financial intermediaries.
    a. What is a financial panic?

    _____

    _____

    b. What are the six types of regulations the government employs in an attempt to ensure the soundness of our financial intermediaries? Explain.

    _____

    _____

    _____

    _____

    _____

    _____

    c. What regulations have been reduced or repealed. Explain.

    _____

    _____

    _____

    _____

SHORT-ANSWER QUESTIONS

1. Explain the difference between direct and indirect finance.

    _____

    _____

    _____

2. Explain the difference between debt and equity markets, primary and secondary markets, exchanges and over-the-counter markets, and money and capital markets.

   _____

   _____

   _____

   _____

   _____

3. Which money market instrument is considered most liquid? Why? Which capital market instrument has the greatest dollar amount outstanding? On an annual basis, which capital market instrument do firms use most to acquire additional capital funds?

   _____

   _____

4. Other things being the same, which of the following instruments are the least risky to own: short-term bonds, long-term bonds, or equities? Why?

   _____

   _____

   _____

   _____

5. What is the difference between a *foreign bond* and a *Eurobond*? What is the relationship between a Eurobond and European currency known as the euro?

   _____

   _____

   _____

   _____

6. Suppose that after John receives an auto loan from his credit union, he takes the money to a casino and gambles instead of using the money to buy a car. What type of asymmetric information problem have we witnessed: adverse selection or moral hazard? Explain.

   _____

   _____

   _____

7. Name three reasons why a financial intermediary might be able to move funds from lenders to borrowers efficiently?

_____

_____

_____

_____

8. What are the main categories of depository institutions? What is their main source of funds (liabilities)? Which category of depository institution is the largest in terms of assets?

_____

_____

_____

9. What type of investment intermediary sells shares and buys money market instruments? What is the most unusual feature of these funds?

_____

_____

_____

10. Which institutions are subject to Federal Deposit Insurance Corporation (FDIC) regulations, and what is the nature of the regulations?

_____

_____

_____

Critical Thinking

Your grandmother dies and bequeaths to you $10,000. When you receive the check, your best friend accompanies you to the bank in which you plan to deposit the money. Once inside the bank, your friend notices that the rate the bank pays on savings deposits is 3% while the rate the bank charges on auto loans is 9%. Your friend suggests, "Why don't you just stand by the door to the auto loan office and offer the next auto loan customer a loan directly from you? You could charge much more than the 3% you would get on your deposit and cut out the middleman."

1. Explain why it would likely be unprofitable for you to make such a loan.

_____

_____

_____

_____

_____

2. Why is it more likely that the bank is able to make the loan profitably?

_____

_____

_____

_____

Self-Test

TRUE/FALSE QUESTIONS

T   1. Financial markets improve efficiency by channeling funds to those with productive uses for them from those with no investment opportunities.

F   2. When an individual buys a bond issued by General Motors through a Merrill Lynch bond dealer, we have seen a demonstration of indirect finance.

F   3. Securities are liabilities for the person that buys them, but assets for the individual or company that issues them.

T   4. The primary market is where new issues of securities are sold, and the secondary market is where previously issued securities are resold.

F   5. Bonds are sold in the equity market while stocks are sold in the debt market.

F   6. Stocks are a less risky investment for savers than bonds because stockholders are residual claimants.

F   7. Commercial paper is considered to be the most liquid money market instrument.

T   8. Eurodollars are dollar denominated deposits in foreign banks that are outside the United States or in foreign branches of U.S. banks.

___ 9. Individuals may find it efficient to save their funds in a financial intermediary because financial intermediaries have lower transactions costs when making loans due to economies of scale in making loans.

___ 10. Moral hazard occurs when risky individuals who are least likely to repay their loans and therefore have the most to gain from getting the loan are the ones that tend to actively seek loans.

___ 11. Asymmetric information in financial markets exists because borrowers know more about the true likelihood of the repayment of the loan than do lenders.

___ 12. More funds flow to corporations through the corporate bond market than through financial intermediaries.

___ 13. Life insurance companies are the largest financial intermediaries in the United States when measured by the size of their assets.

___ 14. Mutual funds sell shares and use the funds to buy diversified portfolios of stocks and bonds.

___ 15. To increase information available to investors and to insure the soundness of the financial system, the government heavily regulates the financial system.

MULTIPLE-CHOICE QUESTIONS

1. Which of the following would be considered direct finance?
   a. You pay life insurance premiums to Franklin Life, and Franklin Life makes a mortgage to a homebuyer.
   b. You buy a bond issued by General Electric through a broker at Smith Barney.
   c. You deposit $100,000 in First National Bank, and First National Bank lends $100,000 to Ace Hardware.
   d. None of the above would be considered direct finance.

2. Which of the following statements regarding direct finance is true?
   a. Direct finance occurs when borrowers sell securities directly to lenders.
   b. Direct finance requires the use of financial intermediaries.
   c. In the United States, more funds flow through the direct financial channels than through indirect financial channels.
   d. Securities are assets for the firm that issues them and liabilities for the individual that buys them.

3. Which of the following is true regarding primary and secondary markets?
   a. Primary markets are for stocks while secondary markets are for bonds.
   b. Primary markets are for long-term securities while secondary markets are for short-term securities.
   c. Primary markets are where new issues of securities are sold while secondary markets are where previously issued securities are resold.
   d. Primary markets are exchanges while secondary markets are over-the-counter.

4. Investment banks facilitate the sale of securities in the
    a. over-the-counter market.
    b. stock exchange.
    c. secondary market.
    d. primary market.

5. Which of the following is an example of a money market instrument?
    a. a mortgage
    b. a share of stock in IBM
    c. a John Deere bond with 20 years to maturity
    d. U.S. government treasury bill with six months to maturity

6. Which of the following is likely to generate the least risk to the purchaser?
    a. a 30-year mortgage
    b. a share of stock in IBM
    c. a short-term bond
    d. a long-term bond

7. Which of the following is true regarding the characteristics of debt and equity?
    a. Equity holders are residual claimants.
    b. Bond holders receive dividends.
    c. Equity securities are considered short term.
    d. A bond is an asset to the firm that issues it.

8. When a bond denominated in dollars is sold in Great Britain, it is known as
    a. a foreign bond.
    b. a Eurobond.
    c. Eurodollars.
    d. foreign exchange.

9. Financial intermediaries
    a. reduce transactions costs for lender-savers and borrower-spenders.
    b. allow for risk sharing for the lender-savers.
    c. solve some of the problems caused by asymmetric information.
    d. achieve all of the above.

10. Which of the following is an example of indirect finance?
    a. You pay life insurance premiums to Franklin Life, and Franklin Life issues a mortgage loan to a homebuyer.
    b. You buy a bond issued by General Electric through a broker at Smith Barney.
    c. You buy stock in Microsoft through a local OTC dealer.
    d. None of the above would be considered indirect finance.

11. In a given year, corporations raise the greatest amount of funds through which of the following instruments?
    a. corporate stocks
    b. commercial paper
    c. corporate bonds
    d. repurchase agreements

12. Before a loan is made, banks screen their prospective loan customers to avoid the problem of
    a. risk sharing.
    b. adverse selection.
    c. moral hazard.
    d. asset transformation.

13. Rick Smith just received an auto loan for $5,000. After he received the loan, he decided to gamble with the money at a nearby casino instead of buying a car. This is an example of
    a. diversification.
    b. asset transformation.
    c. adverse selection.
    d. moral hazard.

14. When a financial intermediary such as a bank borrows from one person and lends to another, we have observed a demonstration of
    a. indirect finance.
    b. direct finance.
    c. foreign finance.
    d. investment banking.

15. When lenders have inferior knowledge relative to borrowers about the potential returns and risks associated with an investment project, it gives rise to the problem known as
    a. financial intermediation.
    b. transaction costs.
    c. asset transformation.
    d. asymmetric information.

16. Which of the following is a depository institution?
    a. pension fund
    b. life insurance company
    c. credit union
    d. finance company

17. Which of the following institutions holds mortgages as their primary asset?
    a. banks
    b. savings and loan associations
    c. money market mutual funds
    d. credit unions

18. Mutual funds
    a. collect deposits and lend for mortgages.
    b. are organized around some common link, usually employment.
    c. sell shares and use the proceeds to buy diversified portfolios of stocks and bonds.
    d. receive premiums from policies and purchase corporate bonds and stock.

19. Which of the following regulatory agencies protects depositors from bank failures by guaranteeing repayment of deposits up to $250,000 per depositor at a bank?
    a. Securities and Exchange Commission (SEC)
    b. Federal Reserve System
    c. Office of Thrift Supervision
    d. Federal Deposit Insurance Corporation (FDIC)

20. Prior to 1986, Regulation Q gave the Federal Reserve the power to
    a. limit competition between banks by placing a ceiling on the interest rates banks could pay on savings deposits.
    b. limit competition between banks by restricting interstate branching.
    c. increase competition among banks by expanding entry into the banking industry.
    d. increase competition among banks by imposing stringent reporting requirement for disclosure of information to the public.

Solutions

Terms and Definitions

 7 adverse selection
20 asset transformation
 4 asymmetric information
31 brokers
24 capital
 9 capital market
28 conflicts of interest
35 currency
33 dealers
27 default
 8 diversification
34 dividends
 3 economies of scale
19 economies of scope
13 equities
23 Eurobond
 5 Eurodollars
12 exchanges
18 federal funds rate
10 financial intermediation
22 financial panic
16 investment banks
25 liabilities
32 liquid
29 maturity
 1 money market
11 moral hazard
 2 over-the-counter (OTC) market
21 portfolio
15 primary market
30 risk sharing
17 secondary market
26 thrift institutions (thrifts)
14 transaction costs
 6 underwriting

Practice Problems

1. a. Indirect finance
   b. Direct finance
   c. Indirect finance
   d. Indirect finance
   e. Direct finance
   f. Direct finance
   g. Direct finance
   h. Indirect finance

2. a. debt, secondary, over-the-counter (all bonds are sold OTC), money
   b. equity, secondary, over-the-counter (Microsoft is traded on NASDAQ, an OTC market), capital
   c. equity, primary, no exchange or OTC market is involved yet, capital
   d. debt, secondary, over-the-counter, capital
   e. equity, secondary, exchange (Ford is traded on the NYSE), capital

3.

	Sources	Uses
Commercial banks	e	i
Savings and loan associations	e	f
Credit unions	e	k
Life insurance companies	c	g
Pension funds, government retirement funds	b	j
Finance companies	a	l
Mutual funds	d	h

4. a. A collapse of financial intermediaries because the providers of funds doubt the health of the intermediaries and pull their funds out of both sound and unsound institutions.

   b. *Restrictions on entry*: the government provides a charter only to upstanding, well-capitalized individuals.

   Disclosure: intermediaries are subject to stringent reporting requirements.

   Restrictions on assets and activities: there are limits on the riskiness of the assets held by intermediaries.

   Deposit insurance: People suffer less of a financial loss when a depository institution fails.

Limits on Competition: branching restrictions limit competition, which was believed to cause failures.

Restrictions on interest rates: Regulation Q set the ceiling on interest rates that banks could pay, limiting their ability to compete.

c. Banks can again be involved in the securities industry (investment banking activities). Branching restrictions have been reduced or eliminated. Regulation Q was abolished and banks can now pay the interest rate they choose.

Short-Answer Questions

1. With direct finance, borrowers acquire funds directly from lenders by selling them securities. With indirect finance, a financial intermediary stands between the lender and borrower and helps transfer the funds from one to the other.

2. A debt security is for borrowing while an equity security is for ownership. The primary market is where new issues are sold, and the secondary market is where existing issues are resold. An exchange is centralized while an OTC market is decentralized and linked by computers. The money market is for short-term debt, and the capital market is for long-term funds.

3. U.S. Treasury bills, because they are the most actively traded security and have no default risk. Corporate stocks. Corporate bonds.

4. Equity holders are residual claimants, so in the event of a bankruptcy, they receive funds only after all of the debt holders have been paid. Short-term debt securities have smaller fluctuations in prices than long-term securities do. Therefore, short-term bonds have the least risk.

5. Foreign bonds are sold in a foreign country and denominated in that country's currency. Eurobonds are denominated in a currency other than the currency of the country in which it is sold. There is no relationship between a Eurobond and the euro. That is, Eurobonds are not denominated in euros.

6. Moral hazard. Moral hazard is the risk that the borrower will engage in activities that are immoral from the lender's point of view. In this case, the borrower is using the money in a riskier manner than was agreed to in the loan contract.

7. They have lower transactions costs due to economies of scale. They provide risk sharing. They reduce the problems associated with asymmetric information by screening and monitoring borrowers.

8. Commercial banks, savings and loan associations and mutual savings banks, and credit unions. Deposits are the main liability. Commercial banks are the largest.

9. Money market mutual funds. Since they buy such safe and liquid instruments with the funds they have acquired, they are able to allow shareholders to write checks against the value of their share holdings.

10. Commercial bank, mutual savings banks, and savings and loan associations. The FDIC provides insurance of up to $250,000 for each depositor at a bank, examines the books of insured banks, and imposes restrictions on assets that banks can hold.

Critical Thinking

1. The transaction costs would be prohibitive because it would be expensive to pay a lawyer to write a loan contract that would be used only once. It would be risky because you would be putting all of your eggs in one basket by lending all of your money to one person. Finally, you are unlikely to know how to avoid the problems of asymmetric information. There could be adverse selection in that risky borrowers desire to borrow. There could be moral hazard in that the borrow may take the loan money and use it to gamble instead of buying a car.

2. Banks make many similar loans, so they pay the lawyer only once for a contract that can be used many times. Banks make a variety of different loans whose returns do not always move together, which reduces their risk on the group of loans. Banks know how to screen and monitor loan customers to reduce adverse selection and moral hazard.

True/False Questions

1. T
2. F
3. F
4. T
5. F
6. F
7. F

8. T
9. T
10. F
11. T
12. F
13. F
14. T
15. T

Multiple-Choice Questions

1. b
2. a
3. c
4. d
5. d
6. c
7. a
8. b
9. d
10. a
11. c
12. b
13. d
14. a
15. d
16. c
17. b
18. c
19. d
20. a

3 What Is Money?[*]

Chapter Review

PREVIEW

Money has always been important to the economy because it promotes economic efficiency. Here we develop a current definition of money by addressing the functions of money, and learning about the different forms of money through history.

MEANING OF MONEY

Money is anything that is generally accepted in payment for goods or services or in the repayment of debts. The definition of money includes currency (notes and coins) and checking account deposits. Money is not the same as wealth or income. A person's wealth includes that person's money, but it also includes other assets such as bonds, stock, art, land, and houses. Income is a flow of earnings per unit of time while money is a stock, which is measured at a given point in time.

FUNCTIONS OF MONEY

Money has three primary functions. Money serves as a

- *medium of exchange*. Money is used to pay for goods and services. The use of a medium of exchange is efficient for two reasons: It reduces transactions costs (the time spent exchanging goods or services), and it allows for specialization and the division of labor. In a barter economy—an economy without money — goods and services are exchanged directly for other goods and services. Transaction costs in a barter economy are high because an exchange requires a "double coincidence of wants."

---

[*]This is also Chapter 3 in the 3rd ed.

- *unit of account*. Money is used to measure value in the economy. As a result, all prices are in terms of money. The use of money as a unit of account is efficient because it reduces transactions costs. In a barter economy, where all goods must be valued in terms of all other goods, the exchange of just a small number of goods requires an enormous number of prices. When money is a unit of account, there is only one price per good, and transaction costs are small.

- *store of value*. Money is used as a repository of purchasing power. This allows people to earn money today, and spend it at a later date. Other assets are a store of value, and they may provide a greater rate of return, but people still hold money because of its liquidity. During inflation, when prices are rising rapidly, people are reluctant to hold money because its value is falling.

EVOLUTION OF THE PAYMENTS SYSTEM

Most economic systems first employed *commodity money,* usually a valuable commodity or precious metal such as gold or silver. Because metals are difficult to transport, societies developed paper currency that was fully convertible into precious metals. More recently, paper currency has evolved into *fiat money,* money decreed by governments as legal tender but not convertible into a precious metal. Since coins and paper currency are easily stolen and hard to transport, modern banking has invented *checks*. Checks instruct your bank to transfer money from your bank account to another person's account. Checks are efficient because some payments cancel each other out so no currency need be physically moved; checks can be easily written for large amounts; checks reduce loss from theft; and checks provide receipts for purchases. But checks take time to move from place to place, so the money is not available immediately when deposited, and checks are expensive to process. Computers now allow for *electronic payment* of bills over the Internet. *E-money* is money that exists only in electronic form, in the form of debit cards, stored-value cards, and e-cash. Each type of money is more efficient than its predecessor because it lowers transactions costs.

MEASURING MONEY

Since there is no single measure of money that is accurate for all times and for all purposes, the Federal Reserve defines two measures of the money supply, known as monetary aggregates.

- M1 = currency + traveler's checks + demand deposits + other checkable deposits

- M2 = M1 + small-denomination time deposits + savings deposits and money market deposit accounts + money market mutual fund shares (retail)

All of the assets in M1 are perfectly liquid. M2 includes some assets that are not quite as liquid as those in M1. These two measures of the money supply do not always move together, so the proper choice of a measure of money by policymakers does matter for the conduct of monetary policy.

Helpful Hints

1. One of the functions of money is to serve as a unit of account. When serving in this capacity, money expresses the relative value between all goods. That is, when all prices are established in terms of money, money is the common denominator across all goods. If an apple costs 25 cents, while an orange costs 50 cents, we know that it takes two apples to get an orange. The relative value between the goods has been established.

2. The M1 monetary aggregate includes demand deposits and other checkable deposits. Note that it is not the check that is part of the money supply. It is the balance in the account that is money. A fresh checkbook with 25 checks is of no value unless there is a positive balance in the account. Similarly, credit card balances are not considered money, since these are loans which must be repaid with some form of money.

3. As we move from M1 to M2, we include slightly less liquid assets. M1 only includes perfectly liquid assets in that the items in M1 don't need to be converted into anything else in order to be exchanged for goods and services. The additional assets in M2 are highly liquid, but they require some small expense or effort to convert them into cash.

Terms and Definitions

Choose a definition for each key term.

Key Terms:

_3_ commodity money

_6_ currency

_11_ electronic money (e-money)

_4_ fiat money

_12_ hyperinflation

_13_ income

_7_ liquidity

_10_ medium of exchange

_8_ monetary aggregates

_1_ payments system

_9_ store of value

_2_ unit of account

_5_ wealth

Definitions:

1. the method of conducting transactions in the economy
2. anything used to measure value in an economy
3. money made of precious metals or another valuable commodity
4. paper currency decreed by a government as legal tender but not convertible into coins or precious metal
5. all resources owned by an individual, including all assets
6. paper money and coins
7. the relative ease and speed with which an asset can be converted into cash
8. the two measures of the money supply used by the Federal Reserve System (M1 and M2)
9. a repository of purchasing power over time
10. anything that can be used to pay for goods and services
11. money in the form of a stored value card, smart card, or balances to purchase goods and services over the internet
12. periods of extreme inflation
13. the flow of earnings over a specific period of time

Problems and Short-Answer Questions

PRACTICE PROBLEMS

1. Which of the three functions of money (medium of exchange, unit of account, store of value) is illustrated by each of the following situations?

    a. Susan purchases a case of soda at the grocery store with a check.

    _____

    b. Bryce puts $3,000 in his checking account and plans to spend it next month when he pays his college tuition.

    _____

    c. To avoid confusion, prisoners in a POW camp value all of their tradable items in terms of cigarettes.

    _____

    d. Joe goes shopping for meat. At the meat counter, he notices that fresh fish is priced at $10 per pound while frozen fish is priced at $5 per pound. He immediately recognizes that he could get twice as much frozen fish as fresh fish for the same expenditure.

    _____

    e. Lisa is willing to specialize as an economics professor and receive payment in dollars because she is confident that she can go to the market and spend those dollars for food, clothing, and shelter.

    _____

    f. A prisoner in a POW (prisoner) camp keeps 100 cigarettes in his locker even though he does not smoke because he believes that he will be able to buy chocolates with them next week when packages from home arrive.

    _____

    g. For tax purposes Jennifer's Flower Shop values the store's inventory, which includes a variety of different types of flowers, at $40,000.

    _____

    h. Joe buys ten gallons of gasoline with a twenty dollar bill.

    _____

2. Suppose there are four goods produced in an economy—apples, oranges, pears, and bananas.

   a. If this is a barter economy, list the prices needed in order to exchange any good for any other good. How many are there?

   _____

   _____

   _____

   b. Suppose dollars are introduced into the economy and universally circulate as money. What are the prices needed in order to exchange any good for any other good? How many are there?

   _____

   _____

   c. Which system has lower transactions costs, the barter system or the one with money? Does the difference in transactions costs increase or decrease as the economy expands? Explain.

   _____

   _____

   _____

3. What type of payment (commodity money, fiat money, checks, electronic payment, or e-money) is employed in each of the following situations?

   a. While in France, you use a 100 euro note to purchase a bottle of wine.

   _____

   b. On the island of Yap, stone wheels are used to purchase all goods and services.

   _____

   c. You have your mortgage and life insurance premiums automatically paid each month by your bank directly out of your checking account.

   _____

   d. One hundred fifty years ago, your great-great grandfather purchased a new suit with a twenty dollar gold piece.

   _____

   e. You write a check each month on your NOW account at your savings and loan and mail it your auto insurance company to pay your premium.

   _____

f.   You buy a new lawnmower at Sears and pay directly out of your checking account with your debit card.

_____

g.   You buy a soda at a Quick Shop with a ten dollar bill.

_____

h.   You purchase $20 worth of subway rides in Washington, D.C. Instead of tickets, you receive a disposable paper card with a magnetic strip on the back (similar to the back of a credit card). You feed it into the turnstile each time you ride the train, and you continue to use it until the $20 has been used up.

_____

4.   List the monetary aggregates (M1 and/or M2) in which each of the following assets belongs. If the asset does not belong in either of the monetary aggregates, write "none."

a.   currency_____

b.   Eurodollars _____

c.   government bonds_____

d.   demand deposits _____

e.   savings deposits_____

f.   large denomination time deposits_____

g.   checkable deposits_____

h.   stocks _____

i.   money market deposit accounts (retail)_____

j.   small denomination time deposits _____

SHORT-ANSWER QUESTIONS

1. What is income? What is wealth? Does someone who has a high income or is wealthy necessarily have a lot of money? Explain.

_____

_____

_____

_____

2. What is a barter economy? What are transactions costs? What are two reasons why transactions costs are high in a barter system?

_____

_____

_____

_____

3. What are the necessary characteristics of a commodity if it is to function effectively as money?

_____

_____

4. Why do people hold money as a store of value when there are many other assets, such as houses and bonds, that earn a greater rate of return and are also a store of value?

_Liquidity_____

_____

5. What are some advantages of using checks as a means of payment? What are some shortcomings?

_____

_____

_____

_____

6. What are the assets included in M1? What separates them from the assets in M2?

_____

_____

_____

7. Which is the larger monetary aggregate, M1 or M2? Why?

_____

_____

8. Does it matter what definition of money policymakers use as the true measure of money when making monetary policy decisions? Why?

_____

_____

9. What is the difference between small-denomination time deposits and savings deposits?

_____

_____

_____

10. Why are money market mutual fund shares and money market deposit accounts considered money and counted in M2?

_____

_____

Critical Thinking

You are with your best friend at the bank when she cashes her paycheck for cash. She takes the $500 of currency, and with a frown on her face, she says, "Money is just becoming paper these days. I should go the United States Treasury and demand that they give me gold in exchange for this paper. Then I'd have some real money."

1. Explain to your friend what type of money she received.

_____

_____

2. What are some of the advantages and disadvantages of this type of money?

_____

_____

_____

3. What type of money does your friend think she wants? Explain. Would the U.S. Treasury redeem her currency in gold? Why or why not?

_____

_____

_____

4. In the modern high-technology world, has money moved beyond paper? Explain.

_____

_____

_____

Self-Test

TRUE/FALSE QUESTIONS

1. Money is anything that is generally accepted in payment for goods and services or in the repayment of debt.

2. Income is the same thing as money, because if someone has a high income, that person earns a lot of money.

3. Of the three functions of money, the function that separates money from all other assets is that money serves as a medium of exchange.

4. Barter is inefficient because it requires that there be a "double coincidence of wants" in order for an exchange to take place.

5. Barter is inefficient because barter requires an enormous number of prices for each good to be valued in terms of all other goods.

6. Money is the most liquid store of value in the economy.

7. Money is an excellent store of value during inflationary times.

8. Fiat money evolved into commodity money because commodity money is less likely to be stolen and is easier to transport.

___F___9. Fiat money is paper money that the government has guaranteed to redeem in terms of a particular precious metal.

___T___10. The driving force behind the movement from checks toward electronic payment is the time and high cost of transporting and processing checks.

___T___11. Savings deposits are included in the monetary aggregate known as M1.

___T___12. M1 contains only perfectly liquid financial assets.

___F___13. Policymakers can use either M1 or M2 as a guide for monetary policy and get the same results because the movements of these monetary aggregates always closely track each other.

___F___14. In a barter economy with 100 goods, there would be 100 prices for those goods.

___F___15. The value of M2 is more than four times that of the M1 money supply in the United States.

MULTIPLE-CHOICE QUESTIONS

1. Which of the following is measured as a flow per unit of time?
   a. money
   b. wealth
   c. income
   d. all of the above

2. Which of the following economies has the least efficient payments system?
   a. an economy using gold as a commodity money
   b. a barter economy
   c. an economy using fiat money
   d. an economy using currency and deposit money

3. In which of the following economies are goods and services traded directly for other goods and services?
   a. an economy using gold as a commodity money
   b. a barter economy
   c. an economy using fiat money
   d. an economy using currency and deposit money

4. Which of the following is not a purpose or function of money?
   a. store of value
   b. medium of exchange
   c. protection against inflation
   d. unit of account

5. A payments system based on money is
   a. more efficient than a barter economy because transactions costs are lower.
   b. more efficient than a barter economy because fewer prices are needed to establish relative values between all commodities.
   c. less efficient than a barter economy because a money economy requires that there be a double coincidence of wants in order for there to be an exchange.
   d. less efficient than a barter economy because money is costly to transport.
   e. Both (a) and (b) are correct.

6. With a payments system based on money, John can specialize as a medical doctor and use the money earned from his efforts to buy all of the things he needs. Which of the functions of money has been most clearly demonstrated by the scenario above?
   a. store of value
   b. medium of exchange
   c. protection against inflation
   d. unit of account

7. Which of the following is not a characteristic of an effective commodity money?
   a. It must be widely accepted.
   b. It must be standardized.
   c. It must be divisible.
   d. It should be able to be easily reproduced by everyone in the economy.
   e. All of the above are characteristics of an effective commodity money.

8. An asset with great liquidity is one that
   a. can be converted into a medium of exchange with relative ease and speed.
   b. generates high transactions costs when liquidating.
   c. is an excellent store of value.
   d. acts as a unit of account.
   e. all of the above

9. Which of the following is an example of commodity money?
   a. a five dollar bill
   b. a check drawn on a bank account in the United States
   c. a credit card
   d. cigarettes in a POW (prison) camp
   e. all of the above

10. Which of the following is an example of fiat money?
    a. a five dollar bill
    b. a twenty dollar gold piece
    c. sea shells used as money in a primitive society
    d. cigarettes in a POW (prison) camp
    e. all of the above

11. Which of the following forms of payment is least efficient because it generates the highest transactions costs?
    a. checks
    b. commodity money
    c. fiat money
    d. electronic payment

12. Which of the following is *not* an example of electronic money?
    a. debit card
    b. stored-value card
    c. smart card
    d. credit card = a loan

13. Which of the following statements about fiat money is false?
    a. Fiat money is paper currency decreed by government as legal tender.
    b. Fiat money is easier to transport than commodity money.
    c. Fiat money is redeemable into a particular precious metal such as gold.
    d. Fiat money should be made difficult to counterfeit.

14. When prices are rising rapidly, money does not act as a good
    a. unit of account.
    b. medium of exchange.
    c. liquid asset.
    d. store of value.

15. Which of the following is not included in the M1 monetary aggregate?
    a. money market deposit accounts
    b. currency
    c. demand deposits
    d. NOW accounts
    e. traveler's checks

16. Checkable deposits are included in which of the following monetary aggregates?
    a. M1 only
    b. M2 only
    c. M1 and M2
    d. Checkable deposits are not included in either of the monetary aggregates.

17. Which of the following is not included in M2?
    a. currency
    b. large-denomination time deposits
    c. small-denomination time deposits
    d. savings deposits

18. Which of the following statements about the monetary aggregates is true?
    a. M1 is greater than M2.
    b. The growth rates of M1 and M2 always track each other very closely.
    c. When you transfer funds from your savings account to your checking account, M2 decreases and M1 stays the same.
    d. When the growth rate of M2 increases, the growth rate of M1 must also increase.

19. Which of the following statements about the liquidity of the assets in the monetary aggregates is true?
    a. The assets in M1 are more liquid than the assets in M2.
    b. The assets in M2 are more liquid than the assets in M1.
    c. All of the assets in the monetary aggregates have equal liquidity because they are all considered money.
    d. The only liquid asset in the monetary aggregates is currency.

20. Which of the following is *not* a characteristic of barter economies?
    a. Barter requires that there be a double coincidence of wants in order for there to be an exchange.
    b. Barter requires an enormous number of prices in order for every good to be valued in terms of every other good.
    c. In a barter economy, it is difficult for people to specialize in the production of just one item.
    d. Barter generates very low transactions costs.
    e. In a barter economy, goods are exchanged directly for other goods.

Solutions

Terms and Definitions

 _3_   commodity money

 _6_   currency

 _11_ electronic money (e-money)

 _4_   fiat money

 _12_ hyperinflation

 _13_ income

 _7_   liquidity

 _10_ medium of exchange

 _8_   monetary aggregates

 _1_   payments system

 _9_   store of value

 _2_   unit of account

 _5_   wealth

Practice Problems

1. a. medium of exchange
    b. store of value
    c. unit of account
    d. unit of account
    e. medium of exchange
    f. store of value
    g. unit of account
    h. medium of exchange

2. a. apples/orange, apples/pear, apples/banana, orange/pear, orange/banana, pears/banana. $[n(n-1)]/2 = (4 \times 3)/2 = 12/2 = 6.$

    b. dollars/apple, dollars/orange, dollars/pear, dollars/banana. Four.

    c. The system with money needs fewer prices so transactions costs are lower. The difference in transactions costs increases as the economy expands because the number of prices needed in a barter economy explodes as the number of goods increases.

3. a. fiat money
    b. commodity money
    c. electronic payment
    d. commodity money
    e. checks
    f. e-money

g. fiat money

h. e-money (stored-value card)

4. a. M1, M2
    b. None
    c. None
    d. M1, M2
    e. M2
    f. None
    g. M1, M2
    h. None
    i. M2
    j. M2

Short-Answer Questions

1. Income is a flow of earnings per unit of time. Wealth is a total collection of property that serves to store value. Money is the asset that is generally accepted in payment for goods or services. It is not necessary that high income or wealthy people have a great deal of money. High income people may spend it all, and wealthy people may hold their wealth in forms other than money.

2. A system without money where goods and services are exchanged directly for other goods and services. Transaction cost is the time spent trying to exchange goods and services. Barter requires a "double coincidence of wants" and an enormous number of prices to establish relative values.

3. It must be easily standardized, widely accepted, easily divisible, easy to carry, and it must not deteriorate quickly.

4. Money is perfectly liquid because it is a medium of exchange. Other assets involve transaction costs when converting them into a medium of exchange.

5. Advantages are that checks increase efficiency since some payments cancel each other out. Checks can be written for large amounts, there is little loss from theft, and checks provide a receipt. Some problems are that it takes time to get checks from one place to another so you do not have access to your money immediately when you deposit a check, and checks are expensive to process.

6. Currency, traveler's checks, demand deposits, and other checkable deposits. All of the assets in M1 are a medium of exchange (perfectly liquid).

7. M2, because M2 includes all of M1 plus additional slightly less liquid assets.

8. Yes, because while the monetary aggregates tend to often move together, sometimes their growth rates diverge greatly.

9. Both are forms of very liquid funds that pay interest. However, the main difference between the two is that holders of small-denomination time deposits must wait until a specified period of time before accessing those funds, otherwise a withdrawal penalty will be incurred. A savings account has no such maturity restrictions or withdrawal penalties.

10. They are considered money because they look and act a lot like a regular checking account, since the funds can be accessed by writing checks against the account balance. However, they are slightly less liquid than a regular checking account, so they are considered in M2 rather than M1.

Critical Thinking

1. Fiat money. It is money that is decreed by government as legal tender, but it is not convertible into a particular precious metal.

2. It is lighter and, therefore, easier to transport. However, it will only be accepted if people trust that the authorities will not print too much of it and that the paper money is difficult to counterfeit.

3. Commodity money, which is a precious metal or another valuable commodity. No. Modern money is fiat money, and it is not redeemable in any particular precious metal.

4. Yes. People can electronically transfer their account balances to pay their bills. Recurring bills can be paid automatically. E-money exists in the form of debit cards, stored-value cards and smart cards, and e-cash.

True/False Questions

1. T
2. F
3. T
4. T
5. T
6. T
7. F
8. F
9. F
10. T
11. F
12. T
13. F
14. F
15. T

Multiple-Choice Questions

1. c
2. b
3. b
4. c
5. e
6. b
7. d
8. a
9. d
10. a
11. b
12. d
13. c
14. d
15. a
16. c
17. b
18. c
19. a
20. d

4 Understanding Interest Rates*

Chapter Review

PREVIEW

This chapter establishes what interest rates are and addresses the ways in which they are measured. The most accurate measure of *interest rates* is *yield to maturity*. The concept of yield to maturity reveals that bond prices and interest rates are negatively related, and the longer the maturity of the bond, the greater the change in the price of the bond from a given change in the interest rate. Interest rates are important because they affect how much people and firms wish to save or borrow. The terms defined in this chapter will be employed throughout the book.

MEASURING INTEREST RATES

Present value (or present discounted value) is today's value of a future cash payment given an interest rate of i. The basic present value formula is:

$$PV(1 + i)^n = CF \text{ or } PV = CF/(1 + i)^n$$

where PV = present value, CF = future cash flow, and n = number of years to maturity.

For example, a simple loan of $100 (the present value) at 6% for one year ($n = 1$) generates a future cash flow payment of $100(1.06) = $106 one year from today. Alternatively, the present value of a future cash payment of $106 to be received one year from today is $106/1.06 = $100 today.

There are four basic types of credit market instruments: a simple loan, a fixed-payment loan (also known as a fully amortized loan), a coupon bond, and a discount bond (also known as a zero-coupon bond). A simple loan and a discount bond require the borrower to make one payment at the end of the loan, which includes both the principle and interest. Fixed-payment loans (installment loans such as auto loans and mortgages) and coupon bonds require the borrower to make

*This is also Chapter 4 in the 3rd ed.

periodic payments to the lender until a maturity date. The payments on a fixed-payment loan are all the same size and each payment includes a combination of interest and principle. The periodic payments on a coupon bond are interest payments alone, and the final payment at maturity includes the face-value or principle of the bond.

The most important and accurate way to calculate the interest rate is *yield to maturity*, which is the interest rate that equates the present value of cash flow payments received from a debt instrument with its price or value today. The price or value today of any instrument is equal to the sum of the present value of all of its future cash flow payments. Since a simple loan and a discount bond generate only one future cash flow payment, yield to maturity on each of those instruments can be calculated with the present value formula provided above. If the value today and the future cash flow values are known, one can use the formula above to solve for i, which is the yield to maturity. For the simple, one-year case, $i = (CF - PV)/PV$, which is also our formula for simple interest.

We follow the same general process for finding the yield to maturity for fixed-payment loans and coupon bonds, but since they generate periodic future cash flow payments, we must sum the present value of each future cash flow payment and equate it to the value or price of the instrument today. The general formula for an instrument generating annual payments until some future maturity date is:

$$\text{Value today (price)} = CF/(1 + i) + CF/(1 + i)^2 + CF/(1 +i)^3 +...+ CF/(1 + i)^n$$

If the price of the instrument and the future cash flow payments are known, we can solve for i and get the yield to maturity. Because this calculation is not easy, many pocket calculators have been programmed to solve this problem.

When the formula above is applied to a coupon bond, the following facts emerge:

- If the yield to maturity equals the coupon rate (coupon/face value), the price of the bond equals its face value.

- If the yield to maturity is above the coupon rate, the price of the bond is below its face value, and vice versa.

- The price of the bond and its yield to maturity are negatively related. This is also true for a discount bond.

A consol or perpetuity is a coupon bond with no maturity. For a perpetuity, $P = C/i$, or $i = C/P$, where P is the price of the perpetuity, C = annual coupon, and i = yield to maturity. This formula is also an approximation of yield to maturity for any long-term coupon bond, and it is know as *current yield* when used in this manner. The greater the maturity of the bond, the better current yield approximates yield to maturity.

THE DISTINCTION BETWEEN INTEREST RATES AND RETURNS

The actual *rate of return* earned by the holder of a coupon bond includes the capital gains or losses on the bond from fluctuations in the price of the bond. The formula for the *return* on a bond held from time t to $t + 1$ is:

$$Return = (C + P_{t+1} - P_t)/P_t$$

where C = coupon payment, P_t = price of the bond at t, and P_{t+1} = price of the bond at $t + 1$. General findings from this concept include:

- The return on a bond equals the yield to maturity if the holding period is equal to maturity (the bond is held to maturity).

- An increase in interest rates causes the price of a bond to fall, resulting in a capital loss on bonds with maturity greater than the holding period.

- The longer to maturity, the greater is the change in price (and capital gain or loss) from a change in interest rates, and the greater is the impact on the return on the bond.

- Thus, a bond with a high yield to maturity can have negative returns if interest rates rise and the bond is sold before maturity (has a short holding period).

Prices (and therefore returns) are more volatile on long-term bonds than short-term bonds. This volatility in returns that results from changes in the interest rate is known as *interest rate risk*.

THE DISTINCTION BETWEEN REAL AND NOMINAL INTEREST RATES

The *nominal interest rate* has not been corrected for the effects of inflation. The *real interest rate* has been adjusted for inflation so that it more accurately reflects the true cost to borrowers and true return to lenders. The Fisher equation shows the necessary adjustment,

$$i_r = i - \pi^e$$

where i = nominal interest rate, i_r = real interest rate, and π^e = expected inflation. Borrowers and lenders respond to real interest rates. When real rates are low, there are greater incentives to borrow and fewer incentives to lend. In practice, real interest rates are difficult to observe since they must be inferred using measures of inflation expectations. One way to they can be estimated is by using the spread between *indexed bonds* and nonindexed bonds.

Helpful Hints

1. We can use the present value formulas in this chapter to solve for the yield to maturity (interest rate) on an instrument if we know the price (value today) of the instrument and its future cash flow payments. Alternatively, and equally important, we can use the present value formulas in this chapter to solve for the price of an instrument given the interest rate and its future cash flow payments. Using the formulas in this alternative way, one can clearly see the main points developed in this chapter. When interest rates rise, the present value of future cash flows decrease and the price of existing instruments fall. Longer-term instruments have more terms to be discounted at higher powers, so the longer to maturity, the greater is the change in the price of an instrument from the same size change in the interest rate. Thus, long-term bonds can generate greater capital gains and losses when held for short holding periods, making them less desirable to hold as short-term investments.

2. *Yield to maturity* is the return the owner of an instrument would realize if the owner held the instrument to maturity. If the holding period is less than maturity, the return to the holder may differ from the yield to maturity. If the yield to maturity on comparable instruments rises (the interest rate rises), then the price of the bond will fall and the returns to the holder of the bond will fall below the bond's original yield to maturity if the holder of the bond sells it before maturity.

Terms and Definitions

Choose a definition for each key term.

Key Terms:

_18_ cash flows

_13_ consol or perpetuity

_7_ coupon bond

_12_ coupon rate

_25_ current yield

_6_ discount bond (zero-coupon bond)

_1_ face value (par value)

_15_ fixed-payment loan (fully amortized loan)

_17_ indexed bond

_9_ interest-rate risk

_10_ nominal interest rate

_4_ present discounted value

_14_ rate of capital gain

_8_ real interest rate

_16_ real terms

_3_ return (rate of return)

_11_ simple loan

_54_ yield to maturity

Definitions:

1. a specified final amount paid to the owner of a bond at the maturity date

2. an approximation of the yield to maturity that equals the yearly coupon payment divided by the price of a coupon bond

3. the payments to the owner of a security plus the change in the security's value, expressed as a fraction of its purchase price

4. today's value of a payment to be received in the future for a given interest rate

5. the interest rate that equates the present value of payments received from a credit market instrument with its value today

6. a credit market instrument that is bought at a price below its face value and whose face value is repaid at the maturity date

7. a credit market instrument that pays the owner a fixed interest payment every year until the maturity date, when a specified final amount is repaid

8. the interest rate adjusted for expected inflation so that it more accurately reflects the true cost of borrowing

9. the possible reduction in returns associated with changes in interest rates

10. an interest rate that does not take inflation into account

11. a credit market instrument providing the borrower with an amount of funds that must be repaid to the lender at the maturity date along with an additional payment of interest

12. the dollar amount of the yearly coupon payment expressed as a percentage of the face value of a coupon bond

13. a bond with no maturity date and no repayment of principle, but makes periodic fixed coupon payments

14. the change in a security's price relative to the initial purchase price

15. a loan in which the borrower makes fixed periodic payments for a set period of time

16. reflecting the actual amount of goods and services that can be purchased

17. a bond where principle and interest payments are adjusted for changes in the price level over time

18. streams of cash payments which can continue indefinitely into the future

Problems and Short-Answer Questions

PRACTICE PROBLEMS

1. Calculate the present value of each of the following.
   a. $1,000, to be received one year from today, and the interest rate is 4%.

   $1000/1.04 = 961.54 \quad PV=FV/(1+i)^n$

   b. $1,000, to be received one year from today, and the interest rate is 8%.

   $1000/1.08 = 925.93$

   c. $1,000, to be received two years from today, and the interest rate is 4%.

   $1000/(1.04)^2 = 924.56$

d. Compare your answers to *a* and *b* above. What happens to the present value of a future cash flow if the interest rate rises? Why?

PV goes down

_____

_____

e. Compare your answers to *a* and *c* above. What happens to the present value of a future cash flow as the future cash flow is received further into the future? Why?

PV falls

_____

_____

2. The following questions are based on a $1,000 face value coupon bond with a coupon rate of 10%.

a. Suppose the bond has one year to maturity and you buy it for $1,018.52. What is the yield to maturity on the bond? Is the yield to maturity above or below the coupon rate of 10%? Why?

_____

_____

_____

b. Since the equation is often considered too difficult to solve, simply write down the equation that one would have to solve to find the yield to maturity if the bond has two years to maturity and you paid $965 for the bond. If this equation were solved, would the resulting yield to maturity be above or below the coupon rate of 10%? Why?

_____

_____

_____

c. What price would the bond sell for if it had two years to maturity and the interest rate (and therefore the yield to maturity) on the bond is 7%?

_____

d. What price would the bond sell for if it had two years to maturity and the interest rate (and therefore the yield to maturity) on the bond is 8%?

_____

e. Compare *c* and *d* above. What happens to the price of a bond if the interest rate rises? Make a general statement with regard to the price of any coupon bond and the interest rate?

_____

_____

f. What price would the bond sell for if it had one year to maturity and the interest rate is 7%? What is the price of the bond if the interest rate is 8%? Using your results from *c* and *d* above, how much did the price change on the two-year bond when the interest rate rose to 8% from 7%? How much did the price change for the one-year bond when the interest rate rose to 8% from 7%? Make a general statement with regard to the sensitivity of bond prices to changes in interest rates.

_____

_____

_____

_____

3. Suppose you purchase a coupon bond with 20 years to maturity for $1,000. It pays coupons of $70 per year.

a. Suppose after one year, you must sell the bond to help pay for tuition. Further suppose that interest rates have risen so that the price of the bond has fallen to $950. What is the rate of return that you earned for holding the bond one year?

$$\frac{70}{1000} = 7\%$$

$$\frac{1000-950}{1000} = 5\%$$
$$+2\% = \$20$$

    $+2\%$
    _____

    _____

b. What was the size of the capital gain or loss on the bond?

    $\$+20$ gain
    _____

c. Is it possible to make negative returns on a long-term U.S. government bond if the holding period is less than maturity? Explain.

    Yes. if interest rates rise
    _____

    _____

d. Do long-term U.S. government bonds generate a sure return if you will need to sell them before maturity? Explain.

    NO. prices could change
    _____

    _____

    e. What name do we apply to the type of risk long-term bondholders bear when the holding period is less than maturity?

_____

   4. What is the value of the real interest rate in each of the following situations?

    a. The nominal interest rate is 15%, and the expected inflation rate is 13%.

_____

    b. The nominal interest rate is 12%, and the expected inflation rate is 9%.

_____

    c. The nominal interest rate is 10%, and the expected inflation rate is 9%.

_____

    d. The nominal interest rate is 5%, and the expected inflation rate is 1%.

_____

    e. In which of the above situations would you prefer to be the lender? Why?

_____

    f. In which of the above situations would you prefer to be the borrower? Why?

_____

SHORT-ANSWER QUESTIONS

   1. If a lender makes a simple loan of $500 for one year and charges 6%, how much will the lender receive at maturity? If a lender makes a simple loan of $500 for one year and charges $40 interest, what is the simple interest rate on that loan?

_____

_____

2. What is the alternative name for a fixed-payment loan? How is it similar to a coupon bond? How is it different?

    _____

    _____

    _____

    _____

3. What is a bond's coupon rate? Does it change over the life of the bond? If a bond's yield to maturity exceeds its coupon rate, what is its price compared to par (or face value)? Why?

    _____

    _____

    _____

    _____

4. What is a consol or perpetuity? What is the price of a perpetuity if it pays an annual coupon of $70, and its yield to maturity is 7%? What is its price if the yield to maturity rises to 14%?

    _____

    _____

5. What is the yield to maturity on a consol that pays an annual coupon of $70 and sells for $700? What is the *current yield* of the consol? Explain the relationship between yield to maturity and current yield on a consol.

    _____

    _____

    _____

6. What are the characteristics of a bond for which current yield is a good estimate of yield to maturity? (Hint: Look at question 5 above.) Why?

    _____

    _____

    _____

7. If you lend money at a 10% nominal interest rate, but you expect inflation to be 6% over the life of the loan, at what rate do you expect your purchasing power to grow? What is the real interest rate on the loan?

   _____

   _____

8. Suppose the interest rate (and therefore the yield to maturity) increases by the same amount on Treasury bills and bonds. Which would you prefer to be holding when the increase in the interest rate takes place: a one-year Treasury bill or a twenty-year Treasury bond? Why?

   _____

   _____

9. If the holder of a bond sells the bond before maturity, will the rate of return on the bond equal its yield to maturity? Why or why not?

   _____

   _____

   _____

10. Suppose long-term U.S. Treasury bonds have no default risk. Does this mean that long-term U.S. Treasury bonds are risk free? Explain.

   _____

   _____

Critical Thinking

Your friend just won a state lottery that claims to pay the winner $30,000. The lottery actually pays the holder of the winning ticket $10,000 per year for the next three years. The first $10,000 payment arrives immediately. The second arrives one year from today. And the third arrives two years from today. Your friend excitedly says to you, "I need all the money right now because I want to make a down payment on a house. Since you have saved some money, why don't you just give me the $30,000 and I'll give you the ticket. Then you can collect the $30,000 and we'll be even."

1. Should you give your friend $30,000 for the winning lottery ticket? Why or why not?

   _____

   _____

2. Suppose the interest rate is 5%. What price would you pay for the winning lottery ticket?

_____

_____

3. Suppose the interest rate is 8%. What price would you pay for the winning lottery ticket?

_____

_____

4. Which interest rate implies a greater present value for the lottery ticket? Why?

_____

_____

Self-Test

TRUE/FALSE QUESTIONS

___F___1. Most people would prefer to receive $100 one year from today than receive $100 today because the present discounted value of a future cash flow is greater than the future cash flow.

___T___2. A fixed-payment loan requires the borrower to make a single payment to the lender when the loan matures, and that single payment includes both the principle and interest.

___T___3. The coupon rate on a bond is the coupon divided by the face value (par) of the bond.

___T___4. Yield to maturity is what economists mean when they use the term "interest rate."

___T___5. If a $1,000 face value bond pays annual coupons of $50, has two years to maturity, and has a yield to maturity of 7%, it will sell for $963.84. = PV

___F___6. If the yield to maturity on a bond exceeds its coupon rate, the price of the bond will be above its face value. P↑ YTM↓   P↓ YTM↑

___T___7. The price of a bond and its yield to maturity are negatively related.

___T___8. The yield to maturity on a U.S. Treasury bill that sells for $9,500 today, has a face value of $10,000, and matures in one year is 5%. $i = \frac{FV - PV}{PV} =$

___F___9. If the nominal interest rate is 7% and expected inflation is 2%, then the real interest rate is 9%. 7 − 2 = 5%

_F__ 10. Current yield is a better estimate of yield to maturity for short-term bonds than for long-term bonds.

_F__ 11. Current yield and yield to maturity on a perpetuity are the same.

_T__ 12. If a bondholder pays $1,000 for a twenty-year bond that pays $40 annual coupons, holds the bond for one year and than sells the bond for $1,050, the rate of return for that year for the bondholder is 9%.

_F__ 13. A security that pays the holder $500 five years from today is preferred to a security that pays the holder $100 per year for the next five years.

_F__ 14. If the interest rate falls the same amount for both short-term and long-term bonds, bondholders would prefer to be holding short-term bonds.

_T__ 15. Borrowers have a greater desire to borrow when the nominal interest rate is 15% and the expected inflation rate is 13% than when the nominal interest rate is 6% and the expected inflation rate is 2%.

MULTIPLE-CHOICE QUESTIONS

1. The most accurate measure of interest rates is
   a. the coupon rate.
   b. yield to maturity.
   c. current yield.
   d. discounted present value.

2. If the interest rate is 5%, the present value of $1,000 to be received five years from today is
   a. $783.53.
   b. $866.66.
   c. $952.38.
   d. $1,000.00.
   e. $1,050.00.

3. If a borrow must repay $106.50 one year from today in order to receive a simple loan of $100 today, the simple interest on this loan is
   a. 65%.
   b. 5.0%.
   c. 6.1%.
   d. 6.5%.
   e. none of the above.

4. You are in a car accident, and you receive an insurance settlement of $5,000 per year for the next three years. The first payment is to be received today. The second payment is to be received one year from today, and the third payment two years from today. If the interest rate is 6%, the present value of the insurance settlement is
   a. $15,000.00.
   b. $14,166.96.
   c. $13,365.06.
   d. $13,157.98.

5. Which of the following instruments pays the holder of the instrument a fixed interest payment every year until maturity, and then at maturity pays the holder the face value (principle) of the instrument?
    a. simple loan
    b. fixed-payment loan
    c. coupon bond
    d. discount bond

6. A U.S. Treasury bill is an example of a
    a. simple loan.
    b. fixed-payment loan.
    c. coupon bond.
    d. discount bond.

7. A coupon bond with a face value of $1,000 that pays an annual coupon of $100 has a coupon rate of
    a. $100.
    b. $1,100.
    c. 10%.
    d. 9.1%.
    e. none of the above.

8. What is the approximate yield to maturity on a coupon bond that matures one year from today, has a par value of $1,000, pays an annual coupon of $70, and whose price today is $1,019.05?
    a. 4%
    b. 5%
    c. 6%
    d. 7%
    e. 8%

9. What price will a coupon bond sell for if it has two years to maturity, a coupon rate of 8%, a par value of $1,000, and a yield to maturity of 12%?
    a. $920.00
    b. $924.74
    c. $932.40
    d. $1,035.71
    e. $1,120.00

10. Which of the following bonds has the highest yield to maturity?
    a. a 20-year, $1,000 par, 5% coupon bond selling for $900.
    b. a 20-year, $1,000 par, 5% coupon bond selling for $1,000.
    c. a 20-year, $1,000 par, 5% coupon bond selling for $1,100.
    d. There is not enough information to answer this question.

11. Which of the following statements is true?
    a. If the yield to maturity on a bond exceeds the coupon rate, the price of the bond is below its face value.
    b. If the yield to maturity on a bond exceeds the coupon rate, the price of the bond is above its face value.
    c. If the yield to maturity on a bond exceeds the coupon rate, the price of the bond is equal to its face value.
    d. None of the above is true.

12. Suppose you purchase a perpetuity for $1,000 that pays coupons of $50 per year. If the interest rate changes and becomes 10%, what will happen to the price of the perpetuity?
    a. The price will not change and will always equal $1,000 because this bond always pays $50 per year.
    b. The price will rise by $50.
    c. The price will fall by $50.
    d. The price will rise by $500.
    e. The price will fall by $500.

13. What is the approximate yield to maturity on a discount bond that matures one year from today with a maturity value of $10,000, and the price today is $9,174.31?
    a. 92%
    b. 10%
    c. 9.2%
    d. 9%
    e. 8%

14. With regard to a coupon bond, the coupon divided by the face value of the bond is known as the
    a. yield to maturity.
    b. current yield.
    c. face value rate.
    d. coupon rate.

15. If market participants expect there to be some inflation in the future,
    a. real interest rates will exceed nominal interest rates.
    b. nominal interest rates will exceed real interest rates.
    c. nominal and real interest rates will be the same.
    d. there will be no relationship between nominal and real interest rates.

16. If the interest rate falls by the same amount on all bonds regardless of the length to maturity, which of the following bonds would you prefer to be holding?
    a. a $10,000 U.S. Treasury bill with one year to maturity
    b. a $10,000 U.S. Treasury note with 10 years to maturity
    c. a $10,000 U.S. Treasury bond with 20 years to maturity
    d. It does not matter which instrument is held because there is no risk associated with any of them.

17. What is the rate of return on a long-term, 5% coupon rate bond that was purchased at its face value of $1000, held for one year, and because interest rates rose sold after one year for $920?
    a. −8%
    b. −3.3%
    c. −3%
    d. 5%
    e. 13%

18. Which of the following statements is true?
    a. Current yield is a better approximation of yield to maturity for long-term bonds when compared to short-term bonds.
    b. Bond prices vary inversely with the interest rate for both coupon bonds and discount bonds.
    c. The longer to maturity, the greater is the change in the price of a bond from the same size change in the interest rate.
    d. The coupon rate on a coupon bond is fixed once the bond is issued.
    e. All of the above are true.

19. Bondholders are displeased when interest rates rise because, on the bonds they currently hold,
    a. the prices will fall.
    b. the coupon payments will fall.
    c. the yield to maturity will fall.
    d. all of the above are true.

20. If the nominal interest rate is 4% and the expected rate of inflation is 2%, then the real interest rate is
    a. -2%.
    b. 2%.
    c. 4%.
    d. 6%.
    e. 8%.

Solutions

Terms and Definitions

18   cash flows

13   consol or perpetuity

7   coupon bond

12   coupon rate

2   current yield

6   discount bond (zero-coupon bond)

1   face value (par value)

15   fixed-payment loan (fully amortized loan)

17   indexed bond

9   interest-rate risk

10   nominal interest rate

4   present discounted value

14   rate of capital gain

8   real interest rate

16   real terms

3   return (rate of return)

11   simple loan

5   yield to maturity

Practice Problems

1. a. $1,000/1.04 = $961.54

    b. $1,000/1.08 = $925.93

    c. $1,000/(1.04)^2 = $924.56

    d.   The present value falls because a larger interest rate means that a value today would grow into a larger value in the future so a value in the future must be discounted to a greater degree to find its value today.

    e.   The present value falls because a value today would grow larger if allowed to grow further into the future so a value further into the future must be discounted to a greater degree to find its value today.

2. a. $1,018.52 = $1,100/(1 + i). Solve for i = $1,100/$1018.52 − 1 = 0.08 = 8%. It would be below. If the price is above the face value (or par), then the yield to maturity must be below the coupon rate.

    b. $965 = $100/(1 + i) + $100/(1 + i)^2 + $1,000/(1 + i)^2 and solve for i. It would be above. If the price is below the face

value (or par), then the yield to maturity must be above the coupon rate.

    c.   P = $100/1.07 + $1,100/(1.07)^2 = $93.46 + $960.78 = $1,054.24

    d.   P = $100/1.08 + $1,100/(1.08)^2 = $92.59 + $943.07 = $1,035.66

    e.   The price of the bond falls. Bond prices and interest rates are negatively related.

    f.   If i = 7%, P = $1,100/1.07 = $1,028.04. If i = 8%, P = $1,100/1.08 = $1,018.52. For the two year case, the price changes is $1,054.24 − $1,035.66 = $18.58. For the one-year case, the price change is $1,028.04 − $1,018.52 = $9.52. The longer to maturity, the greater is the change in the price of a bond from the same size change in the interest rate.

3. a.   Return = ($70 + $950 − $1,000)/$1,000 = $20/$1,000 = 2%.

    b.   Capital loss of $50.

    c.   Yes. If interest rates rise causing a capital loss greater than the gains from the coupons, then the returns could be negative.

    d.   No. Although the coupons are sure, the price of the bond can be volatile.

    e.   Interest rate risk.

4. a.   15% − 13% = 2%

    b.   12% − 9% = 3%

    c.   10% − 9% = 1%

    d.   5% − 1% = 4%

    e.   *d* above, because it generates the largest real interest rate.

    f.   *c* above, because it generates the smallest real interest rate.

Short-Answer Questions

1. $500 × 1.06 = $530.

    $40/$500 = 0.08 = 8%

2. Fully amortized loan. Both require the borrower to make periodic payments to the lender until maturity. The payments on a fixed-payment loan are all the same size and each is part principle and interest. The payments on a coupon bond are each just interest payments, and the last one at maturity is the principle.

3. Yearly coupon/face value. No, because the coupon and face value are fixed. Its price must be below par because the fixed coupons and principle are discounted to the present using a larger interest rate. In addition, the only way to make a bond with fixed coupons and par pay a higher yield to maturity is to have it sell for a lower price (a discount).

4. A coupon bond with no maturity. $P = \$70/0.07 = \$1000$. $P = \$70/0.14 = \$500$.

5. $i = C/P = \$70/\$700 = 0.10 = 10\%$. $i = C/P = \$70/\$700 = 0.10 = 10\%$. They are the same.

6. Current yield is a good estimate for yield to maturity for very long-term bonds (and becomes a perfect estimate for bonds with no maturity, known as perpetuities.) This is because the discounted present value of the many coupons of long-term bonds is similar to a perpetuity, and the principle payment is discounted to such a great degree.

7. 4%. 4%.

8. A one-year Treasury bill. When interest rates rise, the prices of existing instruments fall, but the prices of long-term instruments fall more, causing a greater capital loss on the bond.

9. Usually not. If interest rates have changed during the holding period, then the price of the bond moves inversely with the change in the interest rate, and the bond generates a capital gain or loss in addition to its current yield.

10. No. They have interest rate risk, which is the possible reduction in returns associated with changes in interest rates.

Critical Thinking

1. No. Employing any positive interest rate, the present value of the lottery ticket is less than $30,000.

2. $\$10,000 + \$10,000/1.05 + \$10,000/(1.05)^2 = \$28,594.10$

3. $\$10,000 + \$10,000/1.08 + \$10,000/(1.08)^2 = \$27,832.65$

4. 5%. A smaller interest rate causes a present value to grow more slowly over time, and therefore a future sum would require a smaller discount when it is discounted back to the present.

True/False Questions

1. F
2. F
3. T
4. T
5. T
6. F
7. T
8. F
9. F
10. F
11. T
12. T
13. F
14. F
15. T

Multiple-Choice Questions

1. b
2. a
3. d
4. b
5. c
6. d
7. c
8. b
9. c
10. a
11. a
12. e
13. d
14. d
15. b
16. c
17. c
18. e
19. a
20. b

5 The Behavior of Interest Rates*

Chapter Review

PREVIEW

In this chapter we employ both the bond market and the liquidity preference framework to see how a variety of shocks affects interest rates. We address how a change in the money supply affects the interest rate, both in the near term while other determinants of the interest rate are held constant, and in the long-run when other determinants are allowed to adjust to the change in the money supply.

DETERMINANTS OF ASSET DEMAND

Before we address the demand for bonds, we first address the demand for assets in general, such as money, bonds, stock, and art. Holding everything else unchanged, the quantity demanded of any asset is:

1. Positively related to the wealth of the buyer.

2. Positively related to the expected return on the asset relative to that on an alternative asset.

3. Negatively related to the risk of the asset relative to that of alternative assets.

4. Positively related to the liquidity of the asset relative to that of alternative assets.

These factors help explain *portfolio choice,* which describes why people choose to hold particular types of assets.

---

*This is also Chapter 5 in the 3rd ed.

SUPPLY AND DEMAND IN THE BOND MARKET

The bond demand curve shows the relationship between the quantity demanded of bonds and the price of bonds, holding everything else constant. Recall from the previous chapter that a high price for a bond corresponds to a low interest rate and vice versa. Since the demander of bonds is a lender, at a high price of bonds (a low interest rate), the quantity demanded of bonds is low. Alternatively, at a low price of bonds (a high interest rate) the quantity demanded of bonds is relatively high. As a result, the bond demand curve has the usual downward slope when graphed in price/quantity space.

The bond supply curve shows the relationship between the quantity supplied of bonds and the price of bonds, holding everything else constant. Since the supplier of bonds is the borrower, at a high price of bonds (a low interest rate), the quantity supplied of bonds is high, and the bond supply curve has the usual positive slope when graphed in price/quantity space.

The intersection of bond supply and bond demand determines the equilibrium price and quantity of bonds. The equilibrium price generates a corresponding equilibrium interest rate.

CHANGES IN EQUILIBRIUM INTEREST RATES

Equilibrium interest rates change when there is a shift in the demand or supply of bonds.

The demand for bonds shifts right if there is an increase in wealth (often from a business cycle expansion), a decrease in the riskiness of bonds relative to other assets, an increase in the liquidity of bonds relative to other assets, or an increase in the expected return on bonds relative to other assets. The expected return on bonds could rise due to a reduction in expected inflation (which raises real returns to lenders at each price of bonds) or a decrease in the expected interest rate (which would cause an increase in the price of bonds in the future and increase real returns).

The supply of bonds shifts right if there is an increase in the expected profitability of investment opportunities (from a business cycle expansion), an increase in expected inflation (which reduces real costs of borrowing at each price of bonds), or an increase in government deficits (necessitating the government to issue more bonds to finance the deficit).

A rightward shift in the demand for bonds increases the price of bonds and reduces the interest rate. A rightward shift in the supply of bonds decreases the price of bonds and increases the interest rate. An increase in expected inflation causes bond supply to shift right, bond demand to shift left, the price of bonds to fall, and interest rates to rise. This effect is known as the Fisher effect. Note also that business cycle expansions and contractions affect both the bond supply and demand curves; in theory, the effect on bond prices and interest rates should be ambiguous. However, in practice, the equilibrium effects on interest rates tend to be procyclical, suggesting that the supply curve shifts more than the demand curve due to business cycle factors.

SUPPLY AND DEMAND IN THE MARKET FOR MONEY: THE LIQUIDITY PREFERENCE FRAMEWORK

The liquidity preference framework suggests that the interest rate is determined by the supply and demand for money. While the bond market best shows how expected inflation affects interest rates, the liquidity preference framework best shows how changes in income, the price level, and the money supply affect interest rates.

Because money earns little or no interest, the interest rate on bonds is the opportunity cost of holding money. Therefore, at high interest rates, the opportunity cost of holding money is high, and the quantity demanded of money is low. Using similar logic, at low interest rates, the quantity demanded of money is high. As a result, the demand for money has the usual negative slope when graphed in interest rate/quantity of money space. Since we assume that the central bank controls the supply of money at some fixed quantity, the supply of money is a vertical line at the fixed quantity of money supplied. The intersection of money supply and money demand determines the equilibrium interest rate.

Changes in the supply or demand for money cause changes in the equilibrium interest rate. The demand curve for money shifts right if there is an increase in income or if there is an increase in the price level. An increase in the money supply will shift the money supply curve to the right. Thus, other things held constant, an increase in income during a business cycle expansion will cause interest rates to rise, an increase in the price level will cause interest rates to rise, and an increase in the money supply will cause interest rates to fall. This last result is known as the liquidity effect.

An increase in the money supply, however, might not leave "other things equal." An increase in the money supply is expansionary and has secondary effects, which tend to increase national income (the income effect), raise the price level (price-level effect), and increase expected inflation (expected inflation effect). Therefore, an increase in the growth rate of the money supply generates opposing effects on the interest rate: The liquidity effect suggests that interest rates should immediately fall, while the income, price-level, and expected inflation effects suggest that the interest rate should rise. There are three possible outcomes. If the liquidity effect is larger than the other effects, an increase in the rate of money growth will cause interest rates to first fall, and then rise, but not to the level of the original interest rate. If the liquidity effect is smaller than the other effects, the interest rate will first fall, and then rise above the original interest rate. If the liquidity effect is smaller than the other effects and inflation expectations adjust quickly, then an increase in the rate of money growth only causes interest rates to rise. Empirical evidence suggests that an increase in money growth first causes the interest rate to fall and then rise above the original interest rate.

Helpful Hints

1. When dealing with the bond market, it is always helpful to remember that the bond suppliers are borrowers and that the bond demanders are lenders. This distinction is particularly useful when dealing with disequilibrium. For example, if the price of bonds is above equilibrium, there is an excess supply of bonds. If there is an excess supply of bonds, then *desired borrowing exceeds desired lending*. Interest rates rise and the price of bonds falls until we reach equilibrium.

2. Supply and demand models can address both positive and negative shocks to variables that affect supply and demand. In the text and study guide, we often just explain the results of one direction of shock just to save space. For example, we show how an increase in inflation expectations in the bond market affects bond demand, bond supply, the price of bonds, and the interest rate. It is helpful (and good practice) if you address the opposite shock from that demonstrated in the text and see if you can generate the opposite result. In the case described above, since the text demonstrated the case of an increase in expected inflation, you should see if you are able to demonstrate the case of a decrease in expected inflation in the bond market.

3. The phrase, "liquidity preference" is an alternative term for "money demand." That is, our desire to hold money is our preference to be liquid, or liquidity preference. Therefore, a model that employs the supply and demand for money is termed the "liquidity preference framework."

4. The asset market approach (the bond market) and the liquidity preference framework are generally compatible. That is, they generally provide the same answer to the question of how interest rates should respond to a particular shock. We only employ both markets because each market provides a particularly clear answer for how interest rates respond to a few important shocks. Specifically, the bond market provides a clear answer to how interest rates respond to changes in expected inflation, while the liquidity preference framework (market for money) provides a clear answer to how interest rates respond to changes in income, the price level, and the money supply.

5. In the liquidity preference framework, the price-level and expected-inflation effects are related but distinctly different. For instance, a one-time increase in the overall price level will permanently increase the price level. Inflation (and by extension, expected inflation) will increase temporarily, but once the price level achieves the new, permanently higher level, inflation will return to zero. Thus, the (expected) inflation effect is temporary, but the price-level effect is permanent.

Terms and Definitions

Choose a definition for each key term.

Key Terms:

_____4_____ asset market approach

_____5_____ expected return

_____2_____ Fisher effect

_____7_____ liquidity

_____3_____ liquidity preference framework

_____1_____ opportunity cost

_____8_____ risk

_____9_____ theory of portfolio choice

_____6_____ wealth

Definitions:

1. the amount of interest or expected return sacrificed by not holding an alternative asset

2. the outcome that when expected inflation occurs, interest rates will rise

3. Keynes's theory of the demand for money

4. an approach used to determine asset prices using stocks of assets rather than flows

5. the return on an asset expected over the next period

6. all resources owned by an individual, including all assets

7. the relative ease and speed with which an asset can be converted into cash

8. the degree of uncertainty associated with the return on an asset

9. the theory that the quantity demanded of an asset is positively related to wealth, positively related to the expected return and liquidity of the asset relative to alternatives, and negatively related to the risk of the asset compared to alternatives

Problems and Short-Answer Questions

PRACTICE PROBLEMS

1. Use the theory of portfolio choice to determine whether you would increase or decrease your quantity demanded of bonds in response to the following events. Explain.
   a. Your grandmother dies and leaves you a bequest of $100,000.

   _____

   _____

b. Your brokerage firm lowers its commissions on stock transactions but keeps its commissions the same on bond transactions.

_____

_____

c. You are risk averse. You anticipate more volatility in future stock returns.

_____

_____

d. You become more pessimistic about future returns in the stock market.

_____

_____

e. You wreck your uninsured automobile.

_____

_____

f. Your brokerage firm offers discount commissions if you use the Internet for bond transactions.

_____

_____

g. U.S. brokerage firms close many Middle East offices due to threats from terrorists.

_____

_____

2. a. Information is provided below for the demand and supply of $1,000 face value, one-year discount bonds that pay no coupon, and are held to maturity (for the full year). Complete the table and plot demand and supply in the graph provided below. Record the corresponding interest rates on the graph in the box beside the related price. Quantities are in billions of dollars.

Price	Quantity demanded	Quantity supplied	Corresponding interest rate
$975	100	300	25/975 = 2.6
$950	150	250	5.3
$925	200	200	8.1
$900	250	150	11.1

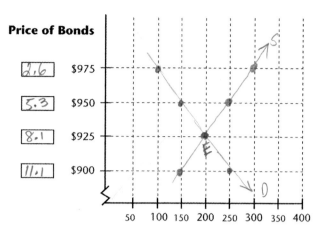

Price of Bonds

2.6	$975
5.3	$950
8.1	$925
11.1	$900

50 100 150 200 250 300 350 400

Quantity of Bonds

b. What is the equilibrium price, interest rate, and quantity demanded of bonds?

925^{a}, 8.1%, 200 Billion

c. Suppose that the price of bonds is above the equilibrium price at, say, $950. Explain why this price is not the market-clearing price, and explain how and why the price of bonds and interest rates adjust to equilibrium.

d. Suppose that wealth in the economy increases causing the demand for bonds to increase by $100 billion at each price. Show this shift on the accompanying graph. What are the new equilibrium price, interest rate, and quantity of bonds?

3. For each of the following events, describe the shift in the supply and/or demand for bonds, and describe the impact on the price of bonds and the interest rate. Use the graph provided to help you determine the answer.

a. There is an increase peoples' wealth.

Demand shifts right and Price gets up

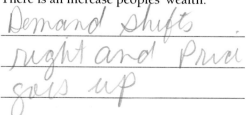

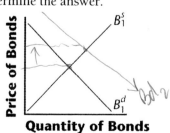

Quantity of Bonds

b. An SEC ruling allows brokerage firms to reduce their commissions on bond transactions but not on stock transactions.

_____

_____

_____

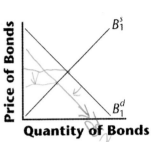

c. The volatility of stock returns decreases.

_____

_____

_____

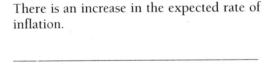

d. People expect higher interest rates in the future.

_____

_____

_____

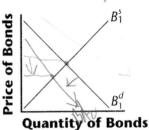

e. There is an increase in the expected rate of inflation.

_____

_____

_____

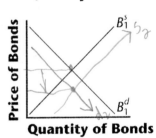

f. People become more pessimistic about stock returns.

_____

_____

_____

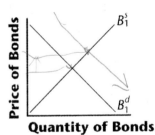

g. The government runs a higher than expected budget deficit.

_____

_____

_____

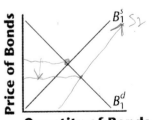

h.   A business cycle expansion occurs.

_____

_____

_____

4.   For each of the following events, use the liquidity preference framework and shift money demand or money supply to determine the change in the equilibrium interest rate.

a.   There is a higher level of income due to a business cycle expansion.

_____

_____

_____

_____

b.   There is a higher price level.

_____

_____

_____

_____

c.   The Federal Reserve increases the money supply.

_____

_____

_____

_____

5.   Suppose that the Federal Reserve increases the growth rate of the money supply. Further, suppose this event causes a liquidity effect, income effect, price-level effect, and expected inflation effect.

a.   In what direction do interest rates move in response to each of these effects?

_____

_____

b. Suppose that the liquidity effect is immediate and smaller than the other effects, and our expectations of inflation adjust slowly. Draw the time path of interest rates on the graph below from an increase in the growth rate of the money supply that occurs at time "T."

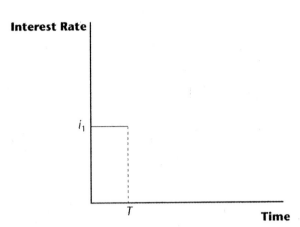

c. Suppose that interest rates adjust to a shock in money growth as suggested in part *b* above. If the Federal Reserve wanted to reduce interest rates over the near term, should it increase or decrease the growth rate in the money supply? Why? If the Fed wanted to reduce interest rates in the long run, should it increase or decrease the growth rate in the money supply? Why?

_____

_____

SHORT-ANSWER QUESTIONS

1. In the theory of portfolio choice, what are the four factors that affect whether to buy one asset rather than another?

_____

_____

2. Suppose you buy a one-year discount bond that pays no coupons, has a face value of $1,000, and you hold it for the entire year. If you pay $963 for it, what is the corresponding interest rate?

_____

3. If there is an excess demand for bonds, is the price of bonds above or below the equilibrium price? Explain the price adjustment to equilibrium.

_____

_____

4. Suppose people expect lower interest rates in the future. Use the bond market to explain the impact of this event on interest rates.

_____

_____

5. What three events would shift the supply of bonds to the right?

_____

_____

6. Suppose there is a decrease in expected inflation. Use the bond market to explain the impact of this event on interest rates.

_____

_____

7. In question 6 above, the change in interest rates that results from a change in expected inflation is known as what?

_____

8. In Keynes's liquidity preference framework, what is the opportunity cost of holding money? Why?

_____

_____

9. According to the liquidity preference framework, in what direction do interest rates move in response to an increase in the money supply, other things unchanging? What is the name of this effect?

_____

_____

10. If the Federal Reserve increases the growth rate of the money supply, which effect works in the opposite direction from the others? Explain.

_____

_____

Critical Thinking

You are watching the national news with your parents. The news anchor says that interest rates are higher than the historical average. Your parents know that you will begin looking to buy a house in a just few years. Your father says, "I hope that someone is appointed soon to run the Fed that will expand the money supply faster. If more money is available, borrowing rates will go down, and it will be much cheaper for you to buy a home."

1. If the liquidity effect is smaller than the income, price-level, and expected inflation effects, is it true that increasing the growth rate in the money supply will decrease interest rates? Explain for both the near term and longer run.

_____

_____

_____

_____

_____

2. If it is going to be a significant amount of time before you buy a home, is a faster or slower growth rate in the money supply likely to create lower interest rates for you? Explain.

_____

_____

_____

_____

_____

Self-Test

TRUE/FALSE QUESTIONS

___T__ 1. According to the theory of portfolio choice, an increase in expected returns in the stock market decreases the quantity demanded of bonds.

___F__ 2. According to the theory of portfolio choice, an increase in the volatility of returns in the stock market decreases the quantity demanded of bonds.

___T__ 3. A one-year discount bond for which the owner pays $937, holds it for the entire one year, and receives $1,000 at maturity, generates an interest rate of 6.7%. $i = FV - PV / PV = 1000 - 937 / 937 = 6.7$

___T__ 4. The price of a bond and the interest rate are always negatively related for any type of bond, whether a discount or coupon bond.

___F__ 5. If the price of bonds is below the equilibrium price, there will be an excess supply of bonds, and interest rates will rise.

_____T_____ 6. An increase in the government's budget deficit shifts the supply of bonds to the right, decreases the price of bonds, and increases the interest rate.

_____F_____ 7. The asset market approach emphasizes flows rather than stocks of assets to determine asset prices.

_____T_____ 8. An increase in expected inflation decreases real returns at each price of bonds causing bond demand to shift left, bond supply to shift right, the price of bonds to fall, and interest rates to rise.

_____F_____ 9. When expected inflation rises, causing interest rates to rise, we have seen a demonstration of the Fisher effect.

_____F_____ 10. An increase in the riskiness of bonds causes bond demand to increase, the price of bonds to rise, and interest rates to fall.

_____T_____ 11. The liquidity preference framework suggests that the interest rate is determined by the supply and demand for bonds.

_____F_____ 12. In the liquidity preference framework, an increase in incomes, *ceteris paribus*, causes money demand to shift left and interest rates to fall.

_____F_____ 13. An increase in the money supply, other things held constant, causes interest rates to fall.

_____T_____ 14. If there is an increase in the growth rate of the money supply and the resulting liquidity effect is smaller than the combined income, price-level, and expected inflation effects, then the interest rate will eventually rise above the initial interest rate.

_____T_____ 15. If there is an increase in the growth rate of the money supply, the resulting liquidity effect is smaller than the combined income, price-level, and expected inflation effects, and inflationary expectations adjust quickly, then the interest rate will immediately rise and rise further over time.

MULTIPLE-CHOICE QUESTIONS

1. In the theory of portfolio choice, which of the following will decrease the quantity demanded of an asset?
    a. an increase in the wealth of the buyer
    b. an increase in the expected return on the asset relative to alternative assets
    c. an increase in the risk of the asset relative to alternative assets
    d. an increase in the liquidity of the asset relative to alternative assets

2. What is the interest rate on a one-year discount bond that pays $1,000 at maturity, is held for the entire year, and the purchase price is $955?
    a. 4.5%
    b. 4.7%
    c. 5.5%
    d. 9.5%

    $$i = \frac{FV - PV}{PV} = \frac{1000 - 955}{955} = \frac{45}{955} = 4.7$$

3. The price of bonds and the interest rate are
    a. uncorrelated.

b. positively correlated.
c. negatively correlated.
d. either positively or negatively correlated depending on whether the market participant is a bond buyer or a bond seller.

4. Along the supply curve for bonds, an increase in the price of bonds
a. decreases the interest rate and increases the quantity of bonds supplied.
b. decreases the interest rate and decreases the quantity of bonds supplied.
c. increases the interest rate and increases the quantity of bonds supplied.
d. increases the interest rate and decreases the quantity of bonds supplied.

5. If the price of bonds is below the equilibrium price, there is an excess
a. supply of bonds, the price of bonds will fall, and the interest rate will rise.
b. supply of bonds, the price of bonds will rise, and the interest rate will fall.
c. demand for bonds, the price of bonds will fall, and the interest rate will rise.
d. demand for bonds, the price of bonds will rise, and the interest rate will fall.

6. Which of the following statements about the bond market is true?
a. Bond demand corresponds to willingness to lend.
b. Bond supply corresponds to willingness to borrow.
c. The supply and demand of bonds are measured in terms of "stocks" of assets, so it can be considered an asset market approach to the determination of asset prices and returns.
d. All of the above are true.

7. If the demand for bonds shifts to the left, the price of bonds
a. decreases, and interest rates fall.
b. decreases, and interest rates rise.
c. increases, and interest rates rise.
d. increases, and interest rates fall.

8. An increase in the riskiness of stocks causes
a. bond demand to shift right.
b. bond demand to shift left.
c. bond supply to shift right.
d. bond supply to shift left.

9. A decrease in wealth in the economy causes
a. bond demand to shift right, the price of bonds to rise, and interest rates to fall.
b. bond demand to shift left, the price of bonds to fall, and interest rates to rise.
c. bond supply to shift right, the price of bonds to fall, and interest rates to rise.
d. bond supply to shift left, the price of bonds to rise, and interest rates to fall.

10. An increase in expected inflation causes
a. bond demand to shift left, bond supply to shift right, and interest rates to fall.
b. bond demand to shift right, bond supply to shift left, and interest rates to rise.
c. bond demand to shift left, bond supply to shift right, and interest rates to rise.

    d. bond demand to shift right, bond supply to shift left, and interest rates to fall.

11. Which of the following would cause the demand for long-term bonds to shift right?
    a. Stocks become less risky.
    b. People expect interest rates to fall in the future.
    c. Brokerage firms reduce their commissions on stock transactions.
    d. People increase their expectations of inflation.

12. Which of the following will cause interest rates to rise?
    a. The stock market has become more volatile.
    b. Firms become pessimistic about the future profitability of new plant and equipment.
    c. People reduce their expectations of inflation.
    d. The government increases its budget deficit.

13. When an increase in expected inflation causes interest rates to rise, this is known as the
    a. liquidity effect.
    b. output effect.
    c. Fisher effect.
    d. deficit effect.

14. A business cycle expansion causes *Creates More Wealth*
    a. both bond demand and bond supply to shift right.
    b. both bond demand and bond supply to shift left.
    c. bond demand to shift right and bond supply to shift left.
    d. bond demand to shift left and bond supply to shift right.

15. In the liquidity preference framework, interest rates are determined by the supply and demand for
    a. bonds.
    b. stocks.
    c. output.
    d. money.

16. Which of the following effects from an increase in the money supply causes interest rates to decrease in the short run?
    a. the income effect
    b. the liquidity effect
    c. the expected inflation effect
    d. the price-level effect

17. An increase in the price level causes
    a. money demand to shift to the right, and interest rates increase.
    b. money demand to shift to the left, and interest rates decrease.
    a. the money supply to shift to the right, and interest rates decrease.
    b. the money supply to shift to the left, and interest rates decrease.

18. Suppose there is an increase in the growth rate of the money supply. If the liquidity effect is smaller than the income, price-level, and expected inflation effects, and if inflationary expectations adjust slowly, then in the *short run*, interest rates
    a. remain unchanged.

b.   rise.
c.   fall.
d.   become unpredictable.

19. Suppose there is an increase in the growth rate of the money supply. If the liquidity effect is smaller than the output, price-level, and expected inflation effects, then in the *long run,* interest rates
   a.   remain unchanged when compared to their initial value.
   b.   rise when compared to their initial value.
   c.   fall compared to their initial value.
   d.   become unpredictable.

20. In the long run, if the output, price-level, and expected inflation effects outweigh the liquidity effect, to reduce interest rates the Federal Reserve should
   a.   maintain the growth rate of the money supply.
   b.   increase the growth rate of the money supply.
   c.   decrease the growth rate of the money supply.
   d.   do none of the above.

Solutions

Terms and Definitions

 4 asset market approach
 5 expected return
 2 fisher effect
 7 liquidity
 3 liquidity preference framework
 1 opportunity cost
 8 risk
 9 theory of asset demand
 6 wealth

Practice Problems

1. a. increase, because your wealth has increased

   b. decrease, because the relative liquidity of bonds has decreased

   c. increase, because bonds are relatively less risky

   d. increase, because bonds have relatively higher expected returns

   e. decrease, because your wealth has decreased

   f. increase, because the bonds have become more liquid

   g. decrease, because bonds have become less liquid

2. a.

Price	Quantity demanded	Quantity supplied	Corresponding interest rate
$975	100	300	($1,000 – $975)/ $975 = 2.6%
$950	150	250	($1,000 – $950)/ $950 = 5.3%
$925	200	200	($1,000 – $925)/ $925 = 8.1%
$900	250	150	($1,000 – $900)/ $900 = 11.1%

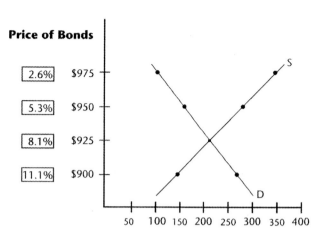

Price of Bonds

Quantity of Bonds

   b. $925, 8.1%, 200 billion dollars

   c. At $950 (or an interest rate of 5.3%), the quantity demanded of bonds is $150 billion while the quantity supplied is $250 billion. The excess supply of bonds means that desired borrowing exceeds desired lending, causing the price of bonds to fall to $925 and the corresponding interest rate to rise to 8.1%.

   d. $950, 5.3%, 250 billion dollars.

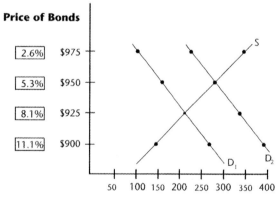

Price of Bonds

Quantity of Bonds

3. a. bond demand shifts right, price of bonds increases, interest rate falls

   b. bond demand shifts right, price of bonds increases, interest rate falls

   c. bond demand shifts left, price of bonds decreases, interest rate rises

   d. due to expected capital losses, expected returns on bonds falls so bond demand shifts left, price of bonds decreases, interest rate rises

e. for each price of bonds, the real interest rate on bonds decreases, causing bond demand to shift left, bond supply to shift right, the price of bonds to fall, interest rates to rise

f. bond demand shifts right, price of bonds increases, interest rate falls

g. bond supply shifts right, price of bonds decreases, interest rate rises

h. this causes an increase in expected profit opportunities and an increase in wealth, bond supply right, bond demand right, and changes in bond prices and interest rates are ambiguous (but bond supply usually shifts right more so price of bonds decreases, interest rate increases)

4. a. money demand shifts right, interest rates rise

b. money demand shifts right, interest rates rise

c. money supply shifts right, interest rates fall

5. a. Liquidity effect causes interest rates to fall. Income, price-level, and expected inflation effects cause interest rates to rise.

b.

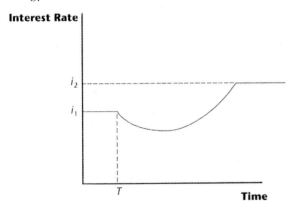

c. Increase money growth because the liquidity effect is immediate, causing interest rates to fall. Decrease money growth because the stronger income, price-level, and expected inflation effects suggest that the interest rate would fall in the long run.

Short-Answer Questions

1. Wealth, expected return relative to alternative assets, risk relative to alternative assets, and liquidity relative to alternative assets.

2. ($1,000 – $963)/$963 = 3.8%

3. The price of bonds is below equilibrium. An excess demand for bonds means that desired lending exceeds desired borrowing, the interest rate falls, and the price of bonds rises.

4. Lower interest rates in the future would mean higher bond prices in the future and an increase in expected returns on bonds purchased today, shifting bond demand to the right today. Bond prices rise and interest rates fall.

5. An increase in the expected profitability of investment opportunities, an increase in expected inflation, and an increase in the budget deficit.

6. For each price of bonds, the real interest rate on bonds increases, causing bond demand to shift right, bond supply to shift left, the price of bonds to rise, and interest rates to fall.

7. The Fisher effect.

8. The interest rate, because since he assumes that money earns no interest, the interest rate is what is sacrificed by holding money.

9. Interest rates decrease. Liquidity effect.

10. The liquidity effect suggests that interest rates should fall, but the income, price-level, and expected inflation effects all suggest that interest rates should rise.

Critical Thinking

1. Not necessarily. In the near term, if people are slow to adjust their expectations of inflation, then interest rates will first fall (liquidity effect). But in the longer run, the interest rate will rise to a point higher than the original interest rate (income, price-level, expected inflation effects). If people adjust their inflationary expectation quickly, then the liquidity effect is overwhelmed by the expected inflation effect even in the near term; interest rates rise in both the near term and long term.

2. The empirical evidence suggests that while there is a small short-term liquidity effect from a change in the growth rate of money, in the long run the liquidity effect is dominated by the income, price-level, and expected inflation effects. Therefore, after all effects are accounted for, a reduction in money growth tends to cause interest rates to decline.

True/False Questions

1. T
2. F
3. T
4. T
5. F
6. T
7. F
8. T
9. T
10. F
11. F
12. F
13. T
14. T
15. T

Multiple-Choice Questions

1. c
2. b
3. c
4. a
5. d
6. d
7. b
8. a
9. b
10. c
11. b
12. d
13. c
14. a
15. d
16. b
17. a
18. c
19. b
20. c

6 The Risk and Term Structure of Interest Rates[*]

Chapter Review

PREVIEW

There are many different interest rates. Due to differences in risk, liquidity, and tax treatment, bonds with the same term to maturity may have different interest rates. The relationship between these interest rates is known as the *risk structure of interest rates*. Bonds with different terms to maturity (but that are otherwise the same) also have different interest rates. The relationship between these interest rates is known as the *term structure of interest rates*.

RISK STRUCTURE OF INTEREST RATES

Bonds with the same term to maturity may have different interest rates because they have differences in:

* Risk of default

* Liquidity

* Income tax treatment

Default occurs when the issuer of a bond is unable to make interest payments or pay off the face value when the bond matures. U.S. Treasury bonds are considered to be *default-free bonds* because they have no risk of default. The *risk premium* is the spread between the interest rate on bonds with default risk and the interest rate on default-free bonds, both of the same maturity. It shows how much bondholders must be compensated to hold a bond with default risk. The risk premium can be demonstrated by analyzing the separate markets for default-free U.S. Treasury bonds and corporate bonds of the same maturity. Suppose the price in each market is originally the same, and therefore the interest rate is the same. Since corporations have some possibility of default, the expected return on corporate bonds is lower.

---

[*]This is also Chapter 6 in the 3rd ed.

The corporate bond's return is also more uncertain. Since the relative expected return is lower and the risk is higher, the theory of portfolio choice tells us that the demand for corporate bonds will decrease, or shift left. At the same time, the relative return on default-free government bonds is higher, and their risk is lower, so the demand for Treasury bonds increases, or shifts right. The price of corporate bonds falls, and their interest rate rises. The price of Treasury bonds rises, and their interest rate falls. The difference between the two interest rates is the risk premium. An increase in default risk on corporate or municipal bonds will increase the risk premium on those bonds. *Credit-rating agencies* rate the quality of corporate and municipal bonds in terms of the probability of default. Similar risk premiums can be calculated between bonds with different bond ratings. Credit-rating agencies have been the subject of criticism recently due to their inability to provide accurate risk assessments leading into the global financial crisis.

According to the theory of portfolio choice, *liquidity* is a desirable attribute. U.S. Treasury bonds are more widely traded and, thus, are easier to sell quickly and at lower cost than comparable corporate bonds. Similar to the analysis of default risk described above, the difference in liquidity between U.S. Treasury securities and corporate bonds causes a further decrease in the demand for corporate bonds and a further increase in the demand for U.S. Treasury bonds. Thus, differences in liquidity across bonds increase the "risk and liquidity premium," which is simply called the *risk premium* by convention.

Interest payments received from holding municipal bonds are exempt from federal income tax. Other things being the same, if a bondholder were in the 35% tax bracket, a 10% return on taxable U.S. Treasury bonds would net the holder 6.5% after tax. In this case, a bondholder might prefer a similar municipal security if it pays more than 6.5%. Alternatively, applying the analysis from above, the tax exempt status of municipal bonds increases the demand for municipal bonds, which increases their price and decreases their interest rate. The taxable status of Treasury bonds decreases their demand and increases their interest rate. Thus, municipal bonds usually pay lower rates than U.S. Treasury bonds.

TERM STRUCTURE OF INTEREST RATES

Bonds that are otherwise the same may have different interest rates if the time to maturity is different. A *yield curve* is a plot of interest rates for a particular type of bond with different terms to maturity. That is, a yield curve shows the term structure of interest rates. A theory of the term structure must explain the following three empirical facts:

- Interest rates on bonds of different maturities move together over time.

- When short-term rates are low, yield curves tend to be upward sloping; when short-term rates are high, yield curves tend to be downward sloping, or inverted.

- Yield curves almost always slope upward.

There are three theories of the term structure of interest rates. The *expectations theory* argues that, if bonds of different maturities are perfect substitutes, then the interest rate on a long-term bond is the average of short-term interest rates that people expect to prevail over the life of the bond. For example, if the one-year interest rate is 6% and next year's expected one-year rate is 7%, the current two-year rate must be (6% + 7%)/2 = 6.5%. As a result, a bondholder would be indifferent between holding sequential one-year bonds earning first 6% and then 7%, and holding a two-year bond earning 6.5%. This theory can explain the first two empirical facts listed above. However, since short-term rates are as likely to rise as fall, the expectations theory suggests that yield curves should generally be flat.

The *segmented markets theory* of the term structure argues that, if bonds of different maturities are not substitutes at all, then interest rates for different maturity bonds are completely separate, and the interest rate for each maturity is determined by the supply and demand for bonds of that maturity. Since the demand for short-term bonds is greater than for long-term bonds, the prices of short-term bonds will be higher and their interest rates lower than long-term bonds. This theory can explain the third empirical fact listed above.

The *liquidity premium theory* of the term structure combines components of the previous two theories. This theory suggests that bonds of different maturities are substitutes but not perfect substitutes. As a result, the liquidity premium theory argues that the interest rate on long-term bonds is an average of short-term interest rates expected to occur over the life of the long-term bond (from the expectations theory) plus a positive term that represents the liquidity premium (from the segmented markets theory). Since people prefer short-term to long-term bonds, the liquidity premium is larger on long-term bonds. The *preferred habitat theory* is the same as the liquidity premium theory if bondholders prefer short-term bonds. While the expectations theory and the segmented markets theories can each explain some of the three empirical facts about the term structure of interest rates, the liquidity premium theory and preferred habitat theories can explain all three. In addition, the liquidity premium/preferred habitat theories allow us to infer future movements in short-term interest rates from the yield curve as follows:

- A steeply upward-sloping yield curve indicates that short-term rates are expected to rise. This often can be an indicator of increases in future inflation.

- A mildly upward-sloping yield curve suggests that short-term rates are expected to stay the same.

- A flat curve indicates that short-term rates are expected to decline slightly.

- An inverted curve (downward sloping) indicates that short-term rates are expected to decline substantially. This can be indicative of future economic weakness and recessionary conditions.

Helpful Hints

1. The segmented markets theory of the term structure is based on the argument that bonds of different maturities are not substitutes. This will be true if people won't accept any interest rate risk. If people won't accept any interest rate risk, they will only buy bonds of a maturity that perfectly matches their expected holding period. If you are saving for next year's vacation, you will only buy bonds in the market for one-year bonds. If you are saving for your retirement, you will only buy bonds in the market for 30-year bonds, and so on. As such, the interest rate for any particular maturity bond is unrelated to the interest rate for any other maturity bond.

2. The preferred habitat theory is a more general theory of the term structure than the liquidity premium theory. The preferred habitat theory leaves open what length to maturity bondholders might prefer. If we argue that, other things the same, bondholders would always prefer short-term bonds, then long-term bonds require an interest rate premium in order to get people to buy them, and the preferred habitat theory and the liquidity premium theory become the same.

Terms and Definitions

Choose a definition for each key term.

Key Terms:

_____ 7 credit-rating agencies

_____ 9 default

_____ 2 default-free bonds

_____ 3 expectations theory

_____ 11 inverted yield curve

_____ 12 junk bonds

_____ 8 liquidity premium theory

_____ 13 preferred habitat theory

_____ 4 risk premium

_____ 6 10 risk structure of interest rates — *Various interest rates with same maturity*

_____ 1 segmented markets theory

_____ 10 6 term structure of ✓ interest rates – DIFF. TER to MATURI

_____ 5 yield curve *to Maturi*

Definitions:

1. A theory of the term structure that argues that markets for different-maturity bonds are completely separate so that the interest rate for bonds of any given maturity is determined solely by supply and demand for bonds of that maturity

2. Bonds with no default risk, such as U.S. Treasury bonds

3. The proposition that the interest rate on a long-term bond will equal the average of short-term interest rates that people expect to prevail over the life of the long-term bond

4. The spread between the interest rate on bonds with default risk and the interest rate on default-free bonds

5. A plot of the interest rates for particular types of bonds with different terms to maturity

6. The relationship among the various interest rates on bonds with the same term to maturity

7. Investment advisory firms that rate the quality of corporate and municipal bonds in terms of the probability of default

8. The proposition that the interest rate on a long-term bond will equal the average of short-term interest rates that people expect to prevail over the life of the long-term bond plus a positive term that represents the liquidity premium

9. A situation in which the party issuing a debt instrument is unable to make interest payments or pay off the face value when the instrument matures

10. The relationship among interest rates on bonds with different terms to maturity

11. A yield curve that is downward sloping

12. Bonds that have a relatively high return due to high default risk

13. The theory that bond holders like to hold specific maturities of bonds, and require a term premium to hold bonds of other maturities

Problems and Short-Answer Questions

PRACTICE PROBLEMS

1. Suppose that the health of the economy improves so that the probability of corporations defaulting on their bonds decreases.
   a. Use the diagrams below to show the shifts in the supply and demand for corporate bonds and U.S. Treasury bonds from the event described above. Describe and explain the shifts in the curves.

   _____

   _____

   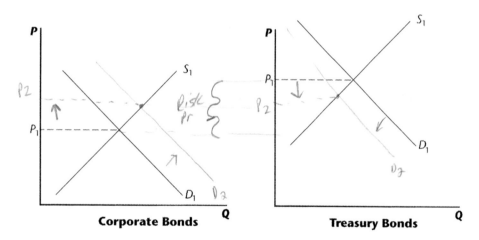

   Corporate Bonds   **Treasury Bonds**

   b. What happens to the price and interest rate on corporate bonds?

   Price goes up and i goes down

   c. What happens to the price and interest rate on Treasury bonds?

   Price goes down i goes up

   d. What happens to the risk premium? Explain.

   Risk premium decreases

   _____

2. Describe the shifts in supply and demand in the financial markets that would result from each of the following events, and then describe the impact on the relevant spread or risk premium.

   a. A major AAA-rated corporation defaults on its bonds. What happens in the markets for corporate bonds and U.S. Treasury bonds and the spread?

   _____

   _____

   _____

   b. The volume of transactions in the corporate bond market increases so that corporate bondholders are more confident that they can find a buyer easily should they decide to sell their corporate bonds. What happens in the markets for corporate bonds and U.S. Treasury bonds and the spread?

   _____

   _____

   _____

   c. The top marginal tax bracket is reduced from 40% to 30%. What happens in the markets for municipal and Treasury bonds and the spread?

   _____

   _____

   _____

   d. A major BBB-rated corporation defaults on its bonds. What happens in the markets for bonds rated BBB and corporate bonds rated AAA and the spread between BBB and AAA bonds?

   _____

   _____

   _____

3. Suppose your marginal tax rate is 30%.

   a. What is your after-tax return from holding (to maturity) a one-year corporate bond with a yield to maturity of 10%?

   _____

   b. What is your after-tax return from holding (to maturity) a one-year municipal bond with a yield to maturity of 8%?

   _____

c. If both of these bonds have the same degree of risk and liquidity, which one would you prefer to own?

_____

d. What does this example suggest about the relationship between the interest rates on municipal bonds versus other bonds?

_____

_____

4. The following questions address the term structure of interest rates.

a. Suppose people expect the interest rate on one-year bonds for each of the next four years to be 4%, 5%, 6%, and 7%. Calculate the implied interest rate on bonds with a maturity of one-year, two-years, three-years, and four-years if the expectations theory of the term structure of interest rates is correct.

$1 year = 4\%$ $2 yr = \frac{4+5}{2} = 4.5\%$ $3 yr = \frac{4+5+6\%}{3} = 5\%$

$4 yr = \frac{4+5+6+7\%}{4} = 5.5\%$

b. Plot the yield curve generated by this data if the expectations theory of the term structure of interest rates is correct.

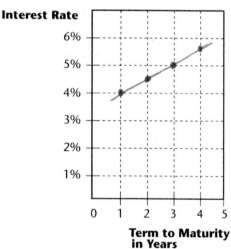

c. Can the yield curve you derived in *b* above be used to explain why yield curves almost always slope upward? Explain.

_____

_____

d. Since short-term interest rates are just as likely to rise as fall, in the long run people on average expect short-term interest rates to be steady. Suppose that people expect the one-year bond rate to remain at 4% for each of the next four years. If the liquidity premium theory of the term structure is correct, what are the liquidity premiums implied by a yield curve that looks like the one you plotted in *b* above?

_____

_____

5. For each of the following descriptions of a yield curve, what is the market predicting about movements in future short-term interest rates, assuming that the liquidity premium theory of the term structure is correct? Explain.

a. The yield curve is perfectly flat. = ST Rates Fall
   decrease

_____

b. The yield curve is moderately upward sloping.
   stay the same

_____

c. The yield curve is inverted.
   fall sharply

_____

d. The yield curve is steeply upward sloping.
   Rise

_____

SHORT-ANSWER QUESTIONS

1. What is the risk premium?

_____

_____

2. What three characteristics of a bond are collectively embedded in the risk structure of interest rates? How does a change in each affect the spread or risk premium?

   Default risk, liquidity, Tax Structure
   _____
   _____
   _____

3. Suppose a corporate bond pays an interest rate of 10%. What interest rate would you expect an identical (same maturity, risk, liquidity, ...) municipal bond to pay if the marginal tax rate is 25%?

   7.5%
   _____

4. What are the two main credit-rating agencies? What are these firms advising investors about? What name do we attach to bonds rated Baa (or BBB) or higher? What name to we attach to bonds rated below Baa (or BBB)?

   Moody's & S&P. The risk these Companies
   will default. Baa or higher = INVESTMENT
   grade. Below Baa = JUNK / SPECULATIVE

5. Why are interest rates on U.S. Treasury bonds usually higher than on municipal bonds when U.S. Treasury bonds are default-free and municipal bonds have some default risk?

   _____
   _____

6. How does the expectations theory of the term structure of interest rates explain the fact that interest rates on bonds of different maturities move together over time?

   _____
   _____

7. How does the expectations theory of the term structure of interest rates explain the fact that yield curves almost always slope upward?

   _____

8. How does the segmented markets theory of the term structure of interest rates explain the fact that yield curves almost always slope upward?

   _____
   _____
   _____

9. Suppose that the Fed has tightened monetary policy and has temporarily pushed short-term interest rates unusually high. People expect the Fed to sharply lower short-term rates in the future. According to the liquidity premium theory of the term structure, what is the likely shape of the yield curve in this situation?

_____

_____

10. If rising interest rates are associated with economic booms and falling interest rates with recessions, what would most likely follow a steeply upward-sloping yield curve— inflation or recession? Why?

_____

_____

Critical Thinking

You are presented with two alternatives: You can buy a three-year bond with a yield to maturity of 7%, or you can buy a one-year bond with a yield to maturity of 6%, then purchase another one-year bond with a yield to maturity of 7%, and when the second bond matures, purchase another one-year bond with a yield to maturity of 8%.

1. What is your expected annual rate of return for the first strategy?

_____

2. What is your expected annual rate return for the second strategy?

_____

3. What can you say about the two expected returns?

_____

4. If the liquidity premium theory of the term structure of interest rates is correct, which one of these choices would you pick? Why?

_____

_____

_____

Self-Test

TRUE/FALSE QUESTIONS

F 1. The spread between the interest rate on a one-year U.S. Treasury bond and a 20-year U.S. Treasury bond is known as the risk premium.

T 2. If General Motors Corporation unexpectedly defaults on a bond issue, the spread between U.S. Treasury bonds and corporate bonds will widen.

T 3. When U.S. marginal income tax rates were very low, municipal bonds generally paid higher interests than U.S. Treasury bonds of the same maturity.

T 4. If more people are participating in the corporate bond market so that corporate bonds are considered to be more liquid, bondholders will increase their demand for corporate bonds, decrease their demand for U.S. Treasury bonds, and the risk premium will fall.

T 5. The difference in the default risk among bonds is the sole determinant of the risk premium.

F 6. When there is a "flight to quality" in the bond market, the spread between bonds rated BBB and U.S. Treasury bonds narrows.

F 7. If a corporate bond pays 10% while a municipal bond pays 7.5%, a bondholder in a 15% marginal income tax bracket would prefer to hold the municipal bond, given that the bonds are otherwise identical.

T 8. The term structure of interest rates is the relationship among interest rates on bonds with different terms to maturity.

F 9. A plot of the interest rates on default-free government bonds with different terms to maturity is known as a term structure curve.

F 10. Yield curves almost always slope downward.

F 11. The expectations theory of the term structure of interest rates assumes that bonds of different maturities are perfect substitutes.

T 12. The segmented markets theory of the term structure of interest rates cannot explain why yield curves usually slope upward.

F 13. If the expectations theory of the term structure of interest rates is true, and if the one-year bond rate is 4% and the two-year bond rate is 5%, then participants in the bond market must think that next year's one-year bond rate will be 6%.

T 14. According to the liquidity premium theory of the term structure of interest rates, people prefer to hold short-term bonds, so they must be compensated with a higher interest rate in order to be induced to hold long-term bonds.

F 15. According to the liquidity premium theory of the term structure of interest rates, a flat yield curve indicates that short-term interest rates are expected to stay the same.

MULTIPLE-CHOICE QUESTIONS

1. The risk premium on a bond may be affected by all of the following except the bond's
   a. liquidity.
   b. risk of default.
   c. income tax treatment.
   d. term to maturity.

2. Which of the following bonds tends to pay the highest interest rate?
   a. U.S. Treasury bonds
   b. corporate Aaa bonds
   c. municipal Aaa bonds
   d. They all pay the same interest rate.

3. Which of the following would cause the risk premium on corporate bonds to fall?
   a. There are fewer participants in the bond markets causing a reduction in the daily volume of transactions.
   b. There is an increase in brokerage commissions.
   c. Forecasters predict that the economy will grow more quickly for the next few years.
   d. U.S. Treasury bonds become more liquid.

4. If the default risk on corporate bonds increases, the demand for corporate bonds shifts
   a. right, the demand for U.S. Treasury bonds shifts left, and the risk premium rises.
   b. left, the demand for U.S. Treasury bonds shifts right, and the risk premium falls.
   c. right, the demand for U.S. Treasury bonds shifts left, and the risk premium falls.
   d. left, the demand for U.S. Treasury bonds shifts right, and the risk premium rises.

5. If the risk premium on corporate bonds increases, then
   a. the price of corporate bonds has increased.
   b. the price of default-free bonds has decreased.
   c. the spread between the interest rate on corporate bonds and the interest rate on default-free bonds has become greater.
   d. the spread between the interest rate on corporate bonds and the interest rate on default-free bonds has become smaller.

6. Municipal bonds tend to pay lower interest rates than U.S. Treasury bonds because
   a. interest payments received from holding municipal bonds are exempt from federal income tax.
   b. municipal bonds are default-free.
   c. municipal bonds are more liquid than U.S. Treasury bonds.
   d. all of the above are true.

7. A reduction in income tax rates shifts the demand for municipal bonds to the
   a. left, shifts the demand for U.S. Treasury bonds to the right, and increases interest rates on municipal bonds relative to U.S. Treasury bonds.
   b. left, shifts the demand for U.S. Treasury bonds to the right, and decreases interest rates on municipal bonds relative to U.S. Treasury bonds.
   c. right, shifts the demand for U.S. Treasury bonds to the left, and increases interest rates on municipal bonds relative to U.S. Treasury bonds.
   d. right, shifts the demand for U.S. Treasury bonds to the left, and decreases interest rates on municipal bonds relative to U.S. Treasury bonds.

8. Suppose your marginal income tax rate is 25%. If a corporate bond pays 10%, what interest rate would an otherwise identical municipal bond have to pay in order for you to be indifferent between holding the corporate bond and the municipal bond?
   a. 12.5%
   b. 10%
   c. 7.5%
   d. 2.5%

9. In which of the following situations would you choose to hold the corporate bond over the municipal bond, assuming that corporate and municipal bonds have the same maturity, liquidity, and default risk?
   a. The corporate bond pays 10%, the municipal bond pays 7%, and your marginal income tax rate is 35%.
   b. The corporate bond pays 10%, the municipal bond pays 7%, and your marginal income tax rate is 25%.
   c. The corporate bond pays 10%, the municipal bond pays 8%, and your marginal income tax rate is 25%.
   d. The corporate bond pays 10%, the municipal bond pays 9%, and your marginal income tax rate is 20%.

10. Which of the following would be considered to be "high-yield bonds"?
    a. junk bonds
    b. speculative-grade bonds
    c. bonds rated Caa
    d. All of the above are correct.

11. A plot of the yields on bonds with different terms to maturity but the same risk, liquidity, and tax considerations is known as
    a. a term-structure curve.
    b. a yield curve.
    c. a risk-structure curve.
    d. an interest-rate curve.

12. Which of the following statements is not true?
    a. Interest rates on bonds of different maturities tend to move together over time.
    b. Yield curves almost always slope upward.
    c. When short-term interest rates are high, yield curves tend to be downward sloping.
    d. When short-term interest rates are low, yield curves tend to be inverted.

13. The expectations theory of the term structure of interest rates implies that yield curves should usually be
    a. upward sloping.
    b. downward sloping.
    c. flat.
    d. vertical.

14. According to the expectations theory of the term structure of interest rates, if the one-year bond rate is 3%, and the two-year bond rate is 4%, next year's one-year rate is expected to be
    a. 3%.
    b. 4%.
    c. 5%.
    d. 6%.

15. The segmented markets theory of the term structure of interest rates is based on the assumption that
    a. bonds of different maturities are not substitutes.
    b. bonds of different maturities are perfect substitutes.
    c. long-term bonds are preferred to short-term bonds.
    d. long-term interest rates are an average of expected short-term rates.

16. According to the segmented markets theory of the term structure of interest rates, if bondholders prefer short-term bonds to long-term bonds, the yield curve will be
    a. flat.
    b. upward sloping.
    c. downward sloping.
    d. vertical.

17. According to the liquidity premium theory of the term structure of interest rates, if the one-year bond rate is expected to be 4%, 5%, and 6% over each of the next three years, what is the interest rate on a three-year bond if the liquidity premium on a three-year bond is 0.5%?
    a. 4%
    b. 4.5%
    c. 5%
    d. 5.5%
    e. 6%

18. According to the liquidity premium and preferred habitat theories of the term structure of interest rates, a flat yield curve indicates that
    a. future short-term interest rates are expected to rise.
    b. future short-term interest rates are expected to stay the same.
    c. future short-term interest rates are expected to fall.
    d. bondholders no longer prefer short-term bonds to long-term bonds.

19. Which of the following theories of the term structure of interest rates best explains the observed empirical facts about the relationship among interest rates on bonds with different terms to maturity?
    a. the liquidity premium theory
    b. the expectations theory
    c. the segmented markets theory
    d. the risk premium theory

20. According to the liquidity premium theory of the term structure of interest rates, a mildly upward-sloping yield curve suggests that
    a. short-term interest rates are expected to rise.
    b. short-term interest rates are expected to fall.
    c. short-term interest rates are expected to stay the same.
    d. bondholders prefer long-term bonds to short-term bonds.

Solutions

Terms and Definitions

_7_ credit-rating agencies

_9_ default

_2_ default-free bonds

_3_ expectations theory

_11_ inverted yield curve

_12_ junk bonds

_8_ liquidity premium theory

_13_ preferred habitat theory

_4_ risk premium

_6_ risk structure of interest rates

_1_ segmented markets theory

_10_ term structure of interest rates

_5_ yield curve

Practice Problems

1. a. The demand for corporate bonds increases while the demand for default-free bonds decreases as funds move from Treasury bonds to corporate bonds.

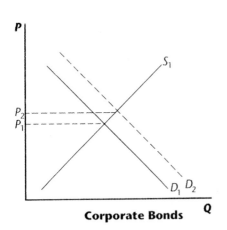

Corporate Bonds

Treasury Bonds

   b. The price increases and the interest rate decreases.

   c. The price decreases and the interest rate increases.

   d. The risk premium decreases because corporate bonds have less default risk.

2. a. The demand for corporate bonds shifts left and the demand for U.S. Treasury bonds shifts right. Interest rates increase on corporate bonds, and interest rates fall on Treasury bonds, so the risk premium or spread increases.

   b. The demand for corporate bonds shifts right, and the demand for U.S. Treasury bonds shifts left. Interest rates decrease on corporate bonds, and interest rates increase on Treasury bonds, so the risk premium or spread decreases.

   c. The tax advantage of municipal bonds decreases, so the demand for municipal bonds shifts left, and the demand for Treasury bonds shifts right. Interest rates on municipal bonds increase, and interest rates on Treasury bonds decrease. If municipal bonds were paying lower interest rates than Treasuries, then interest rates on municipal bonds will rise toward Treasuries or could even rise above Treasuries, causing the spread to increase.

   d. The demand for BBB corporate bonds shifts left and the demand for AAA corporate bonds shifts right. This causes the interest rate to increase on BBB bonds and decrease on AAA bonds, causing the spread between BBB and AAA bonds to increase.

3. a. After paying taxes, you get to keep 70% of the 10%, or 7%.

   b. The interest is tax exempt, so you keep all 8%.

   c. The municipal bond.

   d. Municipal bonds will pay a lower interest rate than corporate or Treasury bonds of similar risk, liquidity, and maturity.

4. a. 1 year = 4%, 2 years = (4% + 5%)/2 = 4.5%, 3 years = (4% + 5% + 6%)/3 = 5%, 4 years = (4% + 5% + 6% + 7%)/4 = 5.5%.

b.

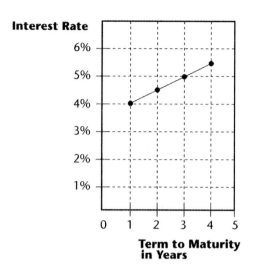

c. No. The expectations theory of the term structure can only explain an upward-sloping yield curve if short-term rates are expected to rise, but rates can't always be expected to rise.

d. 1 year = 4% − 4% = 0%, 2 year = 4.5% − 4% = 0.5%, 3 year = 5% − 4% = 1%, 4 year = 5.5% − 4% = 1.5%.

5. a. Future short-term rates are expected to fall slightly, because if interest rates were expected to be stable, the curve would slope up slightly due to the liquidity premium.

b. Future short-term rates are expected to stay the same, because a stable interest rate plus an increasing liquidity premium will cause a moderately upward slope.

c. Future short-term interest rates are expected to fall sharply. If long-term rates are sharply below short-term rates even with a liquidity premium attached, short-term rates must be expected to fall sharply.

d. Future short-term rates are expected to rise. If the curve is rising faster than can be explained by the liquidity premium, it must be because short-term rates are expected to rise.

Short-Answer Questions

1. The amount of additional interest people must earn in order to be willing to hold a risky bond.

2. Risk of default, liquidity, and income tax treatment. An increase in the risk of default or a decrease in liquidity of a corporate bond

causes the risk premium to increase. A decrease in the tax rate causes an increase in the interest rate on tax-exempt bonds (municipals), which can be considered an increase in the risk premium on municipals.

3. After tax interest rate on corporate = interest rate on municipal. 10%(1 − 0.25) = 7.5%.

4. Moody's Investor Service and Standard and Poor's Corporation. They advise investors about the probability of default on corporate and municipal bonds. Investment-grade securities. Speculative-grade or junk bonds.

5. The tax-exempt status of the municipal bond outweighs the lower risk of the Treasury bond.

6. If long-term rates are an average of expected short-term rates, then an increase in short-term rates and expected future short-term rates will increase long-term rates too.

7. It can't explain it. The expectations theory alone suggests that yield curves should be flat on average.

8. The theory argues that bonds of different maturities are not substitutes and people have a greater demand for short-term bonds than long-term bonds. Thus, the prices are higher on short-term bonds and their interest rates are lower.

9. If people expect short-term rates to fall sharply in the future, the yield curve will be downward sloping.

10. Inflation. An upward-sloping yield curve means people expect future short-term rates to rise, so people expect a boom. Prices tend to rise during an economic boom.

Critical Thinking

1. 7%.

2. (6% + 7% + 8%)/3 = 7%.

3. The expected returns are the same.

4. The three one-year bonds are preferred. Other things the same, people prefer short-term securities. Thus, people require a liquidity premium (a higher interest rate) in order to be induced to hold longer-term bonds, and this three-year bond does not pay a liquidity premium.

True/False Questions

1. F
2. T
3. T
4. T
5. F
6. F
7. F
8. T
9. F
10. F
11. T
12. F
13. T
14. T
15. F

Multiple-Choice Questions

1. d
2. b
3. c
4. d
5. c
6. a
7. a
8. c
9. b
10. d
11. b
12. d
13. c
14. c
15. a
16. b
17. d
18. c
19. a
20. c

7

The Stock Market,
the Theory of
Rational Expectations,
and the Efficient
Market Hypothesis*

Chapter Review

PREVIEW

There are a variety of fundamental theories that underlie the valuation of stocks and other securities. These theories require that we understand how expectations affect stock market behavior because, to value a stock, people must form expectations about a firm's future dividends and the rate to discount future values. The *theory of rational expectations*, when applied to financial markets, implies the *efficient market hypothesis*.

COMPUTING THE PRICE OF COMMON STOCK

Stockholders have voting rights within the firm and are *residual claimants* on the firm's *cash flows*. Stockholders also receive *dividends* from the net earnings of the corporation. The value of any investment is the present discounted value of all expected cash flows the investment will generate over its life. A one-period model of stock price determination would suggest that $P_0 = [Div/(1 + k_e)] + [P_1/(1 + k_e)]$, where P_0 = the current price of the stock, Div = the dividend paid at the end of the year, k_e = the required return on investments on equities, and P_1 = the price of the stock at the end of the period. The *generalized dividend model* extends the single period model by discounting all future expected cash flows. Since the sale price is so far in the future, it is discounted to such a degree that its value is very small and can be ignored. Thus, the generalized dividend model says that the current price of a stock is the sum of the present value of all future dividends. This is difficult to calculate because it requires that we estimate all future dividends. The *Gordon growth model* is a simplified version of the generalized dividend model that assumes a constant growth rate of dividends. Thus, $P_0 = Div_0(1 + g)/(k_e - g) = Div_1/(k_e - g)$, where Div_0 = the most recently paid dividend, Div_1 = the next future dividend, and g = the expected constant growth rate of dividends.

---

*This is also Chapter 7 in the 3rd ed.

HOW THE MARKET SETS STOCK PRICES

On a day-to-day basis, stock prices are set by the interaction of traders in the stock market. As with an auction, the price of a stock is determined by the buyer who values the stock the greatest. Based on the Gordon growth model, the trader who values the stock the greatest either has less uncertainty regarding its future cash flows or estimates its cash flows to be greater than other traders do. New information that causes even small changes in expectations about dividend growth rates or required returns causes large changes in stock prices, so stock markets are often volatile. Monetary policy affects stock prices by altering the required rate of return on equities (k_e) and by altering the performance of the economy, which can affect the expected growth rate of dividends (g).

THE THEORY OF RATIONAL EXPECTATIONS

The evaluation of stock prices requires that people form expectations about firms' future cash flows and the discount rate. An older theory, called *adaptive expectations,* suggests that expectations of a variable are based on an average of past values of that variable. A more modern theory, called *rational expectations,* suggests that expectations are identical to *optimal forecasts* (the best guess of the future), which uses all available information. This does not mean that rational expectations are perfectly accurate. Expectations can still be rational even if an additional factor is important in the prediction but was not available to the forecaster. It would be irrational if additional information were available, but the forecaster ignored it or was unaware of it.

It is logical that people form rational expectations because there is a cost to people whose expectations are not based on the optimal forecast. As a result:

- If there is a change in the way a variable moves, the way in which expectations of this variable are formed will change as well.

- The forecast errors of expectations will on average be zero, and they cannot be predicted ahead of time.

THE EFFICIENT MARKET HYPOTHESIS: RATIONAL EXPECTATIONS IN FINANCIAL MARKETS

The application of the theory of rational expectations to financial markets is called the *efficient market hypothesis.* It suggests that prices of securities fully reflect all available information. The above statement is derived from the following: Since the expected return on a security equals the equilibrium return, if rational expectations hold then the expected return equals the optimal forecast of the return. It then follows that the optimal forecast of the return must equal the equilibrium return. Therefore, current prices in a financial market are set so that the optimal forecast of a security's return equals the equilibrium return.

In an efficient market, since prices of securities fully reflect all available information, all *unexploited profit opportunities* will be eliminated by arbitrage. For example, if the optimal forecast of tomorrow's price of a stock is higher than today's price, buying today at the lower price would generate abnormally high returns. This would cause people to buy the stock, driving its price up and its returns down until the optimal forecast of the returns is reduced and equals the equilibrium return. This does not require that all market participants be well informed. "Smart money" will eliminate any profit opportunities, ensuring equilibrium returns are equivalent to optimal forecasts.

The efficient market hypothesis implies that hot tips and investment advisor's published recommendations cannot help an investor outperform the market because this information is already fully incorporated into the prices of securities. One would need to have the information before others have it in order to outperform the market. In addition, stock prices will respond to announcements only when the information being announced is unexpected. This implies that most investors should engage in a "buy and hold" strategy, which will generate the average market return in the long run but with lower costs due to fewer brokerage commissions.

WHY THE EFFICIENT MARKET HYPOTHESIS DOES NOT IMPLY THAT FINANCIAL MARKETS ARE EFFICIENT

A stronger version of the efficient market hypothesis suggests that not only are the prices of securities the result of optimal forecasts, they reflect the true fundamental value of the securities, or what is known as the *market fundamentals* (the items that have a direct impact on future income streams of the securities). This assertion has several important implications:

- If capital markets are efficient, one investment is as good as any other.

- A security's price reflects all available information about the value of the security.

- Security prices can be used to accurately assess the cost of capital, hence help determine whether a specific investment is desirable.

Some economists think that stock market crashes and bubbles (when the price of an asset differs significantly from its fundamental market value) are evidence that the stronger version of efficient markets is not true and point to market psychology and institutional factors as the source. However, large swings in securities prices could be due to changes in new information, which does not violate the efficient markets theory. Ultimately, as long as bubbles and crashes are unpredictable, efficient markets theory holds.

BEHAVIORAL FINANCE

Behavioral finance applies concepts from other social sciences like psychology to understand securities prices. Loss aversion may stop smart money from engaging in *short sales* even when a stock is overvalued. In addition, investor overconfidence and social contagion can explain why trading volume may be abnormally high, why stocks get overvalued, and why speculative bubbles occur.

Helpful Hints

1. When most people hear the phrase "rational expectations," they think that it cannot be true because they know some very irrational people. However, the theory of rational expectations does not require that all or even most people are rational. It only requires that enough people are rational (following *smart money* strategies) that their behavior removes all profit opportunities by moving securities prices to their equilibrium values. This also helps explains why studies employing survey data will find that many people engage in irrational behavior while stock market studies usually show that market outcomes support the theory of rational expectations.

2. Keep in mind that rational expectations does not mean that forecasts are 100% accurate all the time; it simply requires that, on average, forecast errors are zero on average.

Terms and Definitions

Choose a definition for each key term.

Key Terms:

_____ adaptive expectations

_____ arbitrage

_____ behavioral finance

_____ bubble

_____ cash flows

_____ dividends

_____ efficient market hypothesis

_____ generalized dividend model

_____ Gordon growth model

_____ market fundamentals

_____ optimal forecast

_____ rational expectations

_____ residual claimant

_____ short sales

_____ stockholders

_____ unexploited profit opportunity

Definitions:

1. The application of rational expectations to financial markets

2. The manner by which market participants eliminate unexploited profit opportunities

3. A situation in which the price of an asset differs significantly from its fundamental market value

4. Periodic payments made by equities to shareholders

5. Selling borrowed shares of stock that must be replaced at a later date, thus betting that the stock price will go down

6. A situation in which an investor can earn a higher than normal return

7. Expectations of a variable based on an average of past values of the variable

8. Items that have a direct impact on future income streams of a security

9. Expectations that reflect optimal forecasts using all available information

10. The difference between cash receipts and cash expenditures

11. Those who hold stock in a corporation

12. The best guess of the future using all available information

13. A model of stock price valuation that assumes a constant growth rate of dividends

14. Stockholders rights to receive the remains after all other claims against firm assets have been satisfied

15. Field applying concepts from social sciences to understand the behavior of securities prices

16. Determines the value of stock prices solely by the present discounted value of dividends

Problems and Short-Answer Questions

PRACTICE PROBLEMS

1. Suppose that a stock is expected to pay a $1 dividend at the end of this year and that your required return on equity investments is 9%.

   a. Using a one-period model of stock price determination, what would you pay for the stock if you expect to sell it in one year for $17.50?

   _____

   b. Using the Gordon growth model, what would you pay for the stock if you expected the dividends to grow at 3% per year?

   _____

   c. Suppose that you meet the CEO of the firm and you are so impressed that you consider the company to be of lower risk that you previously thought, and so you reduce your required return on this equity investment to 7%. Using the Gordon growth model, what would you pay for this stock?

   _____

   d. Suppose the CEO provides you with inside information that the dividends are going to grow at 4% per year. Using the Gordon growth model, if your required return on this equity investment remains at 7%, what price would you pay for the stock?

   _____

   e. Compare your answers from *b*, *c*, and *d*. According to the Gordon growth model of stock price determination, for a given dividend payment, what are the only things that can increase the price of a stock?

   _____

   _____

   f. If the Fed engaged in an expansionary monetary policy by lowering interest rates, how would the variables in the Gordon growth model be affected, and what would likely happen to stock prices?

   _____

   _____

   _____

2. If the efficient market hypothesis is true, how will each of the follow events affect the relevant asset or security price? Explain your answer.

    a. IBM announces profits of $100 million. Stock analysts had predicted profits of $300 million. What happens to the price of IBM stock?

    _____

    _____

    b. IBM announces profits of $300 million. Stock analysts had predicted profits of $300 million. What happens to the price of IBM stock?

    _____

    _____

    c. IBM announces a merger with Dell Computer. The deal is so complex that only financial analysts and other financially sophisticated people can correctly assess that it will make both firms much more efficient and profitable. The average person is simply confused. What happens to the price of IBM stock?

    _____

    _____

    d. The price of IBM stock has risen each day for the past three days. What should happen to the price of IBM stock on the fourth day?

    _____

    _____

    e. Your investment advisor calls you and tells you that IBM stock is significantly undervalued and that you should buy it. What will likely happen to the price of IBM stock in the future?

    _____

    _____

    f. Your investment advisor calls you and tells you that the price of IBM stock has risen significantly each of the past two Fridays. He suggests that you should buy IBM stock on Thursday. What will likely happen to the price of IBM stock on Friday?

    _____

    _____

g. A new Federal Reserve chairman is appointed and will take office in three months. The future chairman announces that when he takes over, he plans to tighten monetary policy and raise interest rates. Three months later, the new Fed chair takes his position. What happens to the stock market on the day he takes over?

_____

_____

SHORT-ANSWER QUESTIONS

1. John values ABC stock at $10 per share. Susan values it at $15 per share, and Bill values it at $20 per share. In a free-market auction, who will buy ABC stock? Why? What price range will ABC stock trade in? Explain.

_____

_____

_____

2. Suppose a person has better information about a firm than others and so has greater certainty regarding the future cash flows of the firm. Other things being the same, will that person be willing to pay more, the same, or less than others for stock in that firm? Explain.

_____

_____

3. Are rational expectations always perfectly accurate? Why or why not?

_____

_____

_____

4. Suppose there is a change in the way a variable moves. If adaptive expectations accurately represent how people form expectations, are forecast errors zero on average and unpredictable? Explain.

_____

_____

_____

5. Suppose there is a change in the way a variable moves. If rational expectations accurately represent how people form expectations, are forecast errors zero on average and unpredictable? Explain.

_____

_____

_____

6. If the optimal forecast of tomorrow's stock price is higher than today's price, are there unexploited profit opportunities? If the efficient market hypothesis is correct, how does the behavior of market participants eliminate the unexploited profit opportunity?

_____

_____

_____

7. If the stronger version of the efficient market hypothesis is true so that stock prices reflect the true fundamental value of the stock, what strategy should most investors use when investing? Explain.

_____

_____

_____

8. If the efficient market hypothesis is true, can stock prices be predicted? Explain.

_____

_____

_____

9. Do stock market bubbles and crashes violate the efficient markets hypothesis? Explain.

_____

_____

10. If the efficient market hypothesis is correct, what investment strategy is best for most investors?

_____

_____

Critical Thinking

You are watching a broadcast of the Financial Market Report on CNN with a friend. The host reports that a tropical storm in the Gulf of Mexico has just been upgraded to hurricane status. It is expected to hit the entire gulf coast of the United States and destroy most of the sugar beet farms. Your friend says, "We should purchase stock in C&H Sugar because they produce only pure cane sugar from outside the gulf region, and its stock price will surely rise after the storm damages its competitors."

1. Is it likely that you can make abnormally high returns by using this information to buy stock in C&H Sugar? Why or why not?

   _____

   _____

   _____

2. Suppose another friend works for the U.S. Weather Bureau. She calls you late at night and in casual conversation tells you that weather satellites have detected cloud movements that suggest that an enormous storm is in the process of forming. The weather bureau has not yet reported this information. It is afraid of causing panic because there are no evacuation plans in place. Can you earn abnormally high returns using this information? Why or why not?

   _____

   _____

   _____

3. What will happen to the price and returns to stock in C&H Sugar as you (and later others) buy stock in C&H Sugar? Can abnormally high returns be maintained? Explain.

   _____

   _____

   _____

Self-Test

TRUE/FALSE QUESTIONS

_____1.   Using the one-period valuation model of stock prices, if a share of stock pays an annual dividend of $3, you require a 13% return on equity investments, and if you believe that you can sell the stock next year for $50, then you would be willing to pay $46.90 for the share of stock today.

_____2.   Using the Gordon growth model of stock price determination, if a share of stock will pay a $2 dividend next year, dividends are expected to grow 3%, and people require an 11% return on equity investments, then the price of the stock is $14.29.

_____3.   According to the Gordon growth model of stock price valuation, the trader who values a stock higher than other traders must have less uncertainty regarding the stock's future cash flows or the trader estimates its cash flows to be greater than other traders do.

_____4.   According to the Gordon growth model of stock price determination, a monetary policy that raises interest rates reduces stock prices by increasing the discount rate and reducing the growth rate of the economy and therefore dividends.

_____5.   Other things being the same, if people reduce their required rate of return on investments in equities, stock prices will fall.

_____6.   If adaptive expectations accurately represent how people form their expectations, then people's expectations will be identical to optimal forecasts.

_____7.   Rational expectations are perfectly accurate.

_____8.   The efficient market hypothesis suggests that the prices of securities fully reflect all available information, so the average investor cannot find unexploited profit opportunities.

_____9.   Everyone in a financial market must be well informed and have rational expectations in order for the price of a security to be driven to the optimal forecast of the price of that security.

_____10. According to the stronger version of the efficient market hypothesis (which argues that prices of securities are driven to their fundamental values), one investment is as good as any other because security prices are correct.

_____11. The efficient market hypothesis suggests that published reports of financial analysts will help investors that use this information outperform the market.

_____12. According to the efficient market hypothesis, the most profitable investment strategy requires the continuous buying and selling of stock.

_____13. Some evidence suggests that investors tend to be overconfident and mistakenly attribute the profits they earn to their trading skills, leading them to trade too often.

_____14. According to the efficient market hypothesis, stock prices will respond to an announcement only when the information being announced is new and unexpected.

_____15. The existence of stock market bubbles proves that people are irrational, and thus, the theory of rational expectations is incorrect.

MULTIPLE-CHOICE QUESTIONS

1. Using the one-period model of stock price determination, at what price should a stock sell for if the required return on equity investments is 8%, the stock pays a dividend of $0.50 next year, and the stock is expected to sell next year for $30?
   a. $27.78
   b. $28.24
   c. $30
   d. $30.50

2. According to the Gordon growth model of stock price determination, at what price should a stock sell for if the required return on equity investments is 12%, the stock will pay a dividend of $1.80 next year, and dividends are expected to grow at a constant rate of 3%?
   a. $12
   b. $15
   c. $18
   d. $20
   e. A price cannot be calculated because the future selling price of the stock is unknown.

3. If a company called Advanced Technologies has yet to pay a dividend on its stock, the generalized dividend model predicts that the company's stock may still have value because
   a. the required return on investment for high technology companies is zero.
   b. all companies are legally required to pay dividends within ten years of the initial public offering of stock.
   c. people expect Advanced Technologies to pay dividends in the future.
   d. all companies that have any physical assets have value.

4. According to the Gordon growth model of stock price determination, other things being the same, if the required return on equity investment were to rise, stock prices should
   a. rise.
   b. fall.
   c. be unaffected.
   d. rise or fall because stock prices are unpredictable.

5. Which of the following is true regarding the pricing of assets?
   a. The price is set by the buyer willing to pay the highest price.
   b. The price is set by the buyer who can best take advantage of the asset.
   c. Other things being the same, the price is set by buyers with the best information because the reduced uncertainty allows them to discount cash flows at a lower rate.
   d. All of the above are correct.
   e. None of the above is correct.

6. Suppose that the Fed engages in an expansionary monetary policy, which reduces interest rates. Which of the following statements best describes the impact of this event on the stock market?
   a. There will be a decrease in the required rate of return on equities, an increase in the growth rate on dividends, and stock prices will rise.
   b. There will be an increase in the required rate of return on equities, a decrease in the growth rate on dividends, and stock prices will fall.
   c. There will be a decrease in the required rate of return on equities, a decrease in the growth rate on dividends, and stock prices will fall.
   d. There will be an increase in the required rate of return on equities, a decrease in the growth rate on dividends, and stock prices will rise.

7. The efficient market hypothesis is an application of the theory of
   a. adaptive expectations.
   b. perfect expectations.
   c. rational expectations.
   d. efficient expectations.

8. Interest rates have been at 5% for the past four years. The economy goes into a recession causing the Fed chairperson to announce an expansionary monetary policy with an interest rate target of 3%. You forecast interest rates for next year to be 5%. This is an example of applying the theory of
   a. adaptive expectations.
   b. rational expectations.
   c. fundamental expectations.
   d. forecast expectations.

9. Which of the following statements about rational expectations is true?
   a. Rational expectations are the same as adaptive expectations.
   b. Rational expectations are always accurate.
   c. Rational expectations are identical to optimal forecasts.
   d. Rational expectations theory suggests that forecasts errors of expectations are sizable and can be predicted.
   e. All of the above are true.

10. If stock markets are efficient, then
    a. hot tips are valuable.
    b. a well-diversified mutual fund may be the best investment strategy for the average investor.
    c. investors need the advice of financial analysts in order to make an average return.
    d. the optimal investment strategy is to buy and sell often in order to profit from price swings.

11. An "optimal forecast" is best defined as the
    a. correct forecast.
    b. best guess using all available information.
    c. actual outcome.
    d. best possible forecast using only past values of the variable.

12. Which of the following is *not* true regarding efficient markets?
    a. The prices of securities reflect all available information.
    b. Smart money eliminates unexploited profit opportunities.
    c. Everyone in the market must be well informed.
    d. Hot tips in the stock market are unlikely to bring exceptional returns.

13. Ford Motor Company announces quarterly profits of $200 million. Its stock price immediately falls based on this news. It is likely that
    a. the pre-announcement price reflected higher profit expectations.
    b. expectations are not rational.
    c. markets are not efficient.
    d. stock prices are biased measures of future corporate earnings.

14. According to the efficient market hypothesis, paying a financial analyst for investment advice
    a. will increase your expected returns substantially.
    b. will not affect on your returns.
    c. may decrease your returns somewhat due to high brokerage commissions.
    d. will have no predictable effect on your returns.

15. If the efficient market hypothesis is true,
    a. stock prices should rise every year.
    b. hot tips help investors earn abnormally high returns.
    c. the advice of financial analysts is useful.
    d. a buy and hold investment strategy is best.

16. Unexploited profit opportunities
    a. are often available.
    b. are quickly eliminated by arbitrage.
    c. help investors generate abnormally high returns in the long run.
    d. None of the above is correct.

17. According to the efficient market hypothesis, in order to earn abnormally high returns, an investor would need to
    a. read many published reports of stock analysts.
    b. buy mutual funds that have performed exceptionally well in the past.
    c. have better information than other market participants.
    d. All of the above are correct.

18. Announcements of already-known information
    a. generate unexploited profit opportunities.
    b. improve forecasts of stock prices.
    c. reduce stock returns.
    d. fail to affect stock prices.

19. Stock market bubbles
    a. can occur even if market participants are rational.
    b. prove that the efficient market hypothesis is incorrect.
    c. occur when stock prices move directly with the fundamental value of the stock.
    d. should be able to be predicted by stock analysts.

20. Evidence from studies in behavioral finance suggests that
    a. investors do not fear losing money so they engage in too much short selling.
    b. investors are overconfident so they buy and sell too often.
    c, investment fads cause stock prices to be undervalued most of the time.
    d. All of the above are true.

Solutions

Terms and Definitions

_7_ adaptive expectations

_2_ arbitrage

_15_ behavioral finance

_3_ bubble

_10_ cash flows

_4_ dividends

_1_ efficient market hypothesis

_16_ generalized dividend model

_13_ Gordon growth model

_8_ market fundamentals

_12_ optimal forecast

_9_ rational expectations

_14_ residual claimant

_5_ short sales

_11_ stockholders

_6_ unexploited profit opportunity

Practice Problems

1. a. $P = \$1/1.09 + \$17.50/1.09 = \$18.50/1.09$ $= \$16.97$

    b. $P = \$1/(9\% - 3\%) = \$1/0.06 = \$16.67$

    c. $P = \$1/(7\% - 3\%) = \$1/0.04 = \$25.00$

    d. $P = \$1/(7\% - 4\%) = \$1/0.03 = \$33.33$

    e. A reduction in the required return on equities or an increase in the growth rate of dividends.

    f. Interest rates on bonds would fall causing investors to accept lower returns in the stock market (k_e would fall). The economy would grow more quickly causing the growth rate of dividends to rise (g would rise). Stock prices would rise.

2. a. The price falls. Even though profits appear high, the stock price had fully reflected the greater expected profits, so this was bad news.

    b. The price stays the same (if no other events take place). Expectations were realized. The stock price had fully reflected the correct profits, so the announcement was not news.

c. The price rises. It is not necessary that everyone in a financial market be well informed for unexploited profit opportunities to be eliminated. Smart money can move the market.

d. The price could rise or fall because stock prices have incorporated all available public information.

e. The price could rise or fall because the current price is the best guess of the true value of the stock.

f. The price could rise or fall because regular patterns will be acted upon to remove the unexploited profit opportunities.

g. There should be no impact on the stock market because the Fed Chairman's comments are already fully reflected in the stock prices.

Short-Answer Questions

1. Bill, because assets go to the person who values them the most. The price will exceed $15 and could range up to $20. The price is set by the one that values the asset the most, and that person will bid something greater than the next highest bidder.

2. More. The individual with superior information and certainty will discount the future cash flows at a lower interest rate, increasing the valuation of the stock.

3. No. Forecasts will be accurate on average, but unpredictable events will cause the actual event to randomly deviate from the optimal forecast.

4. No. If an event makes the average value of a random variable permanently larger, adaptive expectations will fail to fully adjust and will under-predict the variable, making forecast errors non-zero and predictable.

5. Yes. If an event makes the average value of a random variable permanently larger, rational expectations will fully reflect the new information, making forecast errors zero on average and unpredictable.

6. Yes. If the price is below the optimal forecast, the return to the stock will exceed the equilibrium return. Smart money will engage in arbitrage, buying the stock and causing the

price to increase until the optimal forecast of the return equals the equilibrium return. The unexploited profit opportunity is eliminated.

7. Since there are no unexploited profit opportunities and the price reflects fundamental value, one stock is as good another. Buy and hold a diversified set of stocks to generate the average market return and avoid excessive brokerage commissions.

8. No. If stock prices reflect all publicly available information, then no unexploited profit opportunities exist.

9. No. As long as there are no exploitable profit opportunities, then the efficient markets hypothesis will hold. In particular, as long as the bubbles and crashes are not predictable, the efficient markets theory will hold.

10. Use a "buy and hold" strategy to generate an average market return at low cost.

Critical Thinking

1. No. If markets are efficient, the current price of the stock incorporates all available information. Since information about the storm is public, the price of the stock will already have risen before you can buy it.

2. Yes. Since the information is not publicly available, it will not be incorporated into the price. You can buy at the low price and make abnormally high returns as the price appreciates.

3. The price will rise, and the returns will return to the equilibrium return. Abnormally high returns cannot be maintained in the long run. The behavior of smart money eliminates the unexploited profit opportunity.

True/False Questions

1. T
2. F
3. T
4. T
5. F
6. F
7. F
8. T
9. F
10. T
11. F
12. F
13. T
14. T
15. F

Multiple-Choice Questions

1. b
2. d
3. c
4. b
5. d
6. a
7. c
8. a
9. c
10. b
11. b
12. c
13. a
14. c
15. d
16. b
17. c
18. d
19. a
20. b

8 An Economic Analysis of Financial Structure[*]

Chapter Review

PREVIEW

The financial system is designed to move funds from savers to borrowers with the most productive uses. Thus, the efficiency of the financial system is an important link in explaining the performance of the macroeconomy.

BASIC FACTS ABOUT FINANCIAL STRUCTURE THROUGHOUT THE WORLD

There are eight basic facts about the financial structure that this chapter will explain.

- *Stocks are not the most important source of external financing for businesses.* In the United States, only 11% of external financing comes from stock. In other developed countries it is much less.

- *Issuing marketable debt and equity securities is not the primary way in which businesses finance their operations.* Stocks and bonds combined only add up to 43% of the external source of funds to U.S. businesses and even less in other countries.

- *Indirect finance, which involves the activities of financial intermediaries, is many times more important than direct finance, in which businesses raise funds directly from lenders in financial markets.* Since most of the newly issued securities of firms are sold to financial intermediaries, less than 10% of external funding is truly direct finance.

---

[*]This is also Chapter 8 in the 3rd ed.

- *Financial intermediaries, particularly banks, are the most important source of external funds used to finance businesses.* While this is true for the United States, it is even more the case in developing nations.

- *The financial system is among the most heavily regulated sectors of the economy.* Regulations promote the provision of information and stability of the system.

- *Only large, well-established corporations have easy access to securities markets to finance their activities.* Small firms obtain their funding primarily from banks.

- *Collateral is a prevalent feature of debt contracts for both households and businesses.* Collateralized debt, known as *secured debt*, requires the borrower to pledge an asset to the lender to guarantee payment of the debt.

- *Debt contracts typically are extremely complicated legal documents that place substantial restrictions on the behavior of the borrower.* Loan contracts usually contain restrictive covenants that restrict the activities in which the borrower can engage.

Understanding transaction costs and information costs will help explain the eight facts above.

TRANSACTION COSTS

People with only a small amount to loan cannot lend through financial markets because the brokerage fees are too large and the denominations of issues may be too large. To lower transaction costs, mutual funds take advantage of *economies of scale* by combining many small savers' funds and buying a widely diversified portfolio. Financial intermediaries also gain *expertise* in carrying out customer transactions, which reduces transaction costs further. This cost reduction allows money market mutual funds to provide *liquidity services*.

ASYMMETRIC INFORMATION: ADVERSE SELECTION AND MORAL HAZARD

Asymmetric information is when each party to a transaction has unequal knowledge about the other party. This leads to two problems: *adverse selection* (which occurs before the transaction) and *moral hazard* (which occurs after the transaction). Adverse selection occurs when bad credit risks are the ones who most desire to borrow. Moral hazard occurs when borrowers engage in activities that are undesirable from the lender's point of view. The analysis of how asymmetric information affects economic behavior is known as *agency theory*.

THE LEMONS PROBLEM: HOW ADVERSE SELECTION INFLUENCES FINANCIAL STRUCTURE

If a buyer can't determine if a product for sale is a lemon, he will pay only a low value. Sellers of good quality products won't want to sell at the lower price. As a result, the market becomes small and inefficient at moving goods from sellers to buyers. In financial markets, the adverse selection problem suggests that risky firms benefit more from borrowing. If lenders can't distinguish between good and bad firms, they will pay only low prices for securities (that is, charge high interest rates). Good firms won't bother to sell securities at the low price, so the market is small and inefficient. This is a reason why stocks and bonds are not the primary source of financing for businesses.

There are tools to help reduce the asymmetric information problem that causes the lemons problem. These tools help lenders distinguish good firms from bad.

- *Private production and sale of information.* Standard and Poor's, Moody's, and Value Line gather information and sell it. However, the *free-rider problem* (those not paying for the information but still benefiting) reduces the production of private information.

- *Government regulation to increase information.* The Securities and Exchange Commission (SEC) requires firms to have independent audits, use standard accounting principles, and disclose information about sales, assets, and earnings. As a result, the financial system is heavily regulated. This reduces the asymmetric information problem, but does not eliminate it.

- *Financial intermediation.* Since it is so hard for individuals to acquire enough information to make completely informed loans, most people lend to financial intermediaries, such as a bank, who then lend to the ultimate borrower. The bank becomes an expert in sorting good credit risks from bad. There is no free-rider problem because the bank makes private, nontraded loans rather than buying securities. The larger and more established the firm, the more likely it is that they will issue securities rather than borrow from an intermediary.

- *Collateral and net worth. Collateral* is property promised to the lender if the borrower defaults, which reduces the consequences to the lender of a default. *Net worth*, or equity capital, is the difference between a firm's assets and liabilities. Large net worth lowers the probability of default and acts as collateral in the event of default.

HOW MORAL HAZARD AFFECTS THE CHOICE BETWEEN DEBT AND EQUITY CONTRACTS

The *principal-agent problem* causes a particular type of moral hazard in equity contracts. Managers (agents) act in their own interests rather than the interests of the stockholders (principals). The following are tools that help solve the principal-agent problem.

- *Production of information: monitoring.* Stockholders can engage in *costly state verification*, which is where individuals monitor the firm through auditing and observing management. It is expensive and suffers from the free-rider problem.

- *Government regulation to increase information.* Governments impose standard accounting principles and punish fraud.

- *Financial intermediation.* Venture capital firms pool resources of their partners and help entrepreneurs start new businesses. In exchange they receive equity and membership on the board of directors, which provides lower-cost verification activities.

- *Debt contracts.* Since a lender receives a fixed amount of interest as opposed to a portion of the profits, the principal-agent problem is much smaller with debt finance when compared to equity finance. This explains why debt contracts are more prevalent than equity contracts.

HOW MORAL HAZARD INFLUENCES FINANCIAL STRUCTURE IN DEBT MARKETS

Although debt contracts suffer from moral hazard less than equity contracts, there is still an incentive for the borrower to behave in a more risky fashion than the lender wants. The following tools help solve the moral hazard problem in debt contracts by making the contracts *incentive compatible.*

- *Net worth and collateral.* When borrowers have more to lose, moral hazard is reduced.
- *Monitoring and enforcement of restrictive covenants.* Covenants can discourage undesirable behavior (avoid risky behavior), encourage desirable behavior (require life insurance for the borrower), keep collateral valuable, and provide information (periodic accounting reports).
- *Financial intermediation.* Monitoring and restrictive covenants still suffer from the free-rider problem. Financial intermediaries make private loans that don't have this problem, which explains why financial intermediaries predominate.

Helpful Hints

1. Transaction costs and information costs explain the proportion of external finance done through stocks, bonds, and intermediation. High transaction costs suggest that only large borrowers and lenders use the direct financial markets, so most people and firms use intermediaries. Information costs due to adverse selection and moral hazard further explain why most external finance is through intermediaries. Information costs also explain why most of the remaining direct finance is done with debt rather than equity.

2. Markets are efficient when all mutually beneficial transactions take place. Therefore, markets become inefficient when there are impediments to trade that reduce the number of participants in the market. In the case of the financial markets, transaction costs and information costs reduce the amount of participants in the direct finance markets, reducing the efficiency of the direct finance markets and providing an opportunity for financial intermediaries to improve efficiency.

Terms and Definitions

Choose a definition for each key term.

Key Terms:

_9_ agency theory

_4_ collateral

_13_ costly state verification

_2_ economies of scale

_7_ free-rider problem

_11_ incentive compatible

_12_ net worth (equity capital)

_5_ principle-agent problem

_8_ restrictive covenants

_1_ secured debt

_3_ state-owned banks

_10_ unsecured debt

_6_ venture capital firm

Definitions:

1. Debt guaranteed by collateral

2. The reduction in transaction costs per dollar of transaction as the size of transactions increases

3. Banks owned by government agencies

4. Property that is pledged to the lender to guarantee payment in the event that the borrower is unable to make debt payments

5. A moral hazard problem that occurs when managers act in their own interest rather than in the interests of the owners due to having different sets of incentives

6. A financial intermediary that pools the resources of its partners and uses the funds to help entrepreneurs start up new businesses

7. The problem that arises when people who do not pay for information take advantage of the information that others have paid for

8. Provisions that restrict and specify certain activities that a borrower can or cannot engage in

9. The analysis of how asymmetric information problems affect economic behavior

10. Debt not guaranteed by collateral

11. Having the interests of both parties to a contract in alignment

12. Difference between a firm's assets and liabilities

13. Monitoring a firm's activities which can be expensive and time consuming

Problems and Short-Answer Questions

PRACTICE PROBLEMS

1. Firms can seek funds through bank and nonbank loans (added together), bonds, and stock. Answer the following questions regarding the preferred method of external finance chosen in different countries.

    a. For the United States, rank the sources of funds from most utilized to least.

    Bank Loans, Debt, equity

    b. Rank the sources of funds from most utilized to least for other industrialized countries and for developing countries.

    c. Compare the sources of funds for U.S. firms to the sources of funds for firms from other industrialized and developing countries. Explain the similarities and differences.

2. The following questions refer to the adverse selection problem generated by asymmetric information known as the "lemons problem."

    a. In general, what is the "lemons problem?"

b. What is the lemons problem as it applies to the direct financial markets?

_____

_____

_____

c. What tools have been developed to reduce the lemons problem in direct financial markets?

_____

_____

_____

d. Have these tools completely solved the problem? Explain.

_____

_____

_____

3. The following questions are based on the principal-agent problem.
   a. What is the principal-agent problem?

_____

_____

b. What tools have been developed to reduce the principal-agent problem in direct financial markets?

_____

_____

_____

_____

c. Have these tools completely solved the problem? Explain.

_____

_____

_____

4. Which of the following, transaction costs, adverse selection, and/or moral hazard, help explain the eight facts about financial structure below? Explain.

   a. Stocks are not the most important source of finance for businesses.

   _____

   _____

   b. Issuing marketable securities is not the primary way businesses finance their operations.

   _____

   _____

   c. Indirect finance is many times more important than direct finance.

   _____

   _____

   d. Financial intermediaries, particularly banks, are the most important source of external funds to business.

   _____

   _____

   e. The financial system is heavily regulated.

   _____

   _____

   f. Only large, well-established corporations have access to securities markets to finance their activities.

   _____

   _____

   g. Collateral is a prevalent feature of debt contracts.

   _____

   _____

   h. Debt contracts are complicated documents often placing restrictions on the behavior of borrowers.

   _____

   _____

5. The following questions address automobile drivers and insurance.
    a. Consider two types of automobile drivers: those who drive with auto insurance, and those who drive uninsured. In this context, briefly explain how the provision of auto insurance exhibits adverse selection.

    _____

    _____

    b. Assume that you are required by law to carry auto insurance when you drive. How does being covered by auto insurance introduce moral hazard? Briefly explain.

    _____

    _____

SHORT-ANSWER QUESTIONS

1. Why are transaction costs high for small savers/lenders?

    _____

    _____

2. How are financial intermediaries able to lower transaction costs?

    _____

    _____

3. How does the free-rider problem reduce efficiency in financial markets?

    _____

    _____

    _____

    _____

4. Is adverse selection a problem before or after a loan transaction? Is moral hazard a problem before or after a loan transaction? Explain each.

    _____

    _____

    _____

5. How does government regulation help reduce adverse selection in stock and bond markets?

    _____

    _____

6. Which are more important sources of external funds to businesses: stocks and bonds, or banks? Are banks becoming more or less important over time? Why?

    _____

    _____

7. When lenders require a borrower to have a high net worth and collateral, are they trying to reduce adverse selection or moral hazard or both? Explain.

    _____

    _____

8. Why do debt contracts have fewer principal-agent problems than equity contracts?

    _____

    _____

9. What are the reasons for restrictive covenants in a debt contract?

    _____

    _____

    _____

10. Why are financial markets in developing countries less efficient than those in developed countries?

    _____

    _____

    _____

Critical Thinking

Suppose that you have worked all summer and accumulated $5,000. You would like to save it, but you might need it one year from this fall for tuition payments. Your friends all have ideas about where you should save it.

1. One friend says, "Lend it to my brother. He's starting a new restaurant that is sure to make big profits." Is this a good choice? Explain.

   _____

   _____

   _____

2. Another friend says, "You should buy stocks and bonds. The market has been doing very well lately. Use my broker. Here's his card." Is this a good choice? Explain.

   _____

   _____

   _____

3. Yet another friend says, "Given your small amount of funds and your need to be liquid, you should buy either a money market mutual fund or simply deposit it in a bank." Is this a good choice? Explain.

   _____

   _____

   _____

Self-Test

TRUE/FALSE QUESTIONS

_____1. Stocks are the most important source of external funds for businesses in the United States.

_____2. In the United States, bonds are a more important source of external funds than stocks.

_____3. Although banks are the most important source of external funds to businesses worldwide, their role is shrinking slightly over time.

_____4. Over 90% of American households own securities.

_____5. Financial intermediaries, such as mutual funds, take advantage of economies of scale to reduce transaction costs by combining many small savers' funds and buying a diversified portfolio.

_____6. Banks reduce the free-rider problem in information production because they make private nontraded loans rather than purchasing securities that are traded in financial markets.

_____F___7. Adverse selection occurs when borrowers use borrowed funds in a manner that lenders find objectionable.

_____F___8. Bonds create a greater moral hazard problem than stocks.

_____F___9. The adverse selection problem in financial markets is eliminated by the private production and sale of information about borrowers by companies such as Standard and Poor's, Moody's, and Value Line.

_____T___10. When lenders cannot sort good borrowers from bad ones, they lend less and financial markets become inefficient.

_____T___11. The principal-agent problem occurs when managers act in their own interests rather than the interests of stockholders.

_____T___12. Firms with relatively low net worth and little collateral are more likely to default on their loans.

_____T___13. To make a debt contract more incentive compatible, lenders may include restrictive covenants requiring the borrower to keep the collateral valuable.

_____T___14. Monitoring the behavior of borrowers after a loan is made is a good way for banks to minimize the adverse selection problem.

_____T___15. Small businesses rely mostly on bank loans, while larger firms rely more on direct finance for funds.

MULTIPLE-CHOICE QUESTIONS

1. The largest source of external finance for U.S. businesses is
   a. stocks.
   b. bonds.
   c. bank and nonbank loans.
   d. venture capital firms.

2. Which of the following statements is true?
   a. Firms raise more funds with bonds than with bank loans.
   b. Firms raise more funds with bonds than with stocks.
   c. Stocks and bonds are the largest source of external funds to businesses.
   d. Direct finance is much more important than indirect finance as a source of external funds to businesses.

3. In which country do firms use direct finance to the greatest degree when compared to the firms of the other countries?
   a. United States
   b. Germany
   c. Japan
   d. Canada

4. Small savers/lenders use intermediaries as opposed to direct lending because intermediaries
   a. reduce transaction costs of the saver.
   b. increase diversification of the saver.
   c. reduce risk of the saver.
   d. do all of the above.

5. Large, well-known companies are more likely than small companies to acquire funds through
   a. direct finance.
   b. banks.
   c. issuing collateral.
   d. nonbank financial intermediaries.

6. Which of the following demonstrates adverse selection? *Moral Hazard*
   a. A borrower takes the funds from a loan to a casino and gambles.
   b. A corporate officer uses the funds from the sale of securities to buy art for his office.
   c. A scientist applies for a loan to research a possible cure for cancer with a low probability of success but a high payoff if successful.
   d. All of the above are true.

7. Your parents loan you money to pay your tuition, and you use the money to play online poker instead. This is an example of
   a. the free-rider problem.
   b. moral hazard.
   c. adverse selection.
   d. financial intermediation.

8. The "lemons problem" is a term used to describe the
   a. free-rider problem in financial markets.
   b. principal-agent problem in financial markets.
   c. moral hazard problem in financial markets.
   d. adverse selection problem in financial markets.

9. When bad credit risks have the most to gain from a loan so they most actively seek a loan, we have a demonstration of
   a. the free-rider problem.
   b. moral hazard.
   c. adverse selection.
   d. financial intermediation.

10. Banks reduce the free-rider problem in information production by
    a. charging others for information about the financial condition of potential borrowers.
    b. buying tradable securities with their depositors' funds.
    c. buying information about smaller borrowers from firms that specialize in gathering information, such as Standard and Poor's and Moody's.
    d. making private, nontraded loans so other lenders cannot benefit from the information they have collected about the borrower.

11. Which of the following is *not* a tool used to reduce adverse selection in the financial markets?
    a. monitoring and enforcement of restrictive covenants
    b. government regulation to increase information about borrowers
    c. private production and sale of information about borrowers
    d. requiring collateral and a high net worth from the borrower
    e. financial intermediation to more efficiently produce information on borrowers

12. The principal-agent problem arises mainly because
    a. principals find it difficult and costly to monitor agents' activities.
    b. agents' incentives are not always compatible with those of the principals.
    c. principals have incentives to free-ride off the monitoring expenditures of other principals.
    d. All of the above are true.

13. The principal-agent problem causes
    a. the collateral problem.
    b. moral hazard.
    c. adverse selection.
    d. the lemons problem.

14. Which of the following is *not* a tool used to reduce the principal-agent problem?
    a. Stockholders engage in costly state verification by auditing and observing management.
    b. Venture capital firms provide funds to new firms in exchange for equity and membership on the board of directors.
    c. Firms issue equity instead of debt because the principal-agent problem is smaller with equity.
    d. Governments regulate firms by imposing standard accounting principles and by punishing fraud.

15. Restrictive covenants
    a. reduce adverse selection.
    b. solve the lemons problem.
    c. make debt contracts more incentive compatible.
    d. are most common in equity contracts.

16. You go into an electronics store to buy a big-screen television. A salesperson rudely tells you that he's too busy to help you now. He says you'll just have to wait. Then you watch him get a cup of coffee and take his break. You've just seen a demonstration of
    a. the principal-agent problem.
    b. adverse selection.
    c. the lemons problem.
    d. how collateral reduces moral hazard.

17. Which of the following is *not* an example of a restrictive covenant in a debt contract?
    a. requiring borrowers to keep their collateral valuable
    b. requiring borrowers to have life insurance
    c. requiring borrowers to provide periodic accounting reports
    d. requiring borrowers to pay a high interest rate

18. Which of the following reduces both adverse selection and moral hazard in a loan arrangement?
    a. requiring that the borrower provide collateral
    b. requiring that the borrower have high net worth
    c. having the borrower use an intermediary, such as a bank, for the loan
    d. all of the above

19. Which of the following is an example of a restrictive covenant?
    a. Government regulations require disclosure of certain information.
    b. A homeowner is required to carry adequate insurance by a mortgage lender.
    c. A lender stipulates that it receive a percentage of a borrowing firm's profits
    d. You tell your neighbor that they cannot park their car on the street in front of your house.

20. When banks are state-owned,
    a. there is little incentive by these banks to efficiently allocate capital.
    b. economic growth tends to be higher.
    c. adverse selection and moral hazard problems tend to be lower.
    d. financial regulation is not necessary.

Solutions

Terms and Definitions

_9_ agency theory

_4_ collateral

_13_ costly state verification

_2_ economies of scale

_7_ free-rider problem

_11_ incentive compatible

_12_ net worth (equity capital)

_5_ principle-agent problem

_8_ restrictive covenants

_1_ secured debt

_3_ state-owned bank

_10_ unsecured debt

_6_ venture capital firm

Practice Problems

1. a. Bank and nonbank loans (together) 56%, bonds 32%, stocks 11%.

   b. Bank and nonbank loans (together) are greatest, followed by bonds and stocks for other industrialized and developing countries.

   c. All countries utilize bank and nonbank loans the most, followed by bonds, and then stocks. The United States relies on direct finance more than other countries do. Developing countries lack the institutions to support sophisticated direct financial markets, so they rely on bank and nonbank loans more.

2. a. Sellers know more than buyers about the quality of the product. Buyers must assume the product may be a lemon (low quality) and bid a low price. At that price, only low-quality products will be offered for sale. The market is too small and is inefficient.

   b. Borrowers know more about the probability of default than lenders. If lenders can't distinguish good firms from bad, lenders bid low prices for securities (charge high interest rates). At the low price, only risky borrowers sell securities. The market is too small and is inefficient.

   c. Private firms produce and sell information; government regulates firms, requiring them to increase information to lenders; lenders require borrowers to pledge collateral against a loan and have high net worth; financial intermediaries use their expertise to sort good firms from bad.

   d. No. The fact that financial intermediaries are larger than direct finance suggests that the adverse selection problems in direct finance have not been completely solved.

3. a. Managers act in their own interests instead of the interests of stockholders.

   b. Stockholders can produce information through audits and by monitoring management; governments can regulate to increase information to stockholders by requiring standardized accounting; funds can be supplied through debt contracts as opposed to equity contracts; financial intermediaries, such as venture capital firms, can monitor at a lower cost with no free-rider problem.

   c. No. The fact that financial intermediaries are larger than direct finance suggests that the principle-agent problems in direct finance have not been completely solved.

4. a. Adverse selection and moral hazard. Stocks suffer from the lemons problem and costly state verification so stocks are not the most important source of funding.

   b. Adverse selection. Stocks and bonds suffer from the lemons problem so they are not the most important source of funding.

   c. Transaction costs, adverse selection, and moral hazard. Indirect finance reduces transaction costs for small lenders and efficiently collects information to reduce adverse selection and moral hazard, while avoiding the free-rider problem.

   d. Adverse selection and moral hazard. Banks make nontraded loans so the information they collect to reduce both adverse selection and moral hazard is less subject to the free-rider problem.

   e. Adverse selection and moral hazard. Governments regulate to increase information to lenders both before the loan and after.

f. Adverse selection. More information is known about large, well-known companies, so they have access to direct finance.

g. Adverse selection. Lenders select borrowers that provide collateral, which lowers the lender's risk.

h. Moral hazard. Debt contracts require complicated restrictive covenants to lower moral hazard.

5. a. Auto insurance exhibits adverse selection in the sense that the drivers who are most likely to get into accidents are also the drivers that are most likely to not be carrying insurance. This is because, often times, uninsured drivers are the most at risk of causing accidents, and therefore, insurance is too expensive or not available to them at all, so they don't bother carrying insurance. This is similar to the banking industry in that the people who are most likely to need loans (need car insurance) are also the ones that pose the highest risk. Insurance companies can reduce adverse selection by gathering information about prior driving history, and other demographic information (like banks do) to determine the riskiness of drivers in setting policy rates.

b. By carrying auto insurance, if you get into an accident you know that the insurance company will pay for losses or medical expenses. This means that you will probably drive less safely than if you had no insurance, since with no coverage you would presumably have to cover all expenses and would have much more to lose in the event of an accident. This is why insurance companies require deductibles in the event of an accident, which requires policyholders to pay a set minimum amount of any expenses for insurance claims. This helps to reduce the moral hazard problem.

Short-Answer Questions

1. Brokerage fees are large, and the denominations of the instruments are too large.

2. They take advantage of economies of scale by combining the funds of many small savers,

and they gain expertise in carrying out repetitious transactions.

3. Due to the problems of adverse selection and moral hazard, lenders need costly information about borrowers. Individual lenders don't want to pay for gathering the information if they can use other's information for free, so little information is produced and too little is loaned.

4. Before. After. Adverse selection occurs when risky borrowers who have the most to gain and little to lose are the ones who want to borrow. Moral hazard occurs when borrowers use the money they borrowed in a manner that lenders would consider undesirable.

5. The SEC requires firms to have independent audits, use standard accounting, and report information on sales, assets, and earnings.

6. Banks. Less important over time because information is getting easier to acquire, so direct finance should continue to grow.

7. Both. Both help banks select a borrower and both help make contracts incentive compatible because borrowers have more to lose in the event of default.

8. The problem is smaller because debt holders receive a fixed payment of interest regardless of the performance of the firm while stockholders share in the profits.

9. Covenants can discourage bad behavior such as taking on risky investments, encourage good behavior such as buying insurance, require that collateral be kept valuable, and provide information in the form of quarterly reports.

10. Developing countries often have weaker property rights, making it difficult to use collateral and restrictive covenants to protect lenders and help solve adverse selection and moral hazard problems. As a result, there is an inefficiently low amount of investment that occurs in developing economies.

Critical Thinking

1. The loan would have high transaction costs because a one-of-a-kind contract would have to be written. Your investment would not be diversified or liquid. It is a poor choice.

2. Your funds are so few and the denominations so large that you cannot buy a diversified portfolio. Transaction costs would be high due to brokerage fees. The funds would not be liquid. It is a poor choice.

3. Either choice would be diversified. Due to economies of scale and expertise of the intermediary, transaction costs are so low that the intermediary can offer liquidity services. Good choice.

True/False Questions

1. F
2. T
3. T
4. F
5. T
6. T
7. F
8. F
9. F
10. T
11. T
12. T
13. T
14. F
15. T

Multiple-Choice Questions

1. c
2. b
3. a
4. d
5. a
6. c
7. b
8. d
9. c
10. d
11. a
12. d
13. b
14. c
15. c
16. a
17. d
18. d
19. b
20. a

9 Financial Crises[*]

Chapter Review

PREVIEW

Financial crises are major disruptions in financial markets characterized by a decline in asset prices and the failure of many firms. This chapter explains why the most recent financial crisis occurred, why these crises are so prevalent, and why these crises tend to be followed by severe economic contractions.

WHAT IS A FINANCIAL CRISIS?

A *financial crisis* occurs when a disruption in the financial system causes an increase in asymmetric information, which increases adverse selection and moral hazard problems. As a result, this causes *financial frictions* in which financial markets fail to channel funds efficiently from savers to productive investment opportunities. A financial crisis occurs when financial frictions are large enough to lead to a sharp reduction in lending and a severe contraction in economic activity.

DYNAMICS OF FINANCIAL CRISES IN ADVANCED ECONOMIES

A full blown financial crisis in most advanced economies involves three stages. The first stage is the initiation of the crisis, which can start from several factors:

- *Mismanagement of Financial Innovation/Liberalization.* When *financial innovation* or *liberalization* occurs, it introduces new products and credit channels into the financial system. And although it can help to improve the efficiency of capital markets, it can also create unexpected imbalances in credit markets and create a *credit boom.* Due to moral hazard and lack of proper regulation, institutions

[*]This is also Chapter 9 in the 3rd ed.

and government regulators are unable to keep credit from being extended to much riskier borrowers. Eventually, riskier borrowers begin to default, creating large losses for banks and financial companies and deterioration in financial firms' balance sheets. This reduces the net worth of financial firms, which prompts *deleveraging* and a sharp contraction in credit. This contraction in credit reduces the financial markets ability to properly address asymmetric information problems, which further limits credit availability. The end result is a sharp reduction in economic activity.

- *Asset-price boom and bust*. When asset prices climb above *fundamental economic values*, this can fuel further investment and create an *asset-price bubble*. Eventually these bubbles burst, sending asset prices tumbling. This reduces the value of assets on financial firms' balance sheets, resulting in a decline in net worth. Financial firms reduce credit to firms with less net worth, and the reduction in lending leads to a decline in economic activity, and a worsening of asymmetric information problems.

- *Increase in uncertainty*. Periods of uncertainty, such as a stock market crash or failure of major financial institutions can trigger a crisis. This has happened periodically in the U.S., for instance with the failure of the Bank of the United States in 1930, and more recently with the failure of Bear Stearns, Lehman Brothers, and AIG in 2008. When this occurs, asymmetric information problems sharply increase, resulting in reduced lending and economic activity.

The second stage is a full-blown banking crisis, in which the contraction in economic activity puts pressure on banks' balance sheets. This is caused through loan defaults and also by reductions in the prices of other assets that banks holds due to the contraction. The end result is that banks become insolvent and fail. Because of the interconnectedness of the banking system, when one bank fails that can lead to other banks failing, causing a *bank panic*. As a result, banks may be forced into *fire sales* in order to raise necessary funds, which further depresses asset prices. As banks fail, credit becomes harder to obtain, and the supply of information needed to mitigate the adverse selection and moral hazard problems becomes even more pronounced. This further deepens the crisis and reduces asset prices. Depending upon the severity of the crisis, the economy may eventually begin to recover, and the process may end here.

If, however, the crisis is strong enough, it may induce a third crisis stage of *debt deflation*. Debt instruments in advanced economies are typically denominated in fixed nominal terms. If the contraction in the economy is severe enough, this could cause a sustained, wholesale decrease in the price level, which further deteriorates firms' balance sheets and net worth by increasing the real debt burden of firms (increasing liabilities). This leads to a further round of credit contraction   and increases in adverse selection and moral hazard. This oftentimes sets the stage for a prolonged, severe economic contraction, as was the case with the Great Depression.

FINANCIAL CRISES: THE GREAT DEPRESSION AND THE GLOBAL FINANCIAL CRISIS OF 2007–2009

Leading up to the 1930s, the U.S. stock market soared. The Federal Reserve responded by tightening monetary policy, which was followed by a stock market crash. As the economy began to recover, the agricultural sector was hit hard by drought, and as with a prototypical financial crisis discussed above, this led to the second stage, a banking crisis. Bank assets (loans to farmers) began to deteriorate, causing banks to fail, which worsened the adverse selection and moral hazard problems. To stem the bank panic, President Roosevelt declared a "bank holiday" in which all banks were closed for several days. Even though the banking system had been stabilized, a third of all commercial banks failed, resulting in less credit availability, and a worsening of asymmetric information problems. This fueled a further decline in stock prices and lead to greater financial frictions and higher *credit spreads*.

The subsequent sharp drop in aggregate demand fueled a 25% decrease in the price level, which triggered the third stage of crisis: debt deflation. As firms' balance sheets deteriorated, this further worsened adverse selection and moral hazard problems, leading to a further restriction in credit and contraction in economic activity.

At the height of the Great Depression in 1933, unemployment reached 25%; other countries around the world were also similarly adversely affected by the bank panics and reduction in demand for goods in the United States. And like the Great Depression, which started in the United States but spread to other countries, the crisis of 2007–2009 followed a similar pattern.

However, instead of being triggered by stock market bubbles, the recent global financial crisis of 2007–2009 was fueled primarily by a housing bubble triggered by several factors:

* *Financial innovation in the mortgage markets.* The development of *securitization* in the form of *mortgage-backed securities* allowed for even the riskiest of borrowers to obtain so-called *subprime mortgages*. Other types of new, more complex financial products expanded the availability of credit, fueling cheap credit that helped to increase access and hence demand for housing.

* *Agency problems in the mortgage markets.* The securitization of mortgages necessitated an *originate-to-distribute* system in which the companies that issued the mortgages sold off the debt. This created *agency problems* where mortgage originators had little incentive to verify credit information or thoroughly evaluate credit risk. This was exacerbated by the holders of the mortgage-backed securities who earned strong returns and, therefore, had little incentive to scrutinize mortgage originators.

* *Asymmetric information and credit-rating agencies.* The agencies that were involved with evaluating the credit risk of borrowers contributed to the asymmetric information problem. In particular, these agencies acted as advisors to the companies that created complex financial instruments and, at the same time, were the ones that rated the credit risk, creating a conflict of interest. This resulted in credit ratings that were much rosier than they actually should have been.

Effects of the crisis were widespread throughout the economy, but there were five key areas that were particularly hard hit. Those include:

- *Residential housing.* Following the 2001 recession, home prices climbed steadily. The expansion of credit through subprime mortgages and other new financial innovation contributed to home price appreciation. And as home prices climbed, credit standards fell, further fueling an increase in demand for housing and rising prices. By 2006, home prices began to peak, the expansion of credit retracted, and the housing market eventually collapsed.

- *Financial institutions' balance sheets.* With the collapse of the housing market, defaults rose substantially. This reduced the value of financial firms' assets, resulting in a decline in net worth. Credit availability declined, and with it came an increase in asymmetric information problems. This led to many homeowners owing more than the value of the house, resulting in millions of mortgages in foreclosure.

- *The shadow banking system.* The strain in the housing market began to take its toll on hedge funds and investment banks, collectively known as the *shadow banking system*, which made their living creating and trading the complex financial instruments supporting the credit boom from the housing market. With the decline in the housing market, the discounts, or *haircuts*, on collateral began to increase, meaning that firms could borrow less. Some firms resorted to quick sales of assets at rock bottom prices to meet obligations, or *fire sales*, which put further downward pressure on the price of these assets. This worsened adverse selection and moral hazard problems by further reducing net worth of households and firms. A decline in credit ensued, and with it a sharp contraction in economic activity.

- *Global financial markets.* Though problems originated in the United States, European markets began to feel the first major effects of the crisis. A major French investment house that held large amounts of mortgage-backed securities began to fail. Central banks around the world pumped substantial liquidity into banks worldwide to prop up failing financial markets, but credit continued to shrink rapidly. A high profile bank in the United Kingdom as well as other European financial firms failed.

- *Failure of high profile firms.* As credit continued to shrink, asymmetric information problems worsened, and asset prices fell, causing the balance sheets of major U.S. financial firms to deteriorate rapidly. Bear Stearns, one of the oldest investment banks in the United States was heavily invested in mortgage-backed securities. Those securities rapidly lost value, and in the spring of 2008 Bear Stearns was forced to sell itself to J.P. Morgan. Later in the summer, Fannie Mae and Freddie Mac, two companies that insure mortgages, had to be bailed out by the U.S. government. At the height of the crisis in September 2008, the investment bank Lehman Brothers failed. The following day, one of the largest insurers in the world, AIG, was propped up by Treasury and Federal Reserve actions due to its holdings of *credit default swaps* tied to the housing market.

Although fiscal policymakers responded to the emerging crisis with a stimulus bill, it was delayed, causing further turmoil in financial markets. The Federal Reserve took a prominent role in trying to stabilize credit and financial markets;

however, the effects of the various policies served only to keep the economy from freefalling further. By the spring of 2009, financial markets finally began to stabilize, and credit spreads began to decline.

DYNAMICS OF FINANCIAL CRISES IN EMERGING MARKET ECONOMIES

Emerging market economies are economies in an earlier stage of market development that have recently opened up their markets for goods, services, and capital to the rest of the world, a process known as *financial globalization*. Financial crises in these economies are initiated through two basic paths: Mismanagement of financial liberalization/globalization or severe fiscal imbalances.

- *Mismanagement of financial liberalization/globalization*: Due to weaker financial supervision in emerging market economies, *financial liberalization* creates an even bigger lending boom than in advanced economies. High risk loans fail, causing a lending crash. The deterioration in banks' balance sheets is even more harmful here because the securities markets are less developed, so there is less ability for financial institutions to hedge and access liquidity or credit markets if needed. As emerging economies grow, macroprudential regulation and supervision may not keep up with financial market liberalization because influential business interests may more easily sway politicians to look the other way or discourage new laws.

- *Severe fiscal imbalances:* Governments in emerging market economies with a fiscal imbalance often force their banks to buy the government's debt. Investors may lose confidence in the ability of the government to repay the debt. This causes the value of the debt to decrease and, consequently, a deterioration of banks' balance sheets. The instability of the government also adds to uncertainty, all of which can lead to bank panics and heightened agency problems.

In addition to the two main factors above, external factors can also play a role in initiating a crisis. For instance, sharp increases in interest rates in the United States can lead to higher interest rates in emerging market countries, reducing *cash flow* and leading to increases in financial frictions. Asset markets in emerging market countries are less liquid and tend to be more susceptible to large swings; business cycle swings tend to be more pronounced, and political systems are more unpredictable, all leading to heightened uncertainty that can worsen the initial effects of a crisis.

In the second stage, a currency crisis ensues. In response to the deterioration in banks' balance sheets, participants in the foreign exchange markets engage in a *speculative attack* on the currency, selling the currency and driving its value down. The speculative attack on the domestic currency could also come from a severe fiscal imbalance where investors fear that the government cannot repay its debts. Eventually, the country will run out of reserves to maintain the overvalued currency, and the country's currency will suffer a rapid depreciation.

In the third stage, a full-fledged financial crisis develops. The decline in the value of the domestic currency causes a sharp rise in the debt burden of firms. This is caused by *currency mismatch*, whereby debt in emerging markets is often denominated in dollars, but assets are denominated in domestic currency. This leads to a decline in firms' net worth, causing an increase in adverse selection and moral hazard. In addition, the depreciation of the currency leads to an increase in import prices and an increase in inflation and interest rates, reducing firm's net worth even more. The inability of firm's to repay their debts to the banks and the increase in the value of the banks' foreign-currency denominated deposits causes a banking crisis, even greater adverse selection and moral hazard problems, a reduction in lending, and a severe contraction in economic activity.

The previous discussion helps explain the recent financial crises that occurred in Mexico, East Asia, and Argentina.

Helpful Hints

1. Financial crises are associated with financial liberalization or innovation, combined with a government safety net. The unregulated financial liberalization causes a lending boom, and the government safety net exaggerates the problem by making the loans appear to be less risky.

2. At some point in a financial crisis, the lending boom turns into a lending crash. Regardless of the source, in the end, an increase in adverse selection and moral hazard in the credit markets reduces lending to a point that it substantially reduces investment and economic activity and increases unemployment.

Terms and Definitions

Choose a definition for each key term.

Key Terms:

_____ asset-price bubble

_____ bank panic

_____ cash flow

_____ credit boom

_____ credit default swaps

_____ credit spread

_____ currency mismatch

_____ debt deflation

_____ deleveraging

_____ emerging market economies

_____ financial crisis

_____ financial engineering

_____ financial frictions

_____ financial globalization

_____ financial innovation

_____ financial liberalization

_____ fire sales

_____ fundamental economic values

_____ haircuts

_____ mortgage-backed securities

_____ originate-to-distribute

_____ repurchase agreements (repos)

_____ securitization

_____ shadow banking system

_____ speculative attack

_____ structured credit products

_____ subprime mortgages

Definitions:

1. a standardized debt security in which the underlying assets are mortgages

2. a situation in which asset prices are driven well above their fundamental economic values

3. a process in which a substantial, unanticipated decline in the price level increases the burden of indebtedness

4. economies at an earlier stage of market development that have recently opened up to the flow of goods, services, and capital from the rest of the world

5. a situation in which financial institutions expand their lending at a rapid pace

6. when deposits are removed from banks causing multiple banks to fail simultaneously

7. the bundling of loans (such as mortgages) into standard debt securities

8. mortgages for borrowers with less-than-stellar credit records

9. when financial institutions cut back on their lending

10. a business model in which a mortgage was originated by a separate party and then distributed to an investor as an underlying asset in a security

11. a major disruption in financial markets characterized by a decline in the prices of assets and the failure of many firms

12. when financial institutions are forced to sell assets quickly at low prices to raise funds

13. increases in asymmetric information problems that reduce the efficient allocation of capital

14. discounts on the value of collateral

15. the difference in interest rates between a risky security and a risk-free security

16. a condition in which debt is denominated in currency of another country, while assets are denominated in the domestic currency

17. arrangements where one party purchases securities with a formal agreement that the seller will repurchase the securities at a point in the near future

18. the process of economies opening up to flows of capital and financial firms from other countries

19. the difference between cash receipts and cash expenditures

20. the values of assets based on realistic expectations of the value of future income streams

21. securities that are derived from cash flows of underlying assets that have specific risk characteristics appealing to a particular investor class

22. a situation in which speculators engage in massive sales of the currency

23. the process of introducing new types of financial products

24. the process of researching and developing new financial products that meet customer demands and are profitable

25. financial insurance that provides payments to holders of securities in the event of default

26. the reduction or elimination of restrictions on financial markets

27. collection of nonbank financial institutions such as hedge funds and investment banks which provide lending through securities markets rather than bank lending

Problems and Short-Answer Questions

PRACTICE PROBLEMS

1. Explain how each of the following events affects the state of a borrowing firm's balance sheet, and thus how it affects the severity of asymmetric information problems in the financial system.
   a. A decline in the stock market

   _____

   _____

   _____

   b. An unanticipated decline in the price level

   _____

   _____

   _____

   c. An unanticipated decline in the value of the domestic currency

   _____

   _____

   _____

   d. A write-down in the value of assets

   _____

   _____

   _____

2. The following questions address debt deflation.
   a. What is debt deflation?

   _____

   _____

b. How does debt deflation affect economic activity? Explain.

_____

_____

_____

_____

c. What event in U.S. history is the greatest example of debt deflation?

_____

d. How much did prices fall during this period? What was the rate of unemployment during this period?

_____

3. The following questions address the global financial crisis of 2007–2009.
    a. What is a subprime mortgage?

    _____

    b. What is a mortgage-backed security?

    _____

    c. Explain the agency problem in the originate-to-distribute business model.

    _____

    _____

    _____

    d. How did the factors described in *a*, *b*, and *c* combine to create a housing price bubble?

    _____

    _____

    _____

    _____

    e.   What happens when an asset-price bubble pops?

_____

_____

_____

_____

SHORT-ANSWER QUESTIONS

1. Why does an increase in adverse selection and moral hazard reduce aggregate economic activity?

_____

_____

2. Why do financial crises in emerging market economies tend to be more severe compared to those in developed economies?

_____

_____

_____

_____

3. How can a government's fiscal imbalance cause a financial crisis?

_____

_____

_____

4. How did financial innovation in mortgage markets help fuel the housing bubble leading into the global financial crisis of 2007–2009?

_____

_____

_____

5. What type of crisis is common to all U.S. financial crises? Why?

_____

_____

6. Why does a financial crisis often begin with financial liberalization or innovation?

   _____

   _____

7. How can currency mismatch worsen a currency crisis?

   _____

   _____

8. What was the source of the recent global financial crisis?

   _____

   _____

   _____

Critical Thinking

You are watching a financial news show on CNN with your roommate. The commentator is discussing the recent global financial crisis in the United States. Your roommate says, "I don't know why we are having difficulty figuring out the causes and cures for our financial crisis. There was a financial crisis in Russia in 1998 and in Argentina 2001–2002. Why don't we just study their crises and copy their solutions. All of these financial crises are the same."

1. What is an "emerging market economy?"

   _____

   _____

2. What was the main source of the financial crises in Russia in the late 1990s and in Argentina in the early 2000s?

   _____

   _____

3. What was the main source of the global financial crisis of 2007–2009 in the United States?

   _____

   _____

4. Are the sources of financial crises (and therefore the solutions to financial crises) the same in countries at different levels of development? Explain.

_____

_____

_____

_____

Self-Test

TRUE/FALSE QUESTIONS

_____F_1. An increase in adverse selection and moral hazard in credit markets tends to increase bank lending.

_____T_2. The shadow banking system includes commercial banks, investment banks, and hedge funds.

_____T_3. Financial crises often begin with financial liberalization or innovation.

_____T_4. An unanticipated decline in the price level raises the real burden of a firm's debt payments when these debt payments are fixed in nominal terms.

_____F_5. Adverse selection and moral hazard problems increase in all three stages of a financial crisis.

_____T_6. The originate-to-distribute system increases the principle-agent problem.

_____T_7. Sooner or later, an asset-price bubble must burst because the price of an asset cannot stay above its fundamental value forever.

_____T_8. The financial crisis in Argentina in 2001 was caused mainly by poor regulation and supervision of the banking system.

_____F_9. The securitization of mortgages reduces the risk that the securitized mortgages will default.

_____F_10. A subprime loan is a loan for which the interest rate is below the prime rate.

_____F_11. Financial crises in emerging market economies are often more severe than those in more developed economies.

_____T_12. In an emerging market economy, the concurrent crises of a financial crisis and a currency crisis are often referred to as the "twin crises."

_T_13. Events that reduce the net worth of a borrowing firm reduce the firm's capital, effectively reducing the borrowing firm's collateral and increasing adverse selection and moral hazard.

_F_14. A reduction in the value of a country's currency improves the condition of domestic firms' balance sheets and reduces the risk of default on loans.

_F_15. Bank panics are a feature of all financial crises in emerging market economies, but bank panics have never been associated with a financial crisis in the United States.

MULTIPLE-CHOICE QUESTIONS

1. South Korea, Malaysia, Indonesia, and the Philippines
   a. experienced speculative attacks.
   b. had sharp devaluations of their currencies occur.
   c. were hit by financial crises.
   d. experienced all of the above.

2. When a fire sale occurs,
   a. financial frictions are low.
   b. uncertainty is reduced.
   c. banks may become insolvent.
   d. adverse selection and moral hazard are reduced.

3. Which of the following does *not* cause a reduction in the net worth of the borrowing firm in a loan market?
   a. a decline in the stock market that reduces the value of the firm
   b. an unanticipated increase in the price level that reduces the value of the firm's liabilities
   c. an unanticipated decline in the value of the domestic currency when the firm's debt is denominated in terms of a foreign currency
   d. asset write-downs on the firm's balance sheet

4. Financial crises
   a. are prevalent in all industrial economies.
   b. only occur in emerging market economies.
   c. rarely have an impact on aggregate economic output.
   d. tend to be more severe in financially advanced countries.

5. Which of the following is an example of debt deflation?
   a. A credit boom deflates into a credit crunch.
   b. An unanticipated decrease in the price level increases the burden of indebtedness.
   c. There is a write-down in the value of assets.
   d. An asset-price bubble bursts and deflates.

6. A subprime mortgage is
   a. a loan with a lower-than-prime interest rate.
   b. a securitized loan.
   c. denominated in a foreign currency.
   d. a loan to someone with less-than-excellent credit.

7. The recent global financial crisis began with
   a. mismanagement of financial innovations in the subprime residential mortgage market.
   b. a spike in interest rates for subprime borrowers.
   c. an excessive government fiscal imbalance where the government forced banks to buy its subprime bonds.
   d. the bailout of subprime Wall Street firms.

8. Financial crises in emerging market economies tend to be more severe than in financially advanced economies because
   a. there is weaker financial supervision in emerging market economies.
   b. bankers in emerging market economies are less experienced with screening and monitoring for adverse selection and moral hazard.
   c. bank panics are more crippling to an emerging market economy because financial markets are less developed.
   d. All of the above are true.

9. Securitization is a process by which
   a. deposits are insured by the FDIC against default.
   b. loans are insured against default.
   c. loans are bundled into standardized securities.
   d. securities are rated as investment grade or less-than-investment grade.

10. The main problem with the originate-to-distribute business model for mortgage lending is that
    a. the interest rate is driven so high that borrowers default.
    b. it reduces funds flowing into the mortgage market.
    c. it is subject to a significant principle-agent problem.
    d. it only works efficiently when packaging subprime mortgages.

11. What economic process is believed to have caused the Great Depression to last so long?
    a. debt deflation
    b. securitization
    c. the stock market crash
    d. the bursting of the asset-price bubble

12. Regardless of the original source of the financial crisis, all credit booms end in a credit crash because of
    a. corruption in the mortgage industry.
    b. an increase in adverse selection and moral hazard in the loan market.
    c. massive government deficits.
    d. collateralized debt obligations.

13. Why does a financial crisis ultimately cause a substantial reduction in economic activity?
    a. The government responds to the crisis with excessive regulation.
    b. Only corrupt bankers survive the crisis.
    c. The financial crisis causes a fiscal deficit.
    d. The resulting credit crash severely reduces investment for productive activities.

14. Which of the following is unlikely to cause a reduction in lending?
    a. a decline in the stock market
    b. a bank panic
    c. a decrease in interest rates
    d. an unanticipated decline in the price level

15. In an emerging market economy, what two types of financial crises are often referred to as the "twin crises?"
    a. a banking crisis and a currency crisis
    b. a fiscal crisis and a monetary crisis
    c. an asset crisis and a liability crisis
    d. a lending crisis and a borrowing crisis

16. Which of the following is one of the main sources of a financial crisis in an emerging market economy?
    a. excessive government regulation
    b. a restriction on the extension of credit
    c. severe government fiscal imbalances
    d. all of the above

17. Which of the following has not been a source of past financial crises in the United States?
    a. severe government fiscal imbalances
    b. mismanagement of financial liberalization or innovation
    c. a spike in interest rates
    d. the bursting of an asset-price bubble

18. Deleveraging occurs when banks
    a. increase their lending.
    b. contract their lending.
    c. increase their capital.
    d. reduce the interest rates they charge on loans.

19. Which of the following statements is true when there is an increase in adverse selection and moral hazard in the loan market?
    a. Banks tend to lend more, which generates an asset-price bubble.
    b. Banks tend to reduce interest rates.
    c. Banks tend to reduce lending because fewer firms want to borrow.
    d. Banks tend to reduce lending because they cannot separate good credit risks from bad ones as efficiently.

20. Severe government fiscal imbalances may cause a financial crisis because the fiscal imbalance may cause the government to
    a. increase taxes.
    b. decrease spending.
    c. sell high-risk government securities to domestic banks.
    d. restrict financial innovations.

Solutions

Terms and Definitions

_2_	asset-price bubble
_6_	bank panic
_19_	cash flow
_5_	credit boom
_25_	credit default swaps
_15_	credit spread
_16_	currency mismatch
_3_	debt deflation
_9_	deleveraging
_4_	emerging market economies
_11_	financial crisis
_24_	financial engineering
_13_	financial frictions
_18_	financial globalization
_23_	financial innovation
_26_	financial liberalization
_12_	fire sales
_20_	fundamental economic values
_14_	haircuts
_1_	mortgage-backed securities
_10_	originate-to-distribute
_17_	repurchase agreements (repos)
_7_	securitization
_27_	shadow banking system
_22_	speculative attack
_21_	structured credit products
_8_	subprime mortgages

Practice Problems

1. a. A decline in the stock market reduces the net worth of a borrowing firm, reducing the collateral pledged against the loan and increasing adverse selection and moral hazard.

    b. A decrease in the price level increases the real burden of a borrowing firm's debt (liabilities), reducing the net worth of a borrowing firm. As in *a* above, a firm has less to lose if it defaults on a loan, increasing adverse selection and moral hazard.

    c. A reduction in the value of the domestic currency raises the real burden of a borrowing firm's debt payments when the debt is denominated in a foreign currency, reducing the net worth of a borrowing firm. As in *a* above, a firm has less to lose if it defaults on a loan, increasing adverse selection and moral hazard.

    d. When asset prices decline, firm's write down (reduce) the value of the assets they own on their balance sheets. This reduces the net worth of the borrowing firm. As in *a* above, the firm has less to lose if it defaults on a loan, increasing adverse selection and moral hazard.

2. a. It is a process in which a substantial, unanticipated decline in the price level increases the burden of indebtedness.

    b. It reduces economic activity because the reduction in the price level reduces the value of the borrowing firm's assets but not its liabilities, causing a deterioration in the firm's balance sheet. Adverse selection and moral hazard problems increase, lending contracts sharply, and aggregate economic activity remains depressed.

    c. The Great Depression.

    d. Prices fell 25% during the Great Depression. The rate of unemployment was 25%.

3. a. It is a mortgage for borrowers with less-than-excellent credit records.

    b. It is a standardized debt security back by mortgages.

    c. The originator of the loan distributes the loan to the ultimate lender (investor), and thus the mortgage originator has little incentive to make sure that the mortgage is a good credit risk.

    d. Mortgage originators loaned money to subprime borrowers, packaged the loans into mortgage-backed securities, and profitably sold them to investors around the world. So much easy credit entered the housing market that it drove housing prices above their fundamental values.

    e. When the price of housing returns to the fundamental value, it causes many borrowers to default because they owe more on their homes than the home is worth. The defaults cause financial firms to become insolvent, reducing lending and economic activity.

Short-Answer Questions

1. Because an increase in adverse selection and moral hazard makes it difficult and more costly for lenders to find low-risk borrowers, lenders contract their lending, which reduces investment and economic activity.

2. Emerging market economies have weaker bank supervision, and their banks lack expertise in screening and monitoring, so the lending boom is greater, and the lending crash is greater. In addition, emerging market banks borrow abroad at higher interest rates, causing a greater crisis when their balance sheets deteriorate. The financial markets are less developed, so a banking crisis is even more harmful.

3. When the government runs a large deficit and private investors fear that the government will default on its debt, the government may force domestic banks to buy its debt. If the value of the debt decreases, it will reduce bank capital, and bank lending will decrease.

4. The development of securitization through mortgage-backed securities allowed for the riskiest of borrowers to obtain loans as subprime mortgages. Financial engineering and the development of structured credit products allowed investors to buy into high risk, high return securities tied to the housing market. These factors pushed down the costs of financing home loans and increased access to many who wouldn't otherwise be able to get mortgages. This continued to increase demand for housing, leading to higher housing prices, which eventually collapsed.

5. Banking crises. When the credit boom turns into a credit crash, the increase in defaults causes depositors to withdraw their funds from banks, causing a bank panic.

6. Financial liberalization or innovation creates a credit boom, which causes financial firms to take on excessive risk and also causes a bubble in asset prices. When the asset-price bubble pops, the credit boom turns into a credit crunch.

7. When a currency crisis occurs, speculative attacks lead to a sharp devaluation of the domestic currency. This sharp, unexpected devaluation leads to an increased debt burden of domestic firms, since debt instruments in emerging market economies are often denominated in foreign currencies (such as the dollar), while assets are typically denominated in the domestic currency. The resulting currency mismatch leads to a sharp decrease in the net worth of domestic firms, and an increase in adverse selection and moral hazard problems, worsening the crisis.

8. Mismanagement of financial innovation in the subprime residential mortgage market and a bursting of a housing price bubble was the source of the recent subprime financial crisis.

Critical Thinking

1. It is an economy at an earlier stage of market development that has recently opened up to the flow of goods, services, and capital from the rest of the world

2. Severe fiscal imbalances caused the governments in Russia and Argentina to force domestic banks to buy their government debt, which later fell in value.

3. Mismanagement of financial innovation in the subprime residential mortgage market and a bursting of the resulting housing price bubble.

4. No. The sources are different so the solutions are different. Russia and Argentina needed to more closely balance the government's budget (raise taxes or cut government spending). The United States may need better regulation and supervision of financial innovations to avoid future crises.

True/False Questions

1. F
2. F
3. T
4. T
5. T
6. T
7. T
8. F
9. F
10. F

11. T
12. T
13. T
14. F
15. F

Multiple-Choice Questions

1. d
2. c
3. b
4. a
5. b
6. d
7. a
8. d
9. c
10. c
11. a
12. b
13. d
14. c
15. a
16. c
17. a
18. b
19. d
20. c

10 Banking and the Management of Financial Institutions[*]

Chapter Review

PREVIEW

This chapter focuses on how commercial banks are managed in order to maximize profits. We concentrate on commercial banks because they are the most important financial intermediaries.

THE BANK BALANCE SHEET

A bank's balance sheet lists its sources of funds (liabilities, such as deposits) and uses of funds (assets, such as loans). It has the characteristic that total assets = total liabilities + bank capital. A bank's liabilities include checkable deposits (demand deposits, NOW accounts, MMDAs), nontransactions deposits (savings deposits, time deposits, or CDs), and borrowings (discount loans, federal funds borrowed, borrowings from their own bank holding company parent, repurchase agreements, Eurodollars). Bank capital is on the liability side of the balance sheet and is the bank's net worth. Checkable deposits have gone from over 60% of bank liabilities in 1960 to only about 6% today. Nontransactions deposits are approximately 53% of bank liabilities.

A bank's assets include reserves (the bank's deposits at the Fed plus its vault cash), cash items in the process of collection, deposits at its correspondent banks (for check clearing, securities purchases, foreign exchange), securities (U.S. government and agency securities known as *secondary reserves,* and state and local government securities), loans (commercial and industrial, real estate, consumer, interbank), and other assets (physical capital). The *required reserve ratio* or *reserve requirement* sets the percent of checkable deposits that must be held as *required reserves.* It is 10% at this time, but banks may choose to hold *excess reserves* above this amount.

---

[*]This is also Chapter 10 in the 3rd ed.

BASIC BANKING

Banks make profits from asset transformation. They borrow short (accept relatively short-term deposits) and lend long (make loans that are relatively longer). When a bank receives additional deposits, it gains an equal amount of reserves. When it loses deposits, it loses an equal amount of reserves. In the simplest case, banks make profits by lending the excess reserves generated from a deposit and charging a higher interest rate on the loan than they pay on the deposit.

A *T-account* is helpful to demonstrate how these transactions affect assets and liabilities of a bank. For example, if a customer deposits $100 into her account at First National Bank, both assets and liabilities for the bank will increase by $100, as shown below. The bank may choose to loan out its $90 in excess reserves, in which the asset then becomes a loan of the same amount.

National Bank

Assets		Liabilities	
Required reserves	+$10	Checkable deposits	+$100
Excess reserves	+$90		

GENERAL PRINCIPLES OF BANK MANAGEMENT

Banks engage in *liquidity management* to be prepared for *deposit outflows*, which can leave banks with inadequate reserve levels. There are four ways that banks can respond to deposit outflows. First, banks can hold excess reserves and secondary reserves to offset deposit outflows, even though they earn less interest than less liquid assets such as loans. Second, the bank could sell some of its securities holdings with relatively low transaction costs. Third, it could get a discount loan from the Fed, but it would have to pay the *discount rate*, the interest rate charged by the Fed. Finally, it could call in loans or sell loans to another bank, but this is the costliest way to acquire funds and is to be avoided.

Banks engage in *asset management* to seek the highest returns possible, reduce risk, and provide liquidity. They do this by seeking borrowers who will pay high rates but are a low risk of default, buying securities with high returns and low risk, buying a variety of assets to lower risk through diversification, and maintaining just enough liquid assets to insure against deposit outflows.

Liability management used to be rather dull because 60% of their liabilities were checkable deposits for which they could not compete by paying interest, and there was no well-developed federal funds market. Post-1960, large *money center banks* began selling negotiable CDs and borrowing from other banks. Thus, banks began to actively seek funds if they found productive loan prospects.

Banks must manage the amount of capital they hold in order to lessen the chance of a bank failure (a condition when its liquid assets are less than its immediate liabilities) and to meet capital requirements set by regulatory authorities, which is known as *capital adequacy management*. Bank capital acts as a cushion against losses on assets that result from bad loans. Other things the same, the greater the capital account, the more bad loans the bank can sustain and remain solvent (have positive net worth). However, the lower the bank capital, the higher the return on equity for the owners of the bank, causing a trade-off between safety and return to equity holders. This relationship is demonstrated by the definition of *return on equity* (ROE), where ROE = net profit after taxes/equity capital. Thus, reducing capital increases ROE and vice versa. A more basic measure of bank profitability is *return on assets* (ROA), where ROA = net profit after taxes/assets. These two measures are related by the formula ROE = ROA × EM, where EM is the *equity multiplier,* representing the ratio of assets to equity capital.

Due to the cost of holding capital, regulatory authorities enforce minimum bank capital requirements. To increase the amount of capital relative to assets, a bank can issue more common stock, reduce the bank's dividends to increase retained earnings, or reduce the bank's assets by selling off loans or securities. In a financial crisis, it is difficult for banks to raise capital, so banks usually reduce loans, causing a credit crunch.

MANAGING CREDIT RISK

Credit risk is the risk associated with the probability of default on a loan. To avoid the asymmetric information problems of adverse selection and moral hazard, banks engage in five activities. First, banks *screen and monitor* borrowers by collecting information on borrowers prior to the loan, specializing in lending to particular industries to gain expertise in screening, and monitoring and enforcing restrictive covenants to ensure that the borrower uses the loan for the prescribed activities. Second, banks develop *long-term customer relationships* to more efficiently gather information on the borrower and to provide the borrower with an incentive to reduce moral hazard for future borrowing. Third, banks issue *loan commitments*, which promote long-term customer relationships. Fourth, banks require *collateral and compensating balances* from the borrower. Compensating balances act as collateral and help the bank monitor the spending of the loan. Finally, the bank can engage in *credit rationing*, refusing to make a loan even at a high interest rate or making a loan for a smaller amount that was originally requested.

MANAGING INTEREST-RATE RISK

Interest-rate risk is the riskiness of earnings associated with changes in interest rates. If a bank has more rate-sensitive (short-term) liabilities than assets, a rise in interest rates will reduce bank profits. This is because the increase in interest a bank pays on its liabilities will exceed the increase in interest it receives on its assets. Alternatively, a decline in interest rates will raise bank profits. Basic *gap analysis* can measure the sensitivity of bank profits to changes in interest rates, where gap = rate-sensitive assets – rate-sensitive liabilities, and gap × change in interest rate = change in bank profits.

Duration analysis measures the interest rate sensitivity of the market value of the bank's assets and liabilities, and thus shows the change in net worth of the bank from a change in interest rates. Duration analysis implies the percent change in market value of security = – percentage-point change in interest rate × duration in years. Both measures indicate that banks with more rate-sensitive liabilities tend to suffer when interest rates rise and gain when they fall. Managing interest-rate risk can be costly if it requires changing the average duration of a bank's assets or liabilities.

OFF-BALANCE-SHEET ACTIVITIES

Off-balance-sheet activities involve trading financial instruments and generating income from fees and loan sales, which affect bank profits but don't appear on the balance sheet. A *loan sale*, or secondary loan participation, is when a bank sells all or part of a loan's cash stream. Fee income is earned from foreign exchange trades for a customer, servicing mortgage-backed securities, guaranteeing debt such as banker's acceptances, providing backup lines of credit, and creating structured investment vehicles (SIVs). Trading activities can be profitable but risky, requiring the bank to put risk assessment procedures in place and restrict employees from taking on too much risk.

Helpful Hints

1. When banks borrow from other banks or from the central bank, these funds represent liabilities to the borrowing bank. However, when a bank extends a loan to a customer (or other bank), this represents an asset to the lending bank. Thus, loans can be both assets and liabilities to a bank, depending on the source of funds.

2. Prior to 1960, more than 60% of a bank's liabilities were checkable deposits. Since banks could not actively compete for those deposits by paying interest on them, a bank's size was largely determined by its local source of funds. Post-1960, banks with exceptionally profitable loan opportunities can actively seek funds by borrowing in ways that didn't exist prior to the 1960s. Thus, a bank now has more influence over its size and growth rate than prior to 1960.

3. Capital protects a bank from bankruptcy or insolvency. Insolvency is when the value of a bank's assets falls below the value of its liabilities. Thus, a bank can sustain a reduction in the value of its assets by the amount of its capital. If a bank has $1 billion in capital, the value of its assets could fall by up to $1 billion, and the bank would still be technically solvent.

Terms and Definitions

Choose a definition for each key term.

Key Terms:

_____5_____ asset management
_____8_____ balance sheet
_____13_____ capital adequacy management
_____18_____ compensating balance
_____14_____ credit rationing
_____3_____ credit risk
_____21_____ deposit outflows
_____10_____ discount loans
_____25_____ discount rate

_____2_____ duration analysis ✓
_____12_____ equity multiplier (EM) ✓
_____7_____ excess reserves
_____17_____ gap analysis
_____4_____ interest-rate risk ✓
_____10_____ liability management ✓
_____15_____ liquidity management
_____22_____ loan commitment
_____19_____ loan sale

_____27_____ money center banks
_____24_____ off-balance-sheet activities
_____1_____ reserve requirements
_____11_____ reserves
_____20_____ return on assets (ROA)
_____6_____ return on equity (ROE) ✓
_____9_____ secondary reserves
_____26_____ T-account ✓
_____23_____ vault cash

Definitions:

1. Regulation making it obligatory for depository institutions to keep a certain fraction of their deposits as reserves

2. A measurement of the sensitivity of the market value of a bank's assets and liabilities to changes in interest rates

3. The risk arising from the possibility that the borrower will default

4. The possible reduction in returns associated with changes in interest rates

5. The acquisition of assets that have a low rate of default and diversification of asset holdings to increase profits

6. Net profit after taxes per dollar of equity capital

7. Holdings of reserves higher than what is required

8. A list of the assets and liabilities of a bank that balances: total assets equal total liabilities plus bank capital

9. Short-term U.S. government and agency securities held by private banks

10. The acquisition of funds at low cost to increase profits

11. A bank's deposits at the Fed plus its vault cash

12. The amount of assets per dollar of equity capital

13. A bank's decision about the amount of capital it should maintain and then the acquisition of that capital

14. When a lender refuses to make a loan or restricts the size of the loan to less than the full amount sought

15. The decisions made by a bank to maintain sufficient liquid assets to meet the bank's obligations to depositors

16. A bank's borrowings from the Federal Reserve System

17. A measurement of the sensitivity of bank profits to changes in interest rates calculated as rate-sensitive assets minus rate-sensitive liabilities

18. A required minimum amount of funds that a firm receiving a loan must keep in a checking account at the lending bank

19. The process by which banks remove loans from its balance sheet

20. After-tax net profit per dollar of assets

21. Occurs when depositors make withdrawals or demand payment

22. Arrangements by a bank to provide loans to certain customers for a specified period of time, up to a given credit limit

23. Currency physically held in bank vaults

24. Activities that generate profits for banks but are not visible on banks' balance sheets

25. The interest rate the Federal Reserve charges for loans to banks

26. A method of representing a balance sheet to keep track of changes in assets and liabilities

27. Large banks in key financial centers

* Duration = the sensitivity of the Bond Mutual fund in terms of interest rate fluctuation.
(ex: rates go up = fund goes down by duration multiple
rates go up 1% on a fund with duration of (8) fund goes down 8%

Problems and Short-Answer Questions

PRACTICE PROBLEMS

1. Record each of the following events in the T-account provided below.
   a. Joe deposits his $3,000 paycheck into his checking account at Local Bank.

   Local Bank

Assets	Liabilities

   b. Local Bank deposits the check at the Fed, and the Fed collects the funds for Local Bank.

   Local Bank

Assets	Liabilities

   c. What happens to a bank's reserves when it receives a deposit?

   _____

   d. Joe withdraws $500 cash and pays his rent. His landlord deposits the $500 in Landlord Bank.

   Local Bank

Assets	Liabilities

   Landlord Bank

Assets	Liabilities

e. What happens to a bank's reserves when it loses a deposit?

_____

f. Suppose the reserve requirement is 10%. Landlord bank lends out the maximum it can from the $500 deposit.

Landlord Bank

Assets	Liabilities

g. For Landlord Bank to make profits, what must be true about the interest rate it pays on deposits compared to the interest rate it receives on loans?

_____

2. Suppose that Liquidity Management Bank has the following balance sheet position and that the required reserve ratio on deposits is 20%. The numbers below are in millions.

Assets		Liabilities	
Reserves	$25	Deposits	$100
Loans	75	Bank capital	10
Securities	10		

a. Show the impact of a $5 million deposit outflow on the bank's balance sheet.

Assets	Liabilities

b. Must the bank make any adjustments in its balance sheet in order to meet its reserve requirement? Explain.

_____

_____

c. Show the impact of another $5 million deposit outflow on the bank's balance sheet (for a total of $10 million deposit outflow).

Assets	Liabilities

d. Must the bank make any adjustments in its balance sheet in order to meet its reserve requirement? Explain.

_____

_____

e. If the bank chooses to sell off securities to meet its reserve requirement, how many dollars of securities must it sell? Explain. Show the bank's balance sheet after the sale of securities.

_____

_____

Assets	Liabilities

f. Why would a bank choose to sell its securities rather than its loans to meet its liquidity needs? What might happen to the bank if there were such a great deposit outflow that it ran out of securities and no one would lend to it, so it had to sell off some of its loans?

_____

_____

_____

_____

3. Below you will find balance sheets for High Capital Bank and Low Capital Bank. Numbers are in millions.

High Capital Bank

Assets		Liabilities	
Reserves	$90	Deposits	$540
Loans	510	Bank capital	60

Low Capital Bank

Assets		Liabilities	
Reserves	$90	Deposits	$560
Loans	510	Bank capital	40

a. How many dollars of bad loans can each bank sustain before it becomes insolvent? As a result, which bank has the lower probability of becoming insolvent?

_____

_____

b. Suppose net profit after taxes is $6 million for each bank. What is each bank's return on assets (ROA)? What is each bank's return on equity (ROE)? Which bank is more profitable to its owners?

_____

_____

c. What does this example say about the relationship between safety and returns to equity holders? How do regulations address this issue?

_____

_____

4. Suppose that Rate-Sensitive Bank has the following balance sheet. All values are in millions of dollars.

Rate-Sensitive Bank

Assets		Liabilities	
Variable-rate Loans	$5	Variable-rate CDs	$30
Short-term Loans	10	Money Market	
Short-term Securities	15	Deposit Accounts	20
Reserves	10	Checkable Deposits	10
Long-term Loans	30	Savings Deposits	10
Long-term Securities	30	Long-terms CDs	20
		Equity Capital	10

a. Employ basic gap analysis to determine this bank's "gap."

_____

b. If interest rates suddenly increase by two percentage points, by how much do the bank's profits change?

_____

c. If, instead, interest rates decrease by three percentage points, by how much do the bank's profits change?

_____

d. If a bank has more rate-sensitive liabilities than assets, how do bank profits move with respect to the interest rate?

_____

e. Suppose the average duration of the assets of this bank is four years while the average duration of the liabilities is two years. Use duration analysis to determine the change in the net worth of the bank if interest rates rise by three percentage points.

_____

_____

_____

(handwritten margin notes:)

$-12nm - (-5.4nm) =$

$-12nm$

$-6.6mm$

ASSETS $+3\%$

$(100m) \times (-.03) =$

$(-3mm)(4yrs) =$

$-12mm$

LIAB $+3\%$

$(90mm)(-.03)(2yrs)$

$(-2.7m) = -5.4$

SHORT-ANSWER QUESTIONS

1. What are secondary reserves? What purpose do they serve? What advantage do they have over excess reserves?

_____

_____

2. What is the largest source of funds to commercial banks? Are checkable deposits a more important or <u>less</u> important source of funds today when compared to 50 years ago?

_____

_____

3. What category of assets generates the greatest profits for commercial banks? Why would banks receive more profit from this type of asset?

_____

_____

4. If a bank has $1,000 in deposits and the required reserve ratio is 10%, how much are the bank's required reserves? In what form must the bank hold them?

Vault Cash and a deposit at the FED

_____

5. When banks engage in asset management, they seek high-return, low-risk, liquid assets. Why is this difficult?

_____

_____

6. If a depositor withdraws $100 from his deposit at a bank, what happens to the bank's reserves?

decreases by same amount

7. How do banks reduce their exposure to credit risk?

KYC, Rationing, screen & monitor

_____

8. What methods can a bank use to increase its capital relative to assets?

stop lending, issue more stock, call loans

_____

9. What are off-balance-sheet activities? Are they growing or diminishing?

_____

_____

10. How can a bank generate liquidity in the face of deposit outflows?

_____

_____

_____

Critical Thinking

You are watching the news with a friend. The news anchor says that the Fed has just increased the interest rate for the eighth meeting in a row. Your friend says, "I bet banks just love these increases in the interest rate. Banks must be making enormous profits charging those high interest rates. Bank stock prices must just be going through the roof."

1. Use a description of gap analysis to explain to your friend how a rising interest rate tends to affect a bank's profits.

_____

_____

_____

_____

_____

2. Use a description of duration analysis to explain to your friend how a rising interest rate tends to affect a bank's net worth.

_____

_____

_____

_____

_____

Self-Test

TRUE/FALSE QUESTIONS

___F___ 1. A bank's assets are its source of funds.

___F___ 2. Checkable deposits are the primary source of bank funds.

_____T__ 3. Bank capital is the net worth of a bank, and it equals the total assets of the bank minus the total liabilities.

_____T__ 4. Borrowings from the Fed are called discount loans, and the interest rate the borrowing bank pays on the loan is known as the discount rate.

_____T__ 5. ✓Required reserves are a fixed percentage of a bank's total liabilities.

_____T__ 6. Loans provide banks with most of their profits.

_____F__ 7. When a bank is faced with deposit outflows, its first choice for acquiring reserves to meet the deposit outflow is to sell off loans.

_____F__ 8. Banks keep over 50% of their assets in excess reserves to insure that they are liquid enough to meet deposit outflows.

_____T__ 9. A bank fails when it cannot pay its depositors and other creditors.

_____T__ 10. Negotiable CDs and bank borrowings have increased as a source of funds to banks since 1960.

_____T__ 11. ✓Increasing a bank's capital increases the bank's safety and increases the bank's return on equity (ROE).

_____T__ 12. To reduce credit risk, banks often require collateral and compensating balances from the borrower.

_____F__ 13. If the average duration of a bank's assets exceeds the average duration of a bank's liabilities, an increase in interest rates will increase a bank's net worth.

_____F__ 14. If a bank has more rate-sensitive liabilities than assets, an increase in interest rates will reduce the bank's profits.

_____F__ 15. Off-balance-sheet activities have declined in importance for banks since 1980.

MULTIPLE-CHOICE QUESTIONS

1. Which of the following is the greatest source of funds to commercial banks today?
   a. checkable deposits
   b. nontransactions deposits
   c. borrowings
   d. bank capital

2. Which of the following was the greatest source of funds to commercial banks in 1960?
   a. checkable deposits
   b. nontransactions deposits
   c. borrowings
   d. bank capital

3. Which of the following bank assets is the most liquid?
   a. state and local government securities
   b. commercial and industrial loans
   c. real estate loans
   d. U.S. government securities

4. Required reserves are a fixed percentage of a bank's
   a. assets.
   b. loans.
   c. checkable deposits.
   d. capital.
   e. liabilities.

5. Which of the following is true about a bank's balance sheet?
   a. A bank's liabilities are its source of funds.
   b. A bank's assets are its use of funds.
   c. Assets – liabilities = bank capital.
   d. All of the above are true.

6. The sum of a bank's vault cash plus its deposits at the Fed is the bank's
   a. capital.
   b. federal funds.
   c. reserves.
   d. cash items in the process of collection.
   e. excess reserves.

7. Which of the following is generally the least expensive way for a bank to acquire funds?
   a. checkable deposits.
   b. federal funds.
   c. nontransactions deposits.
   d. borrowings such as Eurodollars or repurchase agreements.
   e. discount loans.

8. When you deposit your $3,000 paycheck in your bank, which was written on an account at a different bank, the immediate impact on your bank's balance sheet is that your bank's deposits rise by $3,000 and your bank's
   a. reserves rise by $3,000.
   b. cash items in the process of collection rise by $3,000.
   c. loans rise by $3,000.
   d. capital rises by $3,000.
   e. None of the above is correct.

9. When a bank suffers deposit outflows and has no excess reserves, the bank will generally first try to raise the funds by
   a. calling in some loans.
   b. selling some loans.
   c. borrowing from the Fed.
   d. selling some of its securities.

10. Which of the following would not be considered a managed liability?
    a. negotiable certificates of deposit
    b. federal funds borrowed
    c. Eurodollar borrowings
    d. checkable deposits.

11. A bank has $100 in checkable deposits, reserves of $15, and a reserve requirement of 10%. Suppose the bank suffers a $10 deposit outflow. If the bank chooses to borrow from the Fed to meet its reserve requirement, how much does it need to borrow?
    a. $0
    b. $1.50
    c. $4
    d. $5
    e. $10

12. Which of the following is *not* true regarding how banks manage their assets? Banks seek assets that
    a. are liquid.
    b. provide diversification.
    c. have no default risk.
    d. generate high returns.

13. Suppose that a bank's balance sheet consists of the following: On the liability side it has $93 of deposits and $7 of capital, while on the asset side it has $10 of reserves and $90 of loans. How many dollars of bad loans can this bank sustain before it become insolvent?
    a. $0
    b. $7
    c. $9.30
    d. $10
    e. $93

14. Other things being the same, a bank with a greater amount of capital
    a. has a lower risk of failure.
    b. has a higher rate of return on equity to the owners.
    c. is more liquid.
    d. All of the above are true.

15. Which of the following is *not* a method by which banks reduce their *credit risk*?
    a. collect information on prospective borrowers to screen out high-risk borrowers
    b. use gap analysis to help balance a bank's rate-sensitive assets and liabilities
    c. develop long-term relationships with borrowers
    d. enforce restrictive covenants in the loan contract
    e. engage in credit rationing

16. Banks often specialize in providing loans to firms in a particular industry because this activity
    a. reduces the cost of acquiring and analyzing information about the borrower.
    b. reduces the bank's exposure to interest-rate risk.
    c. allows the bank to increase the diversification of its loan portfolio.
    d. is required by law.
    e. All of the above are true.

[handwritten: rate sensitive Assets]
[handwritten: LIAB]

17. Suppose a bank has a "gap" of –$50 million dollars. What will happen to its profits if interest rates rise by 2%?
    a. Profits rise by $100 million.
    b. Profits fall by $100 million.
    c. Profits rise by $1 million.
    d. Profits fall by $1 million.

[handwritten: $(+.02)(-50mm) = -\$1mm$]

18. Which of the following statements about interest-rate risk is true?
    a. A commercial bank usually has a larger "gap" than an equivalent size savings and loan.
    b. An increase in interest rates always increases commercial bank profits.
    c. If a bank has more rate-sensitive liabilities than assets, an increase in interest rates reduces bank profits.
    d. Banks tend to have more rate-sensitive assets than liabilities.
    e. All of the above are true.

19. Which of the following does *not* describe an off-balance-sheet activity?
    a. A bank guarantees a firm's debt by signing a banker's acceptance.
    b. A bank writes a mortgage and sells it to a life insurance company.
    c. A bank makes a loan to a large corporate customer.
    d. A bank exchanges dollars for euros for a large corporate customer.

20. Using duration analysis, if a bank's assets have an average duration of four years and the interest rate rises by 2%, what will happen to the value of the bank's assets?
    a. The value of the assets will rise by 8%.
    b. The value of the assets will fall by 8%.
    c. The value of the assets will rise by 2%.
    d. The value of the assets will rise by 2%.

[handwritten notes:]
✗ Rates go up = ASSET Value ↓
PROFIT ↓
✗ Duration = ASSET Val
✗ GAP = PROFIT
✗ Rates go down = ASSET Val. ↑
PROFIT ↑

Solutions

Terms and Definitions

 5 asset management
 8 balance sheet
13 capital adequacy management
18 compensating balance
14 credit rationing
 3 credit risk
21 deposit outflows
16 discount loans
25 discount rate
 2 duration analysis
12 equity multiplier (EM)
 7 excess reserves
17 gap analysis
 4 interest-rate risk
10 liability management
15 liquidity management
22 loan commitment
19 loan sale
27 money center banks
24 off-balance-sheet activities
 1 reserve requirements
11 reserves
20 return on assets (ROA)
 6 return on equity (ROE)
 9 secondary reserves
26 T-account
23 vault cash

Practice Problems

1. a.

Local Bank

Assets	Liabilities
Cash items in process of collection +$3,000	Checkable deposits +$3,000

b.

Local Bank

Assets	Liabilities
Reserves +$3,000	Checkable deposits +$3,000

c. Its reserves rise by precisely the size of the increase in the deposit.

d.

Local Bank

Assets	Liabilities
Reserves −$500	Checkable deposits −$500

Landlord Bank

Assets	Liabilities
Reserves +$500	Checkable deposits +$500

e. Its reserves fall by precisely the size of the decrease in the deposit.

f.

Landlord Bank

Assets		Liabilities	
Reserves	+$50	Checkable	
Loans	+$450	deposits	+$500

g. It must pay a lower interest rate on its deposits than it receives on its loans.

2. a.

Assets		Liabilities	
Reserves	$20	Deposits	$95
Loans	75	Bank capital	10
Securities	10		

b. No. Required reserves after the deposit outflow are (0.20 × $95) = $19 million so the bank had enough excess reserves to handle the deposit outflow.

c.

Assets		Liabilities	
Reserves	$15	Deposits	$90
Loans	75	Bank capital	10
Securities	10		

d. Yes. Required reserves after the deposit outflow are (0.20 × $90 million) = $18 million, and the bank only has $15 million. The bank has a reserve deficiency of $3 million.

e. $18 million – $15 million = $3 million. The bank should sell $3 million in securities.

Assets		Liabilities	
Reserves	$18	Deposits	$90
Loans	75	Bank capital	10
Securities	7		

f. Transaction costs are small on securities held as secondary reserves. Selling off loans is costly because they usually can't be sold for full value. If the bank had to discount its loans to such a degree that the value of its assets fell below the value of its liabilities, the bank would be insolvent.

3. a. High Capital Bank: $60 million. Low Capital Bank: $40 million. High Capital Bank has a lower probability of becoming insolvent.

   b. ROA for each = $6/$600 = 1%. ROE for High Capital Bank = $6/$60 = 10%. ROE for Low Capital Bank = $6/$40 = 15%. Low Capital Bank is more profitable.

   c. There is a trade-off between profitability and safety. As a result, bank regulations impose bank capital requirements.

4. a. $30 million – $50 million = –$20 million.

   b. 0.02 × –$20 million = –$400,000.

   c. – 0.03 × (– $20 million) = $600,000.

   d. Interest rates and profits are inversely related.

   e. Change in value of assets = –0.03 × 4 × $100 million = –$12 million; Change in value of liabilities = –0.03 × 2 × $90 million = –$5.4 million; Change in net worth = –$12 million – (–$5.4 million) = –$6.6 million.

Short-Answer Questions

1. Short-term U.S. government securities. They provide liquidity in case of deposit outflow and they earn interest while excess reserves generally earn a lower or zero interest rate.

2. Nontransactions deposits supply about 53% of the funds. Checkable deposits are less important, going from 60% of the funds to about 6% in that time period.

3. Loans. Loans are riskier and less liquid than other bank assets.

4. $100. Reserves can be held as deposits at the Federal Reserve or as vault cash.

5. High return assets tend to be higher risk and less liquid.

6. The bank's reserves fall by $100.

7. Banks screen and monitor borrowers, specialize in lending to particular industries, monitor and enforce restrictive covenants, develop long-term customer relationships, issue loan commitments, require collateral and compensating balances, and engage in credit rationing.

8. Issue more common stock, reduce the bank's dividends to increase retained earnings, or reduce the bank's assets by selling off loans or securities.

9. The generation of income from fees and loan sales, which generate profit but don't appear on the balance sheet. They have nearly doubled since 1980.

10. A bank can hold excess reserves, sell secondary reserves, get a discount loan from the Fed or other borrowings, or sell off loans.

Critical Thinking

1. The gap is defined as: rate-sensitive assets – rate-sensitive liabilities. Gap × change in interest rate = change in bank profits. Since banks tend to have more rate-sensitive liabilities than assets, the gap tends to be negative. Thus, an increase in interest rates reduces bank profits because the increase in interest a bank pays on its liabilities exceeds the increase in interest it receives on its assets.

2. Duration is the average lifetime of a security's stream of payments. The percent change in market value of security = – percentage-point change in interest rate × duration in years. Since banks tend to have longer-term assets than liabilities, there is a greater reduction in

the value of the assets than the liabilities in response to an increase in the interest rate. Thus, the net worth of a bank falls when interest rates rise.

True/False Questions

1. F
2. F
3. T
4. T
5. F
6. T
7. F
8. F
9. T
10. T
11. F
12. T
13. F
14. T
15. F

Multiple-Choice Questions

1. b
2. a
3. d
4. c
5. d
6. c
7. a
8. b
9. d
10. d
11. c
12. c
13. b
14. a
15. b
16. a
17. d
18. c
19. c
20. b

11 Economic Analysis of Financial Regulation*

Chapter Review

PREVIEW

In this chapter, we use economic analysis to show why financial institutions and banks are so heavily regulated. Financial regulation, however, is not always successful. Banking and financial crises cause regulators to reform existing regulations.

ASYMMETRIC INFORMATION AND FINANCIAL REGULATION

Much of banking regulation is based on the presence of asymmetric information, which causes adverse selection and moral hazard problems in banking. Banking regulations can be grouped into the following categories:

- *The government safety net*: Depositors lack information about the quality of a bank's private loans. Before deposit insurance, depositors were reluctant to put funds in a bank, and even small negative shocks to the banking system could cause bank panics and the contagion effect. In response, the FDIC was established in 1934. Bank failures are handled through either the payoff method (which pays off all depositors up to a designated cap, currently $250,000) or the purchase and assumption method, which guarantees all deposits (by finding a buyer to take over the bank). In addition to deposit insurance, central banks can act as the "lender of last resort" to troubled institutions. A government safety net fixes one set of problems but causes a moral hazard problem (financial institutions take on excessive risk) and an adverse selection problem (risk-loving entrepreneurs may choose to enter the financial industry). Since the failure of a very big financial institution may cause a financial disruption, some institutions have been considered "too big to fail," so their insolvencies

*This is also Chapter 11 in the 3rd ed.

were handled by the purchase and assumption method, which further increases the moral hazard problem. The consolidation of the financial industry has caused more financial institutions to be deemed "too big to fail," and conglomerate financial firms may receive a safety net for nonbanking activities.

- *Restrictions on asset holdings:* Because depositors and creditors of financial institutions cannot easily monitor the institution's assets, regulations restrict banks from holding risky assets such as common stock, and regulations require banks to diversify.

- *Capital requirements:* Banks have capital requirements that establish a minimum *leverage ratio* (capital asset ratio) of 5%. The *Basel Accord* increases the capital-asset ratio for risky banks by establishing risk-based capital requirements for banks in over 100 countries. Limitations to the original Basel Accord have led to Basel 2 and Basel 3, which increase capital standards even more and make capital requirements less procyclical, among other revisions.

- *Prompt corrective action:* Failing to act quickly when banks have low capital cushions can lead to greater moral hazard problems and an increased risk of bank failure. FDIC provisions require regulators to act promptly and forcefully to avoid aggravating the problem.

- *Financial supervision: chartering and examination:* Chartering financial institutions, through either state or federal regulators, limits adverse selection by preventing undesirable people from controlling them. On-site periodic examinations and the application of the CAMELS rating to a bank's activities reduce moral hazard. The CAMELS rating takes into account six areas of bank operation: capital adequacy, asset quality, management, earnings, liquidity, and sensitivity to market risk. Banks also file quarterly call reports.

- *Assessment of risk management:* Since banks can take on more risk than is apparent from their balance sheets, regulators are interested in a bank's management processes for controlling risk of fraud, risky trading activities, and interest rate risk. *Stress tests* are also administered to gauge the health of banks under various economic and financial conditions.

- *Disclosure requirements:* Due to the free-rider problem, depositors and creditors don't create enough information about the bank's condition. Regulators respond by requiring financial institutions to adhere to standard accounting principles and to disclose substantial information. Financial firms are required to employ mark-to-market accounting (fair-value accounting) where assets are valued at what they would sell for under current market conditions. During a financial crisis, however, prices of financial instruments may fall below their true value, reducing a lender's capital, and causing lender's to reduce their lending, making the crisis worse.

- *Consumer protection:* As a result of asymmetric information, "truth in lending" laws require lenders to be clear about financing charges. Other laws, such as the Equal Credit Opportunity Act of 1974 and the Community Reinvestment Act of 1977, forbid discrimination in lending. Recent additions to the Truth in Lending Act of 2008 require greater information on the borrower's ability to repay and on the true terms of the loan.

- *Restrictions on competition:* Competition may increase moral hazard by causing financial institutions to assume greater risk to maintain profits. In the past, U.S. banks were restricted from branching, and the Glass-Steagall Act kept nonbank institutions from engaging in banking activities. However, these restrictions caused inefficiency and higher charges to consumers; in 1999, Glass-Steagall was repealed.

- *Macroprudential versus microprudential supervision:* Microprudential supervision, as discussed in various capacities above, focuses on the health of individual banks and financial companies. However, during financial crises, these guidelines may not be sufficient to avert a crisis. Macroprudential supervision assesses overall risk to the financial system by monitoring capital adequacy and access to liquidity in the aggregate. This can be done through mitigating leverage cycles through countercyclical capital requirements, implying tighter credit standards during expansions, or requiring new system-wide capital during downturns to ensure lending occurs.

It is difficult to successfully regulate financial institutions because financial institutions have incentives to avoid the regulations, the regulations may have unintended consequences, and regulators are subject to political pressure to regulate more easily.

Because the same types of asymmetric information problems exist in banking everywhere, financial regulation in foreign countries is similar to that in the United States—financial institutions are chartered, supervised, regulated, and insured. International financial institutions are particularly difficult to regulate because they can shift their business from one country to another.

THE 1980S SAVINGS AND LOAN AND BANKING CRISIS

Few banks and S&Ls failed from 1934 to 1980. An increase in adverse selection and moral hazard caused bank failures to increase more than tenfold from the early 1980s to the early 1990s. This happened for a variety of reasons. Financial innovation decreased the profitability of banks by increasing competition for both their source of funds and their use of funds, causing banks to make riskier loans to maintain profits. In addition, riskier assets like junk bonds became available, and the increase in deposit insurance further increased moral hazard. In particular, new legislation (the Depository Institutions Deregulation and Monetary Control Act of 1980) allowed S&Ls to invest in riskier activities such as commercial real estate and junk bonds, raised FDIC insurance from $40,000 to $100,000 per account, and removed the ceiling on interest rates that could be paid on deposits, allowing risky banks to pay higher rates to attract more funds and causing greater moral hazard. Banks and savings and loans took on additional risk and failures rose, causing losses for the FDIC. Regulators responded with the Financial Institutions Reform, Recovery, and Enforcement Act of 1989 and the FDIC Improvement Act of 1991, which bailed out the commercial banking and savings and loan industries and re-regulated the banking industry.

BANKING CRISES THROUGHOUT THE WORLD

Extensive parallels exist between the banking crises in the United States and those in other countries, indicating that similar forces are at work. All banking crises start with financial liberalization or innovation combined with a weak bank regulatory system and a government safety net. Although deposit insurance may increase moral hazard, the incidence of bank failures worldwide suggests deposit insurance as a safety net is not a significant source of risky bank behavior. The costs associated with the U.S. banking crisis of the 1980s appears small when taken as a percent of GDP— only 4% for the United States but over 50% for Argentina and Indonesia.

THE DODD-FRANK BILL AND FUTURE REGULATION

As a result of the recent global financial crisis, the Dodd-Frank Bill was enacted to address shortfalls in five major areas of the financial system.

- *Consumer Protection:* Creates the new Consumer Financial Protection Bureau to regulate the issuance of residential mortgages and other financial products to poor people and to increase transparency and education about financial products to consumers. It also permanently raised the FDIC insured limit on deposits to $250,000.

- *Resolution Authority:* Gives the U.S. government the ability to intervene and take over large, systemically important financial firms to liquidate them in an orderly fashion.

- *Systemic Risk Regulation:* Creates the Financial Stability Oversight Council, which monitors for systemic risk and designates firms as systemically important, subjecting these firms to higher capital standards.

- *Volcker Rule:* Limits certain trading activities by banks in both the size and composition of those assets traded.

- *Derivatives:* Requires standardized derivatives to be traded and cleared through exchanges and customized derivatives to be subject to higher capital standards. Also increases disclosure and margin requirements for firms dealing in derivatives.

Future regulatory changes are likely to further address the gaps in current regulations in several key areas. These may include (i) countercyclical capital requirements, higher overall capital standards, and bringing some off-balance-sheet activities on the balance sheet to more accurately assess risk. (ii) Limits on executive compensation, including delayed bonuses to reduce risky behavior. (iii) Reform of government-sponsored enterprises, which are private corporations that are fully backed by the government in the event its assets become worthless. Fully privatizing their operations is one possible change. (iv) Restricting activities of credit-rating agencies to ensure more reliable ratings. Although bolstering regulations can help improve the safe functioning of financial markets, overly burdensome or poorly designed regulations may do more harm than good by restricting financial market efficiency and beneficial innovation.

Helpful Hints

1. Depositors face the same problems of adverse selection and moral hazard when depositing money in banks as banks face when lending depositors money. To avoid these asymmetric information problems in private financial markets, banks screen borrowers, employ restrictive covenants preventing borrowers from investing in risky activities, employ restrictive covenants requiring that their borrowers maintain a minimum net worth, and monitor borrowers. Similarly, on behalf of depositors, regulators require banks to have a charter, restrict risky asset holdings of banks, impose capital requirements on banks, and examine banks.

2. The moral hazard problem in banking increases when a bank nears insolvency. When a bank is technically insolvent, the bank is lending the depositors' money with no contribution from the owners because the bank no longer has a positive net worth. That is, the owners have nothing to lose. Thus, the incentive is for the bank to seek out the highest risk loans possible. If the loans fail to perform, the depositors or FDIC may lose, but the owners lose nothing. If the loans perform, the owners gain. It is as if the bank is allowed to gamble with someone else's money. If the gamble loses, the bank doesn't care because it's someone else's money. But if the gamble pays off, the bank gets to keep the winnings.

Terms and Definitions

Choose a definition for each key term.

Key Terms:

____4____ bank failure
____5____ Basel Accord
____1____ financial supervision (prudential supervision)

____6____ leverage ratio
____3____ mark-to-market (fair-value) accounting
____2____ off-balance sheet activities

____9____ regulatory arbitrage
____8____ stress tests
____7____ value-at-risk (VaR)

Definitions:

1. Overseeing who operates banks and how they are operated

2. Bank activities that involve trading financial instruments and the generation of income from fees and loan sales, all of which affect bank profits but are not visible on the balance sheet

3. An accounting entry in which assets are valued in the balance sheet at what they would sell for under current market conditions

4. A situation in which a bank cannot satisfy its obligations to pay its depositors and other creditors and so goes out of business

5. An agreement that required banks hold as capital at least 8% of their risk-weighted assets

6. A bank's capital divided by its assets

7. The size of a loss on a trading portfolio that could happen 1% of the time

8. Calculates bank losses under various adverse scenarios and gauges the need for capital cushions

9. Practice where banks hold more risky assets on their balance sheet, and less risky assets off balance sheet as a response to capital requirements

Problems and Short-Answer Questions

PRACTICE PROBLEMS

1. Depositors and regulators face an adverse selection and moral hazard problem that is similar to what banks and private lenders face in their loan markets. (See Helpful Hint #1.)

   a. What are the four main ways that financial regulators reduce the adverse selection and moral hazard problems in banking? What problem does each regulation reduce— adverse selection or moral hazard?

   _____

   _____

   _____

   _____

   b. Match the answers you provided in *a* above to the solutions banks and private lenders have used to reduce the same problems in their loan markets.

   _____

   _____

   _____

   _____

   _____

   _____

2. Some banks in the United States have been considered by regulators to be "too big to fail."

   a. What two ways can the FDIC handle an insolvent bank? If a regulator decides that a bank is "too big to fail," how does the regulator handle an insolvent bank, and what does it mean to the depositors and creditors of the bank?

   _____

   _____

   _____

b. What is the purpose of a policy that designates some banks as "too big to fail?"

_____

_____

c. What asymmetric information problem is exaggerated by a "too big to fail" policy? Explain.

_____

_____

d. How does financial consolidation affect the "too big to fail" policy? Explain.

_____

_____

e. There are two methods the FDIC can use to handle an insolvent bank. Which method generates the least moral hazard? Why?

_____

_____

_____

SHORT-ANSWER QUESTIONS

1. What two problems are solved by deposit insurance? Explain.

_____

_____

_____

2. How does deposit insurance increase adverse selection and moral hazard? Explain.

_____

_____

_____

3. Why do regulators require that banks maintain a minimum capital-to-asset ratio?

_____

_____

4. What does a CAMELS rating measure?

_____

_____

5. What problem is caused by too much competition in banking? How did regulators restrict competition in the past? What problems did these regulations cause?

_____

_____

_____

6. Why is it difficult to regulate international banking? What did the Basel Accord attempt to do?

_____

_____

7. What are the limitations to the Basel 2 Accords? How does Basel 3 attempt to address these limitations?

_____

_____

8. Are the sources of financial crises in other countries similar or different from those in the United States? What are the main sources of financial crises? Are the sizes of the crises similar? Explain.

_____

_____

9. What factors contributed to the increase in the number of bank and savings and loan failures during the 1980s?

_____

_____

_____

10. How does a leverage cycle destabilize the financial system? What macroprudential policy could address this problem?

_____

_____

Critical Thinking

Suppose you are watching television. An advertisement for Risky Bank suggests that it is a bank that seeks risky speculative loans and junk bonds, and it is willing to pay 10% on its certificates of deposit. Immediately following that advertisement is a commercial for Safe Bank. Safe Bank screens and monitors its borrowers so that the loans are sure to be repaid. However, it only pays 5% on its certificates of deposit.

1. If the FDIC insures all deposits, where would you choose to place your deposit? Why?

   Risky Bank. higher % on $

   _____

2. If there were no deposit insurance, where would you likely choose to place your deposit? Why?

   _____

   _____

3. Explain how this example shows why countries charter and supervise their banks. What problems are reduced by requiring bank charters and by supervising banks?

   _____

   _____

   _____

   _____

Self-Test

TRUE/FALSE QUESTIONS

_____F_____ 1. The presence of deposit insurance from the FDIC reduces moral hazard and adverse selection problems in the banking industry.

____2. It is usually cheaper for the taxpayer if the FDIC resolves an insolvent institution by the "purchase and assumption method."

____3. A policy of "too big to fail" provides a competitive advantage to very large banks because the policy effectively guarantees repayment to all depositors and creditors of a large bank in the event of a bank failure rather than just the insured depositors and creditors.

____4. Requiring banks to be chartered reduces adverse selection in banking because it reduces the chances that undesirable or risk-loving people can gain control of a bank.

____5. The Basel Accord requires all signing countries to provide deposit insurance to their depository institutions.

____6. A bank's balance sheet alone provides an accurate picture of the degree of risk to which the bank is exposed.

____7. The requirement that banks employ mark-to-market accounting may cause lenders to contract lending during a financial crisis.

____8. Capital requirements are intended to reduce moral hazard in banking by making a bank failure more costly to the owners of the bank.

____9. The Community Reinvestment Act of 1974 was enacted to prevent "redlining."

____10. A sharp decrease in interest rates at the beginning of the 1980s caused losses for S&Ls and many failures.

____11. Banking crises in different countries almost always begin with embezzlement by corrupt bankers.

____12. Future financial regulations will likely loosen restrictions on credit rating agencies.

____13. The Dodd-Frank Act requires standardized derivatives to be traded on formal exchanges and trades cleared through clearinghouses.

____14. Basel 3 makes capital requirements less procyclical.

____15. The cost of the banking crises in the United States measured as a percent of GDP far exceeds comparable crises in other countries around the world.

MULTIPLE-CHOICE QUESTIONS

1. Which of the following is *not* true of a banking system with deposit insurance?
   a. Depositors are more likely to deposit their money in a bank.
   b. Depositors are less likely to withdraw their money in the event of a crisis.
   c. Depositors are less likely to collect information about the quality of the bank's loans.
   d. The moral hazard problem in banking is reduced.

2. If a bank becomes insolvent and the FDIC reorganizes the bank by finding a willing merger partner, the FDIC resolved this insolvency problem through the
    a. payoff method.
    b. safety net method.
    c. purchase and assumption method.
    d. CAMELS method.

3. The presence of deposit insurance increases the *adverse selection* problem in banking by
    a. attracting risk-loving people into bank ownership.
    b. increasing risky loans in banking.
    c. reducing bank capital.
    d. reducing the amount of deposits in the bank.

4. If the FDIC considers an insolvent bank to be "too big to fail," it will resolve the insolvency through the
    a. payoff method, which guarantees all deposits.
    b. payoff method, which guarantees only deposits that do not exceed $250,000.
    c. purchase and assumption method, which guarantees all deposits.
    d. purchase and assumption method, which guarantees only deposits that do not exceed $250,000.

5. The "too big to fail" policy of the FDIC
    a. decreases the moral hazard incentives for large banks.
    b. increases the moral hazard incentives for large banks.
    c. decreases the moral hazard incentives for small banks.
    d. increases the moral hazard incentives for small banks.

6. Which of the following banking regulations is most focused on reducing adverse selection in banking?
    a. consumer protection laws
    b. disclosure requirements requiring banks to use standard accounting principles
    c. periodic on-site examinations
    d. bank charter requirements

7. A bank's capital-to-asset ratio is also known as its
    a. leverage ratio.
    b. profit ratio.
    c. equity ratio.
    d. liability ratio.

8. Regulators impose capital requirements on banks because a low capital-to-asset ratio dramatically
    a. increases a bank's adverse selection.
    b. increases a bank's moral hazard.
    c. increases a bank's CAMELS rating.
    d. decreases a bank's rate of return on equity.
    e. All of the above are true.

9. The McFadden Act of 1927 and the Glass-Steagall Act of 1933
   a. increased bank competition and increased efficiency in banking.
   b. reduced bank competition and reduced efficiency in banking.
   c. increased bank competition and reduced efficiency in banking.
   d. reduced bank competition and increased efficiency in banking.

10. The primary objective of the Basel Accord was to standardize
    a. deposit insurance across international boundaries.
    b. bank examinations across international boundaries.
    c. bank capital requirements across international boundaries.
    d. branching restrictions across international boundaries.

11. Savings and loans grew rapidly in the 1980s because
    a. of the removal of restrictions on the interest rates depository institutions could pay on deposits.
    b. deposit insurance coverage was raised to $100,000 per account.
    c. the market for large certificates of deposit expanded.
    d. All of the above are true.

12. The Community Reinvestment Act of 1977
    a. prevented "redlining," which is when a bank refuses to lend in a particular area.
    b. put a ceiling on interest rates that banks could charge.
    c. required banks to provide information to borrowers about the true cost of their loan.
    d. did none of the above.

13. Which of the following is *not* a feature of the Dodd-Frank Act?
    a. Stricter regulations on marketing financial products to poor people.
    b. Giving the federal government the ability to dissolve bank holding companies in an orderly fashion.
    c. Lowering margin requirements on derivatives trades.
    d. Creating regulatory oversight to monitor for asset price bubbles.

14. Most banking crises around the world started with
    a. corrupt bankers.
    b. financial liberalization or innovation.
    c. excessive regulation.
    d. a crisis in the United States.

15. The final cost to the taxpayer for the 1980s savings and loan bailout was approximately
    a. $20 million.
    b. $150 million.
    c. $20 billion.
    d. $150 billion.

16. Future financial regulations will likely
    a. take structured investment vehicles off balance sheets.
    b. lower capital requirements for financial institutions.
    c. increase the size and scope of government-sponsored enterprises such as Fannie Mae and Freddie Mac.
    d. provide greater incentives for credit-rating agencies to provide reliable ratings.

17. Which of the following methods used by the FDIC to address a bank failure generates the greatest moral hazard?
    a. payoff method
    b. purchase and assumption method
    c. CAMELS method
    d. safety net method

18. Off-balance-sheet activities of a bank
    a. are illegal.
    b. reduce bank profits.
    c. increase the bank's risk.
    d. are unregulated.

19. Mark-to-market accounting
    a. helps banks lend more during a financial crisis.
    b. requires financial firms to value assets at what they would sell for.
    c. increases a bank's capital in a financial crisis.
    d. does none of the above.

20. Which of the following statements regarding banking crises throughout the world is true?
    a. The causes of banking crises are so unique across countries that any solution must be tailored specifically to the needs of that country.
    b. The 1980s savings and loan and banking crisis in the United States was more costly as a percent of GDP than any modern banking crisis in the rest of the world.
    c. Japan is the only industrialized country to avoid banking crises altogether in the post-WWII period.
    d. None of the above is true.

Solutions

Terms and Definitions

_4_ bank failure

_5_ Basel Accord

_1_ financial supervision (prudential supervision)

_6_ leverage ratio

_3_ mark-to-market (fair-value) accounting

_2_ off-balance-sheet activities

_9_ regulatory arbitrage

_8_ stress tests

_7_ value-at-risk (VaR)

Practice Problems

1. a. Chartering to prevent undesirables from controlling a bank—reduces adverse selection. Restrict asset holdings of banks—reduces moral hazard. Impose capital requirements on banks— reduces moral hazard. Examine banks— reduces moral hazard.

    b. Banks screening borrowers is similar to regulators chartering banks. Banks employing restrictive covenants preventing borrowers from investing in risky activities is similar to regulators restricting asset holdings of banks. Banks employing restrictive covenants requiring borrowers to have a minimum net worth is similar to regulators imposing capital requirements. Banks monitoring borrowers is similar to regulators examining banks.

2. a. The payoff method and the purchase and assumption method. Under a too-big-to-fail scenario, it uses the purchase and assumption method, which provides guarantees of repayment of large uninsured depositors and creditors of the insolvent bank.

    b. To avoid the financial disruption that could occur if depositors of a large bank lost their deposits.

    c. It increases the moral hazard problem because depositors have no incentive to monitor the bank, so the bank might take on even greater risk.

    d. There are more banks that are too big to fail, and there are conglomerate firms that may inadvertently receive a safety net for their nonbanking activities.

    e. The payoff method. With this method some depositors and creditors may not get all of their money back and stockholders lose all of their money, so all participants have a greater incentive to monitor the bank's loans more closely.

Short-Answer Questions

1. Because depositors can't judge the quality of a bank's loans, depositors were afraid to put their money in a bank. In addition, they would withdraw it when an adverse shock hits the economy, causing a bank panic.

2. Adverse selection—risk-loving entrepreneurs may choose to enter banking. Moral hazard— banks take on excessive risk because depositors have no reason to monitor the bank.

3. To reduce moral hazard. The greater the capital-to-asset ratio (leverage ratio), the more the bank has to lose if it fails, and so it pursues less risky activities.

4. It measures the quality of a banking institution in six areas: capital adequacy, asset quality, management, earnings, liquidity, and sensitivity to market risk.

5. Competition may increase moral hazard because banks may try to maintain their profits by assuming greater risk. Regulators restricted competition through branching restrictions and the Glass-Steagall Act. These restrictions reduced efficiency and raised charges and fees to consumers.

6. Because banks that operate in different countries can shift their business from one country to another. The Basel Accords standardized banks' capital requirements across countries to 8% of risk-weighted assets.

7. Under Basel 2, banks were not required to have sufficient enough capital during financial crises. Risk weights were dependent on unreliable credit ratings. Basel 2 was very procyclical and also proved to be insufficient for protecting banks when liquidity was scarce, particularly during financial crises. To

address these limitations, Basel 3 increased the quality and amount of capital required, and made requirements more countercyclical, revises the use of credit ratings, and makes provisions for banks in the event of liquidity shortages.

8. The sources are similar: Financial liberalization or innovation, weak banking regulations, and a government safety net. The crises in the United States have been much smaller when measured as a percent of GDP, compared to most other countries.

9. Savings and loans were allowed to take on newly available risky assets such as junk bonds and commercial real estate loans. FDIC insurance was increased, which increased moral hazard. Financial institutions were allowed to pay market interest rates, which increased the cost of funds.

10. Leverage cycles destabilize the financial system by rapidly increasing credit during booms. This leads to higher asset prices, higher capital buffers, and further extensions of credit which can lead to overleveraging, and eventually a crash in asset prices and financial markets. Countercyclical capital requirements can mitigate leverage cycles by increasing capital requirements during booms, and reducing them during downturns.

Critical Thinking

1. Put the deposit in Risky Bank because the return is higher and your deposit is guaranteed regardless of whether the bank's loans turn out to be good or not.

2. Since there is such a high chance of the bank becoming insolvent, put your money in the safe bank and accept the lower interest rate.

3. To avoid adverse selection, banks are chartered to make sure that excessively risky people and crooks are not allowed to control a bank. To avoid moral hazard, banks are supervised to make sure that they maintain significant capital and hold low-risk assets.

True/False Questions

1. F
2. F
3. T
4. T
5. F
6. F
7. T
8. T
9. T
10. F
11. F
12. F
13. T
14. T
15. F

Multiple-Choice Questions

1. d
2. c
3. a
4. c
5. b
6. d
7. a
8. b
9. b
10. c
11. d
12. a
13. c
14. b
15. d
16. d
17. b
18. c
19. b
20. d

12 Banking Industry: Structure and Competition*

Chapter Review

PREVIEW

Banks are financial intermediaries in business to earn profits. Compared to other countries, the United States has many more small banks. In this chapter we see why there are so many banks in the United States, and we address the competitiveness, efficiency, and soundness of the banking system.

HISTORICAL DEVELOPMENT OF THE BANKING SYSTEM

The first commercial bank in the United States was chartered in 1782. From 1791 to 1811, the Bank of the United States was created to act as both a private bank and a *central bank,* a government institution that has responsibility for the supply of money and credit in the economy. From 1816 to 1832, the Second Bank of the United States acted as the central bank. Until 1863, commercial banks were chartered by the states, and they were called *state banks*. In 1863, the Office of the Comptroller of the Currency federally chartered banks, called *national banks*. Thus, since 1863 the United States has had a *dual banking system* where state and national banks operate side by side. Our current central bank, the Federal Reserve System (the Fed), was created in 1913. In 1933, legislation created the Federal Deposit Insurance Corporation (FDIC) to prevent depositor losses from bank failures. That same year, the Glass-Steagall Act separated the activities of commercial banks from those of the securities industry. At present, the Comptroller of the Currency supervises national banks, the Fed and the state banking authorities supervise the state banks that chose to be Fed members, while the FDIC and state authorities

---

*This is also Chapter 12 in the 3rd ed.

supervise the insured non-Fed members. State authorities alone supervise the few uninsured state banks. The Fed supervises bank holding companies.

FINANCIAL INNOVATION AND THE GROWTH OF THE "SHADOW BANKING SYSTEM"

A change in the financial environment will stimulate a search by financial institutions for innovations that are likely to be profitable. The *shadow banking system*, in which lending occurs through securities markets, has developed into a large and important part of the financial system through financial innovation. The research and development of new financial products and services is known as *financial engineering*. Financial innovation has come from three basic sources that often interact with each other:

- *Responses to changes in demand conditions:* The increasing volatility of interest rates since the 1970s has increased interest-rate risk, resulting in financial innovations such as adjustable-rate mortgages and *financial derivatives* such as *futures contracts* to *hedge* interest-rate risk.

- *Responses to changes in supply conditions:* Improvements in *information technology* have lowered the cost of processing financial transactions so financial institutions can supply new products and services, and improved information acquisition makes it easier for firms to issue securities. As a result, there has been an increase in the use of bank credit and debit cards and electronic banking such as the ATM, ABM, and virtual banks. Better information technology has increasingly allowed for lower cost screening and monitoring so that lesser-known firms are now able to issue junk bonds and commercial paper. *Securitization* has allowed illiquid loans to be bundled into standardized amounts and sold to a third party. This innovation was at the center of the subprime mortgage crisis of the mid 2000s.

- *The desire to avoid costly regulations:* Two particularly burdensome regulations that have caused loophole mining and innovation are reserve requirements, which act as a tax on deposits, and deposit rate ceilings resulting from Regulation Q, which caused deposit withdrawal known as *disintermediation*. As a result, there has been significant growth in money market mutual funds (accounts in which the funds are used to invest in short-term, low-risk securities that are not subject to Regulation Q interest rate caps or reserve requirements) and sweep accounts (accounts that pay interest by using the funds to make overnight loans and are also not subject to reserve requirements).

Financial innovation has reduced banks' cost advantages in acquiring funds and their income advantages on their assets. Banks' cost advantage in acquiring funds was reduced when competitive pressures caused the elimination of Regulation Q. Banks' income advantages on assets have been reduced due to competition from junk bonds, securitization, and commercial paper. As a result, banks' traditional lines of business (making loans funded by deposits) have become less profitable, leading to a decline in traditional banking and an expansion in the shadow banking system. Banks have responded by making riskier loans for real estate and for corporate takeovers and leveraged buyouts, and by pursuing off-balance-sheet activities. These may have been contributing factors to the banking crises in the 1980s and 2007-2009. Declining cost and income advantages has been demonstrating a similar trend internationally for comparable reasons.

STRUCTURE OF THE U.S. COMMERCIAL BANKING INDUSTRY

The United States has a much greater number of commercial banks than other countries due to anti-competitive *branching* restrictions. The McFadden Act of 1927, coupled with the Douglas Amendment of 1956, essentially eliminated branching across state lines. The Midwestern agricultural states restricted branching the most so they have the largest number of small banks. The large number of banks is evidence of a lack of competition generated from protected market areas, not evidence of competition. The growth of bank holding companies and ATMs are responses to branching restrictions that weakened the anti-competitive effects of those restrictions.

BANK CONSOLIDATION AND NATIONWIDE BANKING

After a period of stability in the number of commercial banks from 1934 to the mid-1980s, the number of banks has declined substantially. From 1985 to 1992, bank failures and consolidations both contributed to the reduction in the number of banks. During this period, banks consolidated because loophole mining reduced the effectiveness of branching restrictions. This exposed the gains of diversification, economies of scale, and *economies of scope* that could be made from allowing banks to expand their markets areas. Reciprocal agreements between groups of states allowing expansion across state lines created *superregional banks*. Bank consolidation continued in the 1990s due to the increase in information technology favoring large banks and the Riegle-Neal Interstate Banking and Branching Efficiency Act of 1994, which established a basis for a nationwide banking system through interstate branching. Most economists think that, in the future, the U.S. banking industry will have fewer but still several thousand banks and a larger number of megabanks. Economists also think that the benefits of bank consolidation of gains in efficiency and risk reduction through diversification will outweigh the costs of reduced competition and reduced lending to small businesses. Indeed, most economists see nationwide branching as increasing competition.

SEPARATION OF THE BANKING
AND OTHER FINANCIAL SERVICE INDUSTRIES

The Glass-Steagall Act of 1933 separated banking from other financial services industries such as securities, insurance, and real estate. Over time, both banks and other financial institutions encroached on the other's territory. In 1987, the Fed allowed bank holding companies to underwrite securities as long as the revenue generated was less than a certain amount. Glass-Steagall was repealed by the Gramm-Leach-Bliley Financial Services Modernization Act of 1999 in order to help U.S. banks compete with foreign banks that have fewer restrictions on the type of business in which they can engage. This act has caused further consolidation of the banking industry. The global financial crisis also caused numerous mergers between banks and investment banks, quickly creating more complex banking organizations. Prior to the repeal of Glass-Steagall, the United States was fairly unique relative to the rest of the world by separating banking and financial services. Worldwide, there are three basic bank/finance structures: (i) *Universal banking*, in which there is no separation of the banking and securities industries; (ii) *British-style universal banking*, which has some separation between the two, and is similar to the current U.S. framework; and (iii) a framework similar to (ii), but allowing commercial banks to hold significant equity portfolios, similar to Japan.

THRIFT INDUSTRY:
REGULATION AND STRUCTURE

The regulation and structure of the thrift industry closely parallels that of the commercial bank industry. Savings and loans are primarily supervised by the Office of Thrift Supervision while their deposit insurance is administered by the FDIC. S&Ls have historically had more liberal branching laws than banks and they can get longer-term loans at lower rates from the Federal Home Loan Bank System than banks can from the Fed. Mutual savings banks are regulated by the states and usually receive insurance from the FDIC. Credit unions are organized around a common bond such as employment. They are regulated by the National Credit Union Association and get deposit insurance from the National Credit Union Share Insurance Fund. Credit unions are typically small.

INTERNATIONAL BANKING

International banking has undergone rapid growth due to three factors. First, the rapid growth of international trade and multinational corporations has caused firms to need banking services in foreign countries. Second, American banks have become involved in global investment banking. Third, American banks have become involved in the Eurodollar market. Eurodollars are dollar-denominated deposits in foreign banks outside the United States or foreign branches of U.S. banks. The majority of these deposits are time deposits that are then loaned to U.S. banks in units of $1 million. U.S. banks engage in international banking by opening branches overseas, creating Edge Act corporations, and opening international banking facilities (IBFs) in the United States. Foreign banks operate in the United States by owning an agency office of the foreign bank, a subsidiary U.S. bank, or a branch of the foreign bank. Foreign banks have been very successful in the United States. The International Banking Act of 1978 removed some of the advantage of foreign banks, and put U.S. banks on a more equal footing with foreign banks with regard to reserve requirements and branching.

Helpful Hints

1. Since branching has historically been restricted in the United States, banks have expanded via bank holding companies (BHCs). A holding company is a corporation that exists to hold stock in other companies. A BHC holds stock in banks, and bank-related companies. A lead bank that wishes to expand but cannot open branch offices creates a holding company and sells its stock to the holding company. The original stockholders of the lead bank now own stock in the BHC rather than the bank itself. While the bank could not buy other banks, the BHC can purchase other banks. The banks that are owned by the holding company are considered "affiliates" of the BHC but not branches. That is, the affiliates are still technically separate corporations and the flow of funds between those affiliates is restricted. When banks are allowed to branch, funds can flow freely between branches because each branch is simply a separate office of the same bank, and deposits from one branch can be loaned out from another branch. BHCs are considered inefficient substitutes for branching, and given the option banks will expand through branching rather than through BHCs.

Terms and Definitions

Choose a definition for each key term.

Key Terms:

_____ automated teller machine (ATM)

_____ bank holding companies

_____ branches

_____ central bank

_____ community banks

_____ deposit rate ceilings

_____ disintermediation

_____ dual banking system

_____ economies of scope

_____ Edge Act corporation

_____ financial derivatives

_____ financial engineering

_____ futures contracts

_____ hedge

_____ international banking facilities (IBFs)

_____ large, complex banking organizations (LCBOs)

_____ national banks

_____ securitization

_____ shadow banking system

_____ state banks

_____ superregional banks

_____ sweep account

_____ virtual bank

Definitions:

1. State chartered banks

2. The U.S. banking system where banks supervised by the federal government operate side by side with banks supervised by the state governments

3. Additional offices of banks that conduct banking operations

4. Restriction on the maximum interest rate payable on deposits

5. Federally chartered banks

6. An arrangement in which any balances above a certain amount in a corporation's checking account at the end of a business day are "swept out" of the account and invested in overnight repos that pay the corporation interest

7. The process of transforming illiquid financial assets into marketable capital market instruments

8. Companies that own one or more banks

9. A contract in which the seller agrees to provide a certain standardized commodity to the buyer on a specific future date at an agreed upon price

10. The government agency that oversees the banking system and is responsible for the supply of money and credit in the economy

11. To protect oneself against risk

12. The ability to use one resource to provide many different products and services

13. Bank holding companies similar in size to money center banks, but whose headquarters are not based in a money center city

14. A reduction in the flow of funds into the banking system that causes the amount of financial intermediation to decline

15. Financial system in which bank lending has been replaced by lending via the securities markets

16. Small banks

17. Development of profitable new financial products that meet customer needs

18. An electronic device that provides banking services 24 hours a day

19. Instruments that have payoffs linked to previously issued securities

20. Internet-based banks with no physical branches

21. Large companies that provide banking as well as other financial services

22. A subsidiary of a U.S. bank primarily engaged in international banking

23. Banks in the U.S. that accept time deposits from foreign entities but are not subject to reserve requirements or interest restrictions

Problems and Short-Answer Questions

PRACTICE PROBLEMS

1. The following questions address financial innovation in U.S. banking.

   a. List the three main sources for financial innovation and provide examples of the banking industry's responses to each.

      _____

      _____

      _____

      _____

      _____

      _____

      _____

   b. Prior to 2008, the Fed did not pay interest on bank reserves. For every $1,000 in deposits, how much did banks lose in forgone interest (opportunity cost) because of reserve requirements if banks charged 8% on loans and the required reserve ratio was 10%?

      _____

   c. For every $1,000 in deposits, how much did banks lose in forgone interest (opportunity cost) because of reserve requirements if banks charged 12% on loans and the require reserve ratio was 20%?

      _____

   d. Use your answers to *b* and *c* above to make a general statement regarding how interest rates and reserve requirements affect the cost to banks of holding required reserves.

      _____

      _____

2. The following questions address trends in banks traditional lines of business.
    a. Has there been an increase or a decrease in banks traditional lines of business of making loans funded by deposits? Why?

    _____

    _____

    b. What factor reduced banks cost advantage in acquiring funds? Explain.

    _____

    _____

    c. What three factors reduced banks income advantages on its assets?

    _____

    _____

    _____

    d. How have banks responded to these events?

    _____

    _____

3. The following questions address bank consolidation and nationwide banking.
    a. From the mid-1980s through the early 1990s, what were the sources of the reduction in the number of banks in the United States?

    _____

    b. After the early 1990s, what were the sources of the reduction in the number of banks?

    _____

    c. Prior to 1994, by what method did banks expand? Why?

    _____

    _____

    d. After 1994, by what method did banks generally expand? Why?

    _____

    _____

SHORT-ANSWER QUESTIONS

1. Has the United States always had a central bank? What are the names and dates of the U.S. central banks?

    _____

    _____

2. What is a dual banking system? How did the United States arrive at such a system?

    _____

    _____

    _____

3. What did the Glass-Steagall Act do? Why was it enacted? Why was it repealed?

    _____

    _____

    _____

4. What did Regulation Q do? When was it repealed, and what two effects did it have on the banking system?

    _____

    _____

    _____

5. What did the McFadden Act of 1927 and the Douglas Amendment of 1956 do?

    _____

    _____

6. What two innovations helped banks avoid branching restrictions?

    _____

7. Why has the growth in junk bonds and the commercial paper market reduced the demand for bank loans?

    _____

    _____

8. What are thrifts? How do their regulation and structure compare to commercial banks?

_____

_____

9. What three factors have caused the rapid growth in international banking?

_____

_____

10. What are the three main ways U.S. banks engage in international banking?

_____

_____

Critical Thinking

Your roommate is reading an article in the *Wall Street Journal* about trends in banking. It states that there are about half the number of banks in the United States today when compared to twenty years ago. Due to mergers, acquisitions, and interstate branching, the number of banks is expected to continue to drop in the future. Your roommate says, "The drop in the number of banks is clearly reducing competition. Borrowers are surely to be forced to pay higher interest rates in the future. This drop in the number of banks has to be bad for consumers."

1. How many banks does the United States have when compared to other countries? Why the great disparity?

_____

_____

2. Which banking system would be more competitive: A banking system where 1,000 banks serve 1,000 towns and each town is served by one bank, or a banking system where ten banks, each with 1,000 offices, serve 1,000 towns so each town has ten banks from which to choose? Why?

_____

_____

3. Which are generally more efficient and have lower risk, large banks or community banks? Why?

_____

_____

_____

4. Is the reduction in the number of banks evidence of lack of competition? Explain.

_____

_____

_____

5. Is your roommate's statement correct? That is, is it true that having fewer banks is likely to be bad for the consumer? Explain.

_____

_____

_____

Self-Test

TRUE/FALSE QUESTIONS

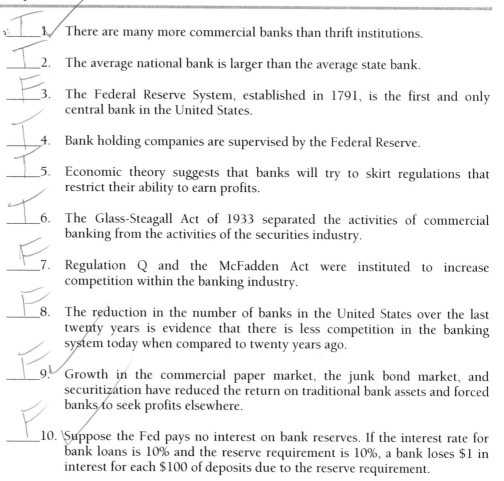

_____ 1. There are many more commercial banks than thrift institutions.

_____ 2. The average national bank is larger than the average state bank.

_____ 3. The Federal Reserve System, established in 1791, is the first and only central bank in the United States.

_____ 4. Bank holding companies are supervised by the Federal Reserve.

_____ 5. Economic theory suggests that banks will try to skirt regulations that restrict their ability to earn profits.

_____ 6. The Glass-Steagall Act of 1933 separated the activities of commercial banking from the activities of the securities industry.

_____ 7. Regulation Q and the McFadden Act were instituted to increase competition within the banking industry.

_____ 8. The reduction in the number of banks in the United States over the last twenty years is evidence that there is less competition in the banking system today when compared to twenty years ago.

_____ 9. Growth in the commercial paper market, the junk bond market, and securitization have reduced the return on traditional bank assets and forced banks to seek profits elsewhere.

_____ 10. Suppose the Fed pays no interest on bank reserves. If the interest rate for bank loans is 10% and the reserve requirement is 10%, a bank loses $1 in interest for each $100 of deposits due to the reserve requirement.

_____F_____ 11. Most economists think that in the long run, the United States will have only five or ten banks, each with thousands of offices, just like most foreign countries.

_____F_____ 12. Large banks are less efficient than community banks and have a greater likelihood of failure.

_____F_____ 13. The Riegle-Neal Interstate Banking and Branching Efficiency Act of 1994 repealed the Glass-Steagall Act.

_____T_____ 14. Branching regulations for savings and loans have historically been more liberal than for commercial banks.

_____T_____ 15. Prior to 1978, foreign banks operating in the United States enjoyed advantages over U.S. banks because foreign banks could branch across state lines and foreign banks were not subject to a reserve requirement.

MULTIPLE-CHOICE QUESTIONS

1. The United States is said to have a dual banking system because
   a. the depository system includes both commercial banks and thrift institutions.
   b. commercial banks offer both banking and securities market services.
   c. state banks and national banks operate side by side.
   d. banks are regulated and examined by both the Federal Reserve and the FDIC.
   e. the banking system includes both bank holding company affiliates and branch banks.

2. The Office of the Comptroller of the Currency charters and supervises
   a. national banks.
   b. state banks.
   c. bank holding companies.
   d. investment banks.

3. At present there are little more than
   a. 5,000 commercial banks in the United States.
   b. 7,000 commercial banks in the United States.
   c. 10,000 commercial banks in the United States.
   d. 15,000 commercial banks in the United States.

4. The Federal Reserve is a
   a. national bank.
   b. dual bank.
   c. state bank.
   d. central bank.
   e. bank holding company.

5. The Glass-Steagall Act of 1933
   a. established the Federal Reserve.
   b. separated the activities of national banks from those of state banks.
   c. separated the activities of commercial banks from those of the securities industry.
   d. separated the activities of commercial banks from those of the thrift industry.

6. Which of the following financial innovations helped banks reduce their interest-rate risk that came from the increased volatility of interest rates since the 1970s?
   a. ATMs
   b. bank holding companies
   c. adjustable-rate mortgages and financial derivatives such as futures contracts
   d. junk bonds and commercial paper

7. Regulation Q
   a. set the ceiling on interest rates that banks could pay on their deposits.
   b. restricted interstate branching.
   c. separated commercial banking and investment banking.
   d. set the ceiling on interest rates that banks could charge on their loans.

8. When depositors fail to deposit funds in banks or withdraw existing deposits because they have found more profitable alternatives, we have observed
   a. securitization.
   b. the effects of economies of scope.
   c. financial innovation.
   d. disintermediation.

9. Suppose the Fed pays no interest on bank reserves. For every $1,000 in deposits, how much do banks lose in forgone interest due to the reserve requirement if the reserve requirement is 10% and the rate at which banks lend is 7%?
   a. $7
   b. $10
   c. $70
   d. $100

10. Which of the following is *not* a source of competition that has reduced the income advantages banks once had on their traditional assets?
    a. growth in the commercial paper market
    b. elimination of Regulation Q
    c. growth in the junk bond market
    d. increasing use of securitization

11. The McFadden Act of 1927
    a. established the FDIC.
    b. established the Fed.
    c. eliminated interstate branching.
    d. eliminated bank holding company expansion across state lines.

12. The decline in traditional banking in the United States has led to
    a. reduced regulation of banks.
    b. an increase in riskier bank loans and off-balance-sheet activities of banks.
    c. an increase in the number of banks.
    d. an increase in the number of savings and loans.

13. Historically in the United States, branching laws have been most restrictive in the
    a. Northeast.
    b. Southwest.
    c. West Coast states.
    d. Midwest.
    e. Southeast.

14. The large number of banks in the United States
    a. is evidence that the banking system in the United States is very competitive.
    b. resulted from restrictive branching laws that reduced competition.
    c. are likely to substantially grow in number over the next few decades.
    d. are roughly equal to the number of banks in most developed countries.

15. Which of the following laws established a basis for a nationwide banking system in the United States?
    a. Riegle-Neal Interstate Banking and Branch Efficiency Act of 1994
    b. Gramm-Leach-Bliley Financial Services Modernization Act of 1999
    c. International Banking Act of 1978
    d. Glass-Steagall Act of 1933
    e. McFadden Act of 1927

16. The bundling of a portfolio of mortgage or student loans in to a marketable capital market instrument is know as
    a. computerization.
    b. consolidation.
    c. economies of scope.
    d. securitization.

17. Which of the following innovations helped banks circumvent restrictive branching laws?
    a. financial derivatives
    b. securitization
    c. bank holding companies and ATMs
    d. sweep accounts

18. Which of the following statements about savings and loans is true?
    a. There are more savings and loans than banks.
    b. Savings and loans do not have deposit insurance.
    c. Savings and loans have historically been subject to more restrictive branching laws than banks.
    d. Savings and loans are supervised by the Office of Thrift Supervision.

19. Compared to banks, credit unions
    a. have customers that share some common bond such as employment.
    b. tend to be larger.
    c. have no deposit insurance.
    d. usually lend to commercial enterprises.
    e. All of the above are correct.

20. Which of the following is *not* true regarding international banking?
    a. International banking has grown in part because of the growth in international trade.
    b. Foreign banks in the United States operate at a disadvantage compared to U.S. banks because they have higher reserve requirements and more restrictive branching rules.
    c. Eurodollars are dollar denominated deposits in foreign banks outside the U.S. or foreign branches of U.S. banks.
    d. U.S. banks can engage in international banking by opening branches overseas, creating Edge Act corporations, and opening IBFs in the United States.

Solutions

Terms and Definitions

18 automated teller machine (ATM)

 8 bank holding companies

 3 branches

10 central bank

16 community banks

 4 deposit rate ceilings

14 disintermediation

 2 dual banking system

12 economies of scope

22 Edge Act corporation

19 financial derivatives

17 financial engineering

 9 futures contracts

11 hedge

23 international banking facilities (IBFs)

21 large, complex banking organizations (LCBOs)

 5 national banks

 7 securitization

15 shadow banking system

 1 state banks

13 superregional banks

 6 sweep account

20 virtual bank

Practice Problems

1. a. Changes in demand conditions: interest rate volatility caused lenders to increase the demand for adjustable-rate mortgages and futures contracts.

Changes in supply conditions: cost reductions from improvements in information technology increased the use of bank credit and debit cards and of electronic banking. It also allowed for expansion of junk bonds, commercial paper, and securitization.

Avoidance of costly regulations: to avoid reserve requirements and Regulation Q, money market mutual funds and sweep accounts were created.

b. $\$1,000 \times 0.08 \times 0.10 = \$8$

c. $\$1,000 \times 0.12 \times 0.20 = \$24$

d. The greater the interest rate and reserve requirement, the greater the opportunity cost of holding required reserves.

2. a. Decrease. More competition has made traditional banking less profitable.

b. The elimination of Regulation Q caused banks to have to pay a competitive market rate for their deposits.

c. Competition from junk bonds, securitization, and commercial paper have reduced the demand for bank loans and reduced profit on bank loans.

d. Banks made riskier loans and pursued off-balance-sheet activities to earn fee income.

3. a. Bank failures and consolidation.

b. Bank consolidation.

c. Bank holding companies, because interstate branching was essentially illegal.

d. Branching, because the Reigle-Neal Interstate Banking and Branching Efficiency Act was passed, making interstate branching legal, and is more efficient than bank holding companies.

Short-Answer Questions

1. No. Bank of the United States (1791–1811), Second Bank of the United States (1816–1832), Federal Reserve System (1913–today).

2. Banks supervised by the federal government operating side by side with banks supervised by the state governments. The federal government passes a law taxing state bank notes with the intention of eliminating state banks. State banks avoided the regulation, survived, and operate along side national banks.

3. It separated the activities of banking from those of the securities industry. It was enacted because investment banking activities of banks were blamed for bank failures during the Depression. It was repealed to put U.S. banks on an equal footing with foreign banks.

4. It set the maximum interest rate banks could pay on deposits. Repeal allowed banks to

compete for deposits to reduce disintermediation, but it made the cost of funds rise to banks so they lost their cost advantage on their source of funds.

5. They made interstate branching illegal and let each state decide branching restrictions within that state.

6. The establishment of bank holding companies and ATMs.

7. It has given less well-known and smaller companies the ability to bypass banks by gaining a direct access to credit through securities markets.

8. Savings and loans, mutual savings banks, and credit unions. The regulation and structure closely parallels commercial banking so that in the case of S&Ls, regulating them separately from banks may no longer make sense.

9. The rapid growth of international trade and multinational corporations, increased involvement of American banks in global investment banking, and the expansion of the Eurodollar market.

10. By opening branches overseas, creating Edge Act corporations, and opening international banking facilities (IBFs) in the United States.

Critical Thinking

1. The United States has thousands more than any other country. The United States restricted branch banking to protect the markets of small banks, particularly in the Midwest.

2. Ten banks each with 1,000 offices would be more competitive because each bank customer would have a choice of ten banks rather than just one local bank.

3. Large banks are more efficient because they can take advantage of economies of scale and scope from advances in information technology. Large banks are better diversified so they have lower risk of failure.

4. No. The large number of banks is evidence of a lack of competition in the past due to branching restrictions. As banks compete, many will fail or be acquired by more efficient banks, reducing the number of banks.

5. No. Fewer banks with more branches is likely to offer the bank customer more choices, greater efficiency, and lower risk.

True/False Questions

1. F
2. T
3. F
4. T
5. T
6. T
7. F
8. F
9. T
10. T
11. F
12. F
13. F
14. T
15. T

Multiple-Choice Questions

1. c
2. a
3. b
4. d
5. c
6. c
7. a
8. d
9. a
10. b
11. c
12. b
13. d
14. b
15. a
16. d
17. c
18. d
19. a
20. b

13 Central Banks and the Federal Reserve System*

Chapter Review

PREVIEW

This chapter describes the institutional structure of the Federal Reserve, the European Central Bank, and other foreign central banks. Knowing the institutional structure of a central bank will help you to understand who controls the central bank, what motivates its behavior, and who holds the reigns of power within the central bank. A key feature of the institutional structure of a central bank is the degree to which it is independent of political pressures from government officials outside of the central bank. This chapter examines the advantages and disadvantages of central bank independence.

ORIGINS OF THE FEDERAL RESERVE SYSTEM

Two attempts to establish central banks in the United States during the nineteenth century failed because the American public feared centralization of power and moneyed interests.

After the charter for the Second Bank of the United States expired in 1836, U.S. financial markets experienced periodic bank panics. The widespread bank panic of 1907 convinced the public that there was a need for a central bank to prevent future panics. The Fed was established in 1913 by an act of Congress. To address the public's fear of centralized power and mistrust of moneyed interests, Congress wrote an elaborate system of checks and balances into the Federal Reserve act. An important feature of the act that was meant to ease fear of centralized power is that it created twelve regional Federal Reserve banks spread throughout the country.

*This is Chapter 16 in the 3rd ed.

STRUCTURE OF THE FEDERAL RESERVE SYSTEM

The Federal Reserve consists of the following entities: *Federal Reserve banks, the Board of Governors* of the Federal Reserve System and the *Federal Open Market Committee,* the Federal Advisory Council and member commercial banks, which represent approximately 40% of all commercial banks. There are twelve Federal Reserve banks, the largest of which (by assets) are New York, Chicago, and San Francisco. The Federal Reserve Bank of New York is the most important, since it is the largest by assets, houses the open market and foreign exchange desks, and is able to closely monitor the health of financial markets due to its proximity to large banks and Wall Street. Each Federal Reserve Bank is part government and part private. The directors of the Federal Reserve banks represent all constituencies of the American public: professional bankers; prominent leaders from industry; labor, agriculture, and the consumer sector; and representatives of the public interest. The twelve Federal Reserve banks are involved in monetary policy in several ways, for instance in the process of setting the discount rate and determining which banks get discount loans in their district.

The twelve Federal Reserve banks also perform the following functions:

- Clear checks

- Issue new currency and withdraw damaged currency from circulation

- Administer and make discount loans to banks in their districts

- Evaluate proposed mergers and applications for banks to expand their activities

- Act as liaisons between the business community and the Federal Reserve System

- Examine bank holding companies and state-chartered member banks

- Collect data on local business conditions

- Use their staffs of professional economists to research topics related to the conduct of monetary policy

The Board of Governors is comprised of seven members who are appointed by the president and confirmed by the senate for fourteen-year nonrenewable terms. The chairman is one of the seven board members and serves a four-year term. The Board of Governors has some duties that are not directly related to the conduct of monetary policy, such as setting margin requirements and approving bank mergers.

The Federal Open Market Committee (FOMC) is comprised of the seven members from the Board of Governors, and five of the twelve Federal Reserve Bank presidents. Due to their special importance and operations, the president of the Federal Reserve Bank of New York is always a member of the FOMC. The remaining four positions on the FOMC rotate annually among the remaining eleven Federal Reserve Bank presidents. Federal Reserve Bank presidents not currently on the FOMC are allowed to sit in on the meetings and provide input, but do not have a vote.

The FOMC meets eight times per year. At each FOMC meeting, detailed national economic forecasts are presented, along with three primary monetary policy alternatives. These previously were presented in separate documents as the "green book" and "blue book," respectively, however they have recently been combined into one document, the "teal book."

Each member on the FOMC votes individually on the direction of monetary policy as well as the monetary policy statement. However, the chairman of the Board of Governors holds considerable sway on the agenda of meetings and acts as the voice for the Fed and so has an important influence on the direction of policy. Once the FOMC meeting concludes, the Committee directs the open market desk at the Federal Reserve Bank of New York to conduct the appropriate *open market operations* necessary to achieve that policy. These policy directives from the FOMC are typically reflected in adjustments to the *federal funds rate*, the overnight bank-to-bank lending rate; a decrease in the federal funds rate represents an *easing of monetary policy*; an increase represents a *tightening of monetary policy*. The FOMC also advises on the setting of the discount rate and reserve requirements.

HOW INDEPENDENT IS THE FED?

A central bank is *instrument independent* if it has the ability to choose and set its monetary policy instruments, and *goal independent* if it has the ability to choose its own goals for monetary policy. The Federal Reserve has both types of independence, and so it enjoys a great deal of independence. One important feature of the Fed that makes it independent is that it funds its own operations mainly through interest earned on its holdings of government securities and so is not subject to budgetary control by Congress or others. However, Congress can still wield some influence over the Federal Reserve through legislation, as the charter under which the Federal Reserve operates from Congress can be changed at any time. The president can influence the Federal Reserve to a limited extent through appointments to the Board of Governors in three primary ways:

- The president can wield influence over Congress and hence indirectly affect Federal Reserve policy and procedures.

- In practice, a sitting president usually appoints more than one or two members to the Board of Governors during a four-year term.

- The president can appoint a new chair of the Board of Governors every four years.

SHOULD THE FED BE INDEPENDENT?

An independent Federal Reserve is less subject to political pressures, which could lead to excessive inflation or a political business cycle. Furthermore, an independent Federal Reserve is more likely to resist pressure to help the Treasury finance deficit spending by purchasing government securities. A third argument for Fed independence is that politicians often lack the expertise in economic matters to make hard decisions that have significant economic implications and so are better left to the Fed.

Opponents of Federal Reserve independence argue that it is undemocratic to have monetary policy controlled by an elite group responsible to no one and that the inability to replace members of the Board of Governors leads to a lack of accountability. Another argument against Fed independence is that by placing the Fed under the control of Congress, fiscal and monetary policy could be better coordinated, leading to better economic outcomes. In addition, independence does not imply that the Fed will always be successful, as evidenced by the Great Depression and the high inflation of the 1970s. Recent research supports the prediction that greater central bank independence is associated with lower inflation rates. Furthermore, those lower inflation rates have not come at the expense of higher unemployment or greater output fluctuations.

EXPLAINING CENTRAL BANK BEHAVIOR

The theory of bureaucratic behavior suggests that the objective of a bureaucracy is to maximize its own welfare. As predicted by this theory, the Fed has fought vigorously to preserve its autonomy. In addition, it has tried to avoid conflict by gradually, rather than abruptly, increasing interest rates to slow the economy, and has increased the frequency, speed, and scope of information that it communicates with the public over time. Finally, it has successfully expanded its jurisdiction to cover all banks, thereby increasing its power.

STRUCTURE AND INDEPENDENCE OF THE EUROPEAN CENTRAL BANK

The European Central Bank (ECB) rivals the Federal Reserve in terms of importance in the central banking world. The ECB has a structure similar to the structure of the Federal Reserve, but there are important differences between the two central banks. In contrast to the Federal Reserve, the ECB has less centralized power; the National Central Banks in the Eurosystem control both its own budgets and that of the ECB; monetary operations are controlled by the National Central Banks; and the ECB is not involved in supervision and regulation of financial institutions.

The Governing Council is the committee within the ECB that plays a role similar to that of the FOMC. The Governing Council decides on monetary policy by consensus rather than by vote as in the FOMC, to avoid the appearance of favoring a policy beneficial to one particular country. Another difference is that the Governing Council holds a press conference following each monetary policy meeting, held monthly. The FOMC typically just releases a statement announcing its decision about the course for monetary policy but has recently began holding a press conference following policy meetings once per quarter. Finally, due to the sheer number of countries in the Eurosystem, there are many more voting members on the Governing Council (currently 21) than there are on the FOMC, which can pose problems for reaching consensus on policy matters.

The ECB is the most independent central bank in the world, with many institutional structures similar to the Federal Reserve that give it great independence. The Maastricht Treaty specifies "price stability" as the single goal of the ECB, but due to the difficulty in modifying the Maastricht treaty, this gives the ECB a greater amount of goal independence than the Federal Reserve.

STRUCTURE AND INDEPENDENCE OF OTHER FOREIGN CENTRAL BANKS

On paper, the Bank of Canada has less instrument independence than the Federal Reserve because the minister of finance can issue a directive that the Bank must follow. However, in practice this has not happened. The Bank of Canada has less goal independence than the Fed because it has a single target of low inflation.

In 1997 the Bank of England was granted the power to set the interest rate, but the Bank of England does not have complete instrument independence because the government has the power to overrule the Bank's interest rate decisions "for a limited period in extreme economic circumstances." The Bank of England is also less goal independent than the Federal Reserve because it has a single goal of low inflation that is set by the Chancellor of the Exchequer (the equivalent of the Treasury Secretary in the United States).

The Bank of Japan was granted greater instrument and goal independence in 1998. Before that time the government had voting members sitting on the monetary policy committee. Representatives from the government still attend monetary policy meetings but no longer have voting rights, and the government still has some budgetary control over the Bank.

Overall, there is a worldwide trend towards greater central bank independence. Both theory and experience suggest that more independent central banks produce better monetary policy, so this trend seems to validate the evidence from greater independence.

Helpful Hints

1. The key point to understand about the institutional structure of the Federal Reserve and other central banks is how institutional structure relates to independence. Independent central banks are less likely to create excessive inflation and a *political business cycle*. On the other hand, an independent central bank is potentially less accountable for its policies. Worldwide there has been a greater movement toward central bank independence in recent years. As predicted by theory, greater central bank independence has been associated with lower inflation.

Terms and Definitions

Choose a definition for each key term.

Key Terms:

_____ Board of Governors of the Federal Reserve System

_____ easing of monetary policy

_____ federal funds rate

_____ Federal Open Market Committee

_____ Federal Reserve banks

_____ goal independence

_____ instrument independence

_____ open market operations

_____ political business cycle

_____ tightening of monetary policy

Definitions:

1. The committee that is comprised of the Board of Governors, the president of the Federal Reserve Bank of New York, and four other Federal Reserve Bank presidents

2. The ability of the central bank to set goals of monetary policy

3. The seven-member board that heads the Federal Reserve System

4. The purchase and sale of government securities by the Federal Reserve that affect both interest rates and the amount of reserves in the banking system

5. A situation in which monetary policy is expansionary prior to an election and contractionary after an election

6. The ability of the central bank to set monetary policy instruments

7. The twelve banks of the Federal Reserve System

8. Increasing the federal funds rate

9. The overnight interest rate which banks charge other banks for loans

10. Decreasing the federal funds rate

Problems and Short-Answer Questions

PRACTICE PROBLEMS

1. The first two attempts at establishing a central bank in the United States failed.
   a. What characteristics of American politics before the twentieth century resulted in their demise?

   _____

   _____

b. What recurring economic problem was attributed to the lack of a central bank in the later half of the nineteenth century?

_____

_____

c. When was the Federal Reserve founded?

_____

d. What specific features of the Federal Reserve were a response to the characteristics of American politics at the time of its founding?

_____

_____

_____

2. The authors of the Federal Reserve Act of 1913 designed a decentralized banking system that reflected their fears of centralized financial power. Today, this decentralization is still evident in the allocation of responsibilities and duties among the various Federal Reserve entities. Match the Federal Reserve entity to its responsibilities and duties given on the left by placing the appropriate letter in the space provided.

Responsibilities and Duties

Federal Reserve Entity

_C_ 1. clears checks

a. Board of Governors

_C_ 2. "establishes" discount rate

b. Federal Open Market Committee

_A_ 3. reviews and determines discount rate

c. Federal Reserve banks

_A_ 4. appointed by the president of the United States

_B_ 5. appointed for fourteen-year _A_ terms

_B_ 6. meets eight times a year

_B_ 7. decides monetary policy

_C_ 8. evaluates bank merger applications

_C_ 9. determines margin _A_ requirements

_C_ 10. issues new currency

3. An important reason to study the institutional structure of central banks is to understand how that institutional structure relates to central bank independence.

   a. What are the two types of central bank independence?

   _____

   b. What institutional features of the Federal Reserve make it independent?

   _____

   _____

4. In just the last decade or two, the Federal Reserve has substantially increased its transparency and communication with the public.

   a. Why, prior to these changes, was the Federal Reserve so secretive about its policies and providing information to the public?

   _____

   b. Describe four ways in which the Federal Reserve's communication strategy has evolved to become more transparent.

   _____

   _____

5. The European Central Bank, which was started in January 1999, was patterned after the Federal Reserve, but there are some important differences between the two central banks as well.

   a. In what ways are the ECB and the Federal Reserve similar?

   _____

   _____

   b. In what ways are the ECB and the Federal Reserve different?

   _____

   _____

   c. Is the ECB more independent or less independent than the Federal Reserve? Why?

   _____

   _____

6. On paper, both the Bank of Canada and the Bank of England appear to lack instrument independence.
   a. Explain why both central banks appear on paper to lack instrument independence, and explain why in practice the two central banks essentially do have instrument independence.

   _____

   _____

   b. What institutional feature of the Bank of Canada and the Bank of England make both banks less goal independent than the Federal Reserve?

   _____

   _____

7. When studying the behavior of a central bank, it is important to understand the objectives facing a bureaucracy.
   a. What does the theory of bureaucratic behavior suggest is the objective of a bureaucracy?

   _____

   _____

   b. Name two ways that the Fed has acted that are consistent with the theory of bureaucratic behavior?

   _____

   _____

8. There are arguments for and against Federal Reserve independence.
   a. What are the arguments in favor of an independent Federal Reserve?

   _____

   _____

   b. What are the arguments against an independent Federal Reserve?

   _____

   _____

SHORT-ANSWER QUESTIONS

1. Why was there no central bank in the United States between 1836 and 1913?

   _____

   _____

2. Why is the New York Federal Reserve Bank so important to the Federal Reserve system?

   _____

   _____

3. What does it mean for a commercial bank to be a member of the Federal Reserve System?

   _____

   _____

4. What is the significance of the Depository Institutions Deregulation and Monetary Control Act of 1980?

   _____

   _____

5. What is the relationship between the FOMC, the New York Federal Reserve Bank, and the System Open Market (trading) desk?

   _____

   _____

6. What factors allow the Chair of the Board of Governors to have so much influence over monetary policy?

   _____

   _____

7. What are the purposes of the "beige book" and "teal book" in FOMC meetings?

   _____

   _____

8. In what ways can the president and Congress influence the Federal Reserve?

   _____

   _____

9. How did the Bank of Japan Law, which took effect in 1998, affect the independence of the Bank of Japan?

_____

_____

10. Do countries with greater central bank independence have higher unemployment or greater output fluctuations?

_____

_____

Critical Thinking

Suppose the Senator from your state introduces a bill to Congress that would require the Federal Reserve to establish a single goal of low inflation.

1. How would passage of this bill affect the Fed's goal and instrument independence?

_____

_____

_____

2. Would passage of this bill make the Fed more or less like the European Central Bank? Explain your answer.

_____

_____

_____

3. Would passage of this bill make it more or less likely that the Fed would pursue policies that would lead to a political business cycle? Explain your answer.

_____

_____

_____

Self-Test

TRUE/FALSE QUESTIONS

_____ F 1. All Federal Reserve district bank presidents are allowed to participate in policy discussions during FOMC meetings.

_____ F 2. The FOMC sets the federal funds rate, but not the discount rate.

_____ T 3. Members on the Board of Governors cannot serve more than fourteen years.

_____ F 4. A tightening of monetary policy typically involves raising reserve requirements.

_____ T 5. The New York Federal Reserve Bank contains the largest gold depository in the United States.

_____ T 6. The Federal Reserve Act, which created a central bank with regional banks, reflected a compromise between traditional distrust of moneyed interest and concern for elimination of financial panics.

_____ T 7. The president of the Federal Reserve Bank of New York is always a member of the Federal Open Market Committee.

_____ T 8. The Governing Council of the European Central Bank plays a role similar to role played by the Federal Open Market Committee of the Federal Reserve.

_____ F 9. The European Central Bank is less independent than the Federal Reserve.

_____ F 10. The Bank of England has more goal independence than the Federal Reserve.

_____ T 11. The Bank of Japan was granted greater instrument and goal independence in 1998.

_____ T 12. In recent years central banks around the world have moved toward greater independence.

_____ T 13. The theory of bureaucratic behavior may help explain why the Federal Reserve has resisted attempts by Congress to control its budget.

_____ T 14. An independent central bank is less likely to produce a political business cycle.

_____ F 15. A disadvantage of central bank independence is that it tends to result in higher inflation.

MULTIPLE-CHOICE QUESTIONS

1. The Federal Reserve System was established in 1913
   a. because of distrust of moneyed interests and centralized power.
   b. because the public became convinced a central bank was needed to avoid bank panics.
   c. to keep the stock markets from crashing.
   d. to ensure banking services for the Treasury.

2. The first central bank in the United States was
   a. the Federal Reserve.
   b. the Bank of United States.
   c. the First Bank of the United States.
   d. The Second Bank of the United States.

3. Reserve requirements are set by the _____ and advised upon by the _____.
   a. Board of Governors; FOMC
   b. Federal Advisory Council; open market desk
   c. New York Federal Reserve Bank; member banks
   d. Chair of the Board of Governors; twelve regional Federal Reserve banks

4. The Board of Governors is involved in which of the following activities?
   a. effectively sets the discount rate through the review and determination process
   b. setting margin requirements
   c. approval of bank mergers
   d. determining open market operations
   e. all of the above

5. The Maastricht Treaty
   a. subjects Federal Reserve monetary policy actions to audits by the GAO.
   b. established the unique structure of central banking in the United States.
   c. gives the ECB more independence than the Federal Reserve.
   d. enhances the ability of Eurozone countries to influence the ECB.

6. The Federal Reserve System is comprised of the following three entities:
   a. Federal Reserve banks, Board of Governors, and the U.S. Treasury.
   b. Federal Reserve banks, the Governing Council, and the U.S. Treasury.
   c. Federal Reserve banks, the Governing Council, and the Federal Open Market Committee.
   d. Federal Reserve banks, the Board of Governors, and the Federal Open Market Committee.

7. The Federal Open Market Committee is comprised of
   a. the five members of the Board of Governors plus seven of the twelve Federal Reserve Bank presidents.
   b. the seven members of the Board of Governors plus five of the twelve Federal Reserve Bank presidents.
   c. the five members of the Board of Governors plus the twelve Federal Reserve Bank presidents.
   d. the seven members of the Board of Governors plus the twelve Federal Reserve Bank presidents.

8. The directors of the Federal Reserve banks
   a. represent all constituencies of the American public.
   b. are all professional bankers.
   c. are appointed by the president of the United States.
   d. are all stockholders of the Federal Reserve Bank.

9. Monetary policy is determined by
   a. the Board of Governors.
   b. the twelve Federal Reserve banks.
   c. the Federal Open Market Committee.
   d. the Federal Reserve Advisory Committee.

10. Which of the following statements concerning the fourteen-year term for members of the Board of Governors is false?
    a. The fourteen-year term is nonrenewable.
    b. The fourteen-year term allows significant independence from political pressures.
    c. Members of the Board of Governors are appointed by the president for fourteen-year terms.
    d. Most members of the Board of Governors serve out the entire fourteen-year term.

11. The Federal Reserve is remarkably free from political pressure because
    a. it has an independent source of revenue.
    b. its structure cannot be changed by Congress through legislation.
    c. like members of the Supreme Court, members of the Board of Governors serve lifetime appointments.
    d. the chairman of the Board of Governors is appointed by the Federal Reserve Bank presidents.

12. The ability of the central bank to set reserve requirements is an example of
    a. goal independence.
    b. instrument independence.
    c. the theory of bureaucratic behavior.
    d. independent review.

13. While the Fed enjoys a relativity high degree of independence for a government agency, it feels political pressure from the president and Congress because
    a. Congress must reappoint Fed Governors every three years.
    b. the Fed must go to Congress each year for operating revenues.
    c. Congress could limit Fed power through legislation.
    d. the president can dismiss a Fed Governor at any time.

14. The Bank of Canada is
    a. less instrument independent than the Federal Reserve on paper and less goal independent than the Federal Reserve.
    b. more instrument independent than the Federal Reserve on paper and less goal independent than the Federal Reserve.
    c. less instrument independent than the Federal Reserve on paper and more goal independent than the Federal Reserve.
    d. more instrument independent than the Federal Reserve on paper and more goal independent than the Federal Reserve.

15. The Bank of Japan
    a. has two goals: price stability and low unemployment.
    b. has a single goal: low unemployment.
    c. has a single goal: price stability.
    d. is not an independent central bank.

16. The theory of bureaucratic behavior may help explain why the Fed
    a. is sometimes slow to increase interest rates.
    b. limits reserve requirements to member banks.
    c. has moved toward greater transparency in recent years.
    d. is currently lobbying to give Congress authority over its budget.

17. The principal–agent problem
    a. is greater for an independent central bank than for politicians.
    b. is greater for politicians than for an independent central bank.
    c. explains why the Fed sets reserve requirements.
    d. explains why the Fed is sometimes slow to increase interest rates.

18. An independent Federal Reserve
    a. is more likely to produce higher inflation and less likely to produce a political business cycle.
    b. is more likely to produce higher inflation and more likely to produce a political business cycle.
    c. is less likely to produce higher inflation and less likely to produce a political business cycle.
    d. is less likely to produce higher inflation and more likely to produce a political business cycle.

19. Proponents of a Fed under greater control of the president or Congress argue that
    a. greater control would help coordinate fiscal and monetary policies.
    b. the Fed has not always used its independence successfully.
    c. it is undemocratic to have monetary policy controlled by an elite group.
    d. All of the above are arguments for putting the Fed under greater control of the president or Congress.

20. Greater central bank independence is associated with
    a. lower inflation and lower unemployment.
    b. lower inflation and no change in unemployment.
    c. lower inflation and higher unemployment.
    d. no change in either unemployment or inflation.

Solutions

Terms and Definitions

_3_ Board of Governors of the Federal Reserve System

_10_ easing of monetary policy

_9_ federal funds rate

_1_ Federal Open Market Committee

_7_ Federal Reserve banks

_2_ goal independence

_6_ instrument independence

_4_ open market operations

_5_ political business cycle

_8_ tightening of monetary policy

Practice Problems

1. a. Before the twentieth century, American politics was characterized by a fear of centralized power and a mistrust of moneyed interests.

    b. Nationwide bank panics

    c. 1913

    d. The Federal Reserve act of 1913 specified an elaborate system of checks and balances and the power of the Federal Reserve was spread throughout the country by establishing twelve regional Federal Reserve banks.

2.
    _c_ 1. clears checks

    _c_ 2. "establishes" discount rate

    _a_ 3. reviews and determines discount rate

    _a_ 4. appointed by the president of the United States

    _a_ 5. appointed for fourteen-year terms

    _b_ 6. meets eight times a year

    _b_ 7. decides monetary policy

    _c_ 8. evaluates bank merger applications

    _a_ 9. determines margin requirements

    _c_ 10. issues new currency

3. a. Instrument independence, which describes the ability of a central bank to choose its monetary policy instruments;

and goal independence which describes the ability of a central bank to choose its monetary policy goals.

    b. Institutional features of the Federal Reserve which make it independent are: it has an independent source of revenue, and members of the Board of Governors are appointed for fourteen-year (technically) nonrenewable terms.

4. a. The theory of bureaucratic behavior indicates that the Fed has an incentive to hide its actions from the public and politicians to avoid conflict. For a long time, this was a feature of the way the Fed operated.

    b. There are at least seven: (1) in 1994, it began to immediately release policy directives after FOMC meetings; (2) in 1999, it began providing policy "bias" in its statements to indicate possible future policy actions; (3) in 2002, the Fed began reporting voting records of those on the FOMC; (4) in 2004, it reduced the delay in releasing previous meeting minutes from six weeks to three; (5) in 2007, it increased the forecast horizon of FOMC projections from two to three years, and produces them four times per year instead of two; (6) in addition, the FOMC projections are released with narrative descriptions that include risks to the outlook; (7) in 2011, the Fed began holding press conferences following policy decisions four times per year.

5. a. Central banks in each country of the European monetary union, which are called National Central Banks, have a similar role to that of the Federal Reserve banks. The ECB has an Executive Board which is similar in structure to the Board of Governors. The ECB's Governing Council which is comprised of the Executive Board and the presidents of the National Central Banks is similar to the FOMC and makes the decisions on monetary policy.

    b. The budgets of the Federal Reserve are controlled by the Board of Governors, while the National Central Banks control their own budgets and the budget of the ECB so the ECB has less power than the Board of Governors. Monetary operations in the Eurosystem are conducted by the National Central Banks in each country. Unlike the Federal Reserve, the ECB is not involved in supervision and regulation of financial institutions.

c. The ECB is more independent than the Federal Reserve. Like the Fed, the ECB controls is own budgets and the governments of the member countries are not allowed to issue instructions to the ECB. But unlike the Federal Reserve, the Eurosystem's charter cannot be changed by legislation; it can be changed only by revision of the Maastricht Treaty, which is a difficult process.

6. a. In both Canada and England, if the bank and the government disagree about the direction of monetary policy, the government can overrule the bank. But economic circumstances would have to be "extreme" and the government's ability to overrule monetary policy is constrained to a limited period of time so in practice it is unlikely that such overruling would occur.

b. The Bank of Canada and the Bank of England have inflation targets which makes them less goal-independent than the Fed.

7. a. According to the theory of bureaucratic behavior, the objective of a bureaucracy is to maximize its own welfare.

b. The Fed continually counterattacks congressional attempts to control its budget. When the Fed raises interest rates to slow the economy, it does so slowly in order to minimize conflict with Congress and the president.

8. a. Subjecting the Fed to more political pressure might lead to more inflation in the economy and could possibly lead to a political business cycle. A less independent Fed might also be pressured to help finance deficit spending. Another argument supporting Federal Reserve independence is that the principal-agent problem is worse for politicians than for the Fed because politicians have fewer incentives to act in the public interest.

b. Independence means less accountability, which some argue is inconsistent with a democracy. A less independent Fed would be more likely to pursue monetary policy that is consistent with fiscal policy. Finally, the Fed has not always used its independence successfully.

Short-Answer Questions

1. Due to distrust of moneyed interests, there was open hostility by the American public to the existence of central banks. As a result, the first two attempts to create a central bank eventually failed. This led to a long period between 1836 and 1913 where no formal central bank existed in the United States.

2. There are many reasons why the New York Federal Reserve bank is important to the Fed: (1) Some of the largest commercial banks are located in New York; (2) the New York Fed houses the open market desk and foreign exchange trading desk; (3) it is located close to Wall Street and many major financial companies, making monitoring conditions convenient; (4) it is also a member of the Bank for International Settlements; (5) it holds the largest gold deposits in the United States; (6) the New York Fed has a permanent vote on the FOMC, unlike other regional Federal Reserve banks.

3. All national banks are required to be members of the Federal Reserve System. State banks can choose to be members.

4. This subjected all depository institutions, regardless of charter, to the same reserve requirements putting all banks on a more equal footing. In addition, it gave all depository institutions access to discount window lending and check clearing functions.

5. The FOMC decides on a monetary policy action. After this, it directs the System Open Market (trading) desk which is housed at the New York Federal Reserve bank to conduct open market operations in order to achieve the particular policy chosen by the FOMC.

6. The Chair is the spokesperson for the Fed, who negotiates with Congress and the president. In addition, the Chair sets the agendas for the Board and FOMC meetings, and can be influential through sheer force of personality. Finally, the Chair can influence monetary policy through direction and supervision of the staff of Board economists,

who provide analysis and input for FOMC meetings.

7. The "teal book" contains the Board staff's national economic forecast as well as different possible scenarios for monetary policy that the FOMC typically considers. The "beige book" gives a summary of economic conditions in each of the twelve Federal Reserve districts.

8. The president can influence the Federal Reserve through his appointments to the Board of Governors. Congress can influence the Federal Reserve by passing legislation to make the Fed more accountable for its actions.

9. It increased the independence of the Bank of Japan by giving it more goal and instrument independence.

10. No. Evidence indicates that countries with greater central bank independence do not have higher unemployment or greater output fluctuations.

Critical Thinking

1. Passage of this bill would reduce the Fed's goal independence. Current law does not require the Fed to pursue a specific inflation target. Passage of a bill requiring the Fed to pursue a specific inflation target would, therefore, reduce the Fed's goal independence, but it would not affect the Fed's instrument independence because the Fed would still have the ability to use any instrument it deems appropriate to achieve the specified inflation goal.

2. This bill would make the Fed more like the ECB. The Maastricht Treaty currently specifies that the overriding, long-term goal of the ECB is price stability.

3. Passage of this bill would make it less likely that the Fed would pursue policies that would lead to a political business cycle because it would make Fed policy more transparent. Both elected officials and the public would be able to evaluate whether the Fed is meeting its goal for inflation. Under current law, the Fed does not have an explicitly stated goal for inflation and so elected officials and the public are less able to evaluate whether the Fed is pursuing policies that would lead to a political business cycle.

True/False Questions

1. T
2. T
3. F
4. F
5. T
6. T
7. T
8. T
9. F
10. F
11. T
12. T
13. T
14. T
15. F

Multiple-Choice Questions

1. b
2. c
3. a
4. e
5. c
6. d
7 b
8. a
9. c
10. d
11. a
12. b
13. c
14. a
15. c
16. a
17. b
18. c
19. d
20. b

14

The Money Supply Process*

Chapter Review

PREVIEW

This chapter describes the money supply process. Bank deposits are by far the largest component of the money supply. This chapter begins by showing how banks create deposits and how deposit creation affects the money supply. It then derives the *money multiplier*. After deriving a more realistic money multiplier, this chapter describes the sources of movement in the monetary base, the money multiplier and the money supply.

Throughout this chapter, money (M) is defined as M1, which is currency plus checkable deposits.

THREE PLAYERS IN THE MONEY SUPPLY PROCESS

The money supply process involves three players: the central bank (the Federal Reserve), banks (depository institutions), and depositors. Of these three players, the central bank—the Federal Reserve System—is the most important.

THE FED'S BALANCE SHEET

The simplified Fed balance sheet is as follows:

Federal Reserve System

Assets	Liabilities
Securities	Currency in circulation
Loans to Financial Institutions	Reserves

---

*This is Chapter 17 in the 3rd ed.

The sum of the Fed's liabilities, currency in circulation (*C*) plus *reserves* (*R*) is called the *monetary base* (*MB*). Reserves equal *required reserves* plus *excess reserves*. The ratio of required reserves to deposits is called the *required reserve ratio* (*rr*). The *required reserve ratio* is established by the Federal Reserve and plays an important role in the deposit creation process.

The Fed holds two primary types of assets. The first are securities, which are typically government securities such as U.S. Treasury debt or agency debt, but in unusual circumstances may also include corporate securities. The second are loans to financial institutions, which are typically to banks, but may also be to other nonbank financial institutions. Fed loans to banks, or discount loans, are provided at the *discount rate*. The Fed makes money through interest income on its asset holdings, while its liabilities cost nothing.

CONTROL OF THE MONETARY BASE

The Federal Reserve exercises control over the monetary base through its buying and selling of securities on the open market, called *open market operations* and through its extension of loans to financial institutions. The Fed has significant (but not complete) control over the total of the monetary base more so than the individual components of the monetary base (currency and reserves). Actions by the nonbank public can change the mix of currency and reserves in the monetary base, but those actions leave the total monetary base unchanged.

When the Fed conducts an *open market purchase* of a $100 bond from a bank, reserves and therefore the monetary base, increase by $100. When the Fed conducts an open market purchase of a $100 bond from the nonbank public, the monetary base again increases by $100. But the increases could take the form of an increase in reserves if the nonbank public deposits the proceeds of the sale into a checking account, or it could take the form of an increase in currency in circulation if the nonbank public decides to hold the proceeds of the sale in currency. Obviously some intermediate case is possible as well; the nonbank public can hold some currency and some deposits, but the main point is that the Fed is able to precisely increase the monetary base by $100, but actions by the nonbank public, not the Fed, determine the mix of reserves and currency in circulation. When the Fed makes a $100 discount loan to a bank, the monetary base increases by $100. When a bank pays off a $100 discount loan from the Fed, the monetary base decreases by $100.

Two sources of change in the monetary base that are outside of the Fed's control are Treasury deposits at the Fed and *float*. When the Treasury moves its deposits from commercial banks to the Fed (it must do this before it can spend the funds), reserves in the banking system and therefore the monetary base decline temporarily (reserves move back up once the money is spent by the Treasury). Float occurs when the Fed clears checks. The Fed often credits the account of the bank presenting the check for payment before it debits the account of the bank that the check is drawn on. For that brief period of time before the debit occurs, reserves in the banking system rise. Treasury purchases and float complicate but do not prevent the Fed from accurately controlling the monetary base.

The Fed does not have complete control over the monetary base because banks decide when they want to borrow from the Fed at the discount rate. Financial institutions' borrowing from the Fed is called *borrowed reserves* (*BR*). If we subtract borrowed reserves (BR) from the monetary base we get the *nonborrowed monetary base* (MB_n). The nonborrowed monetary base is directly under the control of the Fed and is affected only by open market operations.

MULTIPLE DEPOSIT CREATION: A SIMPLE MODEL

In order to derive the *simple deposit multiplier,* we assume that banks hold no excess reserves (they loan them out as soon as they get them) and the nonbank public holds no currency (only deposits). To illustrate how the deposit multiplier works, suppose the Fed makes an open market purchase of a $100 bond from First National Bank. First National Bank will loan out that extra $100 in reserves by creating a $100 checking account deposit for the borrower. By creating that checking account balance, First National Bank has created $100 of new money and the money supply, which includes checking account balances, has increased by $100. This "creation" of money by the bank is key to understanding the *multiple deposit creation* process.

But the creation of money does not stop with First National Bank's creation of a deposit. Presumably, the borrower of the $100 will spend that money and by doing so, that money will work its way into some other bank account (the bank account of the store owner where the purchase was made). Assuming that the store owner banks at Bank A, Bank A will now find itself with $100 in new deposits, and assuming the required reserve ratio is 10%, Bank A will keep $10 of that $100 deposit in reserves and loan out the remaining $90 to a new borrower. As was the case with the First National Bank, Bank A will make the loan by creating a checking account deposit for the borrower. Thus, at this stage of the process, Bank A has created an additional $90 of money. That $90 gets spent, and the process continues. At the next stage, Bank B will receive a $90 deposit, and it will keep 10% or $9 in required reserves and loan out the remaining $81. Thus, Bank B creates $81 of new money. This process continues with Banks C, D, E creating money each time they lend the excess reserves. Once this process is complete, the total amount of deposits (and therefore money) that will have been created by the banking system will be $1,000. A summary of this process is shown in Table 1 below.

Table 1

Bank	Increase in Deposits ($)	Increase in Loans ($)	Increase in Reserves ($)
First National	0.00	100.00 m	0.00
A	100.00 m	90.00 m	10.00 m
B	90.00 m	81.00 m	9.00 m
C	81.00 m	72.90 m	8.10 m
D	72.90 m	65.61 m	7.29 m
E	65.61 m	59.05 m	6.56 m
F	59.05 m	53.14 m	5.91 m
.	.	.	.
.	.	.	.
.	.	.	.
Total for all banks	1,000.00 m	1,000.00 m	100.00 m

In general, the relationship between the initial change in reserves and the total change in deposits in this simple example is given by the simple deposit multiplier: $\Delta D = (1/rr) \times \Delta R$, where ΔR is the initial change in reserves, rr is the required reserve ratio, and ΔD is the total change in deposits by the banking system. Although this formula is helpful for understanding the multiple deposit creation process, the actual creation of deposits is much less mechanical than the simple model indicates. If some of the proceeds from loans are held as currency, or if banks choose to hold all or some of their excess reserves, the money supply will not increase by as much as the simple model of multiple deposit creation tells us. This is because, in these instances, banks will not be willing or able to use as much reserves to extend loans to customers, which means less deposits at other banks. This also underscores the fact that the money supply can be influenced by depositor and bank behavior, which is not under the direct control of the Fed.

FACTORS THAT DETERMINE THE MONEY SUPPLY

The money supply is positively related to the *nonborrowed monetary base* (MB_n) as well as the level of *borrowed reserves* (*BR*) from the Fed. Thus, an open market purchase of securities or an increase in loans to financial institutions will increase reserves, the monetary base, and the money supply (and vice versa). The money supply is negatively related to the required reserve ratio, rr, currency holdings by the nonbank public, and the amount of excess reserves held by banks. An increase in any of these three factors restricts the amount of loans that are made by banks, mitigating the multiple deposit creation process, and thus decreasing the money supply.

OVERVIEW OF THE MONEY SUPPLY PROCESS

Three players—the Federal Reserve, depositors and banks—directly influence the money supply. The Federal Reserve influences the money supply by controlling *borrowed reserves*, the *nonborrowed monetary base*, and the required reserve ratio, rr. Depositors influence the money supply through their decisions about currency holdings, and banks influence the money supply with their decisions about excess reserves. Depositors' behavior also influences bankers' decisions to hold excess reserves. A summary of these factors are shown in Summary Table 1 below.

Player	Variable	Change in Variable	Money Supply Response	Reason
Federal Reserve System	Nonborrowed monetary base, MB_n	↑	↑	More MB for deposit creation
	Required reserve ratio, rr	↑	↓	Less multiple deposit expansion
Banks	Borrowed reserves, *BR*	↑	↑	More MB for deposit creation
	Excess reserves	↑	↓	Less loans and deposit creation
Depositors	Currency holdings	↑	↓	Less multiple deposit expansion

Note: Only increases (c) in the variables are shown. The effects of decreases on the money supply would be the opposite of those indicated in the "Money Supply Response" column.

THE MONEY MULTIPLIER

The relationship between the monetary base and the money supply is $M = m \times MB$, where m denotes the money multiplier. The monetary base is also called *high-powered money* because a $1 change in the monetary base leads to a more than $1 change in the money supply. The size of the money multiplier, m, is negatively related to the *required reserve ratio, rr*. The money multiplier is also negatively related to the *currency ratio, c*, which is the ratio of the publics' holdings of currency to deposits (C/D); and the *excess reserves ratio, e*, which is the ratio of excess reserves held by banks to deposits (ER/D). The formula for the money multiplier is $m = (1 + c)/(rr + e + c)$.

An important difference between the money multiplier and the deposit multiplier is that the money multiplier is smaller because currency holdings and excess reserves reduce loans and, hence, reduce deposit creation. In particular, if a portion of an increase in the monetary base ends up as currency holdings, multiple expansion of deposits will still occur; however, there will be no such expansion from the currency component, so the multiplier will be smaller.

When e is small, as is typically the case, changes in e have a small impact on the money supply and the multiplier. However, during the Great Depression, both e and c increased dramatically. Depositors worried about bank failures chose to hold cash rather than deposits at banks, and banks, due to credit risk and fear of bank runs, held on to more excess reserves. The result was that even though the monetary base increased 20% between 1931 and 1933, the money supply fell by 25%, indicating these factors had a substantial effect on the money supply and the money multiplier. Somewhat similar circumstances played out during the financial crisis of 2007–2009. Even though the currency deposit ratio was relatively stable, the excess reserve ratio increased dramatically, leading to a decline in the money multiplier similar to the Great Depression. However, unlike the Great Depression, during the financial crisis, the monetary base increased more than 200% between 2007 and 2009, resulting in the money supply increasing by a bit less than 25% during this time.

Helpful Hints

1. The monetary base is the sum of the two Federal Reserve liabilities: reserves and currency in circulation. The two primary ways that the Fed causes changes in the monetary base are through open market operations and discount lending.
2. Loans to financial institutions are primarily from discount loans, but the Fed can under some circumstances extend loans to nonbank financial institutions, which has an equivalent effect on (borrowed) reserves as discount lending. Securities holding by the Fed typically are of government securities such as U.S. Treasury bonds, but may also be other types of debt instruments, such as government agency debt or corporate securities during unusual periods.
3. The Fed has more precise control over the monetary base than the mix of reserves and currency. The mix of currency and reserves is determined by the nonbank public.
4. The key to understanding the deposit multiplier is to understand that when a bank makes a loan, it creates a deposit, which is part of the money supply.

5. The money multiplier tells us what multiple of the monetary base is transformed into the money supply. Anything that reduces the amount of loans that banks make reduces the size of the multiplier and therefore the money supply. Increases in *rr, e,* or *c* reduce the quantity of funds that banks have available to lend, which reduces the size of the multiplier and the money supply.

6. Note that the money multiplier process takes place over time and is not instantaneous; the effects of a given open market operation or other institutional factors that affect the multiplier may not immediately have the predicted impact on the money supply. This is because the multiplier effect crucially depends on the creation of deposits through the loan process, both of which take time to be achieved.

Terms and Definitions

Choose a definition for each key term.

Key Terms:

_4_ borrowed reserves
_5_ currency ratio
_13_ discount rate
_12_ excess reserves
_2_ excess reserves ratio
_15_ float
_14_ high-powered money

_1_ monetary base
_3_ money multiplier
_18_ multiple deposit creation
_1_ nonborrowed monetary base
_17_ open market operations
_8_ open market purchase

_16_ open market sale
_9_ required reserves
_10_ required reserves ratio
_6_ reserves
_11_ simple deposit multiplier

Definitions:

$MB_n = MB - BR$

1. The monetary base minus borrowed reserves

2. The ratio of excess reserves to deposits $\frac{ER}{D}$

3. A ratio that relates the change in the money supply to a given change in the monetary base

4. Banks' borrowings from the Fed

5. The ratio of the public's holdings of currency to checkable deposits $\frac{C}{D}$

6. Deposits at the Fed plus currency that is held by banks

7. The total of Federal Reserve liabilities, which is the sum of currency in circulation and reserves

8. The purchase of securities by the Fed

9. Reserves that the Fed requires banks to hold

10. The ratio of required reserves to deposits

11. The multiple increase in deposits generated from an increase in the banking system's

reserves in a simple model with no excess reserves and no currency holdings

12. Reserves that banks hold in addition to what is required by the Fed

13. The interest rate charged on loans that the Fed makes to banks

14. Another name for the monetary base

15. The temporary net increase in bank reserves occurring from the Fed's check-clearing process

16. The sale of securities by the Fed

17. The purchase and sale of securities by the Federal Reserve on the open market

18. The process whereby, when the Fed supplies the banking system with $1 of additional reserves, deposits increase by a multiple of that amount

Problems and Short-Answer Questions

PRACTICE PROBLEMS

1. a. Draw a simplified Fed balance sheet.

    b. Define each of the entries listed in the Fed's balance sheet.

        _____

        _____

        _____

        _____

    c. Which balance sheet entries comprise the monetary base?

        _____

        _____

2. a. Show the T-account entries for the Federal Reserve and a commercial bank that would result from an open market purchase of a $100 government security from the bank.

    b. What was the exact change in the monetary base?

_____

3. a. Show the T-account entries for the Federal Reserve, the banking system, and the nonbank public that would result from an open market purchase of a $100 government security from the nonbank public. Assume that the nonbank public deposits the proceeds from the sale of the government security in a local bank account.

    b. What was the exact change in the monetary base?

_____

    c. Now assume that the nonbank public cashes the check that it receives from selling the government security to the Federal Reserve and holds currency instead of bank deposits. Show the T-account entries for the Federal Reserve and the nonbank public.

    d. What was the exact change in the monetary base?

_____

e. Compare the effects on the monetary base in *a* and *c*. What does this comparison say about the Fed's ability to control the level and the composition of the monetary base?

_____

_____

_____

_____

4. Suppose the Federal Reserve purchases a $100 government security from First National Bank. Further suppose that banks hold no excess reserves and the nonbank public holds no currency (only deposits).
    a. Show the T-account entries for First National Bank as a result of the sale of the security to the Fed.

    b. Show the T-account entries for First National Bank when it loans out the excess reserves created by the sale of the government security to the Fed.

    c. Show the T-account entries for First National Bank and Bank A when the borrower withdraws their loan funds from First National Bank and it gets deposited into Bank A.

d. Show the T-account entries for Bank A when it loans out the excess reserves created by the new deposit, assuming a required reserve ratio of 10%.

e. How much "new" money is created as a result of the loans made by First National Bank and Bank A?

_____

f. Assume this process continues through Bank B, Bank C, and Bank D. How much new money would Banks B, C, and D create as a result of their loans?

_____

g. Calculate the total change in deposits resulting from the $100 open market purchase by the Fed.

_____

5. a. Write the formula for the money multiplier.

_____

b. Calculate the currency ratio, the excess reserve ratio, and the money multiplier given the following values:

$rr = 0.20$	$C = \$320$ billion
$D = \$1000$ billion	$ER = \$60$ billion

$c = \dfrac{C}{D} = \dfrac{320}{1000} = .32$

$e = \dfrac{ER}{D} = \dfrac{60}{1000} = \dfrac{6}{100} = .06$

$m = \dfrac{1+c}{rr+e+c} = \dfrac{1.32}{.20+.06+.32} = \dfrac{1.32}{.58} = 2.28$

c. Calculate the required reserves (RR), total reserves (R), and the monetary base (MB).

RR = $ $rr \times D = 200mm$

R = $ $RR + ER = 260mm$

MB = $ $C + R = 580$

$320 + 260 = 580$

d. Now assume that the Fed lowers the required reserve ratio to 0.10. Calculate the new money multiplier and the new money supply.

$m =$ _____

$M = \$$ _____

e. Calculate the new level of deposits (D) and currency in circulation (C) after the change in reserve requirements.

$D = \$$ _____

$C = \$$ _____

f. Calculate the new level of required reserves (RR) and excess reserves (ER) after the change in reserve requirements.

$RR = \$$ _____

$ER = \$$ _____

6. a. Explain what would happen to the money supply and the money multiplier if there was an increase in the currency ratio. Be sure to describe the intuition behind these changes.

_____

_____

_____

_____

b. Explain what would happen to the money supply and the money multiplier if there was an increase in the excess reserves ratio. Be sure to describe the intuition behind these changes.

_____

_____

_____

_____

7. Assume that the monetary base is \$800 billion and borrowed reserves are \$5 billion.
a. Calculate the quantity of nonborrowed monetary base.

_____

_____

b. Over which quantity, the monetary base or the nonborrowed monetary base, does the Fed have more precise control?

_____

_____

c. What monetary policy tool does the Fed use to control the quantity of nonborrowed monetary base?

_____

_____

d. What happens to the money supply if the nonborrowed monetary base increases, holding borrowed reserves constant?

_____

e. What happens to the money supply if borrowed reserves increase, holding the nonborrowed monetary base constant?

_____

8. Fill in the missing pieces of information in the table below.

Player	Variable	Change in Variable	Money Supply Response
	rr		
Depositors		↓	
	Excess reserves	↑	

SHORT-ANSWER QUESTIONS

1. List the three players in the money supply process. Which of these players is most important?

_____

_____

2. Describe the change in the composition of the monetary base that would result from someone withdrawing $100 in currency from a checking account. Does this withdraw affect the overall monetary base?

_____

_____

3. What happens to the monetary base when the Federal Reserve sells a $100 government security?

_____

_____

4. What happens to the monetary base when the Federal Reserve gives a $100 discount loan to a bank?

_____

_____

5. Use the simple deposit multiplier to show what would happen to total deposits in the banking system as a result of a $100 open market purchase by the Federal Reserve. Assume that the banking system holds no excess reserves, the nonbank public holds no currency, and the required reserve ratio is 10%

_____

_____

_____

6. What is the primary factor that influences banks' decision to hold excess reserves? How will a change in that factor affect excess reserves?

_____

_____

_____

_____

7. How does an increase in the monetary base, which arises from an increase in currency, affect the overall money supply compared to an increase in the monetary base, which arises from an increase in reserves?

_____

_____

8. How does an increase in currency holdings affect the money multiplier and the money supply?

_____

_____

9. Why is it important to distinguish between the nonborrowed monetary base and borrowed reserves?

_____

_____

10. Which of the Fed's monetary policy tools affects the nonborrowed monetary base?

_____

_____

Critical Thinking

Back in the 1950s, economist Milton Friedman proposed setting the required reserve ratio equal to 100%.

1. What would the value of the multiplier be under Friedman's proposal?

_____

_____

2. Describe the roles of banks, depositors, and the Fed in controlling the money supply under Friedman's proposal.

_____

_____

3. Compare the Fed's ability to control the money supply under Friedman's proposal to the current situation in which reserve requirements are much lower.

_____

_____

4. How would Friedman's proposal change the nature of banking?

_____

_____

_____

_____

_____

_____

Self-Test

TRUE/FALSE QUESTIONS

_T_ 1. Reserves consist of deposits at the Fed plus vault cash.

_T_ 2. High-powered money is another name for the monetary base.

_F_ 3. Discount loans are an asset of the banking system.

_T_ 4. The effect of an open market operation on the monetary base is much more certain than the effect on reserves.

_F_ 5. If you withdraw $100 from your checking account, deposits in the banking system will initially fall by $100, but eventually reduce deposits in the banking system by more than $100.

_T_ 6. If you withdraw $100 from your checking account, the monetary base will fall by $100.

_T_ 7. Changes in float and Treasury deposits at the Fed prevent the Fed from accurately controlling the monetary base.

_T_ 8. When a bank chooses to purchase securities instead of making loans, deposit expansion is diminished.

_T_ 9. The ratio that relates the change in the money supply to a given change in the monetary base is called the money multiplier. $M = m \times MB$

_F_ 10. An increase in the monetary base that goes into currency is multiplied, whereas an increase that goes into supporting deposits is not multiplied.

_T_ 11. An increase in the required reserve ratio causes the multiplier to fall.

_F_ 12. An increase in both the excess reserves ratio and the currency ratio causes the multiplier to rise.

_T_ 13. The money multiplier is smaller than the simple deposit multiplier.

_T_ 14. The excess reserves ratio, *e*, fell sharply during the Great Depression and the financial crisis of 2007–2009.

_F_ 15. The monetary base increased during both the Great Depression and the financial crisis of 2007–2009, leading to an increase in the money supply.

MULTIPLE-CHOICE QUESTIONS

1. The three players in the money supply story are
   a. the Federal Reserve, banks, and depositors.
   b. the Federal Reserve, the U.S. Treasury, and commercial banks.
   c. the Federal Reserve, the comptroller of the currency, and depositors.
   d. the comptroller of the currency, the U.S. Treasury, and commercial banks.

2. Which of the following are found on the liability side of the Fed's balance sheet?
   a. government securities
   b. discount loans
   c. reserves
   d. none of the above

3. Which of the following are found on the asset side of the Fed's balance sheet?
   a. government securities
   b. currency in circulation
   c. reserves
   d. none of the above

4. The monetary base is comprised of
   a. discount loans plus government securities held by the Fed.
   b. currency in circulation plus total reserves.
   c. currency in circulation plus deposits in the banking system
   d. discount loans plus excess reserves held by banks.

5. The sum of vault cash and bank deposits at the Fed minus required reserves is called
   a. the monetary base.
   b. the money supply.
   c. excess reserves.
   d. total reserves.

6. When the Federal Reserve sells a government security on the open market, it is called
   a. an open market purchase.
   b. a discount loan.
   c. float.
   d. an open market sale.

7. When the Fed wants to reduce reserves in the banking system, it will
   a. purchase government bonds.
   b. sell government bonds.
   c. extend discount loans to banks.
   d. print more currency.

8. When the Fed gives a discount loan of $100 to a bank,
   a. the Fed's liabilities decrease by $100.
   b. currency in circulation increases by $100.
   c. the monetary base decreases by $100.
   d. the monetary base increases by $100.

9. If Steffi withdraws $400 in cash from her checking account, then
    a. the monetary base declines by $400.
    b. the monetary base rises by $400.
    c. the monetary base stays the same.
    d. it is impossible to tell what happens to the monetary base.

10. When float increases,
    a. currency in circulation falls.
    b. the monetary base rises.
    c. the money supply falls.
    d. none of the above occurs.

11. A bank creates money when it
    a. sells a security to the Fed.
    b. makes a loan and creates a checkable deposit.
    c. borrows reserves from the Fed.
    d. holds excess reserves.

12. On a bank's balance sheet, a checkable deposit is
    a. an asset.
    b. a liability.
    c. neither an asset nor a liability.
    d. both an asset and a liability.

13. If the nonbank public holds currency in addition to deposits, then an open market operation will result in
    a. a smaller change in total deposits than is predicted by the simple deposit multiplier.
    b. a larger change in total deposits than is predicted by the simple deposit multiplier.
    c. greater control of the monetary base by the Fed.
    d. less control of the monetary base by the Fed.

14. The money multiplier tells us how much the
    a. nonborrowed monetary base changes for a given change in the monetary base.
    b. money supply changes for a given change in deposits.
    c. nonborrowed monetary base changes for a given change in deposits.
    d. money supply changes for a given change in the monetary base.

15. A decrease in the excess reserves ratio will cause the money multiplier
    a. to rise and the money supply to fall.
    b. to rise and the money supply to rise.
    c. to fall and the money supply to fall.
    d. to fall and the money supply to rise.

16. The monetary base less borrowed reserves is called
    a. the nonborrowed monetary base.
    b. high-powered money.
    c. reserves.
    d. the borrowed monetary base.

$$MB_n = MB - BR$$

[Handwritten at top right:]
$$\frac{1+.86}{.03+1.43+.86} = \frac{1.86}{2.32}$$

[Handwritten at left:]
Currency Ratio =

$$C = \frac{C}{D} = \frac{600}{700} = .86$$

$$e = \frac{ER}{D} = \frac{1b}{700\,b} = .14$$

$$\frac{1+.86}{.03+\underset{.0014}{.14}+.86} =$$

$$\frac{1.86}{.8914} = \boxed{2.09}$$

17. If the required reserve ratio is 0.03, currency in circulation is \$600 billion, deposits are \$700 billion, and excess reserves is \$1 billion, then the money multiplier is equal to
    a. 3.09.
    b. 3.29.
    c. 2.29.
    d. 2.09.

[Handwritten:]
$$M = \frac{1+C}{rr+e+c}$$

$$C = \frac{600}{700} \overset{C}{\underset{D}{}} .86$$

$$e = \frac{ER}{D} = \frac{1b}{700} = \#$$

$$e = \frac{1}{700}$$

18. Which of the following will lead to a decrease in bank reserves?
    a. an increase in the required reserve ratio
    b. an increase in the excess reserve ratio
    c. an increase in the currency ratio
    d. an increase in the monetary base

19. Suppose the required reserve ratio is 0.12, the currency ratio is 0.6, and the excess reserves ratio is 0.03. If the Fed decreases the monetary base by \$5 billion, the money supply will fall by
    a. \$15.34 billion.
    b. \$10.67 billion.
    c. \$9.87 billion.
    d. \$5.67 billion.

[Handwritten:]
$$m = \frac{1+C}{rr+e+c} = \frac{1.6}{.12+.03+.6}$$

$$e = \frac{ER}{D} =$$

$$C = \frac{C}{D}$$

$$m = \frac{1.6}{.75} = 2.13$$

$$(\$5\,bil)(2.13) = \$10.67b$$

20. The nonborrowed monetary base is controlled by
    a. depositors.
    b. banks.
    c. the Fed.
    d. all of the above.

Solutions

Terms and Definitions

_4_ borrowed reserves

_5_ currency ratio

_13_ discount rate

_2_ excess reserves ratio

_12_ excess reserves

_15_ float

_14_ high-powered money

_7_ monetary base

_3_ money multiplier

_18_ multiple deposit creation

_1_ nonborrowed monetary base

_17_ open market operations

_8_ open market purchase

_16_ open market sale

_10_ required reserves ratio

_9_ required reserves

_6_ reserves

_11_ simple deposit multiplier

Practice Problems

1. a.   A simplified Fed balance sheet:

Federal Reserve System

Assets	Liabilities
Securities Loans to Financial Institutions	Currency in circulation Reserves

 b.   Assets: securities, which typically are securities issued by the U.S. Treasury; and loans to financial institutions, which are typically discount loans (loans that the Fed makes to commercial banks), but can also be to other nonbank financial institutions. Liabilities: currency in circulation is the amount of currency in the hands of the public and reserves are bank reserves that are held at the Fed plus vault cash.

 c.   The monetary base is the sum of the Fed's liabilities: reserves and currency in circulation.

2. a.   An open market purchase of $100 government security from a commercial bank results in the following T-account entries.

Federal Reserve System

Assets		Liabilities	
Securities	+$100	Reserves	+$100

Commercial Bank

Assets		Liabilities
Securities	−$100	
Reserves	+100	

 b.   The monetary base increased by $100.

3. a.   An open market purchase of $100 government security from the nonbank public when the nonbank public deposits the proceeds from the sale of the government security in a local bank account results in the following T-account entries.

Federal Reserve System

Assets		Liabilities	
Securities	+$100	Reserves	+$100

Commercial Bank

Assets		Liabilities	
Reserves	+$100	Checkable Deposits	+$100

Nonbank Public

Assets		Liabilities
Securities	−$100	
Checkable Deposits	+100	

 b.   The monetary base increased by $100.

c. If the nonbank public cashes the check that it receives from selling the government security to the Federal Reserve, the T-account entries for the Fed and the nonbank public are as follows.

Federal Reserve System

Assets		Liabilities	
Securities	+$100	Currency in Circulation	+$100

Nonbank Public

Assets		Liabilities
Securities	−$100	
Currency	+100	

d. The monetary base increased by $100.

e. The monetary base increased by $100 in both cases (*a* and *c*). These examples illustrate that the Fed can precisely affect the total monetary base through open market operations, but it cannot affect the mix of currency and reserves in the monetary base. That mix is determined by the nonbank public's desire to hold currency versus deposits.

4. a. First National Bank sells a $100 government security to the Fed:

First National Bank

Assets		Liabilities
Securities	−$100	
Reserves	+100	

b. First National Bank loans out excess reserves:

First National Bank

Assets		Liabilities	
Securities	−$100	Checkable	
Reserves	+100	Deposits	+100
Loans	+100		

c. Borrower withdraws funds from First National Bank and deposits funds into Bank A:

First National Bank

Assets		Liabilities
Securities	−$100	
Loans	+100	

Bank A

Assets		Liabilities	
Reserves	+$100	Checkable Deposits	+$100

d. Bank A loans out the excess reserves created by the new deposit:

Bank A

Assets		Liabilities	
Reserves	+$100	Checkable	
Loans	+90	Deposits	+$100

e. First National Bank creates $100 in "new" money. Bank A creates $90 in "new" money.

f. Bank B would create $81, Bank C would create $72.90, and Bank D would create $65.61.

g. The total increase in deposits resulting from this $100 open market operation is $1,000 = $100/0.1.

5. a. $m = (1 + c)/(rr + e + c)$

   b. $c = 0.32$

   $e = 0.06$

   $m = 2.28 = 1.32/0.58$

   c. $RR = \$200$ billion

   $R = \$260$ billion

   $MB = \$580$ billion

   d. $m = 2.75 = 1.32/0.48$

   $M = \$1,595$ billion

   e. $D = \$1,208.33$ billion. Note that since $M = C + D$, this implies that $D = M/(1 + c)$. Using the answers from (b) and (d) above gives the answer for deposits.

   $C = \$386.67$ billion

f. RR = $120.83 billion

ER = $72.5 billion = eD = $0.06 × $1,208.33 billion

6. a. Deposits are subject to the multiplier effect, but currency is not. An increase in the currency ratio means that depositors are holding more of their money in the form of currency rather than deposits, so less of their money is subject to the multiplier effect. As a result, the multiplier declines, and the overall money supply declines as well.

   b. Like currency, excess reserves are not subject to the multiplier process because they are held in reserve by banks and are therefore not part of the lending and deposit creation process. An increase in the excess reserves ratio implies that lending and deposit creation will decline, and therefore, the money multiplier and the overall money supply will both decline as well.

7. a. $795 billion

   b. the nonborrowed monetary base

   c. open market operations

   d. It increases.

   e. It increases.

8.

Player	Variable	Change in Variable	Money Supply Response
Fed	rr	↓	↑
Depositors	Currency holdings	↓	↑
Banks	Excess reserves	↑	↓

Short-Answer Questions

1. The three players in the money supply process are the central bank (the Fed), banks, and depositors. The Federal Reserve is the most important.

2. When someone withdraws $100 from a checking account, currency in circulation increases by $100, and reserves decrease by $100, but the total monetary base remains unchanged.

3. The monetary base declines by $100.

4. The monetary base increases by $100.

5. According to the simple deposit multiplier, $\Delta D = (1/rr)\Delta R$. An open market purchase by the Fed will cause reserves to increase by $100. Assuming the required reserve ratio is 10%, $\Delta D = (1/0.10)100 = $1,000$.

6. The main factor that influences excess reserve holdings is banks' expectation of deposit outflows. If banks fear that deposit outflows are likely to increase, they will increase their holdings of excess reserves.

7. An increase in the monetary base arising from currency has no multiplier effect, while an increase in the monetary base arising from reserves does have a multiplier effect.

8. An increase in currency holdings causes both the money multiplier and the money supply to decline, for a given monetary base.

9. Because the Fed has precise control over the nonborrowed monetary base but it does not have precise control over borrowed reserves, which are determined by financial institutions' need for loans.

10. open market operations

Critical Thinking

1. The multiplier would be 1.

2. Banks and depositors would play no role in the money supply process. Only the Fed would play a role in controlling the money supply under Friedman's proposal, since banks by definition would hold no excess reserves, and no loans would be created through reserve increases.

3. The Fed would have much more control over the money supply under Friedman's proposal because the multiplier would always be equal to 1.

4. Friedman's proposal would completely change how banks earn a profit. Banks currently earn a profit by loaning out a fraction of the funds they receive from depositors. Under Friedman's proposal, banks would have no excess funds to loan out because they would be required to hold 100% of the deposits on reserve. There would be no deposit creation by the banking system, and the money supply would essentially be set by the Fed. Banks would earn a profit by charging depositors a fee for holding their funds and providing check services. Banks would be more like the warehouse banks that existed in the Middle Ages simply to safeguard depositors' money.

True/False Questions

1. T
2. T
3. F
4. T
5. T
6. F
7. F
8. F
9. T
10. F
11. T
12. F
13. T
14. F
15. F

Multiple-Choice Questions

1. a
2. c
3. a
4. b
5. c
6. d
7. b
8. d
9. c
10. b
11. b
12. b
13. a
14. d
15. b
16. a
17. d
18. c
19. b
20. c

15 Tools of Monetary Policy*

Chapter Review

PREVIEW

The Fed uses four tools to manipulate the money supply and interest rates: open market operations, discount lending, interest paid on reserves, and reserve requirements. This chapter looks at how the Fed uses these *conventional monetary policy tools* to influence the market for reserves and the *federal funds rate*. However, as seen during the recent global financial crisis, these conventional policy tools have limitations, and so *nonconventional monetary policy tools* are also examined. The chapter ends with a discussion of the tools of monetary policy used by the European Central Bank and other central banks.

THE MARKET FOR RESERVES AND THE FEDERAL FUNDS RATE

The federal funds rate is the interest rate that banks charge each other for overnight lending in the market for reserves. The federal funds rate is determined by the intersection of the demand and supply of reserves, which are influenced by open market operations, discount lending, interest on reserves, and reserve requirements. The demand for reserves (R^d in Figure 15.1) is downward sloping until the point that it reaches the interest rate the Fed pays on reserves, i_{or}. After that point, the demand curve for reserves becomes horizontal; the quantity of reserves demanded by banks is the amount of required reserves, plus the quantity of excess reserves desired at any fed funds rate.

Reserve supply (R^s) is a vertical line up to the discount rate (i_d) at which point it becomes a horizontal line, representing the Fed's ability to provide a potentially unlimited amount of loans to financial institutions. The vertical portion of the

---

*This is Chapter 18 in the 3rd ed.

reserve supply curve is determined by the quantity of *nonborrwed reserves* (NBR). NBR are the reserves that the Fed controls through its open market operations.

When the intersection of the demand and supply of reserves occurs along the vertical part of the reserve supply curve and the downward-sloping part of the reserve demand curve (as shown in Figure 15.1), then the federal funds rate will be determined by the quantity of *NBR,* which is affected by open market operations.

More generally, the effects of the four primary monetary policy tools are summarized below.

- Open Market Operations. An open market purchase of securities increases NBR and shifts the vertical part of R^s to the right, reducing the equilibrium federal funds rate. An open market sale of securities reduces NBR, shifting the vertical part of R^s to the left, and raising the equilibrium federal funds rate.

- Discount Lending. A sharp increase in demand for bank reserves, due to financial frictions or other unpredictable events may raise the equilibrium federal funds rate to the discount rate, which places a ceiling on the federal funds rate. If the downward sloping portion of reserve demand crosses reserve supply along the horizontal portion of supply, the equilibrium amount of reserves along the horizontal portion of supply represents borrowed reserves. By raising the discount rate i_d, borrowing directly from the Fed would become less attractive relative to borrowing from other banks at the lower federal funds rate, so borrowed reserves would decrease. Lowering the discount rate would have the opposite effect, once the equilibrium crosses the horizontal portion of reserve supply.

- Reserve Requirements. Increasing reserve requirements would shift the reserve demand curve horizontally to the right, resulting in a higher equilibrium federal funds rate, and vice versa.

- Interest on Reserves. If the Fed increases i_{or} enough, the flat portion of reserve demand will shift up such that it will raise the intersection point with the vertical portion of reserve supply. In this case, the equilibrium fed funds rate will increase with the higher interest on reserve level. However, under normal circumstances the interest on reserves would be below the federal funds rate, meaning that this portion of reserve demand would not directly affect the market for reserves.

In theory, the discount rate places an upper limit on the federal funds rate, and the interest rate paid on reserves places a lower limit on the federal funds rate. Under the Fed's current operating procedures, therefore, fluctuations in the federal funds rate should be limited to between i_{or} and i_d. However, in practice the federal funds rate has on occasion operated outside these bounds, for two main reasons. The upper bound may be breached, particularly during periods of financial stress, if there is a stigma associated with banks borrowing directly from the Fed; this would imply a 'stigma premium' with banks willing to borrow at the higher federal funds rate to avoid public scrutiny. The lower bound can be breached because many nonbank financial companies put funds in the fed funds market, but are not subject to reserve requirements, and are therefore not eligible to receive interest on reserves. This can push the effective federal funds rate below that paid on reserves.

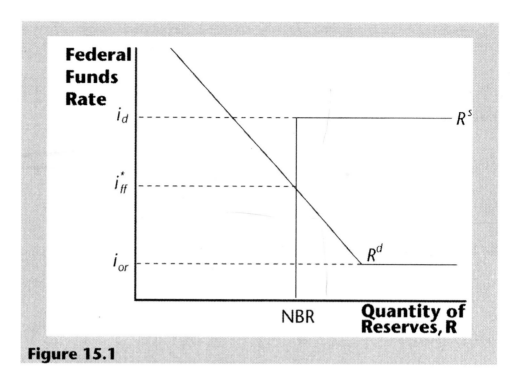

Figure 15.1

CONVENTIONAL MONETARY POLICY TOOLS

The following outlines the main tools used for conventional monetary policy. The most important of these tools are open market operations, which affect the federal funds rate as discussed above.

There are two types of open-market operations: *dynamic open-market operations*, which are intended to change the level of reserves and the monetary base, and *defensive open-market operations*, which are intended to offset movements in reserves and the monetary base due to other factors such as Treasury deposits at the Fed and float. Open-market operations are conducted by the trading desk of the Federal Reserve Bank of New York. Early each day the Fed forecasts the demand for reserves for that day. Once the Fed has decided on the appropriate course of action (increase or decrease reserves), they transmit their buy or sell orders to a group of private sector bond dealers called *primary dealers*. To temporarily increase reserves, the Fed uses *repurchase agreements* (also called repos). In a repo, the Fed purchases securities with an agreement that the seller will repurchase them after a short period of time (1 to 15 days). To temporarily reduce the supply of reserves, the Fed uses *matched sale–purchase transactions* (also called reverse repos). Repos and reverse repos are used for defensive open-market operations.

There are three types of discount loans to banks: primary credit, which healthy banks can borrow from the Fed's *standing lending facility* at the discount rate; secondary credit, which are loans to financially troubled banks at an interest rate 50 basis points above the discount rate; and seasonal credit, which the Fed is considering eliminating in the future. Discount lending allows the Fed to serve as the *lender of last resort*, which is especially important during financial crises. Since bank failures can be very damaging to an economy, providing funding to banks during times of financial stress to keep bank panics from occurring is important. One downside to the Fed providing lender-of-last-resort services is that it can increase moral hazard among banks and nonbank financials, who may take on excessive risk expecting that, during financial panics, they will be able to access the Fed's discount lending facilities.

Reserve requirements affect the money multiplier, so in principle the Fed could manipulate reserve requirements to change the money supply and interest rates. But reserves have become much less important in recent years and for many banks, required reserves are not binding. In addition, raising reserve requirements can cause severe liquidity problems for banks. The Fed no longer uses reserve requirements as a policy tool for changing the money supply and interest rates.

The fourth tool, interest on reserves, was first implemented in 2008, so has a relatively short history. In the aftermath of the recent global financial crisis, the Federal Reserve introduced a large amount of reserves into the banking system, which poses difficulties in unwinding quickly if need be. In this case, the interest rate on reserves can be raised to push the fed funds rate up, when large scale open market operations may be necessary but not possible.

Of the four policy tools discussed above, open market operations are the most important, and have some advantages over the other tools because they can be quickly and easily initiated by the Fed, they are flexible and precise, and can be easily reversed. However, when reserves need to be drained from the banking system on a large scale, interest on reserves can be raised to more effectively increase the fed funds rate compared to traditional open market operations. In addition, discount window lending has a distinct advantage over open market operations when there is need to intervene through the Fed's role as lender of last resort because the funds can be targeted to the banks that need it most.

NONCONVENTIONAL MONETARY POLICY TOOLS DURING THE GLOBAL FINANCIAL CRISIS

During financial crises, conventional monetary policy may be ineffective for two reasons. First, financial frictions lead to a sharp decline in investment due to inefficient allocation of capital. Secondly, the sharp contractions that follow can constrain monetary policy due to the *zero-lower-bound problem* and the inability of monetary policy to push nominal interest rates below zero. As a result, *nonconventional monetary policy tools* in the form of liquidity provision, asset purchases, and commitment to future policy actions may be necessary.

During the recent global financial crisis, the Federal Reserve enhanced liquidity provision in several ways. First, it reduced the gap between the federal funds rate and the discount rate from 100 to 25 basis points; this had a limited impact on discount window borrowing. As a result, the Fed introduced the Term Auction Facility (TAF), which was more widely used because the borrowing rate was set through an auction process which was lower than the discount rate. Ultimately, more than $400 billion was borrowed through TAF. Due to the virulent nature of the financial crisis, as credit markets seized up, the Federal Reserve also introduced a host of new temporary emergency lending programs to banks and nonbank financial companies to keep credit and financial markets from further deteriorating. Ultimately, these new lending programs added over $1 trillion to the Federal Reserve's balance sheet.

In November 2008, and again in November 2010, the Federal Reserve instituted several large scale asset purchases. The first asset purchases included $1.25 trillion in mortgage-backed securities to help mortgage and housing markets. The second round of purchases included $600 billion in long-term U.S. Treasury securities, which was intended to push long-term interest rates lower and help stimulate investment spending. These asset purchase programs are referred to as *quantitative easing* measures, because they are designed to increase the monetary base and money supply. However, quantitative easing may be ineffective because banks may choose to hold the higher level of reserves as excess reserves, which does not increase the money supply or translate into higher lending. In addition, as was seen in the global financial crisis, short term rates were at the zero lower bound, so additional quantitative easing was unable to lower short term rates further. However, these asset purchases may have had the benefit of *credit easing*, not by increasing the monetary base through a larger balance sheet, but rather altering the composition of the Federal Reserve's existing balance sheet to enhance the flow of credit.

A third nonconventional measure used during the global financial crisis was committing to future policy actions. For instance, at the last monetary policy meeting in 2008, the Federal Reserve committed to keeping the federal funds rate "at exceptionally low levels for some time," which was eventually revised to "through at least mid-2013". Through this *management of expectations*, committing to ultra-low short-term interest rates for an extended period of time helps reduce longer-term interest rates in order to stimulate spending and strengthen the economy. These types of policy commitments can be either conditional on the state of the economy, or unconditional. Conditional commitments are not as strong, and so carry less force to influence expectations, however they offer more policy flexibility should conditions change. Unconditional commitments are stronger in that they provide more clarity to future policy action, however they are less flexible should conditions change; if policymakers decided later to reverse the policy prematurely, this could have implications for policy credibility and the effective management of expectations in the future.

MONETARY POLICY TOOLS OF THE EUROPEAN CENTRAL BANK

The European Central Bank's target for the overnight lending rate, called the *target financing rate* is used to control the *overnight cash rate* (similar to the Fed's control of the federal funds rate).it's the primary monetary policy tools of the ECB are similar to those used by the Federal Reserve (open-market operations, lending to banks, and reserve requirements). Open-market operations that are reversed within two weeks are called *main refinancing operations*. These operations, which are similar to the Fed's repos and reverse repos, are the ECB's primary tool for targeting the overnight lending rate. The ECB also operates a standing lending facility called the *deposit facility* that pays interest on reserves and is set 100 basis points below the target financing rate. The interest rate paid on reserves places a lower limit on the ECB's target financing rate.

Helpful Hints

1. The federal funds rate is determined by the demand and supply for reserves. The key to understanding how the Fed's monetary policy tools affect the federal funds rate is to understand how those tools affect the demand and supply for reserves. The Fed mostly uses open market operations to manipulate nonborrowed reserves in order to target the federal funds rate. The discount rate serves as an upper limit on the federal funds rate and allows the Fed to serve its role as lender of last resort. The interest rate the Fed pays on reserves serves as a lower bound on the federal funds rate. Reserve requirements are not used to manipulate the money supply and interest rates.

2. The zero-lower-bound problem can introduce additional complexities into the process of monetary policymaking, since controlling short-term interest rates will no longer be possible. In this case, nonconventional monetary policy measures may need to be employed in order to beneficially impact the economy. These nonconventional policies include liquidity provision, asset purchases, and communication strategies. Unlike conventional interest rate policy, with nonconventional policies there are no constraints as to the size and scope of these types of policy approaches, making them particularly useful when conventional policy has run its course.

Terms and Definitions

Choose a definition for each key term.

Key Terms:

___21___ conventional monetary policy tools

___19___ credit easing

___18___ defensive open-market operations

___1___ deposit facility

___3___ discount window

___8___ dynamic open-market operations

___17___ federal funds rate

___14___ lender of last resort

___13___ longer-term refinancing operations

___10___ main refinancing operations

___20___ management of expectations

___4___ marginal lending facility

___5___ marginal lending rate

___11___ matched sale–purchase transaction (reverse repo)

___2___ nonconventional monetary policy tools

___15___ overnight cash rate

___9___ primary dealers

___22___ quantitative easing

___6___ repurchase agreement (repo)

___16___ reverse transactions

___12___ standing lending facility

___7___ target financing rate

Definitions:

1. The European Central Bank's standing facility that pays interest on bank reserves

2. Non-interest-rate tools used to stimulate aggregate demand when a central bank faces the zero-lower-bound problem

3. The Fed facility from which banks are allowed to borrow all they want

4. The European Central Bank's standing facility that provides loans to banks

5. The interest rate charged on loans by the national central banks of the ECB

6. An agreement whereby the Fed, or another party, purchases securities with the understanding that the seller will repurchase them in a short period of time

7. The overnight interest rate target set by the European Central Bank

8. Open-market operations intended to change the level of reserves and the monetary base

9. Private sector government securities dealers

10. The predominant form of open-market operations used by the European Central Bank

11. An agreement whereby the Fed, or another party, sells securities with the understanding that the buyer will sell them back in a short period of time

12. The Fed facility from which banks borrow reserves

13. The secondary type of open-market operations used by the European Central Bank

14. Provider of reserves to financial institutions when no one else would provide them in order to prevent a financial crisis

15. The interest rate on very short-term interbank loans that is targeted by the European Central Bank

16. The European equivalent to the repurchase agreement

17. The name given in the United States to the interest rate on overnight lending between banks

18. Open-market operations that are intended to offset movements in other factors that affect reserves and the monetary base

19. Altering the composition of the central bank's balance sheet to improve the functioning of credit markets

20. The process of committing to future policy actions in order to affect current behavior to help better achieve policy objectives

21. The use of open market operations, discount lending, and reserve requirements to control the money supply and interest rates

22. Expansion of a central bank's balance sheets through the purchase of assets, leading to a large increase in the monetary base

Problems and Short-Answer Questions

PRACTICE PROBLEMS

1. Suppose the demand for reserves is initially R^d_0 in Figure 15.2.
   a. Use Figure 15.2 to determine the following:

   Nonborrowed reserves = $ _____ 40 bil _____

   Borrowed reserves = $ _____ 0 _____

   The federal funds rate = _____ 5.5 _____ %

   The discount rate = _____ 6.5 _____ %

   The interest rate on reserves = _____ 4.5 _____ %

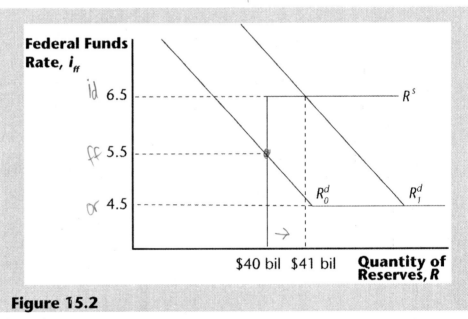

Figure 15.2

   b. Now assume that the demand for reserves increases to R^d_1. Recalculate the following given this new higher demand for reserves:

   Nonborrowed reserves = $ _____ 40 bil _____

   Borrowed reserves = $ _____ 1 bil _____

   The federal funds rate = _____ 6.5 _____ %

   The discount rate = _____ 6.5 _____ %

   The interest rate on reserves = _____ 4.5 _____ %

2. a. Draw the demand and supply diagram for reserves assuming that the equilibrium federal funds rate is below the discount rate and above the interest rate on reserves.

    b. Re-draw the diagram you drew for part *a* and illustrate the effect of an open market purchase by the Fed on the equilibrium federal funds rate. Explain why the federal funds rate changes.

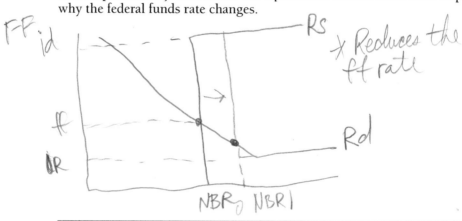

    c. Re-draw the diagram you drew for part *a* and illustrate the effect of an increase in the discount rate. Did the increase in the discount rate affect the federal funds rate? Why or why not?

    d. Now draw the demand and supply diagram for reserves assuming that the equilibrium federal funds rate is equal to the discount rate. Illustrate the effect of a reduction in the discount rate on the equilibrium federal funds rate. What happens to nonborrowed and borrowed reserves in this case?

    e. Explain why a change in the discount rate sometimes causes the federal funds rate to change and sometimes has no effect on the federal funds rate.

_____

_____

_____

_____

_____

_____

    f. Re-draw the diagram you drew for part *a* and illustrate the effect of an increase in reserve requirements on the equilibrium federal funds rate. Explain why this happens.

_____

_____

_____

_____

3. Suppose the Fed expects a change in Treasury deposits will cause reserves to decline by $2 billion for a one-week period after which reserves will return to their initial level.
   a. Describe the open market operation that the Fed would use to maintain the level of reserves in the banking system during this one-week decline in reserves due to the change in Treasury deposits.

   _____

   _____

   _____

   _____

   _____

   b. Now assume that bad weather delays the delivery of checks causing float to increase for one day. How will this increase in float affect reserves? Describe the open market operation that the Fed would use to maintain the level of reserves in the banking system during this temporary change in reserves due to the increase in float.

   _____

   _____

   _____

   _____

   _____

   _____

4. a. What is primary credit?

   _____

   b. Where does primary credit lending take place?

   _____

c. What role does primary credit lending through the discount rate play in the market for federal funds?

_____

_____

_____

_____

_____

d. What is secondary credit? How does it differ from primary credit?

_____

_____

_____

5. a. What is the name of the interest rate targeted by the European Central Bank?

_____

b. What is the difference between the main refinancing operations and longer-term refinancing operations by the European Central Bank?

_____

_____

_____

_____

c. Explain how the ECBs marginal lending facility and deposit facility set limits on how far short-term interest rates can move in relation to the target.

_____

_____

_____

_____

_____

SHORT-ANSWER QUESTIONS

1. What monetary policy tool does the Fed use to control the amount of nonborrowed reserves?

    _____

    _____

2. What will happen to nonborrowed reserves and the federal funds rate when the Fed conducts an open market purchase?

    _____

    _____

3. Under what conditions will a change in the discount rate affect the federal funds interest rate?

    _____

    _____

4. Under what conditions would the federal funds rate equal the interest rate paid on reserves?

    _____

    _____

    _____

5. How will a decrease in reserve requirements affect the demand for reserves and the federal funds rate?

    _____

    _____

6. What are the advantages of open market operations over other conventional monetary policy tools?

    _____

    _____

7. Explain why the existence of FDIC insurance does not make the lender-of-last resort function of the Fed unnecessary.

    _____

    _____

8. What are the advantages and disadvantages of the Fed's discount policy?

    _____

    _____

    _____

    _____

9. What are the disadvantages of using reserve requirements as a policy tool to change the federal funds rate?

    _____

    _____

    _____

    _____

10. Why is the Fed's implementation of paying interest on reserves important?

    _____

    _____

Critical Thinking

1. Use the demand and supply diagram for reserves to illustrate and explain how the Fed's use of the discount rate and the rate they pay on reserves should limit the fluctuations in the federal funds rate.

    _____

    _____

    _____

    _____

2. In practice, the fed funds rate occasionally strays above the discount rate, or below the interest rate paid on reserves. Why might this happen?

    _____

    _____

Self-Test

TRUE/FALSE QUESTIONS

_T_ 1. Open market operations are the Fed's most important monetary policy tool.

_T_ 2. Changes in the discount rate usually affect the equilibrium federal funds rate.

_F_ 3. The federal funds rate can never rise above the interest rate that the Fed pays on reserves.

_T_ 4. The Fed controls nonborrowed reserves through open market operations.

_T_ 5. Dynamic open market operations are intended to offset movements float.

_T_ 6. Defensive open market operations are intended to offset changes in Treasury deposits.

_T_ 7. A matched sale-purchase transaction is used by the Fed to conduct a temporary open market purchase.

_F_ 8. The zero-lower-bound problem implies real interest rates cannot go below zero, but nominal interest rates can.

_T_ 9. Credit easing works by increasing the central bank's balance sheet, thereby lowering interest rates of all maturities.

_T_ 10. The Term Auction Facility was more widely used during the global financial crisis than the discount window because the interest rate was determined competitively.

_T_ 11. The marginal lending rate provides a ceiling for the overnight market interest rate in the European Monetary Union.

_F_ 12. Swap lines allow commercial banks to borrow from each other directly and bypass the federal funds market.

_F_ 13. The European Central Bank signals its monetary policy stance by setting a target financing rate.

_F_ 14. The European Central Bank's predominant form of open market operations is called longer-term refinancing operations.

_F_ 15. Announcements about the future course of monetary policy are one of the four main tools used in conventional monetary policy by the Federal Reserve.

MULTIPLE-CHOICE QUESTIONS

1. An open market purchase will cause
    a. nonborrowed reserves to fall and the federal funds rate to rise.
    b. nonborrowed reserves to rise and the federal funds rate to fall.
    c. borrowed reserves to fall and the federal funds rate to rise.
    d. borrowed reserves to rise and the federal funds rate to fall.

2. An increase in reserve requirements
    a. increases nonborrowed reserves and increases the federal funds rate.
    b. decreases nonborrowed reserves and decreases the federal funds rate.
    c. leaves nonborrowed reserves unchanged and increases the federal funds rate.
    d. leaves nonborrowed reserves unchanged and decreases the federal funds rate.

Figure for questions 3-7

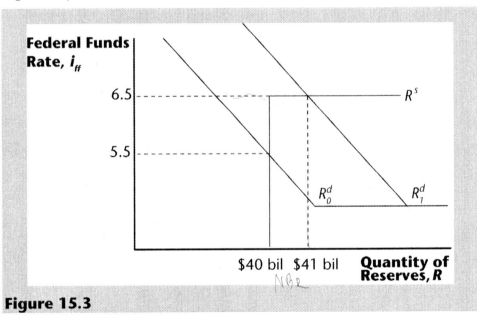

Figure 15.3

3. The rightward shift in reserve demand depicted in Figure 15.3 most likely resulted from
    a. an increase in required reserves.
    b. a decrease in required reserves.
    c. an open market purchase.
    d. an open market sale.

4. When reserve demand is R^d_1 in Figure 15.3, borrowed reserves are
    a. $40 billion.
    b. $41 billion.
    c. $0.
    d. $1 billion.

5. When reserve demand is R^d_0 in Figure 15.3, borrowed reserves are
   a. $40 billion.
   b. $41 billion.
   c. $0.
   d. $1 billion.

6. When reserve demand is R^d_1 in Figure 15.3, nonborrowed reserves are
   a. $40 billion.
   b. $41 billion.
   c. $0.
   d. $1 billion.

7. When reserve demand is R^d_0 in Figure 15.3, nonborrowed reserves are
   a. $40 billion.
   b. $41 billion.
   c. $0.
   d. $1 billion.

8. To lower the federal funds rate, the Fed would
   a. increase the reserve requirement.
   b. increase the discount rate.
   c. conduct an open market purchase.
   d. all of the above

9. Which of the following will shift the supply of reserves to the right?
   a. increase the reserve requirement
   b. increase the discount rate
   c. conduct an open market purchase
   d. all of the above

10. By paying interest on reserves, the Fed is able to keep the federal funds rate
    a. equal to the interest rate on reserves
    b. equal to the discount rate
    c. at or below the interest rate on reserves
    d. at or above the interest rate on reserves

11. An open market operation by the Federal Reserve aimed at maintaining the level of reserves is called a
    a. defensive open market operation.
    b. dynamic open market operation.
    c. longer-term refinancing operation.
    d. reverse transaction.

12. An open market operation by the European Central Bank aimed at maintaining the level of reserves is called a
    a. defensive open market operation.
    b. dynamic open market operation.
    c. longer-term refinancing operation.
    d. reverse transaction.

13. To temporarily raise reserves in the banking sector, the Fed engages in a
    a. repurchase agreement.
    b. reverse repo.
    c. matched sale-purchase transaction.
    d. reverse transaction.

14. Which of the following tools does the Fed use in its role as lender of last resort?
    a. discount lending
    b. reserve requirements
    c. open market operations
    d. FDIC insurance

15. The interest rate on secondary credit is
    a. set below the federal funds rate.
    b. above the discount rate to penalize financially troubled banks.
    c. equal to the federal funds rate.
    d. below the discount rate but above the federal funds rate to help financially troubled banks.

16. The Fed's primary credit lending facility keeps the federal funds rate from rising high above its target because
    a. the Fed routinely sets the discount rate below the federal funds rate.
    b. the Fed will extend unlimited credit to healthy banks at the discount rate, which means that the federal funds rate will not rise above its target.
    c. banks are prohibited by Fed regulators from charging interest rates to other banks above its target rate.
    d. secondary credit lending kicks in whenever the federal funds rate rises too high.

17. The Fed buys and sells government securities through
    a. the U.S. Treasury.
    b. the standing lending facility.
    c. the discount lending facility.
    d. primary dealers.

18. A repurchase agreement by the Fed is
    a. an agreement by the Fed to repurchase securities from the Treasury.
    b. a temporary open market sale that will be reversed shortly.
    c. a temporary open market purchase that will be reversed shortly.
    d. especially desirable way of conducting a dynamic open market operation.

19. Reserve requirements are no longer used by the Fed to manage the money supply and interest rates because
    a. reserve requirements are no longer binding for most banks.
    b. raising reserve requirements can cause immediate liquidity problems for banks.
    c. changing reserve requirements would create uncertainty for banks.
    d. all of the above

20. Which of the following policy changes would be considered a conventional monetary policy change?
    a. Federal Reserve lending through the Term Auction Facility.
    b. An open market sale of securities to increase the fed funds rate.
    c. Purchases of long-term securities to lower long-term interest rates.
    d. Announcing a firm policy to conduct large scale open market purchases in the future.

Solutions

Terms and Definitions

_21_ conventional monetary policy tools

_19_ credit easing

_18_ defensive open-market operations

_1_ deposit facility

_3_ discount window

_8_ dynamic open-market operations

_17_ federal funds rate

_14_ lender of last resort

_13_ longer-term refinancing operations

_10_ main refinancing operations

_20_ management of expectations

_4_ marginal lending facility

_5_ marginal lending rate

_11_ matched sale–purchase transaction (reverse repo)

_2_ nonconventional monetary policy tools

_15_ overnight cash rate

_9_ primary dealers

_22_ quantitative easing

_6_ repurchase agreement (repo)

_16_ reverse transactions

_12_ standing lending facility

_7_ target financing rate

Practice Problems

1. a. Nonborrowed reserves = $ _40_

      Borrowed reserves = $ _0_

      The federal funds rate = _5.5%_

      The discount rate = _6.5%_

      The interest rate on reserves = _4.5%_

   b. Nonborrowed reserves = $ _40 billion_

      Borrowed reserves = $ _1 billion_

      The federal funds rate = _6.5%_

      The discount rate = _6.5%_

      The interest rate on reserves = _4.5%_

2. a. The equilibrium federal funds rate is i_{ff}^0 and the equilibrium quantity of reserves is NBR_0 (because the equilibrium federal funds rate is below the discount rate, the quantity of borrowed reserves equals zero).

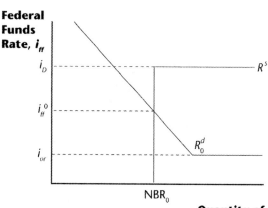

b. An open-market purchase increases nonborrowed reserves from NBR_0 to NBR_1. At the initial equilibrium federal funds rate, i_{ff}^0 there is now an excess supply of reserves, which causes the equilibrium federal funds rate to fall to i_{ff}^1.

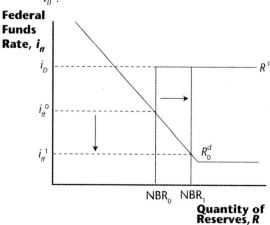

c. An increase in the discount rate as shown below has no effect on the federal funds rate because reserve demand intersects reserve supply below the discount rate.

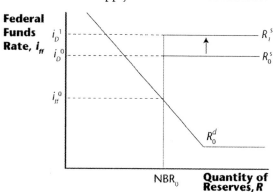

d. In this case, the demand for reserves intersects the supply of reserves along the horizontal portion of the reserve supply curve, which means that the federal funds rate is equal to the discount rate. If the Fed lowers the discount rate from i_D^0 to i_D^1 the federal funds rate will fall from i_{ff}^0 to i_{ff}^1. Nonborrowed reserves will remain at NBR_0, however borrowed reserves will increase, since the cost of borrowing directly from the Federal Reserve has decreased.

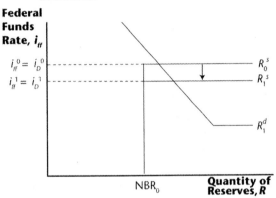

e. The change in the discount rate in problem c did not affect the federal funds rate because the demand for reserves intersected the supply of reserves along the vertical portion of the reserve supply curve. In this case, banks will not borrow from the Fed so changes in the discount rate have no effect on the reserve market or the federal funds rate. The change in the discount rate in problem d did affect the federal funds rate because the demand for reserves intersected the supply of reserves along the horizontal portion of the reserve supply curve. In this case, a portion of total reserves in the banking sector is borrowed from the Fed and the federal funds rate is equal to the discount rate so changes in the discount rate affect the federal funds rate.

f. An increase in reserve requirements causes the demand for reserves to increase from R_0^d to R_1^d, which leads to an increase in the equilibrium federal funds rate from i_{ff}^0 to i_{ff}^1.

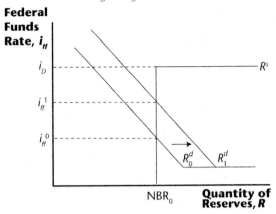

3. a. The Fed would use a repurchase agreement, which is an agreement to purchase securities on the open market (which increases reserves in the banking system) and then resell them to the original owner of the securities (which decreases reserves in the banking system). In this case, the securities would be resold to the original owner after one week, so the net result would be that total reserves in the banking system would remain unchanged.

b. The increase in float will cause reserves to increase. In this case, the Fed would use a matched sale–purchase transaction or reverse repo to offset the temporary increase in reserves. With the reverse repo, the Fed sells securities to a buyer (which decreases reserves in the banking system) and then buys them back (which increases reserves in the banking system) after a short period of time. In this case, the Fed would buy the securities back after one day. This reverse repo would keep reserves in the banking system unchanged in the face of the temporary increase in float.

4. a. Primary credit is the discount lending that the Fed extends to healthy banks.

b. Primary credit takes place at the standing lending facility at the Federal Reserve.

c. The discount rate is the interest rate that the Fed charges on primary credit loans to healthy banks. The discount rate places an upper limit on the federal funds rate. If the demand for reserves rises (unexpectedly, say due to an unexpected increase in deposits) to exceed the quantity of nonborrowed reserves in the banking system, banks will simply borrow from the Fed at the discount rate. Thus, the federal funds rate cannot exceed the discount rate.

d. Secondary credit loans are given to banks that are in financial trouble and are experiencing severe liquidity problems. The interest rate on secondary credit is 50 basis points higher than the discount rate.

5. a. The European Central Bank sets a target financing rate for the overnight cash rate.

b. The main refinancing operations are the European Central Bank's main form of open market operations and are similar to the Fed's repo transactions. The longer-term refinancing operations are a much smaller source of liquidity in the euro area banking system.

c. The ECB lends to banks at the marginal lending rate, which is set 100 basis points above the target financing rate. Banks can deposit reserves in the ECB and earn interest on reserves. The interest paid on reserves is 100 basis points below the target financing rate. The overnight lending rate will not fall below the rate that the ECB pays on reserves, and it will not rise above the rate that the ECB lends at.

Short-Answer Questions

1. The Fed uses open market operations to control the amount of nonborrowed reserves.

2. An open market purchase increases the quantity of nonborrowed reserves and lowers the federal funds rate.

3. A change in the discount rate will only affect the federal funds rate when the demand for reserves is high enough to be on the horizontal portion of the reserve supply curve.

4. The federal funds rate would equal the interest rate paid on reserves when the vertical portion of the supply for reserves

intersects the horizontal portion of the demand for reserves. This could occur as a result of a large decrease in the demand for reserves, or large increase in nonborrowed reserves.

5. A decrease in reserve requirements will decrease the demand for reserves and cause the federal funds rate to fall.

6. The main advantages of open market operations are that they occur at the initiative of the Fed, they are flexible and precise, they are easily reversed, and they can be implemented quickly.

7. FDIC insurance amounts to only about 1% of deposits outstanding. In addition, accounts over $250,000 are not covered by FDIC insurance.

8. The most important advantage of discount lending is that it allows the Fed to play the role of lender of last resort. The main disadvantages are that the Fed does not completely control the quantity of discount loans since borrowing at the discount rate is initiated by banks, and it could introduce moral hazard by increasing risky behavior in the financial system.

9. The main disadvantage of using reserve requirements as a policy tool is that reserve requirements are no longer binding for most banks. In addition, raising reserve requirements can cause immediate liquidity problems for banks, and fluctuating reserve requirements create uncertainty for banks.

10. There are several primary benefits of paying interest on reserves. First, it reduces the effective tax that banks implicitly pay by having to hold required reserves. Second, it allows the Fed to more precisely control excess reserves, which gives greater control over the money multiplier and hence the money supply. Third, it puts a theoretical floor on movements of the federal funds rate similarly allowing greater control over fluctuations in the federal funds rate. Finally, it allows the Fed to decouple balance sheet expansion with decreases in the federal funds rate, which gives it greater policy flexibility to lend as much as it needs to without affecting the main policy instrument.

Critical Thinking

1. The Fed currently pays interest on reserves equal to i_{or} and discount loans are made at

interest rate i_D. The federal funds interest rate is limited to fluctuating between these two rates as illustrated below. If the demand for reserves rises from R^d_0 to R^d_1, the federal funds interest rate will be equal to i_D. If the demand for reserves falls from R^d_0 to R^d_2, the federal funds interest rate will fall to i_{or}.

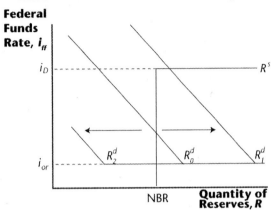

2. The federal funds rate may increase above the discount rate if banks are worried about the perceived stigma associated with borrowing directly from the Fed rather from other banks in the federal funds market. In this case, some banks may prefer to pay a higher federal funds rate than to borrow at a lower rate through the discount window. The federal funds rate my drop below the interest rate paid on reserves because there are many nonbank financial companies who provide funding to the federal funds market, but who are not eligible to receive interest on reserves. If this funding source is large enough, it could push the federal funds rate below that paid to interest on reserves.

True/False Questions

1. T
2. F
3. F
4. T
5. F
6. T
7. F
8. F
9. F
10. T
11. T
12. F
13. T

14. F
15. F

Multiple-Choice Questions

1. b
2. c
3. a
4. d
5. c
6. a
7. a
8. c
9. c
10. d
11. a
12. d
13. a
14. a
15. b
16. b
17. d
18. c
19. d
20. b

16

The Conduct of Monetary Policy: Strategy and Tactics*

Chapter Review

PREVIEW

The last chapter described how the tools of monetary policy affect the market for reserves and the interest rate. This chapter looks at the goals of monetary policy, and the strategies and tactics central banks use to reach those goals.

THE PRICE STABILITY GOAL AND THE NOMINAL ANCHOR

Price stability, which is typically defined as low and stable inflation, is increasingly viewed as the most important goal of monetary policy. Unstable prices create uncertainty, which hampers economic growth. Achieving price stability requires the use of a *nominal anchor,* which ties down the price level and limits the *time-inconsistency problem.* The time-inconsistency problem arises when monetary policy is conducted using discretion and re-evaluated on a day-to-day basis without considering the potential long-run consequences of those day-to-day decisions. Policymakers are always tempted to pursue a discretionary policy that is more expansionary than firms or workers expect in order to boost output in the short run. But firms and workers would eventually come to expect such policy and would increase their wages and prices, which would counteract any expansionary effect of monetary policy on output and lead only to higher inflation. Therefore, a central bank is better off if it does not try to surprise people in the first place and instead tries to keep inflation under control. A nominal anchor helps a central bank avoid the time-inconsistency problem by focusing on the long-term goal of controlling inflation.

*This is Chapter 19 in the 3rd ed.

OTHER GOALS OF MONETARY POLICY

Although price stability is generally the most important objective of central banks, other important goals of monetary policy are (1) high employment and output stability, (2) economic growth, (3) stability of financial markets, (4) interest-rate stability, and (5) stability in foreign exchange markets.

High employment means a level of employment that is consistent with the *natural rate of unemployment*—the unemployment rate that would exist when the demand for labor equals the supply of labor, taking the frictions in the labor market into account. This is generally consistent with output stability, since when the economy is at the natural rate of unemployment, output is also at *potential output*. The second goal, economic growth, is consistent with low unemployment. Financial market stability is important in order to avoid financial crises, which interfere with the ability of financial markets to channel funds to people with productive investment opportunities. Interest rate stability is desirable because it makes it easier for firms and households to plan for the future. International trade is increasingly important in both the U.S. economy as well as elsewhere. Stabilizing extreme movements in the value of the dollar in foreign exchange markets is therefore an important goal for monetary policy. In smaller countries that are largely dependent on trade, this can be an even more important goal.

SHOULD PRICE STABILITY BE THE PRIMARY GOAL OF MONETARY POLICY?

In the long run, price stability is consistent with the other five goals mentioned above. But in the short run, price stability often conflicts with these other goals. Central banks such as the European Central Bank, the Bank of England, the Bank of Canada, and the Reserve Bank of New Zealand have a *hierarchical mandate* that states that as long as price stability is achieved, other goals can be pursued by the central bank. The Federal Reserve has a *dual mandate* that states that price stability and maximum employment are co-equal objectives. Both types of mandates can work equally well as long as central banks maintain price stability as their long-run goal.

INFLATION TARGETING

One way to help achieve long-run price stability is to adopt an *inflation targeting* framework. New Zealand, Canada, and the United Kingdom adopted inflation targeting in the early 1990s. Most inflation-targeting countries share several common elements:

- Public announcement of medium-term numerical inflation objectives.

- Institutional commitment to price stability as the primary long-run goal of monetary policy

- Reliance on many different informational variables when making monetary policy decisions

- Increased transparency and communication with the public and markets

- Increased accountability of the central bank

Inflation targeting has the advantage that it is more transparent and more readily understood by the public, and inflation targeting has the potential to reduce the likelihood that the central bank will fall into the time-inconsistency trap. Inflation-targeting countries also place great emphasis on communication and transparency, which allows the central bank to explain the goals and limitations of policy, how numerical objectives were determined, how inflation targets will be achieved given current conditions, and why the central bank might deviate from specified targets.

There are four claimed disadvantages of inflation targeting: delayed signaling due to lags in the effects of monetary policy, a perceived lack of flexibility in the policy process, potential for increased output fluctuations due to a heightened focus on price stability as the primary objective, and low economic growth as a consequence of achieving low, desirable rates of inflation. But there is little evidence to support these claimed disadvantages.

THE FEDERAL RESERVE'S MONETARY POLICY STRATEGY

Monetary policy affects real output and inflation with a substantial lag. As a result, to prevent inflation from getting started, monetary policy needs to be forward-looking and preemptive. Under Federal Reserve Chairmen Alan Greenspan and Ben Bernanke, the Fed has pursued preemptive monetary policy. The Fed has no explicit nominal anchor, but it has some of the same elements of inflation targeting, including forward-looking behavior and a stress on price stability. This approach has proved to be fairly successful despite a lack of formal commitment mechanisms.

A disadvantage of the Fed's "just do it" monetary policy strategy is that it is less transparent than inflation targeting and, therefore, leads to more volatility in financial markets because financial markets are left to guess what the Fed is going to do in any particular situation. Another disadvantage of the "just do it" approach is that its success is highly dependent on the skills of the Fed chair. Thus, continued success is not guaranteed when a new chair takes over the Fed. A final disadvantage of the Fed's approach is that it is inconsistent with democratic principles and lacks accountability. Inflation targeting would make the Fed more accountable to elected officials and therefore inflation targeting would be more consistent with democratic principles.

LESSONS FOR MONETARY POLICY STRATEGY FROM THE GLOBAL FINANCIAL CRISIS

There are four main lessons that can be drawn from the global financial crisis:

1. Developments in the financial sector have a far greater impact on economic activity than was earlier recognized.

2. The zero-lower-bound on interest rates can be a serious problem.

3. The cost of cleaning up after a financial crisis is very high.

4. Price and output stability do not ensure financial stability.

These factors imply that the use of an inflation target may need to be more carefully considered. In particular, a somewhat higher inflation target may be desirable to help avoid the zero-lower-bound problem in the future. However, if such events are rare, the higher costs over time to higher average inflation may not be worth it. In addition, inflation reduction in the future may be more difficult with a higher inflation target designed to avoid the lower bound on interest rates. A second consideration is that a "flexible inflation targeting" approach may be more appropriate, which gives more scope for the central bank to pay more attention to secondary objectives such as financial stability.

Since *asset-price bubbles* can be extremely damaging to the financial system and the economy, avoiding such bubbles is important to the health of the economy. However, the use of monetary policy to pop bubbles is controversial and may not be effective. These opposing approaches to using monetary policy are summarized by the "lean versus clean" debate: Some economists believe monetary policy should actively "lean" against bubbles to prevent them altogether. Others, such as former Federal Reserve chairman Alan Greenspan believe that central banks should "clean" up after bubbles have popped. This view is summarized in the "Greenspan Doctrine," which argues the following five points:

1. Asset-price bubbles are nearly impossible to identify in real time.

2. Raising interest rates may be very ineffective in restraining bubbles.

3. Monetary policy actions are blunt and may not be able to effectively target specific asset prices.

4. Monetary policy actions to prick bubbles can have harmful effects on the aggregate economy.

5. Harmful aftereffects of bursting asset-price bubbles are manageable if monetary policy responds in a timely fashion.

There are two types of asset-price bubbles: those driven by credit and those driven solely by irrational exuberance. Credit-driven bubbles pose a greater threat to the financial system than bubbles driven solely by irrational exuberance. Policymakers will likely recognize a credit-driven bubble that is in progress but not a bubble driven solely by irrational exuberance. For these reasons, and given the severity of the credit-driven global financial crisis, this has provided a much stronger case for leaning against credit-driven bubbles rather than cleaning up afterward. However, the case for leaning against irrational exuberance driven bubbles is less compelling.

Macroprudential regulation appears to be the right tool for reigning in credit-driven bubbles, since credit booms are often a signal of market failure or poor financial regulation or supervision. In particular, countercyclical capital requirements that prevent leverage cycles may be the most effective type of macroprudential regulation to avoid credit-driven bubbles. However, due to political pressure and efforts to avoid regulation through loopholes, macroprudential policies may be less effective. In this context, monetary policy may be better placed to play a role. Even if monetary policy is less effective at addressing bubbles, it may be a more practical tool to ensure a "risk-taking channel" of monetary policy does not develop from a search for yield in low-interest rate environments.

TACTICS: CHOOSING THE POLICY INSTRUMENT

Central banks use tools such as open market operations, reserve requirements, and the discount rate to achieve their goals. But the connection between tools and goals is not direct and immediate so central banks use the tools of monetary policy to affect *policy instruments* (also called *operating instruments*) to indicate whether monetary policy is tight or easy. Operating instruments give more immediate feedback to the central bank about whether it is moving toward its goals. Examples of policy instruments are reserve aggregates or interest rates. The policy instrument might be linked to an intermediate target, which is more directly related to the goals of monetary policy but less related to the actual tools of monetary policy than the operating instruments. The connection between tools, instruments, targets, and goals are summarized in the figure below.

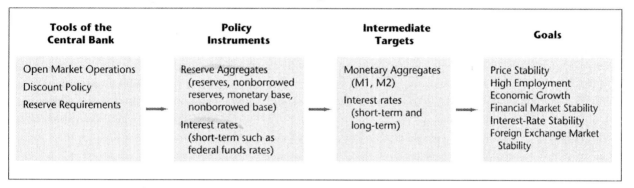

Tools of the Central Bank	Policy Instruments	Intermediate Targets	Goals
Open Market Operations Discount Policy Reserve Requirements	Reserve Aggregates (reserves, nonborrowed reserves, monetary base, nonborrowed base) Interest rates (short-term such as federal funds rates)	Monetary Aggregates (M1, M2) Interest rates (short-term and long-term)	Price Stability High Employment Economic Growth Financial Market Stability Interest-Rate Stability Foreign Exchange Market Stability

A central bank can choose either a reserve aggregate or an interest rate as its policy instrument, but it cannot choose both because targeting one implies that the central bank must be free to move the other. There are three criteria for choosing a policy instrument: (1) It must be observable and measurable; (2) it must be controllable by the central bank; (3) and it must have a predictable effect on the goals. Most central banks use short-term interest rates as their policy instrument, since it meets the three criteria above reasonably well.

TACTICS: THE TAYLOR RULE

The *Taylor rule* is a mathematical equation which describes how the Fed sets the federal funds target. According to the Taylor rule, the federal funds rate equals an "equilibrium" real fed funds rate plus a weighted average of the inflation and output gaps. The output gap appears in the Taylor rule because the Fed is concerned about stabilizing output fluctuations in addition to maintaining low and stable inflation. Another possible reason that the output gap appears in the Taylor rule is that it indicates future inflationary pressures.

When the monetary authority responds to an increase in inflation by raising the nominal interest rate by more than the rise in inflation, it is said to follow the *Taylor principle.* Failure to follow the Taylor principle results in unstable inflation. According to the *Phillips curve theory,* when output is above potential (the gap is positive), inflationary pressures rise, and when output is below potential (the gap is negative), inflationary pressures fall. The Taylor rule does a pretty good job of describing the Fed's setting of the federal funds rate under Chairmen Greenspan and Bernanke but does not perfectly match the actual behavior of the federal funds rate. But there are several reasons why the Fed should not set monetary policy solely based on a mechanical Taylor rule formula. In particular, the conduct of monetary policy requires careful analytics and human judgment, since the structure of the economy is constantly evolving and severe shocks to the economy may not be easily dealt with through a mechanical policy rule.

Helpful Hints

1. Price stability is the most important goal of monetary policy. Central banks have successfully achieved price stability using inflation targeting, dual mandates, and hierarchical mandates.
2. Monetary policy strategies and tactics vary across countries and over time. It is important to keep in mind that each strategy has advantages and disadvantages.

Terms and Definitions

Choose a definition for each key term.

Key Terms:

_12_ asset-price bubble
_16_ dual mandate
_18_ hierarchical mandates
_4_ inflation targeting
_5_ intermediate target
_11_ international policy coordination
_13_ macroprudential regulation

_15_ natural rate of output
_20_ natural rate of unemployment
_14_ nominal anchor
_3_ nonaccelerating inflation rate of unemployment (NAIRU)
_8_ operating instrument
_17_ potential output

_7_ Phillips curve theory
_2_ policy instrument
_19_ price stability
_10_ real bills doctrine
_9_ Taylor principle
_1_ Taylor rule
_6_ time-inconsistency problem

Definitions:

1. A monetary policy rule that describes the setting of the federal funds rate target under Chairmen Greenspan and Bernanke

2. Any of a set of variables such as reserve aggregates or interest rates that the Fed seeks to influence and that are responsive to its policy tools

3. The rate of unemployment when demand for labor equals supply, consequently eliminating the tendency for the inflation rate to change

4. Monetary policy aimed at achieving a certain inflation rate

5. Any of a set of variables, such as monetary aggregates or interest rates, that have a direct effect on employment and the price level and that the Fed seeks to influence

6. Results when discretionary monetary policies are pursued that are expansionary or beneficial in the short run but that have poor outcomes in the long run

7. A theory suggesting that changes in inflation are influenced by the state of the economy relative to its production capacity, as well as other factors

8. An alternative term used to describe a policy instrument

9. The practice of conducting monetary policy so that the nominal interest changes by more than changes in the inflation rate

10. The practice of conducting monetary policy to facilitate the production and sale of goods and services

11. The practice of countries agreeing to enact policies cooperatively

12. Pronounced increases in asset prices that depart from fundamental values

13. Regulatory policy to affect what is happening in credit markets in the aggregate

14. Nominal variable such as the inflation rate, exchange rate, or money supply that policymakers use to tie down the price level

15. Level of output produced at the natural rate of unemployment, at which there is no tendency for prices or wages to change

16. Central bank mandate that features two co-equal objectives: price stability and maximum employment

17. Level of output synonymous with the natural rate of output

18. Central bank mandate that puts the goal of price stability first, but as long as it is achieved other goals can be pursued

19. A condition of low and stable inflation

20. The rate of unemployment consistent with full employment at which the demand for labor equals the supply of labor

Problems and Short-Answer Questions

PRACTICE PROBLEMS

1. a. Give an example of a nominal anchor.

_____

_____

b. Describe the time-inconsistency problem as it applies to monetary policy.

_____

_____

_____

_____

c. Explain how a nominal anchor helps a central bank avoid the time-inconsistency problem.

_____

_____

_____

_____

_____

_____

_____

_____

2. a. What are the advantages of inflation targeting?

_____

_____

b. What are the disadvantages of inflation targeting?

_____

_____

3. a. Describe the Fed's "just do it" approach to monetary policy.

_____

_____

_____

b. What are the advantages of the Fed's approach?

_____

_____

c. What are the disadvantages of the Fed's approach?

_____

_____

_____

_____

_____

4. a. Draw the demand and supply for reserves and show what happens to the federal fund rate when the Fed targets nonborrowed reserves.

b. Draw the demand and supply for reserves and show what happens to the quantity of nonborrowed reserves when the Fed targets the federal funds rate.

c. Use your answers in parts (a) and (b) to explain why the Fed cannot target both the federal funds rate and the quantity of nonborrowed reserves at the same time.

_____

_____

_____

_____

_____

_____

5. Suppose the inflation rate is 2%, the equilibrium real federal funds rate is 2%, the output gap is –1.5%, and the target inflation rate is 2.5%.

   a. Use the Taylor Rule to predict the target federal funds rate given the above data.

   _____

   _____

   b. According to the data given above, is the unemployment rate at, above, or below NAIRU? Does this mean that inflation is expected to rise, fall, or remain unchanged in the future?

   _____

   _____

   c. Based on your Taylor rule calculation, is monetary policy neutral, contractionary, or expansionary?

   _____

   _____

6. Suppose the inflation rate increases by one percentage point above target.

   a. Use the Taylor rule to predict what will happen to the nominal federal funds rate, and the real federal funds rate.

   _____

   _____

   b. Suppose that the weight on the inflation gap in the Taylor rule was [–0.25] instead of [+0.5]. What will happen to the nominal federal funds rate, and the real federal funds rate?

   _____

   _____

   c. How does your answers to parts (a) and (b) demonstrate the Taylor principle?

   _____

   _____

7. a. List and describe the two types of bubbles.

   _____

   _____

b. Which type of bubble poses a larger risk to the financial system?

_____

_____

c. What are the arguments against using monetary policy to burst an asset-price bubble that is driven solely by irrational exuberance?

_____

_____

d. What are the appropriate policy responses to a credit-driven bubble?

_____

_____

_____

SHORT-ANSWER QUESTIONS

1. Why is price stability desirable?

_____

_____

2. Why is interest rate stability desirable?

_____

_____

3. Define the natural rate of unemployment and describe how it relates to a central bank's goals.

_____

_____

_____

_____

_____

_____

4. Does the Fed have a dual mandate or a hierarchical mandate? Does the European Central Bank have a dual mandate or a hierarchical mandate?

_____

5. What typically common features are found with inflation targeting central banks?

_____

_____

_____

6. How can a higher inflation target help avoid the zero-lower-bound on interest rates?

_____

_____

_____

7. What are the three criteria that a central bank uses to choose a policy instrument? In what ways does a short-term interest rate meet those criteria?

_____

_____

8. What is the "Greenspan Doctrine," and what are the arguments to support this view?

_____

_____

_____

_____

9. Which type of bubble are policymakers more likely to identify while it is happening?

_____

_____

_____

10. What is the difference between an operating instrument and an intermediate target?

_____

_____

_____

Critical Thinking

Suppose the central bank's goal for inflation is 2%, and the equilibrium federal funds rate is 2%.

1. Assume that GDP is currently at potential and inflation is 2%. Use the Taylor rule to calculate the target federal funds rate and the value of the *real* federal funds rate that is implied by that target rate. Is monetary policy expansionary, contractionary, or neutral? How will GDP growth and inflation be affected by this monetary policy?

_____

_____

_____

_____

_____

_____

2. Now assume that GDP is 1% below potential and inflation is 1%. Use the Taylor rule to calculate the target federal funds rate and the value of the *real* federal funds rate that is implied by that target rate. Is monetary policy expansionary, contractionary, or neutral? How will GDP growth and inflation be affected by this monetary policy?

_____

_____

_____

_____

_____

_____

3. Now assume that GDP is 1% above potential and inflation is 3%. Use the Taylor rule to calculate the target federal funds rate and the value of the *real* federal

funds rate that is implied by that target rate. Is monetary policy expansionary, contractionary, or neutral? How will GDP growth and inflation be affected by this monetary policy?

_____

_____

_____

_____

_____

_____

_____

Self-Test

TRUE/FALSE QUESTIONS

_____ 1. Inflation in the United Kingdom was 9% in 1991, but fell to 2.2% shortly after this coinciding with the adoption of an inflation target.

_____ 2. One disadvantage of inflation targeting is that it leads to lower economic growth than noninflation targeting countries.

_____ 3. Inflation targeting reduces the likelihood that a central bank will fall into the time-inconsistency trap.

_____ 4. Pursuing price and output stability is a good way to ensure financial stability.

_____ 5. The Fed's "just do it" strategy is consistent with democratic principles.

_____ 6. Following the Taylor principle will result in more stable inflation.

_____ 7. A central bank can target either the federal funds rate or nonborrowed reserves but not both.

_____ 8. Both interest rates and reserve aggregates have observability and measurability problems.

_____ 9. Bubbles driven solely by irrational exuberance pose a much larger risk to the financial system than bubbles driven by credit.

_____ 10. Monetary policymakers are more likely to identify a bubble driven by irrational exuberance than a bubble driven by credit.

_____11. Leaning against asset-price bubbles is a preemptive approach to dealing with bubbles.

_____12. Countercyclical capital requirements are one type of macroprudential regulation to address credit-driven bubbles.

_____13. A weakness of macroprudential regulation to address credit driven bubbles is that it can be subject to lobbying of politicians who may be pressured to minimize regulation.

_____14. An intermediate target could be nonborrowed reserves or the monetary base.

_____15. The Fed has successfully used the Taylor rule to conduct monetary policy in the Greenspan and Bernanke eras.

MULTIPLE-CHOICE QUESTIONS

1. If a central bank pursues a time-inconsistent policy, it will eventually lead to
   a. lower inflation and higher output.
   b. lower inflation and no gain in output.
   c. higher inflation and higher output.
   d. higher inflation and no gain in output.

2. Which of the following is not a goal of monetary policy?
   a. high employment
   b. economic growth
   c. low interest rates
   d. an unemployment rate as close to zero as possible

3. A central bank that follows a hierarchical mandate
   a. mostly uses open-market operations and occasionally uses the discount rate.
   b. uses open-market operations and discount lending equally.
   c. will first achieve its primary goal before it pursues it secondary goals.
   d. places equal weight on all goals.

4. Which of the following is not an essential element of inflation targeting?
   a. public announcement of a numerical target for inflation
   b. an institutional commitment to price stability as the primary, long-run goal of monetary policy
   c. increased transparency of monetary policy
   d. a mechanism for firing the head of the central bank if the inflation target is not achieved

5. Which of the following is a disadvantage of inflation targeting?
   a. There is a long lag between monetary policy actions and inflation.
   b. Inflation targeting is more likely to result in the time-inconsistency problem than monetary targeting is.
   c. Inflation targeting leads to increased exchange rate fluctuations.
   d. Inflation targeting is less transparent than monetary targeting.

6. If the Fed follows the Taylor principle, it will
   a. increase the nominal interest rate by less than an increase in inflation.
   b. increase the nominal interest rate by more than an increase in inflation.
   c. follow the Taylor rule when inflation is below the nominal interest rate.
   d. follow the Taylor rule when inflation is above the nominal interest rate.

7. The Fed should not base monetary policy solely on the Taylor rule conducted in a mechanical fashion because
   a. the Fed looks at a much wider range of information than is contained in the Taylor rule.
   b. no one knows what the true model of the economy is.
   c. times of economic crisis may require very different monetary policy.
   d. All of the above are true.

8. Under Fed Chairmen Greenspan and Bernanke, the Fed has followed
   a. an inflation target.
   b. a money target.
   c. a explicit nominal anchor.
   d. an implicit nominal anchor.

9. Which of the following is a disadvantage of the Fed's "just do it" strategy?
   a. It lacks transparency.
   b. It does not rely on a stable money-inflation relationship.
   c. It uses many sources of information.
   d. It has performed poorly over the past twenty years.

10. Which of the following is a policy instrument?
    a. open market operations
    b. reserve aggregates
    c. inflation
    d. discount rate

11. Intermediate targets
    a. stand between policy tools and policy instruments.
    b. stand between policy instruments and policy goals.
    c. indicate whether policy is tight or easy.
    d. are inconsistent with inflation targeting.

12. The most important characteristic of a policy instrument is that it
    a. is observable and measurable.
    b. is controllable.
    c. has a predictable impact on goals.
    d. is a nominal anchor.

13. According to the Taylor rule, if the equilibrium real federal funds rate is 2%, the inflation rate is 3%, the target inflation rate is 2%, and the output gap is 1%, the federal funds rate target will be
    a. 2.
    b. 4.
    c. 5.
    d. 6.

14. When the unemployment rate rises above NAIRU,
    a. output is below potential and inflation rises.
    b. output is below potential and inflation falls.
    c. output is above potential and inflation rises.
    d. output is above potential and inflation falls.

15. According to the Taylor rule, if inflation falls below its target and output falls below potential,
    a. the federal funds target will decrease.
    b. the federal funds target will increase
    c. the equilibrium real federal funds rate will decrease.
    d. the equilibrium real federal funds rate will increase.

16. Credit-driven bubbles are ____ to identify and pose a ____threat to the financial system compared to bubbles driven solely by irrational exuberance.
    a. easier; smaller
    b. easier; larger
    c. harder; smaller
    d. harder; larger

17. In the presence of a credit-driven asset price bubble, the appropriate policy is
    a. monetary policy tightening.
    b. monetary policy easing.
    c. macroprudential regulation.
    d. nothing; it is best to let the bubble run its course.

18. Flexible inflation targeting is best described as
    a. changing the desired inflation target as economic conditions change.
    b. allowing short-run deviations in inflation from target to better promote output stability.
    c. an intermediate target which is rarely used by central banks.
    d. the monetary policy strategy employed by the Federal Reserve.

19. The Greenspan Doctrine
    a. advocates that monetary policymakers respond to asset-price bubbles only insofar as it affects its price stability and output objectives.
    b. suggests monetary policy can play a role in eliminating asset-price bubbles.
    c. applies only to credit-driven bubbles.
    d. summarizes the "leaning" against asset-price bubbles view.

20. The risk-channel of monetary policy
    a. is caused by the incentives for asset managers to search for yield.
    b. is propagated by low interest rates from overly easy monetary policy.
    c. suggests that monetary policy should be used to lean against credit bubbles.
    d. is all of the above.

Solutions

Terms and Definitions

 12 asset price bubble

 16 dual mandate

 18 hierarchical mandates

 4 inflation targeting

 5 intermediate target

 11 international policy coordination

 13 macroprudential regulation

 15 natural rate of output

 20 natural rate of unemployment

 14 nominal anchor

 3 nonaccelerating inflation rate of unemployment (NAIRU)

 8 operating instrument

 17 potential output

 7 Phillips curve theory

 2 policy instrument

 19 price stability

 10 real bills doctrine

 9 Taylor principle

 1 Taylor rule

 6 time-inconsistency problem

Practice Problems

1. a. The inflation rate and the money supply are both nominal anchors.

    b. The time-inconsistency problem is when policymakers are tempted to pursue a discretionary monetary policy that is more expansionary than expected by firms or people. Monetary policymakers will initially attempt to pursue such policies in order to boost output, but once people and firms catch on to this strategy, inflation rises and there is no gain in output.

    c. Nominal anchors such as inflation or the money supply keep the central bank from pursuing overly expansionary monetary policy and thus help avoid the time-inconsistency problem.

2. a. The advantages of inflation targeting are: It is highly transparent; it increases accountability; and it reduces the likelihood of a central bank falling into the time-inconsistency trap.

    b. The disadvantages of inflation targeting are: delayed signaling, too much rigidity, potential for increased output fluctuations, low economic growth.

3. a. The Fed has an implicit rather than explicit inflation target. The Fed is forward-looking in the sense that they continuously monitor the economy for signs of future inflation. The Fed is also preemptive, tightening monetary policy before inflation rises.

    b. The main advantage of the Fed's approach is that it has been highly successful and shares some of the key advantages of formal inflation targeting frameworks.

    c. A disadvantage of the Fed's approach is that it lacks transparency, which might lead to excess volatility in financial markets. The Fed's current policy relies heavily on the skills of the chair of the Fed. Finally, the Fed's current system lacks accountability and therefore may be inconsistent with democratic principles.

4. a. If the Fed targets nonborrowed reserves, NBR is held constant at NBR*. As illustrated in the figure below, changes in the demand for reserves (R_d) will therefore cause the federal funds rate (i_{ff}) to fluctuate when nonborrowed reserves is held constant.

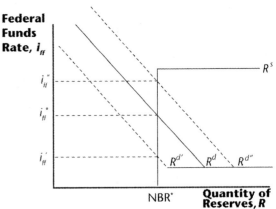

    b. If the Fed targets the federal funds rate, i_{ff} is held constant at i_{ff}*. As illustrated in Figure 2, changes in the demand for reserves (R^d) will therefore cause nonborrowed reserves (NBR) to fluctuate when the federal funds rate is held constant.

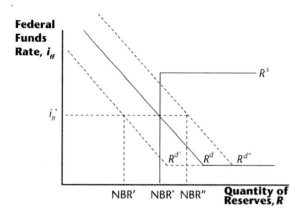

c. The answers to (a) and (b) illustrate how the Fed can target either the federal funds rate (i_{ff}) or nonborrowed reserves (*NBR*), but it cannot target both at the same time. The reason the Fed cannot target both at the same time is that the demand for reserves fluctuates daily. So if the Fed targets (holds constant) *NBR*, fluctuations in the demand for reserves (R^d) will cause the federal funds rate to move up and down. And if the Fed targets (holds constant) i_{ff}, fluctuations in the demand for reserves (R^d) will cause *NBR* to move up and down.

5. a. According to the Taylor-rule, the target federal fund rate = 2 + 2 + 0.5 × (–0.5) + 0.5 × (–1.5) = 3%.

 b. The output gap is negative, which means that the unemployment rate is above NAIRU, which means that there is a tendency for inflation to fall.

 c. Monetary policy is expansionary. Neutral policy would be achieved when the inflation rate is at the target inflation rate and the output gap is zero.

6. a. According to the Taylor-rule, the nominal federal fund rate will increase by = 1 + 0.5% = 1.5%. This implies that the real federal funds rate will increase by 1.5% – 1% = 0.5%.

 b. According to the Taylor-rule, the nominal federal fund rate will increase by = 1 – 0.25% = 0.75%. This implies that the real federal funds rate will change by 0.75% – 1% = –0.25%; in other words, the real federal funds rate will decrease by 25 basis points.

 c. In (a), the Taylor principle is adhered to: increases in the inflation rate are met with more than one-for-one increases in the federal funds rate. As a result, the contractionary effects of the higher real fed funds rate act to stabilize the inflation rate. In (b), the Taylor principle is violated since higher inflation leads to lower real interest rates, which encourage an expansionary monetary policy leading to more inflation.

7. a. The two types of asset price bubbles are credit-driven bubbles and bubbles driven solely by irrational exuberance.

 b. Credit-driven bubbles pose a larger risk to the financial system.

 c. The argument against bursting a bubble driven solely by irrational exuberance is that they are nearly impossible to identify.

 d. The appropriate policy response is macroprudential regulation.

Short-Answer Questions

1. Price stability is desirable because a rising price level creates uncertainty in the economy, and uncertainty might hamper economic growth.

2. Interest rate stability is desirable because fluctuations in interest rates create uncertainty in the economy, which makes it harder to plan for the future.

3. The natural rate of unemployment is the rate of unemployment that is consistent with full employment (the demand for labor equals the supply of labor). One of the goals of a central bank is full employment, so achieving an unemployment rate that is near the natural rate of unemployment is consistent with that goal. Another goal of a central bank is price stability. When unemployment is below the natural rate, inflation tends to rise, and when unemployment is above the natural rate, inflation tends to fall. Thus, keeping unemployment near the natural rate is also consistent with the goal of price stability.

4. The Fed has a dual mandate. The European Central Bank has a hierarchical mandate.

5. Most inflation targeting central banks have public announcements of medium-term numerical inflation targets, an institutional commitment to price stability as the primary long-run objective, they use many different informational variables to determine the appropriate monetary policy, have enhanced transparency and communications mech-

anisms, and have increased accountability to achieve its goals and objectives.

6. A higher average inflation rate would lead to higher average short-term nominal interest rates. Having higher short-term nominal interest rates gives the central bank more room on the downside to reduce the policy interest rate, so that the zero-lower bound would be less binding.

7. The three criteria that a central bank uses to choose a policy instrument are: (1) observability and measurability; (2) controllability; and (3) predictable effect on goals. The nominal fed funds rate is easily observable and measurable; however, the real fed funds rate, which is what matters for the policy stance, is more difficult to observe and measure. Similarly, the nominal fed funds rate is relatively easily controllable, but the real fed funds rate is what matters for the effectiveness of policy and that is much less controllable. The short-term nominal interest rate appears to have a fairly tight link to inflation and, therefore, meets the predictability criteria very well.

8. The Greenspan doctrine was championed by Federal Reserve chairman Alan Greenspan, and laid out arguments for why a central bank should not try to pop asset-price bubbles. There are five main arguments to why central banks should not intervene to address bubbles: (1) Asset-price bubbles are nearly impossible to identify in real time; (2) interest rate increases may be ineffective in restraining bubbles; (3) monetary policy actions are blunt and may not be able to effectively target specific assets; (4) pricking bubbles can have harmful secondary effects on the aggregate economy; (5) the aftereffects of asset-price bubbles can be effectively managed with prudent, timely policy, mitigating the need for a proactive stance on asset-price bubbles.

9. The Fed is more likely to recognize a credit-driven asset price bubble while it is happening.

10. An operating instrument is directly affected by the central bank's tools. An intermediate target is less directly affected by the central bank's tools but more directly related to the goals of monetary policy.

Critical Thinking

1. According to the Taylor rule, $i_{ff}^* = 2 + 2 + 0.5 \times (2 - 2) + 0.5 \times 0 = 4$. If the economy is operating at potential and inflation is at its target of 2%, the Taylor rule calls for a federal funds rate target (i_{ff}^*) of 4%. This target rate for the nominal federal funds rate implies a real federal funds rate that is equal to 2% (real federal funds rate equals nominal federal funds rate – inflation). This would be neutral monetary policy because the real federal funds rate implied by the Fed's target is equal to the equilibrium federal funds rate. Under neutral monetary policy, monetary policy is neither stimulating or dampening GDP growth nor inflation.

2. According to the Taylor rule, $i_{ff}^* = 2 + 1 + 0.5 \times (1–2) + 0.5 \times (–1) = 2$. If the economy is operating below potential and inflation is below its target of 2%, the Taylor rule calls for a federal funds rate target (i_{ff}^*) of 2%. This target rate for the nominal federal funds rate implies a real federal funds rate that is equal to 1%. This would be expansionary monetary policy because the real federal funds rate implied by the Fed's target is less than the equilibrium federal funds rate. Under expansionary monetary policy, GDP growth and inflation will tend to rise.

3. According to the Taylor rule, $i_{ff}^* = 2 + 3 + 0.5 \times (3 – 2) + 0.5 \times (1) = 6$. If the economy is operating above potential and inflation is above its target of 2%, the Taylor rule calls for a federal funds rate target (i_{ff}^*) of 6%. This target rate for the nominal federal funds rate implies a real federal funds rate that is equal to 3%. This would be contractionary monetary policy because the real federal funds rate implied by the Fed's target is greater than the equilibrium federal funds rate. Under contractionary monetary policy, GDP growth and inflation will tend to fall.

True/False Questions

1. T
2. F
3. T
4. F
5. F
6. T
7. T
8. T

9. F
10. F
11. T
12. T
13. T
14. F
15. F

Multiple-Choice Questions

1. c
2. d
3. c
4. d
5. a
6. b
7. d
8. d
9. a
10. b
11. b
12. c
13. d
14. b
15. a
16. b
17. c
18. b
19. a
20. d

17 The Foreign Exchange Market[*]

Chapter Review

This is the first chapter in a two chapter sequence on international finance and monetary policy. This chapter looks at the foreign exchange market. The next chapter looks at the International Financial System.

PREVIEW

The price of one currency in terms of another is called the *exchange rate*. Fluctuations in the exchange rate affect both inflation and output and are an important concern for monetary policymakers. This chapter looks at how the exchange rate is determined in the *foreign exchange market*.

FOREIGN EXCHANGE MARKET

When a U.S. firm buys a foreign good or asset, it first must exchange dollars (or dollar denominated deposits) for the foreign currency (or foreign denominated deposits). That exchange takes place in the foreign exchange market. Two kinds of transactions take place in that market: *spot transactions*, which involve the immediate exchange of bank deposits and *forward transactions*, which involve the exchange of bank deposits at some specified future date. The *spot exchange rate* is the exchange rate on spot transactions, and the *forward exchange rate* is the exchange rate on forward transactions. When a currency increases in value, it experiences an *appreciation*; when it falls in value, it experiences a *depreciation*. When a country's currency appreciates, its goods become more expensive for foreign buyers, and foreign goods become less expensive for domestic buyers. When a country's currency depreciates, its goods become less expensive for foreign buyers, and foreign goods become more expensive for domestic buyers.

---

[*]This is Chapter 20 in the 3rd ed.

EXCHANGE RATES IN THE LONG RUN

According to the *law of one price,* if transportation costs and trade barriers are low, the price of identical goods should be the same throughout the world. If a candy bar costs $1 in the United States and the same candy bar costs 10 pesos in Mexico, then according to the law of one price, the exchange rate between pesos and dollars should be 10 pesos per dollar. The law of one price applied to national price levels (rather than prices of individual goods such as candy bars) is called the *theory of purchasing power parity (PPP).* According to PPP, if the Mexican price level rises 10% relative to the U.S. price level, the dollar will appreciate 10% relative to the peso. Another way to think about purchasing power parity is through the concept called the *real exchange rate,* which is the price of domestic goods relative to the price of foreign goods denominated in the domestic currency.

PPP does not fully explain movements in exchange rates, even in the long run since some goods, and particularly services, may not be easily traded between countries. There are four major factors that affect exchange rates in the long run:

- **Relative price levels:** a rise in a country's price level relative to another country's price level causes the domestic currency to depreciate, and vice versa.

- **Trade barriers:** increasing trade barriers through *tariffs* or *quotas* causes a country's currency to appreciate.

- **Preferences for domestic versus foreign goods:** increased demand for a country's exports causes the currency to appreciate; increased demand for imported goods causes the currency to depreciate.

- **Differences in productivity across countries:** as a country becomes more productive relative to other countries, its currency appreciates.

EXCHANGE RATES IN THE SHORT RUN: A SUPPLY AND DEMAND ANALYSIS

In the short run, exchange rates are determined mainly by the demand and supply for domestic assets. The supply of assets, such as bonds, equities, and bank deposits are fixed, implying a vertical supply curve. The quantity of assets demanded depends on the relative expected return on domestic assets. To understand the demand for domestic assets, think about starting at a point on the demand curve where the euro/dollar exchange rate is 1 and the future euro/dollar exchange rate (E^e_{t+1}) is expected to remain constant at 1 as well. A decrease in the current exchange rate to 0.8 will increase the return on dollar assets relative to European assets and lead to a rise in the quantity of dollar assets demanded. Thus, the demand curve in the foreign exchange market is downward sloping. The equilibrium exchange rate occurs where the supply and demand for assets intersect.

EXPLAINING CHANGES IN EXCHANGE RATES

The supply for domestic assets is fixed and does not shift in the short run. Thus, factors that change the demand for assets are what affect the equilibrium exchange rate. There are seven primary explanations for why demand for dollar assets will shift:

- Domestic interest rate, i^D: an increase in domestic interest rates makes domestic investment more attractive; demand for domestic assets increases, and the domestic currency appreciates.

- Foreign interest rate, i^F: an increase in foreign interest rates makes foreign investment more attractive; demand for domestic assets decreases, and the domestic currency depreciates

- Changes in the expected future exchange rate E^e_{t+1}: an expected appreciation of the domestic currency increases current demand for domestic currency, leading to an appreciation of the domestic currency.

- Expected price level: a higher expected price level will cause a future depreciation of the domestic currency, leading to a decrease in current demand and a depreciation of the currency.

- Expected trade barriers: with greater expected trade barriers, future appreciation will occur and the return on domestic assets will rise. This increases current demand for assets, and the domestic currency appreciates.

- Expected import demand: if imports are expected to increase in the future, this will lead to an expected depreciation of currency in the future. This decreases current demand for assets, and the domestic currency depreciates.

- Expected export demand: if exports are expected to increase in the future, this will lead to an expected appreciation of currency in the future. This increases current demand for assets, and the domestic currency appreciates.

- Expected domestic productivity: higher expected domestic productivity relative to another country will lead to an expected appreciation of the domestic currency. This increases current demand for assets, and the domestic currency appreciates.

The above analysis assumes that changes in the interest rate arise from changes in the real interest rate. If the increase in interest rates is due to an increase in the expected inflation rate instead of the real interest rate, then demand for domestic assets will decrease and the domestic currency will depreciate.

Earlier models of exchange rate fluctuations were based on the goods market and did not predict substantial movements in exchange rates because they did not emphasize changing expectations as a source of exchange rate movements. The weakness of the dollar in the late 1970s and the strength of the dollar in the early 1980s can both be explained by movements in real interest rates but not movements in nominal interest rates. As the global financial crisis spread to the rest of the world in 2008, the dollar increased in value relative to a wider basket of currencies. This occurred because foreign central banks began reducing their interest rates and there was a "flight to quality" which increased the demand for U.S. Treasury securities.

Helpful Hints

1. The supply of domestic assets is fixed and vertical at any given point in time, and does not shift. This is because the value of domestic assets is so large in size and scope, that the exchange rate does not have an influence on the quantity of assets supplied domestically. This implies that exchange rate movements are due to changes in demand for a country's assets.

2. In the long run, movements in exchange rates are mainly driven by relative inflation rates between countries. In the short run, movements in exchange rates are mainly driven by relative rates of returns on assets between countries. The volatility of exchange rates in the short run is due in large part to changes in expectations, which significantly affect demand for assets and hence the exchange rate.

Terms and Definitions

Choose a definition for each key term.

Key Terms:

_____ appreciation

_____ capital mobility

_____ depreciation

_____ effective exchange rate index

_____ exchange rate

_____ foreign exchange market

_____ forward exchange rate

_____ forward transaction

_____ interest parity condition

_____ law of one price

_____ quotas

_____ real exchange rate

_____ spot exchange rate

_____ spot transaction

_____ tariffs

_____ theory of purchasing power parity (PPP)

Definitions:

1. The immediate exchange of bank deposits in the foreign exchange market

2. A fall in the value of a currency

3. The situation in which foreigners can easily purchase American assets and Americans can easily purchase foreign assets

4. The idea that the prices of identical goods should be identical throughout the world

5. The price of one currency in terms of another

6. The exchange rate for forward transactions

7. Taxes on imported goods

8. The exchange of bank deposits in the foreign exchange market at some future specified date

9. An increase in the value of a currency

10. The theory that exchange rates between any two countries will adjust to reflect changes in the price levels of the two countries

11. The requirement that the domestic interest rate equals the foreign interest rate minus the expected appreciation of the domestic currency

12. The value of the dollar in terms of a basket of foreign currencies

13. The market in which the exchange rate is determined

14. The exchange rate for spot transactions

15. Restrictions on the quantity of foreign goods that can be imported

16. The price of domestic goods relative to the price of foreign goods denominated in the domestic currency

Problems and Short-Answer Questions

PRACTICE PROBLEMS

1. Suppose the dollar/euro exchange rate is 1.20.
   a. What is the euro/dollar exchange rate?

   _____

   b. What would the new euro/dollar exchange rate be if the euro appreciated by 5% relative to the dollar?

   _____

   c. Starting from the original exchange rate you calculated in part (a), what would the new euro/dollar exchange rate be if the euro depreciated by 5% against the dollar?

   _____

2. a. Suppose the law of one price holds for wheat and the price of wheat is $4.50 per bushel in the United States, and the peso/dollar exchange rate is 10. Calculate the price of wheat in terms of pesos.

   _____

   b. Now suppose that purchasing power parity holds between the United States and Mexico. Calculate the new peso/dollar exchange rate if the price level in Mexico rises 10% relative to the price level in the United States.

   _____

   c. Now suppose a basket of goods in the United States costs $100, while the cost of the same basket of goods in Mexico costs 950 pesos. Calculate the real exchange rate assuming the peso/dollar exchange rate is 15.

   _____

3. In the second column of the following table, indicate with an arrow whether the exchange rate will rise (↑) or fall (↓) as a result of the change in the factor. (Recall that a rise in the exchange rate is viewed as an appreciation of the domestic currency).

Change in Factor	Response of the Exchange Rate
Domestic interest rate ↓	_____
Foreign interest rate ↓	_____
Domestic price level ↓	_____
Tariffs and quotas ↓	_____
Import demand ↓	_____
Export demand ↓	_____
Domestic productivity ↓	_____

4. Use the demand-and-supply diagram for domestic assets to demonstrate the following.
    a. Show what happens to the exchange rate E_t when the domestic interest rate i^D decreases.

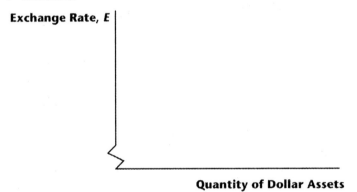

    b. Show what happens to the exchange rate E_t when the foreign interest rate i^F increases.

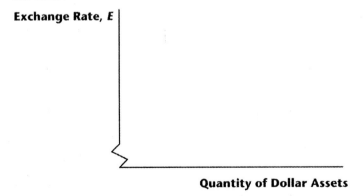

c. Show what happens to the exchange rate E_t when the expected future exchange rate E_{t+1} increases.

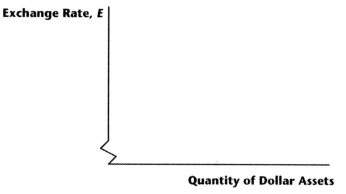

Exchange Rate, E

Quantity of Dollar Assets

SHORT-ANSWER QUESTIONS

1. What happens to the price of foreign imports into the United States when the dollar depreciates?

   _____

   _____

2. What is likely to happen to the quantity of imports demanded by Americans as a result of the dollar depreciating?

   _____

   _____

3. What happens to a country's currency if that country increases its trade barriers and becomes more productive relative to other countries?

   _____

   _____

4. What determines the demand for domestic assets?

   _____

   _____

5. What will happen to the exchange rate today if the expected future exchange rate declines?

   _____

   _____

6. What will happen to the value of the domestic currency when the domestic real interest rate rises?

    _____

    _____

7. What will happen to the value of the domestic currency when the domestic nominal interest rate rises and the increase is due to an increase in expected inflation?

    _____

    _____

8. Why do net exports decrease when a country's currency appreciates?

    _____

    _____

9. What does it mean for the "law of one price" to hold?

    _____

    _____

    _____

    _____

    _____

10. Why did the dollar appreciate during the global financial crisis?

    _____

    _____

Critical Thinking

Most of the analysis in this chapter looks at how a single factor, such as a change in domestic interest rates, affects the exchange rate, holding all other factors constant. But in the real world, many factors change at once, and so sometimes it is not possible to predict the impact on exchange rates. For each of the following combinations of factors, state whether it is possible to predict the direction of the effect on the domestic exchange rate. For the cases where it is possible to predict the direction of effect, state what that direction is.

a. The domestic interest rate rises, foreign interest rate falls, and expected import demand falls as well.

_____

_____

_____

b. The domestic price level rises, quotas are placed on imports, and productivity is expected to rise.

_____

_____

_____

c. Export demand is expected to rise, the domestic price level is expected to fall, and foreign interest rates are expected to fall as well.

_____

_____

_____

Self-Test

TRUE/FALSE QUESTIONS

_____1. Most trades in the foreign exchange market involve the buying and selling of bank deposits.

_____2. When a country's currency appreciates, its goods abroad become less expensive, and foreign goods in that country become more expensive, all else constant.

_____3. Forward exchange rates involve the immediate exchange of bank deposits.

_____4. The theory of purchasing power parity explains most of the movements in exchange rates in the short run.

_____5. If purchasing power parity holds, the real exchange rate equals 1.

_____6. The quantity of domestic assets supplied increases as the exchange rate E_t rises.

_____7. The quantity of domestic assets demanded increases as the exchange rate E_t falls.

_____8. If the price level in the United States rises relative to the price levels in other countries, the dollar will appreciate.

_____9. Increasing trade barriers causes a country's currency to appreciate in the long run.

_____10. In the long run, as a country becomes more productive relative to other countries, its currency appreciates.

_____11. When export demand rises, the domestic currency appreciates.

_____12. When the domestic real interest rate rises, the domestic currency depreciates.

_____13. When the domestic interest rate rises because of an expected increase in inflation, the domestic currency depreciates.

_____14. When the exchange rate falls, there is expected future appreciation of the currency, and the quantity demanded of domestic assets decreases.

_____15. The weakness of the dollar in the late 1970s and the strength of the dollar in the early 1980s can be explained by movements in nominal interest rates but not movements in real interest rates.

MULTIPLE-CHOICE QUESTIONS

1. When the euro appreciates (holding everything else constant), then
    a. European chocolate sold in the United States becomes more expensive.
    b. American computers sold in Europe become more expensive.
    c. European watches sold in the United States become less expensive.
    d. American toothpaste sold in Europe becomes less expensive.
    e. (a) and (c)
    f. (a) and (d)

2. If the Mexican peso depreciates against the dollar, then
    a. it takes more dollars to buy a peso.
    b. it takes fewer pesos to buy a dollar.
    c. the dollar has appreciated against the peso.
    d. U.S. goods are less expensive in Mexico.

3. If transportation costs and trade barriers are low and the exchange rate is 0.80 euros per dollar, then according to the law of one price, a computer that costs $1,000 in the United States will cost
   a. 1,000 euros in Europe.
   b. 1,250 euros in Europe.
   c. 800 euros in Europe.
   d. 1,800 euros in Europe.

4. According to the theory of purchasing power parity, if the price level in the United States rises by 5% while the price level in Mexico rises by 6%, then the dollar will
   a. appreciate 1% relative to the peso.
   b. depreciate 1% relative to the peso.
   c. appreciate 5% relative to the peso.
   d. depreciate 5% relative to the peso.

5. Reasons why the theory of purchasing power parity might not fully explain exchange rate movements include
   a. differing monetary policies in different countries.
   b. changes in the prices of goods and services not traded internationally.
   c. changes in the domestic price level that exceed changes in the foreign price level.
   d. changes in foreign price levels that exceed changes in the domestic price level.

6. If the cost of a market basket of goods in the United States is $80, the cost of that same market basket in France is 90 euros, and the euro/dollar exchange rate is 0.77, the real exchange rate will be
   a. 0.68.
   b. 1.46.
   c. 1.
   d. 0.77.

7. If, in retaliation for "unfair" trade practices, Congress imposes a tariff on Chinese imports, but at the same time Chinese demand for American goods increases, then in the long run
   a. the Chinese yuan will appreciate relative to the dollar.
   b. the Chinese yuan will depreciate relative to the dollar.
   c. the dollar will depreciate relative to the yuan.
   d. it is not clear whether the dollar will appreciate or depreciate relative to the yuan.

8. If U.S. products become popular in Europe and exports of U.S. products to Europe increase, then in the long run,
   a. the euro per dollar exchange rate will fall.
   b. European goods will become more expensive in the United States.
   c. U.S. goods will become less expensive in Europe.
   d. the euro per dollar exchange rate will rise.

9. Holding everything else constant, an increase in the expected future exchange rate will cause the
   a. expected return on dollar assets in terms of foreign currency to rise.
   b. expected return on dollar assets in terms of foreign currency to fall.
   c. expected return on foreign assets in terms of dollars to rise.
   d. expected return on foreign assets in terms of dollars to fall.
   e. (a) and (c)
   f. (a) and (d)

10. All else held constant, an increase in the exchange rate E_t will lead to
    a. a rightward shift in the demand for domestic assets.
    b. a leftward shift in the demand for domestic assets.
    c. an increase in the quantity of domestic assets demanded.
    d. a decrease in the quantity of domestic assets demanded.

11. If the exchange rate is above the equilibrium exchange rate, then
    a. the quantity of domestic assets supplied is greater than the quantity of domestic assets demanded, and the domestic currency will appreciate.
    b. the quantity of domestic assets supplied is less than the quantity of domestic assets demanded, and the domestic currency will appreciate.
    c. the quantity of domestic assets supplied is greater than the quantity of domestic assets demanded, and the domestic currency will depreciate.
    d. the quantity of domestic assets supplied is less than the quantity of domestic assets demanded, and the domestic currency will depreciate.

12. A rise in the expected future exchange rate shifts the demand for domestic assets to the _____ and causes the domestic currency to_____.
    a. right; appreciate
    b. right; depreciate
    c. left; appreciate
    d. left; depreciate

13. A rise in the domestic interest rate shifts the demand for domestic assets to the _____ and causes the domestic currency to_____.
    a. right; appreciate
    b. right; depreciate
    c. left; appreciate
    d. left; depreciate

14. A rise in the foreign interest rate shifts the demand for domestic assets to the _____ and causes the domestic currency to_____.
    a. right; appreciate
    b. right; depreciate
    c. left; appreciate
    d. left; depreciate

15. If the domestic real interest rate rises, then
    a. the nominal interest rate will rise if there is no change in expected inflation.
    b. the return on domestic assets falls.
    c. the return on foreign deposits rises.
    d. the domestic currency depreciates.

16. If the exchange rate between the United States and Europe is $1.35/euro, and the exchange rate between Europe and Japan is 105 Yen/euro, in order for PPP to hold, the exchange rate between the United States and Japan should be
    a. $1 = 135 Yen.
    b. $1 = 105 Yen.
    c. $1 = 77.8 Yen.
    d. $1 = 100 Yen.

17. Exchange rates are volatile because
    a. central banks are constantly manipulating the value of foreign exchange.
    b. inflation rates are volatile.
    c. expectations about the variables that influence exchange rates change frequently.
    d. real interest rates are volatile.

18. If the central bank reduces short-term interest rates more than inflation expectations are reduced,
    a. the real interest rate decreases.
    b. demand for domestic assets increases.
    c. the domestic currency appreciates.
    d. imports will increase, and exports will decrease.

19. The rise in nominal interest rates in the United States in the 1970s caused the dollar to
    a. appreciate because the increase in nominal interest rates was due mainly to an increase in the real interest rate.
    b. appreciate because the increase in nominal interest rates was due mainly to an increase in expected inflation.
    c. depreciate because the increase in nominal interest rates was due mainly to an increase in the real interest rate.
    d. depreciate because the increase in nominal interest rates was due mainly to an increase in expected inflation.

20. Early models of exchange rate behavior could not predict substantial fluctuations in exchange rates because
    a. they assumed purchasing power parity always holds.
    b. they did not emphasize changing expectations.
    c. they assumed the supply of domestic assets is fixed.
    d. they did not take into account trade barriers.

Solutions

Terms and Definitions

_9_ appreciation

_3_ capital mobility

_2_ depreciation

_12_ effective exchange rate index

_5_ exchange rate

_13_ foreign exchange market

_6_ forward exchange rate

_8_ forward transaction

_11_ interest parity condition

_4_ law of one price

_15_ quotas

_16_ real exchange rate

_14_ spot exchange rate

_1_ spot transaction

_7_ tariffs

_10_ theory of purchasing power parity (PPP)

Practice Problems

1. a. 0.83

    b. 0.79

    c. 0.877

2. a. 45 pesos per bushel.

    b. 11 pesos per dollar.

    c. real exchange rate = 1.58

3.

Change in Factor	Response of the Exchange Rate
Domestic interest rate ↓	↓
Foreign interest rate ↓	↑
Domestic price level ↓	↑
Tariffs and quotas ↓	↓
Import demand ↓	↑
Export demand ↓	↓
Domestic productivity ↓	↓

4. a. A decrease in the domestic interest rate i^D causes the demand for dollar assets to shift left and the exchange rate to fall from E_1 to E_2.

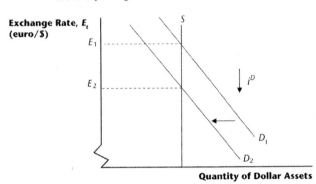

b. An increase in the foreign interest rate i^F causes the demand for dollar assets to shift left and the exchange rate to fall from E_1 to E_2.

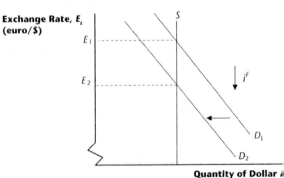

c. An increase in the expected future exchange rate E_{t+1} causes the demand for dollar assets to shift right and the exchange rate to rise from E_1 to E_2.

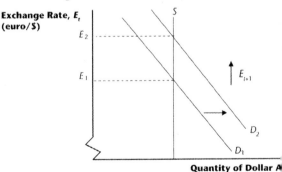

Short-Answer Questions

1. When the dollar depreciates, the price of imports (into the United States) rises.

2. When the dollar depreciates, the quantity of imports demanded by Americans will decline.

3. Both an increase in trade barriers and an increase in productivity will cause a country's currency to appreciate.

4. The demand for domestic assets is determined by the relative expected return of domestic assets.

5. A fall in the expected future exchange rate E^e_{t+1} will cause a depreciation of the currency.

6. When domestic real interest rates rise, the domestic currency appreciates.

7. When domestic interest rates rise due to an expected increase in inflation, the domestic currency depreciates.

8. When a country's currency appreciates, you get more foreign currency per domestic currency, making foreign goods less expensive to domestic consumers and imports increase. Likewise, the appreciation of the currency means foreigners get fewer dollars per foreign currency, making domestic goods more expensive to foreigners and decreases exports. With both exports decreasing and imports increasing, net exports decreases.

9. If two countries produce an identical good and transportation costs and trade barriers are very low, the price of the good should be the same throughout the world no matter which country produces it.

10. Two reasons: Foreign central banks cut their interest rates, which reduced the return on foreign assets, and there was a "flight to quality" as foreign investors bought U.S. Treasury securities.

Critical Thinking

a. An increase in domestic interest rates will cause the exchange rate to rise. A decrease in foreign interest rates will cause the exchange rate to rise and a decrease in expected import demand will cause the exchange rate to rise. Since all three factors cause the exchange rate to rise, their combined effect is unambiguous.

b. An increase in the domestic price level will cause the exchange rate to fall. Quotas will cause the exchange rate to rise, and an expected rise in productivity will cause the

exchange rate to rise as well. Since the impact of a rise in the domestic price level has the opposite effect as quotas and productivity, the overall effect of these changes is ambiguous.

c. An increase in export demand will cause the exchange rate to rise. A fall in the expected domestic price level will cause the exchange rate to rise and a fall in foreign interest rates will cause the exchange rate to rise as well. Since all three factors cause the exchange rate to rise, their combined effect is unambiguous.

True/False Questions

1. T
2. F
3. F
4. F
5. T
6. F
7. T
8. F
9. T
10. T
11. T
12. F
13. T
14. F
15. F

Multiple-Choice Questions

1. f
2. c
3. c
4. a
5. b
6. a.
7. b
8. d
9. f
10. d
11. c
12. a
13. a
14. d
15. a
16. c

17. c
18. a
19. d
20. b

18 The International Financial System[*]

Chapter Review

PREVIEW

This is the second chapter in a two chapter sequence on international finance and monetary policy. The previous chapter looked at the foreign exchange market. This chapter looks at the structure of the international financial system and how that structure affects monetary policy. This chapter also looks at the evolution of the international financial system during the past half century.

INTERVENTION IN THE FOREIGN EXCHANGE MARKET

Central banks regularly engage in *foreign exchange interventions* in order to influence exchange rates. Central banks hold *international reserves*, which are holdings of assets denominated in a foreign currency. When a central bank sells $1 billion of its international reserves, the monetary base declines by $1 billion, and when it buys $1 billion of foreign assets in order to add to its international reserves, the monetary base increases by $1 billion. A central bank can either allow the monetary base to change when it intervenes in the foreign exchange market (this is called an *unsterilized foreign exchange intervention*), or it can offset the effect of the intervention on the monetary base by conducting an offsetting open market operation (this is called a *sterilized foreign exchange intervention*).

An unsterilized intervention in which the central bank sells domestic currency to purchase foreign assets leads to a depreciation of the domestic currency because this results in lower domestic interest rates. An unsterilized intervention in which the central bank sells foreign assets to purchase domestic currency leads to an appreciation of the domestic currency due to higher domestic interest rates. A sterilized intervention leaves the monetary base unchanged and, therefore, has

---

[*]This is Chapter 21 in the 3rd ed.

almost no effect on the exchange rate. The table below shows the effect on the Federal Reserve's balance sheet due to a sterilized intervention of $1 billion.

Federal Reserve System

Assets		Liabilities	
Foreign assets (international reserves)	-$1 billion	Monetary base	0
Government bonds	+$1 billion		

BALANCE OF PAYMENTS

The *balance of payments* is the bookkeeping system for the movements of funds between a nation and foreign countries. It is comprised of three main parts: the *current account*, the *capital account*, and the *official reserve transactions balance*. The current account records the movements of funds in exchange for currently produced goods and services. The capital account records the movements of funds in exchange for capital transactions, and the official reserve transactions balance records the net change in international reserves. The sum of the current account and the capital account equals the official reserve transactions balance.

EXCHANGE RATE REGIMES IN THE INTERNATIONAL FINANCIAL SYSTEM

In a *fixed exchange rate regime*, the central bank pegs its currency to another currency (called the *anchor currency*). In a *floating exchange rate regime*, the value of a currency is allowed to fluctuate in value relative to all other currencies. In a *managed* (or *dirty*) *float regime*, a country influences (but does not strictly peg) the value of its currency relative to another currency.

Prior to World War I the world economy operated under a *gold standard*, which is a type of fixed exchange rate regime in which currencies are convertible into gold at a fixed rate. From 1945 until 1971, exchange rates between countries were fixed under the *Bretton Woods system*, where the convertibility of gold was in terms of U.S. dollars. Due to the dollar convertibility under Bretton Woods and the fact that the U.S. emerged from World War II as an economic powerhouse, the dollar was used as a *reserve currency*. Under Bretton Woods, the *International Monetary Fund* (IMF) and *World Bank* were created. The Bretton Woods system collapsed in 1971 because many smaller economies refused to follow the inflationary monetary policy of the United States.

Under a fixed exchange rate regime, the central bank offsets shifts in the demand for domestic assets in order to keep the exchange rate fixed, at some desired level called the par value of the exchange rate. For instance, if the exchange rate increases above the exchange rate peg, the central bank must intervene by selling domestic currency (increasing the monetary base) and buying international reserves. The effect is to reduce domestic interest rates, which decreases demand for domestic assets, and the currency depreciates until the exchange rate reaches par value.

This process works in reverse if the country is trying to maintain an overvalued exchange rate. In this case, the central bank must buy domestic currency and sell international reserves, which will lead to higher interest rates and an appreciation of the currency until the peg is restored. One problem with this approach is that by keeping the exchange rate overvalued, the central bank may run out of international reserves, which can lead to a *devaluation*.

One important implication of fixed exchange rate regimes is that smaller economies have to follow the same monetary policy as the larger economy to which the currency is pegged. More generally, monetary policy flexibility is limited by the *policy trilemma,* which implies that a country can have any two but not all three of the following characteristics: (1) free capital mobility, (2) a fixed exchange rate, and (3) an independent monetary policy.

The United States has chosen to pursue an independent monetary policy with free capital mobility and a free floating exchange rate. China has chosen to pursue a fixed exchange rate and independent monetary policy and instituted capital controls, which has allowed it to maintain the exchange rate at a low level. The advantage to this strategy for China is that it supports the country's exports sector and has allowed them to accumulate a large amount of international reserves to defend a potential future speculative attack. The disadvantage to this approach for China is that it now holds a large amount of low return U.S. treasury assets, the low yuan value has made it the subject of potential trade disputes with other countries, and the increase in international reserves has also resulted in a large increase in the monetary base, which is potentially inflationary for China.

One risk of maintaining a fixed exchange rate is a *balance of payments crisis*. A balance of payments crisis occurs when there is a decline in the demand for a country's currency that is large enough to make currency speculators believe that the central bank will deplete its international reserves. The expectation that the central bank will eventually allow the currency to depreciate leads to an even greater decline in the demand for the country's currency (as currency speculators sell assets denominated in the country's currency), which speeds the depletion of international reserves.

This happened to several countries who were members of the *Exchange Rate Mechanism (ERM),* a precursor to the present day European Monetary Union. In the case of the ERM, member countries' monetary policies were tied to that of Germany. Inflationary pressures caused the Bundesbank to raise interest rates. Member countries such as Spain, Italy, and Great Britain were faced with two choices: pursue contractionary policy in the face of a weak economy to maintain the peg or abandon the peg through devaluation. *Speculative attacks* against the countries' currencies depleted the central banks' international reserves and sped up the process of abandoning the peg. Similar speculative attacks have occurred in Mexico, East Asia, Brazil, and Argentina.

CAPITAL CONTROLS

Some politicians in emerging market countries have recently found capital controls particularly attractive. But controls on capital outflows suffer from several disadvantages. In particular, they may not actually be effective during a crisis due to efforts to evade the controls, capital flight may speed up as a result of controls, and corruption may limit the ability of governments to maintain strong controls on capital flows. Controls on capital inflows may be more effective, particularly at limiting lending booms and excessive risk taking, but also has disadvantages. Capital inflow controls can discourage foreign direct investment, create distortions in capital markets, and may also lead to corruption.

THE ROLE OF THE IMF

The *International Monetary Fund* (IMF) was originally established to make loans to countries participating in the Bretton Woods exchange rate system. That system was abandoned in 1971, and since then the IMF has taken on new roles. The IMF has served as the lender of last resort for countries experiencing balance of payments crises. Central banks in emerging markets sometimes lack credibility and are, therefore, unable to function as a lender of last resort. The IMF, serving as an international lender of last resort, has the credibility to prevent a balance of payments crisis from getting worse or spreading to other countries. But the IMF may also create a moral hazard problem. Countries may take on too much risk if they believe that the IMF will ultimately bail them out if they get into financial trouble. However, if the IMF does not intervene, the country may experience extreme hardship and political instability. Countries have avoided borrowing from the IMF in recent years because they did not want to be subjected to harsh austerity programs. As a result, the IMF was at risk of becoming irrelevant—until the global financial crisis. Many countries were affected, and the IMF was able to provide billions of dollars to countries that were basically sound, but under stress, to help stabilize their financial systems.

INTERNATIONAL CONSIDERATIONS AND MONETARY POLICY

There are many considerations in the conduct of monetary policy through the impact on exchange rates. When central banks intervene in the foreign exchange market, the monetary base and the level of international reserves can be affected. Moreover, intervention, even if somewhat temporary, means the central bank gives up control over monetary policy in order to maintain a desired peg. These issues are particularly relevant for most countries, other than the United States due to its reserve currency status.

Nonreserve currency countries can also experience sharp balance of payments fluctuations, which can create instability in domestic markets. Although balance of payments deficits can also be a problem for reserve currency countries such as the United States, they are not as problematic since it is not necessary to offset the balance of payments deficits by selling off large amounts of international reserves.

Exchange rate considerations are an important aspect of the conduct of monetary policy because an appreciation of the currency can hurt domestic industry. This has lead to pressure by many central banks around the world, particularly in emerging markets, to manipulate exchange rates to favorable terms. In the past, this has also lead to waves of protectionism by countries such as the United States to defend against a strong dollar that hurts American industry.

TO PEG OR NOT TO PEG: EXCHANGE-RATE TARGETING AS AN ALTERNATIVE MONETARY POLICY STRATEGY

Exchange rate targeting is an alternative to inflation targeting or the Federal Reserve's implied nominal anchor strategy. Advantages of exchange rate targeting are that it ties inflation expectations to the inflation rate in the anchor country, it helps reduce the time-inconsistency problem, and it is highly transparent. There are several serious disadvantages to exchange rate pegging. First, the targeting country can no longer pursue monetary policy to stabilize the domestic economy. Moreover, shocks that occur in the anchor country can be transmitted to the targeting country through pegging. In addition, pegging countries are susceptible to speculative attacks on its currency. Finally, pegging can have the perverse effect of actually weakening the accountability of policymakers by eliminating the signals that help constrain inflationary monetary policy in the first place through exchange rate movements.

Due to these disadvantages, industrialized economies typically are not better off targeting exchange rates as a monetary policy strategy unless (1) domestic monetary and political institutions are not conducive to good monetary policymaking, or (2) an exchange rate target can provide other benefits that are not related to monetary policy.

Emerging market economies with weak political and monetary institutions sometimes opt for a stricter form of fixed exchange rates by either adopting a *currency board* or *dollarization*. A currency board is a monetary policy strategy in which the domestic currency is backed 100% by a foreign currency. Currency boards have the advantage of solving the transparency and commitment problems inherent in an exchange rate targeting regime, and because of this are less subjected to speculative attacks, but have the disadvantage of loss of monetary policy independence, are subject to greater exposure to anchor country shocks, and there is no ability for lender-of-last resort functions by the central bank. Dollarization is when a country adopts the dollar as its official currency and provides a stronger commitment than a currency board. In particular, it completely eliminates the possibility of a speculative attack, but it has the same disadvantages as a currency board. In addition, under dollarization there is no ability to collect *seignorage* revenue because the country does not actually issue currency.

Helpful Hints

1. Unsterilized exchange rate interventions have exactly the same effect on the monetary base as open market operations. International reserves and government securities are both assets on the Fed's balance sheet. When the Fed conducts an open market purchase of securities, the monetary base increases. When the Fed purchases international reserves, the monetary base increases. When the Fed conducts an open market sale of government securities, the monetary base decreases. And when the Fed sells international reserves, the monetary base decreases as well.

2. Sterilized interventions do not affect the monetary base and only affect the composition of the central banks' balance sheet by altering the composition of its holdings between government securities and international reserves.

Terms and Definitions

Choose a definition for each key term.

Key Terms:

_____ anchor currency	_____ fixed exchange rate regime	_____ policy trilemma
_____ balance of payments	_____ floating exchange rate regime	_____ reserve currency
_____ balance-of-payments crisis	_____ foreign exchange intervention	_____ revaluation
_____ Bretton Woods System	_____ gold standard	_____ seignorage
_____ capital account	_____ impossible trinity	_____ special drawing rights (SDRs)
_____ capital controls	_____ International Monetary Fund (IMF)	_____ sterilized foreign exchange intervention
_____ currency board	_____ international reserves	_____ trade balance
_____ current account	_____ managed float regime (dirty float)	_____ unsterilized foreign exchange intervention
_____ devaluation	_____ official reserve transactions balance	_____ World Bank
_____ dollarization		_____ World Trade Organization (WTO)
_____ exchange rate peg		
_____ exchange rate targeting		

Definitions:

1. The difference between merchandise exports and imports

2. A regime in which central banks buy and sell their own currencies to keep their exchange rate fixed at a certain level

3. An account that shows international transactions involving currently produced goods and services

4. The term used to describe the currency that another currency is pegged to in a fixed exchange rate regime

5. Central bank holdings of assets denominated in foreign currencies

6. The bookkeeping system for recording all payments that have a direct bearing on the movement of funds between a country and foreign countries

7. A regime in which central banks allow their currencies to fluctuate in value against all other currencies

8. A regime under which currency is directly convertible into gold

9. The current account balance plus items in the capital account

10. A foreign exchange intervention that leads to a change in the monetary base

11. A regime in which central banks buy and sell their own currencies to influence (but not fix) the value of their currency relative to another country's currency

12. The international monetary system in use from 1945 to 1971 in which exchange rates were fixed and the U.S. dollar was freely convertible into gold

13. A foreign exchange crisis stemming from problems in a country's balance of payments

14. The adoption of a sound currency, like the U.S. dollar, as a country's money

15. A foreign exchange intervention that is offset by a domestic open market operation, which keeps the monetary base unchanged

16. The international organization created by the Bretton Woods agreement whose objective is to promote growth of world trade by making loans to countries experiencing balance-of-payments difficulties

17. A monetary regime in which the domestic currency is backed 100% by a foreign currency

18. The revenue a government receives by issuing money

19. An account that describes the flow of capital between the United States and other countries

20. An international financial transaction in which a central bank buys or sells currency to influence foreign exchange rates

21. Resetting the fixed value of a currency at a lower level

22. The inability of monetary policymakers to pursue simultaneously the goals of a fixed exchange rate, free capital mobility, and independent monetary policy

23. Fixing the value of the domestic currency to the value of another currency

24. A graphical interpretation of the policy trilemma

25. An organization that monitors rules for the conduct of trade between countries

26. Restrictions on the free movement of capital across borders

27. An international organization that provides long-term loans to assist developing countries to improve infrastructure that contributes to economic development

28. Resetting of the fixed value of a currency at a higher level

29. A currency such as the U.S. dollar which is used by other countries to denominate the assets they hold as international reserves

30. A monetary policy strategy designed to provide a strong nominal anchor to promote price stability through pegging of its currency

31. An IMF-issued paper substitute for gold that functions as international reserves

Problems and Short-Answer Questions

PRACTICE PROBLEMS

1. a. Show the T-account transactions for the case where the Federal Reserve buys $1 billion in foreign assets in exchange for $1 billion in currency.

Federal Reserve System

Assets	Liabilities

b. What is the impact of this transaction on the monetary base?

_____

_____

c. Show the T-account transactions for the case where the Federal Reserve buys $1 billion in foreign assets in exchange for $1 billion in deposits.

Federal Reserve System

Assets	Liabilities

d. What is the impact of this transaction on the monetary base?

_____

_____

e. Show the T-account transactions for the case where the Federal Reserve buys $1 billion in foreign assets in exchange for $1 billion in deposits. Assume that the Fed sterilizes this exchange rate intervention by selling $1 billion in government bonds.

Federal Reserve System

Assets	Liabilities

f. What is the impact of these transactions on the monetary base?

_____

_____

2. a. Draw the demand and supply curves for dollar assets and show what happens to the exchange rate when the Fed conducts an unsterilized sale of foreign assets.

Exchange Rate, *E*

Quantity of Dollar Assets

b. Explain what happens to the monetary base, international reserves, and domestic interest rates to affect the demand for domestic assets in response to this exchange rate intervention.

_____

_____

_____

_____

_____

_____

c. Draw the demand and supply curves for dollar assets and show what happens to the exchange rate when the Fed conducts a sterilized sale of foreign assets.

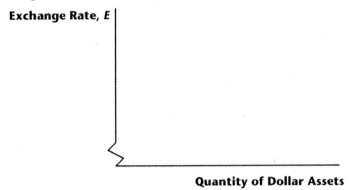

3. a. Draw the demand and supply for dollar assets and show what happens to the exchange rate if the return on foreign assets increases, everything else held constant.

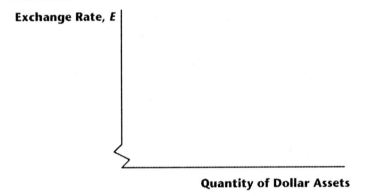

   b. Now assume that the central bank wishes to fix the exchange rate at its original level (the level it was at before the return on foreign assets increased). Describe the type of foreign exchange intervention that the central bank would undertake, and use the diagram you constructed for part (a) to show the effect of this intervention on the exchange rate.

   _____

   _____

   _____

   _____

4. Consider an emerging market country with a fixed exchange rate that experiences a sudden decrease in the demand for its domestic assets. Despite the decrease in demand, the central bank continues to keep the exchange rate at its original value (its value before the decrease in demand for its assets).
   a. Is this country's currency overvalued or undervalued?

   _____

b. Describe the exchange rate intervention that this country would undertake in order to keep its exchange rate at par.

_____

_____

c. What will happen to this country's international reserves as a result of this intervention?

_____

d. Under what circumstances would this country likely experience a speculative attack on its currency as a result of the decrease in demand for its domestic assets?

_____

_____

e. How would a speculative attack affect this county's balance of payments? How would this country's central bank likely respond to such an attack?

_____

_____

f. What possible action would the International Monetary Fund take to halt the speculative attack on this country's currency?

_____

_____

g. Explain how that action by the IMF might create a moral hazard problem for emerging market economies.

_____

_____

SHORT-ANSWER QUESTIONS

1. What is the difference between a sterilized exchange rate intervention and an unsterilized exchange rate intervention?

_____

_____

2. What is the difference between the current account and the trade balance?

    _____

    _____

3. Suppose the current account balance is –$725 billion and the capital account balance is $720 billion. Calculate the net change in government international reserves.

    _____

4. What role does an anchor currency play in a fixed exchange rate regime?

    _____

    _____

5. What is a dirty float exchange rate regime?

    _____

    _____

6. Under the Bretton Woods system, the U.S. dollar was the reserve currency. What did that mean?

    _____

    _____

    _____

7. When did the Bretton Woods system collapse? Why did the Bretton Woods system collapse?

    _____

    _____

    _____

    _____

    _____

8. Explain why economists are more likely to support controls on capital inflows rather than controls on capital outflows.

_____

_____

_____

_____

_____

_____

9. What are the advantages and disadvantages of using an exchange rate target to promote price stability?

_____

_____

_____

_____

10. Why might a country choose to dollarize instead of adopting a currency board? What is the main disadvantage of dollarization relative to a currency board?

_____

_____

Critical Thinking

The U.S. current account deficit has approached nearly $1 trillion in recent years.

1. What does a current account deficit of nearly $1 trillion dollars imply about foreign claims on U.S. wealth?

_____

_____

2. Is the United States increasing or decreasing its claims on foreign wealth?

_____

_____

3. How will the U.S. current account deficit affect the wealth of future Americans? Why?

_____

_____

Self-Test

TRUE/FALSE QUESTIONS

_____1. When the Fed sells international reserves in exchange for currency the monetary base increases by more than if it sells international reserves in exchange for funds drawn from a checking account.

_____2. Sterilized exchange rate interventions leave the monetary base unchanged.

_____3. An unsterilized intervention in which domestic currency is purchased by selling foreign assets leads to a drop in international reserves, a decrease in the money supply, and a depreciation of the domestic currency.

_____4. The U.S. current account deficit implies that foreigners' claims on U.S. assets are falling.

_____5. One disadvantage of the gold standard was that monetary policy was greatly influenced by the production of gold and discoveries of gold.

_____6. The Bretton Woods system was a managed float regime.

_____7. When the domestic currency is undervalued, the central bank must sell domestic currency to keep the exchange rate fixed, but as a result it gains international reserves.

_____8. The importance of gold in international financial transactions has grown in recent years.

_____9. Great Britain pulled out of the exchange rate mechanism in 1992 because it did not want to follow the same inflationary monetary policy as Germany.

_____10. Economists are more likely to favor controls on the outflow of capital rather than controls on the inflow of capital.

_____11. In recent years countries have avoided borrowing from the IMF because they did not want to be subjected to harsh austerity programs.

_____12. Under the current managed float exchange rate system, balance of payments considerations have a larger influence on monetary policy than do exchange rate considerations.

_____13. Special drawing rights are a paper substitute for gold that serve as international reserves.

_____14. Exchange rate targeting is sometimes used as a monetary policy strategy to achieve price stability.

_____15. An advantage of dollarization over a currency board is that it completely eliminates the possibility of a speculative attack on a country's currency.

MULTIPLE-CHOICE QUESTIONS

1. When a central bank buys its currency in the foreign exchange market,
    a. it loses international reserves.
    b. it acquires international reserves.
    c. the money supply increases.
    d. the quantity of international reserves remains unchanged.

2. An unsterilized intervention in which domestic currency is sold to purchase foreign assets leads to a
    a. loss of international reserves and a depreciation of the domestic currency.
    b. gain of international reserves and a depreciation of the domestic currency.
    c. loss of international reserves and an appreciation of the domestic currency.
    d. gain of international reserves and an appreciation of the domestic currency.

3. A sterilized intervention in which domestic currency is sold to purchase foreign assets leads to a
    a. loss of international reserves and a depreciation of the domestic currency.
    b. gain of international reserves and a depreciation of the domestic currency.
    c. loss of international reserves and almost no change in the exchange rate.
    d. gain of international reserves and almost no change in the exchange rate.

4. Which of the following will most likely lead to an increase in the exchange rate from 3.5 Brazilian real per dollar to 3.7 Brazilian real per dollar?
    a. The Brazilian central bank sells Brazilian government bonds.
    b. The Brazilian central bank buys international reserves.
    c. The U.S. Federal Reserve sells dollars.
    d. The U.S. Federal Reserve buys U.S. Treasury bonds.

5. Which of the following appears in the current account part of the balance of payments?
    a. a German's purchase of a share of Google stock
    b. a loan by a Swiss bank to an American corporation
    c. income earned by Barclay's Bank of London England from subsidiaries in the United States
    d. a purchase by the Federal Reserve System of a U.K. Treasury bond

6. If the current account balance is −$530 billion and the official reserve transactions balance is $10 billion, then the capital account balance is
    a. −$540 billion.
    b. $540 billion.
    c. −$520 billion.
    d. $520 billion.

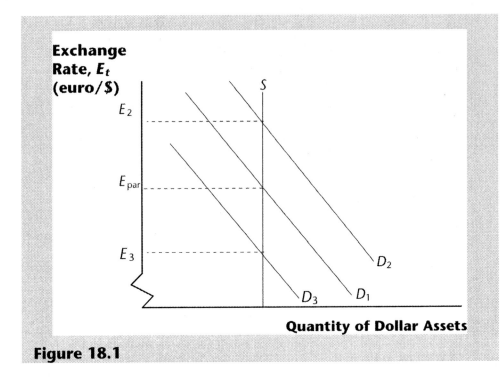

Exchange
Rate, E_t
(euro/$)

Figure 18.1

7. Starting from exchange rate E_{par} in Figure 18.1, an increase in the foreign interest rate, holding everything else constant, will
    a. shift the demand for domestic assets right causing the exchange rate to become overvalued.
    b. shift the demand curve for domestic assets right causing the exchange rate to become undervalued.
    c. shift the demand for domestic assets left causing the exchange rate to become overvalued.
    d. shift the demand curve for domestic assets left causing the exchange rate to become undervalued.

8. Starting from exchange rate E_{par} in Figure 18.1, an increase in the domestic interest rate, holding everything else constant, will
    a. shift the demand for domestic assets right, causing the exchange rate to become overvalued.
    b. shift the demand curve for domestic assets right, causing the exchange rate to become undervalued.
    c. shift the demand for domestic assets left, causing the exchange rate to become overvalued.
    d. shift the demand curve for domestic assets left, causing the exchange rate to become undervalued.

9. In a fixed exchange rate regime, when the domestic currency becomes overvalued, in order to keep the exchange rate at par the central bank must
    a. sell domestic currency, which leads to a gain of international reserves.
    b. sell domestic currency, which leads to a loss of international reserves.
    c. buy domestic currency, which leads to a gain of international reserves.
    d. buy domestic currency, which leads to a loss of international reserves.

10. If there is perfect capital mobility, then a sterilized exchange rate intervention
    a. can only be used for devaluation.
    b. can only be used for revaluation.
    c. is much more effective than an unsterilized exchange rate intervention.
    d. cannot keep the exchange rate at par.

11. The Bretton Woods system of fixed exchange rates collapsed because
    a. inflationary U.S. monetary policy forced other countries to lose international reserves, which led to inflation in those countries as well.
    b. inflationary U.S. monetary policy forced other countries to gain international reserves, which led to inflation in those countries as well.
    c. inflationary U.S. monetary policy forced other countries to lose international reserves, which led to recession in those countries.
    d. inflationary U.S. monetary policy forced other countries to gain international reserves, which led to recession in those countries.

12. An important advantage for a reserve currency country is that
    a. it has more control of its monetary policy than nonreserve currency countries.
    b. it will always have a balance of payments surplus.
    c. it has more control over its exchange rate than nonreserve countries.
    d. it will experience lower inflation than nonreserve currency countries.

13. When a country experiences a speculative attack on its currency, it
    a. loses international reserves and may be forced to revalue its currency.
    b. gains international reserves and may be forced to revalue its currency.
    c. loses international reserves and may be forced to devalue its currency.
    d. gains international reserves and may be forced to devalue its currency.

14. A central bank that wants to _____ its currency is likely to adopt a _____ monetary policy.
    a. strengthen; more contractionary
    b. strengthen; less contractionary
    c. weaken; less expansionary
    d. weaken; neutral

15. When a currency depreciates, then exports become
    a. more expensive for foreigners to purchase, and imports become less expensive for domestic consumers to purchase.
    b. less expensive for foreigners to purchase, and imports become less expensive for domestic consumers to purchase.
    c. more expensive for foreigners to purchase, and imports become more expensive for domestic consumers to purchase.
    d. less expensive for foreigners to purchase, and imports become more expensive for domestic consumers to purchase.

16. Countries experiencing a foreign exchange crisis, such as Mexico, Brazil, and Thailand did in the 1990s,
    a. are also experiencing a balance of payments crisis.
    b. may turn to the World Bank for help.
    c. are gaining international reserves.
    d. can revalue their currencies to end the crisis.

17. Since 1994, the IMF has stepped into the role of lender-of-last-resort because
    a. central banks in emerging markets lack experience with open market operations.
    b. it has been authorized by the world trade organization to perform this function.
    c. it is less likely to create a moral hazard problem than the World Bank.
    d. central banks in emerging markets often lack credibility as inflation fighters.

18. A case can be made for controls on capital inflows because capital inflows
    a. can lead to a lending boom and encourage excessive risk taking.
    b. never go to financing productive investments.
    c. do more harm than good.
    d. are easier to control than capital outflows.

19. A disadvantage of exchange rate targeting is that
    a. it is likely to cause monetary policy to be time inconsistent.
    b. the exchange rate is not a nominal anchor.
    c. the central bank loses the ability to conduct independent monetary policy.
    d. the exchange rate is more difficult to target than either inflation or the money supply.

20. The main difference between a currency board and dollarization is that
    a. with a currency board a country gives up seignorage, but with dollarization it does not.
    b. with dollarization a country gives up seignorage, but with a currency board it does not.
    c. with dollarization a country's currency is 100% backed by the dollar, but with a currency board it is less than 100% backed by the dollar.
    d. a currency board is a firmer commitment to a fixed exchange rate than dollarization.

Solutions

Terms and Definitions

Practice Problems

1. a. The T-account when the Fed buys $1 billion in foreign assets in exchange for $1 billion in currency:

   Federal Reserve System

Assets	Liabilities
Foreign assets (international reserves) +$1 billion	Currency in circulation +$1 billion

   b. The monetary base will increase by $1 billion as a result of this foreign exchange transaction.

   c. The T-account when the Fed buys $1 billion in foreign assets in exchange for $1 billion in deposits:

   Federal Reserve System

Assets	Liabilities
Foreign assets (international reserves) +$1 billion	Deposits with the Fed (reserves) +$1 billion

   d. The monetary base will increase by $1 billion as a result of this foreign exchange transaction.

   e. The T-account when the Fed buys $1 billion in foreign assets in exchange for $1 billion in deposits, and then sells $1 billion in government bonds to sterilize the exchange rate intervention:

   Federal Reserve System

Assets	Liabilities
Foreign assets (international reserves) +$1 billion Government bonds −$1 billion	Monetary base (reserves) $0 billion

f. Sterilized exchange rate interventions leave the monetary base unchanged.

2. a. The long-run and short-run effects of an unsterilized sale of foreign assets.

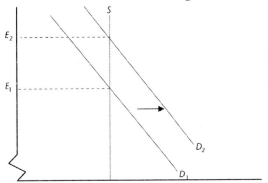

Quantity of Dollar Assets

b. An unsterilized sale of foreign assets reduces the monetary base, which leads to a rise in the domestic interest rate. The increase in the domestic interest rate acts to push the exchange rate up (from E_1 to E_2).

c. A sterilized intervention in the foreign exchange market leaves the monetary base unchanged, and so the interest rate and price level remain unchanged as well. As a consequence, the demand for dollar assets remains unchanged and the exchange rate remains unchanged as shown below.

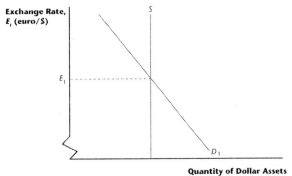

Quantity of Dollar Assets

3. a. An increase in the return on foreign assets will shift the demand curve for dollar assets to the left, and the exchange rate will fall from E_1 to E_2.

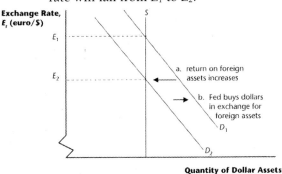

Quantity of Dollar Assets

b. To keep the exchange rate at its original level (E_1) the Fed would buy dollars in exchange for foreign assets. This transaction would reduce the monetary base, which would cause the domestic interest rate to rise, which would in turn cause the exchange rate to rise back to E_1 as the demand for dollar assets shifts back to D_1.

4. a. overvalued

b. The central bank would need to purchase domestic currency to keep the exchange rate fixed at par.

c. It would lose international reserves.

d. If currency traders fear that the central bank will run out of foreign assets, then they may mount a speculative attack on the currency.

e. A speculative attack on a country's currency will lead to a balance of payments deficit. The central bank will respond by raising interest rates.

f. The IMF may provide loans to the country in order to shore up its international reserves.

g. Countries may come to expect that the IMF will bail them out and as a result they may use macroeconomic policies that are more likely to lead to a balance of payments deficit.

Short-Answer Questions

1. In the case of a sterilized exchange rate intervention, the central bank offsets the intervention with an open market operation so that the monetary base remains unchanged. In the case of an unsterilized intervention, the central bank does not offset the intervention with an open market operation, and so the monetary base does change.

2. The current account balance includes everything that is included in the trade balance plus three additional categories of net receipts: investment income, service transactions, and unilateral transfers.

3. The net change in government international reserves = –$5 billion.

4. The anchor currency is the currency that other currencies are pegged to.

5. A dirty float (also called a managed float) is an exchange rate regime in which the central bank intervenes to keep the exchange rate within a certain range (rather than keeping the exchange rate fixed at a particular value).

6. The other countries (other than the United States) that fixed their exchange rates under the Bretton Woods System held international reserves denominated in dollars.

7. The Bretton Woods System broke down in 1971 when the United States pursued inflationary monetary policies. In order to maintain fixed exchange rates with the United States, other countries would have had to pursue inflationary policies as well. Countries with balance of payments surpluses refused to adopt inflationary policies, and so they abandoned the fixed exchange rate system.

8. Evidence suggests that controls on capital outflows are seldom effective during a crisis and may even increase capital flight. Controls on capital outflows often lead to corruption, and controls on capital outflows may keep the government from undertaking meaningful reforms, which would prevent capital outflows. Economists are more likely to support controls on capital inflows reasoning that if speculative capital cannot come in, then it cannot go out quickly.

9. The advantages of an exchange rate target are: The exchange rate is a nominal anchor; an exchange rate target provides an automatic rule for conducting monetary policy; and an exchange rate target is simple, clear and easily understood by the public. The disadvantages of exchange rate targeting are: The country loses independent monetary policy; economic shocks in the anchor-currency country are easily transmitted to the domestic economy; and it opens the country to the possibility of a speculative-attack on its currency.

10. Dollarization is a firmer commitment to a fixed exchange rate than a currency board because a currency board can be abandoned. Countries that suffer credibility problems may therefore choose dollarization because it sends a strong signal that the country is committed to low inflation. The main disadvantage of dollarization is that the country gives up the opportunity to earn revenue from money creation, which is called seignorage.

Critical Thinking

1. Foreign claims on U.S. wealth are increasing.
2. U.S. claims on foreign wealth are decreasing.
3. At some point, America will have to pay back those claims on its wealth and that will make Americans poorer.

True/False Questions

1. F
2. T
3. F
4. F
5. T
6. F
7. T
8. F
9. F
10. F
11. T
12. F
13. T
14. T
15. T

Multiple-Choice Questions

1. a
2. b
3. d

4. b
5. c
6. b
7. c
8. b
9. d
10. d
11. b
12. a
13. c
14. a
15. d
16. a
17. d
18. a
19. c
20. b

19 Quantity Theory, Inflation, and the Demand for Money[*]

Chapter Review

PREVIEW

Earlier chapters looked at how the Federal Reserve, the public, and commercial banks all influence the money supply. This chapter looks at what determines money demand; putting money supply and demand together in order to study how money affects inflation and production in the economy is known as *monetary theory*. The central question in monetary theory is whether and to what extent money demand is affected by interest rates.

QUANTITY THEORY OF MONEY

The quantity theory of money is based on the *equation of exchange*: $M \times V = P \times Y$, where M is the quantity of money, P is the price level, Y is aggregate income and V is the *velocity of money*. The velocity of money is the average number of times per year a dollar is spent in buying the total amount of goods and services in the economy. The equation of exchange is simply an identity that the total amount of spending in a year ($P \times Y$) equals the total amount of money (M) multiplied times the number of times that money is spent (V).

Irving Fisher, an early twentieth century economist, reasoned that velocity was constant in the short run due to institutional and technological features of the economy. With the assumption that velocity is reasonably constant in the short run, the equation of exchange becomes the *quantity theory of money,* which states that nominal income is determined solely by movements in the quantity of money. If V is fixed and M doubles, $P \times Y$ will double as well. The quantity theory of money is not only a theory about how money affects the economy, but it is also a theory of money demand. Rearranging the equation gives:

$$M = (1/V) \times PY \text{ or } M^d = k \times PY$$

---

[*]This is Chapter 22 in the 3rd ed.

Since V is assumed constant, k is constant as well, so nominal income determines money demand. According to the quantity theory of money, interest rates play no role in determining the quantity of money demanded.

The early classical economists went one step further with this theory by assuming that wages and prices were perfectly flexible, implying that the level of output Y was always at full-employment. This assumption implies that movements in the price level result solely from changes in the quantity of money. Moreover, the quantity theory of money can help explain movements in inflation by transforming it into growth rates:

$$\%\Delta M + \%\Delta V = \%\Delta P + \%\Delta Y$$

which implies that if velocity is constant, then $\pi = \%\Delta M - \%\Delta Y$.

The quantity theory of money holds well in the long run, as there is a strong relationship between long-run inflation rates and money growth. However, short-run movements in inflation are not predicted well by money growth, so the quantity theory of money is not supported in the short run.

BUDGET DEFICITS AND INFLATION

Another possible source of inflation is government budget deficits. The government faces a budget constraint: $DEF = G - T = \Delta MB + \Delta B$, where DEF is the government budget deficit, G is government spending, T is tax revenue, ΔMB is the change in the monetary base, and ΔB is the change in government bonds held by the public.

According to this *government budget constraint,* the government can finance a deficit by increasing bonds (borrowing from the public) or increasing the monetary base. In the United States as well as many other countries, the government (Congress, the president, and the U.S. Treasury) cannot simply increase the monetary base to finance the deficit. The only option for the government is to issue bonds to finance the deficit. If the central bank decides to conduct an open market purchase of those bonds, then bonds are removed from the hands of the public, and the monetary base increases. This method of financing the deficit is called *monetizing the debt.* Budget deficits in and of themselves do not lead to persistent inflation. But persistent budget deficits that are financed by money creation will lead to a sustained inflation.

Countries generally resort to monetizing their debt when they do not have sufficient access to capital markets or they face huge budget deficits, which can lead to *hyperinflations,* or periods of extremely high inflation of more than 50% per month. Neither describes the United States; however, hyperinflations in both poor and developed economies have occurred over the past century.

KEYNESIAN THEORIES OF MONEY DEMAND

Keynes assumed that there are three motives for holding money: the transactions motive, the precautionary motive, and the speculative motive. The transactions and precautionary motives are both positively related to income. The more income you earn, the more money you will hold for transactions (the transactions motive), and the more money you will hold to make unexpected purchases (the precautionary motive). These two motives for holding money alone are not too different from the classical view of money demand because they are both related to income. But Keynes went one step further by assuming that there is a third motive for holding money called the speculative motive. The speculative motive assumes that people also hold money as a store of wealth, which simply means that people treat money as an asset in their financial portfolio.

To keep things simple, Keynes assumed that there are only two types of assets that people can choose from: bonds and money. Bonds earn interest, and money does not. At first you might think, why would anyone ever hold money when bonds pay interest? But recall from earlier in the text that the total return on a bond is comprised of the interest payment and the capital gain or loss. When the interest rate is below normal, people naturally expect it to rise, and so they will hold money because if they purchased a bond, they would experience a capital loss once the interest rate does rise (which would cause the price of the bond to fall). When the interest rate is above normal, the opposite happens. People will expect the interest rate to fall, so they will hold bonds and not money (at least for this purpose, they will still hold money for transactions and as a precaution against unexpected purchases). In sum, according to the speculative motive for holding money, the demand for money is negatively related to the interest rate. When the interest rate falls, people hold more money and vice versa.

This was an important innovation in the theory of money demand because, unlike the classical theory, it provided a rationale for why the demand for money depends on the interest rate. Other economists, such as James Tobin and William Baumol, later provided rationale for why the transactions and precautionary motives would be inversely affected by the interest rate. Combing all three motives for holding money, the Keynesian money demand function is $M^d/P = L(i, Y)$, where M^d/P represents *real money balances*. If we substitute Keynes's money demand function into the equation of exchange, we get the following expression for the velocity of money: $V = Y/L(i, Y)$. This equation demonstrates how the Keynesian money demand function can be used to explain why velocity is not constant. When the interest rate rises, $L(i, Y)$ falls and velocity rises. Since interest rates experience substantial fluctuations, velocity experiences substantial fluctuations. Keynes's theory of money demand is called *liquidity preference theory*.

PORTFOLIO THEORIES OF MONEY DEMAND

Since money is an asset, it can be viewed in a similar context to the theory of portfolio choice. This approach supports the conclusion that real money balances are positively related to income and negatively related to interest rates.

There are other factors that affect the relative return on money versus other assets. For example, as wealth rises, money demand is likely to increase; however, this effect is likely to be small because money is a *dominated asset*. As the riskiness of alternative assets increases, people are more likely to want to hold more money and less in alternative assets. However, higher inflation can be viewed as increasing the riskiness of holding money, and so people may wish to hold less money and more *inflation hedges*, such as TIPS, gold, and real estate. Finally, as the liquidity of alternative assets increases, demand for money will fall.

EMPIRICAL EVIDENCE ON THE DEMAND FOR MONEY

The more sensitive money demand is to the interest rate, the less aggregate demand is determined by the quantity of money. The extreme case, where money demand is infinitely responsive to changes in interest rates, is called a *liquidity trap*. When the economy is in a liquidity trap, changes in the quantity of money have no effect on aggregate spending. The empirical evidence suggests that money demand is somewhat but not infinitely responsive to interest rates. There is no evidence of a liquidity trap where money demand is infinitely responsive to interest rates; however, there is evidence of a liquidity trap of a different sort. When the interest rate hits zero, monetary policy becomes ineffective because interest rates cannot go below zero. Japan experienced this type of liquidity trap in recent years, as well as the United States during the global financial crisis, which explains the need for nonconventional monetary policy during such episodes.

The demand for money appeared to be stable through the early 1970s. Since that time, money demand has become unstable and velocity has been hard to predict due to the rapid pace of financial innovation. This implies that setting rigid money supply targets in order to control aggregate spending may not be an effective way to conduct monetary policy and, consequently, helps explain the shift to controlling interest rates instead.

Helpful Hints

1. Does money demand depend on the interest rate? The early classical economists said no. Keynes said yes. Why does it matter? The more sensitive the demand for money is to the interest rate, the less influence the Fed has over aggregate spending. What is the evidence? Interest rates do influence money demand, but the demand for money is not extremely (or infinitely) sensitive to interest rates, which means the Fed can influence, but not completely control, aggregate spending.

2. When governments are unable to raise taxes, there are two ways of financing deficit spending: through issuance of bonds or increasing the monetary base. Issuance of bonds does not directly affect the monetary base and so is not inflationary. However, the extent to which governments are able to monetize the debt can be inflationary if deficits and monetization of the debt are persistent.

Terms and Definitions

Choose a definition for each key term.

Key Terms:

_8_ demand for money

_11_ dominated assets

_1_ equation of exchange

_14_ government budget constraint

_4_ hyperinflations

_9_ inflation hedges

_7_ liquidity preference theory

_13_ liquidity trap

_5_ monetary theory

_12_ monetizing the debt

_15_ payment technology

_10_ printing money

_2_ quantity theory of money

_6_ real money balances

_3_ velocity of money

Definitions:

1. The equation $MV = PY$, which relates nominal income to the quantity of money

2. The theory that nominal income is determined solely by movements in the quantity of money

3. The rate of turnover of money

4. Periods of extreme inflation in which the inflation rate exceeds 50% per month

5. The theory that relates changes in the quantity of money to changes in economic activity

6. The quantity of money in real terms

7. John Maynard Keynes's theory of the demand for money

8. The quantity of money people want to hold

9. Assets whose real returns are affected less than that of money as inflation varies

10. The process by which monetizing the debt occurs

11. Any assets that are just as safe as other assets, but have a lower return

12. Method of financing government spending where government debt issued to finance government spending is removed from the hands of the public and replaced by high-powered money

13. Extreme case of ultrasensitivity of money demand to interest rates in which conventional monetary policy has no direct effect on aggregate spending

14. The requirement that the government budget deficit equal the sum of the change in the monetary base and the change in government bonds held by the public

15. New methods for payment

Problems and Short-Answer Questions

$$MV = PY$$

Money Supply ↑   NOMINAL (New) GDP (output)

PRACTICE PROBLEMS

1. a. Suppose nominal GDP is $15 trillion and the quantity of money is $5 trillion. Calculate the velocity of money.

_____

b. Now suppose that velocity is 5 and nominal GDP is $25 trillion. Calculate the quantity of money.

_____

c. What assumption transforms the equation of exchange into the quantity theory of money?

_____

d. According to the quantity theory of money, what will happen to the price level if the money supply increases from $1 trillion to $1.3 trillion?

_____

e. According to the quantity theory of money, what will the demand for money be if nominal income is $20 trillion and velocity is 2?

_____

2. Suppose that people have come to expect that interest rates are normally 2% but interest rates are currently 4%.
   a. What will people expect to happen to the price of bonds as the interest rate returns to normal?

   _____

   b. What will happen to the return on bonds as the interest rate returns to normal?

   _____

   c. According to Keynes, what will happen to the demand for money if interest rates are above normal? Why?

   _____

   _____

3. Suppose the growth rate of the money supply is 6%, velocity is constant, and real GDP grows at 4% per year on average.
   a. What does the quantity theory of money predict will be the inflation rate?

   _____

   b. Suppose the money growth rate increases to 15%. What does the quantity theory of money predict will be the inflation rate?

   _____

c. What does your answers to parts (a) and (b) say about the relationship between high rates of money growth and inflation?

_____

_____

d. Based on your response to part (c), would you expect this relationship to hold in the short run, the long run, or both? Briefly explain.

_____

_____

4. a. What are three basic ways that an economy can finance government spending?

_____

b. Which of the three would most likely lead to hyperinflation?

_____

c. Why is it unlikely that the option described in your answer to part (b) would occur in the United States?

_____

_____

d. What circumstances related to the three basic ways to finance government spending occurred in the case of Zimbabwe that led to hyperinflation?

_____

_____

SHORT-ANSWER QUESTIONS

1. What reasoning did Irving Fisher use to argue that the velocity of money is constant?

_____

_____

2. Why do classical economists believe that the level of output in the economy in normal times is at full employment?

   _____

   _____

3. Is the velocity of money constant?

   _____

   _____

4. According to Keynes, what are the three motives for holding money? Which of these motives is related to the interest rate?

   _____

   _____

5. What is the difference between nominal money balances and real money balances, and what was Keynes's argument for why people desire to hold a certain level of real money balances?

   _____

   _____

6. Why do people hold precautionary money balances, and how are those money balances related to income?

   _____

   _____

7. What does Keynes's liquidity preference theory predict about the relationship between interest rates and the velocity of money?

   _____

   _____

8. Why has the apparent instability of money demand led to a reduced focus on the money supply when conducting monetary policy?

   _____

   _____

9. According to the theory of portfolio choice, what would happen to money demand if wealth increases and inflation also increases substantially?

   _____

   _____

10. When payment technologies improve, what does the theory of portfolio choice predict will happen to money demand? Why?

_____

_____

Critical Thinking

Suppose you read in the paper that the Fed just increased the money supply by 20%. You decide to figure out what this means for the economy, but having just learned about three possible money demand functions, you know that your answer will depend on how money demand responds to the interest rate.

1. Analyze how this increase in the supply of money will affect the economy if the demand for money is the
   a. quantity theory of money demand.

   _____

   _____

   b. Keynesian liquidity preference function when there is a liquidity trap.

   _____

   _____

   c. Keynesian liquidity preference function but the interest sensitivity of money demand is somewhere between ultrasensative and completely insensitive.

   _____

   _____

2. Which one of your descriptions of the effect of the increase in the money supply on the economy is closest to what would likely happen in the real world? Why?

   _____

   _____

   _____

   _____

3. What does you answer to question 2 imply about the Fed's ability to influence nominal income?

_____

_____

_____

_____

Self-Test

TRUE/FALSE QUESTIONS

_____1. A central question in monetary theory is whether, and to what extent, the quantity of money demanded is affected by changes in interest rates.

_____2. Classical economists believed that wages and prices were inflexible.

_____3. The most important implication of the quantity theory of money is that interest rates affect the demand for money.

_____4. If velocity is constant and money growth and real GDP both grow by 5%, then inflation will be 5%.

_____5. Monetizing the debt leads to a decrease in the monetary base.

_____6. The demand for money and the velocity of money are positively related.

_____7. According to the speculative demand for money, people will hold money instead of bonds when the interest rate is above normal.

_____8. The velocity of money has become more volatile since the early 1970s.

_____9. It is not clear whether the speculative demand for money even exists because Treasury securities pay interest and are risk free.

_____10. The quantity theory supports a strong connection between money growth and inflation in the short run but not the long run.

_____11. During inflationary periods, assets such as TIPS, gold, and real estate are used as inflation hedges.

_____12. Government budget deficits always lead to inflation.

_____13. The more sensitive the demand for money is to interest rates, the more predictable velocity will be.

_____14. A liquidity trap exists when the demand for money is ultrasensitive to interest rates.

_____15. The fact that money demand has become unstable implies that setting rigid money supply targets to control aggregate spending in the economy may be an effective way to conduct monetary policy.

MULTIPLE-CHOICE QUESTIONS

1. The velocity of money is best defined as
    a. the average real money balances that are held in a month.
    b. the average number of times per year that a dollar is spent buying aggregate output.
    c. the average amount of money that a person spends over one year.
    d. the average number of months that a currency bill circulates.

2. According to the quantity theory of money, if the quantity of money falls by one-third,
    a. output will decline by one-third.
    b. velocity will decline by one-third.
    c. the price level will decline by one-third.
    d. output will decline by one-sixth, and the price level will decline by one-sixth.

3. Classical economists believed that velocity could be regarded as constant in the short run because
    a. the opportunity cost of holding money was close to zero.
    b. the historical data on velocity showed that it was constant.
    c. financial innovation tended to offset changes in interest rates.
    d. institutions that affect the way individuals conduct transactions change slowly over time.

4. If real income is $5 trillion, the price level is 2, and the velocity of money is 4, then the quantity of money is
    a. $8 trillion.
    b. $2 trillion.
    c. $2.5 trillion.
    d. $20 trillion.

    $$\frac{5 \times 2}{4} = \frac{10}{4} = 2.5$$

5. The classical economists made the following two assumptions in order to transform the equation of exchange into the quantity theory of money:
    a. velocity is constant, and wages and prices are sticky.
    b. velocity is variable, and wages and prices are sticky.
    c. velocity is constant, and wages and prices are flexible.
    d. velocity is variable, and wages and prices are flexible.

6. According to the quantity theory of money, movements in _____ result solely from changes in _____.
    a. the price level; interest rates
    b. real output; interest rates
    c. the price level; the quantity of money
    d. real output; the quantity of money

7. According to the quantity theory of money demand, if the price level is 1.2, real income is $8 trillion, and velocity is 2, then the demand for money will be
   a. $6.67 trillion.
   b. $16 trillion.
   c. $4 trillion.
   d. $4.8 trillion.

$$\frac{8 \times 1.2}{2} = 4.8$$

8. According to Keynes's liquidity preference theory, the three motives for holding money are
   a. unit of account, store of value, and medium of exchange.
   b. transactions, precautionary, and speculative.
   c. positive, normative, and speculative.
   d. transactions, precautionary, and liquidity.

9. Keynes's _____ motive states that people hold real money balances as a cushion against unexpected need.
   a. quantity
   b. speculative
   c. precautionary
   d. transactions

10. Keynes's liquidity preference theory explains why velocity is expected to rise when
    a. income increases.
    b. wealth increases.
    c. brokerage commissions increase.
    d. interest rates increase.

11. Keynes's liquidity preference theory implies that velocity
    a. has substantial fluctuations.
    b. is zero in the long-run.
    c. is constant.
    d. is not constant but is predictable.

12. According to Keynes's speculative demand for money, if the interest rate is above normal, people will hold
    a. money because they anticipate capital losses on bonds.
    b. bonds because they anticipate capital gains on bonds.
    c. money because they anticipate capital gains on bonds.
    d. bonds because the anticipate capital losses on bonds.

13. Periods of high money growth and low inflation, such as during 2008–2009 indicate
    a. cross-country support for the long-run view of the quantity theory of money.
    b. that prices and wages are flexible.
    c. a breakdown in the quantity theory of money in the short run.
    d. that inflation is always and everywhere a monetary phenomenon.

14. If a government deficit is financed by an increase in bond holdings by the public, the monetary base
    a. increases.
    b. decreases.
    c. could increase or decrease.
    d. does not change.

15. If government spending is $7 trillion and tax revenue is $4 trillion,
    a. the monetary base must increase $3 trillion.
    b. the government must immediately raise $3 trillion in new taxes to cover the shortfall.
    c. the government can monetize the debt by issuing $3 trillion in new bonds, then having the central bank conduct an equivalent open market purchase of bonds.
    d. hyperinflation will occur.

16. Which of the following is illustrative of the speculative motive?
    a. Money is convenient for purchasing goods and services.
    b. Money can be used to buy goods at a later date for unexpected purchases.
    c. Money balances held are proportional to income, according to Keynes.
    d. Money earns no interest, so can be costly to hold.

17. If both stocks and bonds became more risky, you would expect
    a. the demand for money to increase.
    b. the demand for money to decrease.
    c. the demand for gold to decrease.
    d. real money balances to remain constant.

18. When nominal interest rates hit zero,
    a. a liquidity trap has occurred.
    b. the demand for money is completely flat.
    c. nonconventional monetary policy must be used instead.
    d. all of the above are true.

19. Empirical evidence on money demand shows that money demand is
    a. ultrasensitive to interest rates.
    b. unaffected by changes in interest rates.
    c. highly volatile but predictable.
    d. somewhere in between ultrasensitive and unresponsive to changes in interest rates.

20. Since the early 1970s, money demand has become _____, which implies that the best way to conduct monetary policy is by targeting _____.
    a. stable; interest rates
    b. unstable; interest rates.
    c. stable; the quantity of money
    d. unstable; the quantity of money

Solutions

Terms and Definitions

 8 demand for money

11 dominated assets

 1 equation of exchange

14 government budget constraint

 4 hyperinflations

 9 inflation hedges

 7 liquidity preference theory

13 liquidity trap

 5 monetary theory

12 monetizing the debt

15 payment technology

10 printing money

 2 quantity theory of money

 6 real money balances

 3 velocity of money

Practice Problems

1. a. Velocity = 3
    b. The quantity of money = $5 trillion
    c. Velocity is constant.
    d. The price level will rise by 30%.
    e. The demand for money will be $10 trillion.

2. a. The price of bonds will rise as the interest rate falls back to normal.
    b. The return on bonds will increase.
    c. If interest rates are above normal, people will hold bonds instead of money because they will expect the interest rate to fall back to normal in the future, and as interest rates fall back to normal, the return on bonds will increase.

3. a. $\pi = 6 - 4 = 2\%$
    b. $\pi = 15 - 4 = 11\%$
    c. As the money growth rate increases, the inflation rate will rise, implying a direct connection between money growth and inflation.
    d. This relationship will hold in the long run, but not the short run. This is because wages and prices are perfectly flexible in the long run, but is not a good assumption in the short run. As a

consequence, inflation and output behavior is not well explained by the quantity theory of money in the short run.

4. a. Government spending can be supported by higher taxes, issuance of bonds (borrowing from the public), or by increases in the monetary base.
    b. Increases in the monetary base through printing money are likely to lead to hyperinflation because the quantity theory of money implies high money growth would lead to high inflation in the long run.
    c. This is unlikely because the U.S. government does not have the ability to issue currency to raise the monetary base. However, the Federal Reserve can monetize the debt by buying up bonds that are held by the public, but it cannot buy these bonds directly from the government, and so this impedes the ability for the government to simply print money to support its spending.
    d. In Zimbabwe, the government was unable to raise tax revenues due to the poor economy and weak tax laws. And due to distrust of the government, it was unable to issue bonds or borrow from the public or international institutions. The only option was to print money to pay for spending, which led to hyperinflation.

Short-Answer Questions

1. Irving Fisher reasoned that velocity is determined by the institutions in an economy that affect the way individuals conduct transactions, and those institutions evolve slowly over time. Therefore, velocity is roughly constant.

2. Classical economists believed that wages and prices were perfectly flexible, and as a result, the economy will remain at full employment.

3. No, velocity is not constant.

4. Keynes postulated three motives for holding money: the transactions motive, the precautionary motive, and the speculative motive. Keynes reasoned that the speculative motive is related to the interest rate.

5. Nominal money balances refers to the actual dollars that you hold. Real money balances equal the dollars you hold divided by the price level. Keynes reasoned that people desire to hold a certain amount of real money balances because real money balances measure how much a person can buy with their money. If prices in the economy double, the same nominal quantity of money will buy only half as many goods.

6. People hold precautionary money balances in order to make unexpected purchases. Precautionary money balances are positively related to income.

7. As interest rates rise, people will reduce their money holdings (because of the speculative motive) and therefore velocity will rise. Interest rates and velocity will be positively related.

8. If money demand is stable, then velocity will be relatively stable. This implies that changes in the money supply will have relatively predictable effects on nominal spending and income. However, velocity and money demand has been relatively unstable, leading to a weak link between the money supply and aggregate spending.

9. It is possible that this would lead to lower money demand, but it is unclear without knowing the magnitude effects of changes in wealth and inflation on money demand. However, since money is a dominated asset, as wealth rises, money demand will increase modestly. With a substantial increase in inflation, money demand will decrease as people look for inflation hedges. If the latter effect is (as is likely to be) larger than the former, then money demand will decrease.

10. When payment technologies improve, money demand decreases since there is less need for money to make transactions occur.

Critical Thinking

1. a. The quantity theory of money implies that a 20% increase in the money supply will result in a 20% increase in nominal income, and if prices and wages are flexible, a 20% increase in the price level and no change in real output.

   b. If there is a liquidity trap, a 20% increase in the money supply will have no impact on real income, the price level, or nominal income.

   c. If the Keynesian liquidity preference function best describes money demand, but the interest sensitivity of money demand is somewhere between ultrasensitive and completely insensitive, then the increase in the money supply will lead to an increase in nominal income. However the increase in nominal income will be something less than the 20% increase in the money supply because there is some interest sensitivity of money demand. Once again, the split between a change in real income and the price level depends on whether prices and wages are flexible.

2. The Keynesian money demand function in part (c) best describes the real world. Neither extreme case (ultrasensitive or completely insensitive) is consistent with the data.

3. Since money demand is a function of interest rates, the Fed does not have precise control over nominal income. Nonetheless, the interest sensitivity of money demand also does not appear to be ultrasensitive, and so the Fed does have some, but not complete, influence over nominal income.

True/False Questions

1. T
2. F
3. F
4. F
5. F
6. F
7. F
8. T
9. T
10. F
11. T
12. F
13. F
14. T
15. F

Multiple-Choice Questions

1. b
2. c
3. d
4. c

5. c
6. c
7. d
8. b
9. c
10. d
11. a
12. b
13. c
14. d
15. c
16. d
17. a
18. d
19. d
20. b

20 The *IS* Curve[*]

Chapter Review

PREVIEW

This chapter develops the *IS* curve, which is the first building block for understanding aggregate demand. The *IS* curve describes the equilibrium relationship between real interest rates and aggregate output demanded, and helps explain fluctuations in economic activity and the effects of fiscal policy. In later chapters, the *IS* curve will be useful to understand the role of monetary policy in economic fluctuations.

PLANNED EXPENDITURE AND AGGREGATE DEMAND

Total planned expenditure in the economy is the sum of four types of spending:

1. *Consumption expenditure (C)*: total demand for consumer goods and services

2. *Planned investment spending (I)*: total planned spending by businesses on new physical capital plus planned spending on new homes

3. *Government spending (G)*: spending by all levels of government on goods and services, not including transfer payments

4. *Net exports (NX)*: exports minus imports

The total quantity demanded of an economy's output is called *aggregate demand* (Y^{ad}) and is synonymous with planned expenditure:

$$Y^{ad} = C + I + G + NX.$$

As will be seen, equilibrium is where actual expenditure, or total output produced (Y), equals total output demanded (Y^{ad}): $Y = Y^{ad}$.

---

[*]This chapter is unique to the 10th ed.

THE COMPONENTS OF AGGREGATE DEMAND

Consumption spending is based on *disposable income,* which equals aggregate income (Y) minus taxes (T). This relationship is described by the *consumption function:* $C = \overline{C} + mpc \times Y_D$. The slope of the consumption function is $\Delta C/\Delta Y = mpc$, which stands for *marginal propensity to consume.* The mpc is a constant between 0 and 1 that measures the change in consumer expenditures resulting from an additional dollar of disposable income. The $\overline{C}$ in the consumption function represents autonomous consumer expenditures, that is, consumer spending that is *exogenous* and therefore unrelated to disposable income.

Planned investment spending is the sum of two types of investment: (1) *fixed investment,* which is spending on structures and equipment by firms, plus planned spending on new residential housing, and (2) planned *inventory investment,* which is the change in inventories held by firms in a given time period. Inventory investment plays an important role in the adjustment of total production to planned spending. In particular, any production in excess of planned expenditure (which includes planned inventory spending) represents unplanned inventory investments and, as will be seen, will prompt firms to reduce production.

Planned investment spending is negatively related to the real interest rate, since the real interest rate represents the opportunity costs for firms to purchase capital equipment or hold inventories, or for individuals to purchase new housing. Investment can also change due to noninterest rate factors, such as waves of optimism and pessimism, or *animal spirits.* These noninterest related factors affecting investment are referred to as *autonomous investment,* $\overline{I}$. Altogether, this implies an investment function given by $I = \overline{I} - dr_c$, where d reflects the responsiveness of investment to changes in the real cost of borrowing, r_c. During financial crises, however, the effective cost of borrowing can be decoupled from the real interest rate, so the real cost of borrowing can be represented by $r_c = r + \overline{f}$, where $\overline{f}$ represents the effect of financial frictions from asymmetric information problems on the real cost of borrowing. This implies an investment function of the form $I = \overline{I} - d(r + \overline{f})$.

Net exports are affected by the *exchange rate,* which is implicitly affected by the real interest rate. For example, when real interest rates increase, this increases the demand for domestic assets, leading to an appreciation of the domestic currency. This makes domestic goods more expensive to foreigners and foreign goods less expensive to domestic consumers. Both of these factors lead to a decrease in net exports, implying an inverse relationship between the real interest rate and net exports. There are other exogenous factors that affect net exports independent of the exchange rate, given as autonomous net exports, or $\overline{NX}$. These imply the net export function $NX = \overline{NX} - xr$, where x represents the effect of changes in the real interest rate on net exports.

Government purchases and taxes are assumed exogenous and are given as $G = \overline{G}$ and $T = \overline{T}$, respectively.

GOODS MARKET EQUILIBRIUM

The goods market equilibrium is found where the amount of output (Y) is equal to planned expenditure (Y^{ad}). To derive the IS curve, substitute the expressions for consumption, planned investment, government purchases, and net exports into the planned expenditure function, and solve for Y as a function of the real interest rate: $Y = Y^{ad} = C + I + G + NX$. Substitution from the spending components above gives the *IS* curve as:

$$Y = \left[\overline{C} + \overline{I} - d\overline{f} + \overline{G} + \overline{NX} - mpc \times \overline{T} \right] \times \frac{1}{1-mpc} - \frac{d+x}{1-mpc} \times r$$

UNDERSTANDING THE *IS* CURVE

Given the *IS* curve derived above, it is important to note that all factors in the equation are exogenous except the relation between the real interest rate and the (equilibrium) amount of aggregate output demanded. As the real interest rate increases, net exports and planned investment decrease, and represent a movement up and to the left of the *IS* curve, implying the downward slope of the *IS* curve.

Any point on the *IS* curve is a goods market equilibrium, and if the economy were to deviate off the curve, planned spending would no longer be equal to actual expenditure. More generally, any point to the right or above the *IS* curve means actual expenditure (goods produced) is greater than planned expenditure. This means that unplanned inventory accumulation occurs; this prompts firms to cut back on production, and the economy eventually ends up back on the *IS* curve and at a goods market equilibrium. Similarly, when the economy is operating at a point below or to the left of the *IS* curve, production and actual expenditure are less than desired by households, firms, government, and the net export sector; unplanned inventory investment is negative, and prompts firms to increase production and the economy eventually moves to a point back on the *IS* curve.

FACTORS THAT SHIFT THE *IS* CURVE

Note that if the real interest rate changes, this represents a movement along a given *IS* curve. Any other factors identified in the *IS* equation will result in a shift of the *IS* curve.

If autonomous spending increases (for instance, due to an increase in $\overline{C}$, $\overline{I}$, $\overline{G}$, or $\overline{NX}$), aggregate output (Y) will increase by a multiple of that change, holding all other factors, including the real interest rate constant. The ratio of the change in aggregate output to the change in planned expenditures, $\Delta Y/\Delta$(autonomous spending), is called the *expenditure multiplier*, which is equal to $1/(1 - mpc)$.

Keynes viewed the economy as inherently unstable (due to animal spirits), and he reasoned that government spending and taxes should be used to offset decreases in autonomous spending (particularly investment spending) and, therefore, restore the economy to full-employment equilibrium. Changes in government spending have the same multiplier effect as changes in autonomous spending: $\Delta Y/\Delta G = 1/(1 - mpc)$. Changes in taxes have a slightly different effect. When taxes are reduced by $1, consumer spending rises by $1 \times (mpc)$ [consumers save the remaining $1 \times (1 - mpc)$]. Therefore, $\Delta Y/\Delta T = -mpc/(1 - mpc)$. The minus sign appears because decreases in taxes increase consumer spending.

Thus, the following factors shift the IS curve to the right: increases in autonomous consumption, increases in autonomous investment, increases in autonomous net exports, increases in government purchases, decreases in taxes, or a decrease in financial frictions. The table below summarizes these relationships as it affects the *IS* curve.

Variable	Change in Variable	Shift in *IS* Curve	Reason
Autonomous consumption expenditure, $\overline{C}$	↑	r — IS_1 → IS_2 (shift right), Y	C↑ Y↑
Autonomous investment, $\overline{I}$	↑	r — IS_1 → IS_2 (shift right), Y	I↑ Y↑
Government spending, $\overline{G}$	↑	r — IS_1 → IS_2 (shift right), Y	G↑ Y↑
Taxes, $\overline{T}$	↑	r — IS_2 ← IS_1 (shift left), Y	T↑ ⇨ C↓ Y↓
Autonomous net exports, $\overline{NX}$	↑	r — IS_1 → IS_2 (shift right), Y	$\overline{NX}$↑ Y↑
Financial frictions, $\overline{f}$	↑	r — IS_2 ← IS_1 (shift left), Y	I↓ Y↓

Note: Only increases (↑) in the variables are shown; the effects of decreases in the variables on aggregate output would be the opposite of those indicated in the last two columns.

Helpful Hints

1. When actual spending is the same as planned spending, the goods market is in equilibrium, and unplanned inventory investment is zero. However, when the economy is not in a goods market equilibrium (i.e. not on a point on the *IS* curve), actual spending is different than planned spending, and thus, unplanned inventory is either negative or positive. This misalignment signals firms to adjust production to ensure it is meeting demand for goods.

2. Changes in autonomous spending have a multiplier effect on aggregate output, and represent the horizontal shift of the *IS* curve, holding all other factors constant.
3. Movements along the *IS* curve happen because an increase in the interest rate causes planned investment spending and net exports to decline, which leads to lower aggregate output (Y).

Terms and Definitions

Choose a definition for each key term.

Key Terms:

_____ aggregate demand

_____ "animal spirits"

_____ autonomous consumption expenditure

_____ autonomous investment

_____ autonomous spending

_____ consumption expenditure

_____ consumption function

_____ disposable income

_____ exchange rate

_____ exogenous

_____ fixed investment

_____ government purchases

_____ inventory investment

_____ *IS* curve

_____ marginal propensity to consume

_____ net exports

_____ planned expenditure

_____ planned investment spending

Definitions:

1. The total quantity demanded of an economy's output
2. Net foreign spending on domestic goods and services
3. The relationship between disposable income and consumption expenditure
4. Spending by firms on equipment and structures and planned spending on residential homes
5. The slope of the consumption function line that measures the change in consumption expenditures resulting from an additional dollar of disposable income
6. Combinations of aggregate output and the real interest rate for which the goods market is in equilibrium
7. Total spending on consumer goods and services
8. Spending by all levels of government on goods and services
9. Spending by firms on additional holdings of raw materials, parts, and finished goods

10. Spending that is independent of income
11. Waves of optimism and pessimism that affect consumers' and businesses' willingness to spend
12. Total income available for spending (aggregate income minus taxes)
13. Total planned spending by businesses on new physical capital and planned inventory investment plus planned spending on new homes
14. The price of one currency in terms of another currency
15. The amount of consumption expenditure that is independent of disposable income
16. Investment spending which is independent of output and interest rates
17. The total amount of spending on domestically produced goods and services that households, businesses, the government, and foreigners want to make
18. Independent of variables in the model

Problems and Short-Answer Questions

PRACTICE PROBLEMS

1. Suppose the economy is described by the following equations:

    $C = 100 + 0.8Y$

    $I = 50 - 0.5r$

    $G = 200$

    $NX = -50 - 1.5r$

    a. Calculate and solve for the *IS* curve

    _____

    b. Use the table below to fill in equilibrium values of aggregate output, consumption, planned investment, and net exports for different values of *r*.

r	Aggregate Output, *Y*	Consumption Expenditure, *C*	Planned Investment, *I*	Government Spending	Net Exports, *NX*
0	_____	_____	_____	200	_____
2	_____	_____	_____	200	_____
4	_____	_____	_____	200	_____
6	_____	_____	_____	200	_____
8	_____	_____	_____	200	_____
10	_____	_____	_____	200	_____

    c. Why does consumption decrease as the real interest rate increases, if the consumption function is not dependent on *r*?

    _____

    _____

d. Graph the *IS* curve below, labeling the points from the table in part (b).

2. Assume that the marginal propensity to consume is 0.90 and autonomous consumption expenditures equal $100 billion. Further, assume that planned investment spending is $300 billion and government spending, taxes, and net exports are zero.

a. Calculate equilibrium output.

b. Now suppose that autonomous consumption expenditures drop by $50 billion to $50 billion. Calculate the new equilibrium output.

c. Calculate the expenditure multiplier for this economy.

d. Now consider an economy with government spending. Assume that the marginal propensity to consume is 0.90. Calculate the change in equilibrium output that would result from a $100 billion increase in government spending.

e. How would your answer to part (d) change if instead there were a $100 billion decrease in government spending?

_____

_____

3. Consider the economy described by the equations below.

$\bar{C}$ = $3.3 trillion
$\bar{I}$ = $1 trillion
$\bar{G}$ = $4.2 trillion
$\overline{NX}$ = $0.5 trillion
$\bar{T}$ = $4 trillion
$\bar{f}$ = 0
mpc = 0.75
d = 0.4
x = 0.1

a. Write out expressions for the consumption function, investment function, and net export function.

_____

_____

b. Calculate and solve for the *IS* curve.

_____

_____

c. At an interest rate of $r = 2$, what is total output Y, consumption C, planned investment I, and net exports NX?

_____

_____

d. Suppose the interest rate is $r = 2$. If actual production is $Y = \$21.5$ trillion, then what is unplanned inventory investment? If actual production is $Y = \$19$ trillion, then what is unplanned inventory investment? In each of these cases, how will the economy get back to the goods market equilibrium? Draw the *IS* curve, labeling the goods market equilibrium at $r = 2$, and the disequilibrium points where $Y = \$21.5$ trillion and $Y = \$21.5$ trillion.

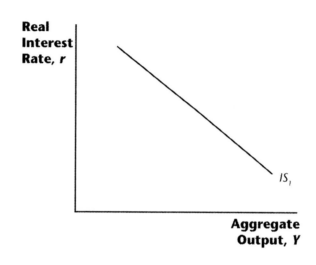

4. For each of the following factors, briefly describe which component of spending is affected and why. Show the effects in the graph of the *IS* curve.

a. A recession occurs in a foreign country.

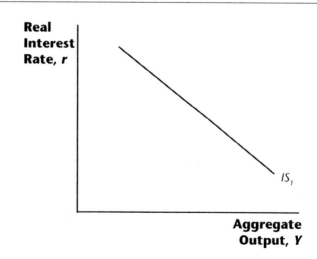

b. Taxes increase.

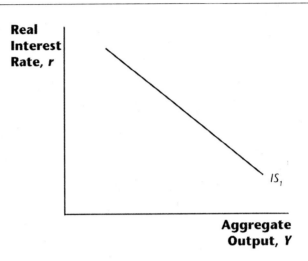

c. Firms become more optimistic about the future of the economy.

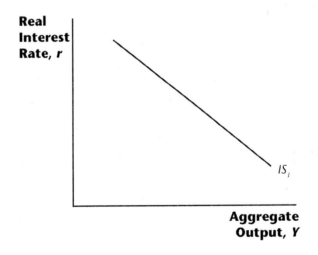

d.   A stock market boom increases household wealth.

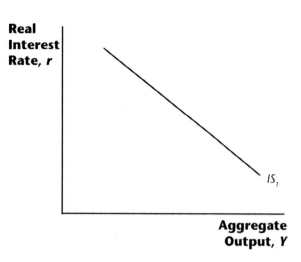

e.   A financial crisis occurs, increasing asymmetric information problems.

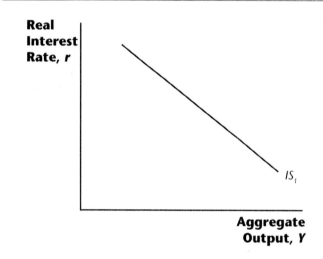

    f.   The real interest rate decreases.

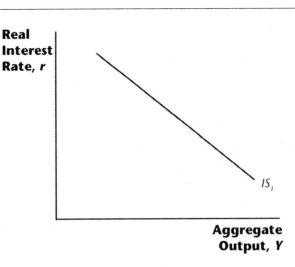

5.   For each of the following scenarios, describe how fiscal policymakers can separately change both taxes and government spending to keep aggregate output from changing.

    a.   A recession occurs in a foreign country.

        _____

    b.   Consumers become pessimistic about the state of the economy.

        _____

    c.   Firms become more optimistic about the future of the economy.

        _____

    d.   A stock market boom increases household wealth.

        _____

    e.   A financial crisis occurs, increasing asymmetric information problems.

        _____

SHORT-ANSWER QUESTIONS

1. What are the four types of spending that sum to total quantity demanded of the economy's output?

   _____

   _____

2. Suppose a consumption function is given by the equation C = 300 + 0.75(Y − 75). What are autonomous consumption, taxes, and the marginal propensity to consume?

   _____

   _____

3. Suppose that aggregate demand is $900 billion and aggregate output is $850 billion. What is the value of unplanned inventory investment in this economy, and what will happen to bring this economy back to equilibrium?

   _____

   _____

4. According to Keynes, what is the dominant source of instability in autonomous expenditures?

   _____

   _____

5. Suppose the *mpc* is 0.80 and net exports falls by $20 billion. Calculate the change in aggregate output.

   _____

   _____

6. Why does a change in taxes have a smaller impact on aggregate output than a change in government spending?

   _____

   _____

7. Why are interest rates and aggregate output negatively related along the *IS* curve?

   _____

   _____

8. Why do changes in taxes and government spending have opposite effects on aggregate output and shifts of the *IS* curve?

_____

_____

9 Suppose the economy is to the left of the *IS* curve. Is there an excess supply or an excess demand for goods? Describe the adjustment of the economy back to the *IS* curve.

_____

_____

10. How does a decrease in asymmetric information affect planned investment?

_____

_____

Critical Thinking

Suppose you get a job working for one of your Senators. The economy has just entered a recession, and she asks you to propose three different plans for increasing aggregate output by $200 billion. Under plan 1, government spending would increase holding taxes constant. Under plan 2, taxes would decrease, holding government spending constant, and under plan 3, government spending would increase, but taxes would increase by the same amount in order to keep the budget deficit unchanged. Assume that the *mpc* is 0.80.

1. How much would government spending have to rise by under plan 1?

_____

_____

2. How much would taxes have to fall by under plan 2?

_____

_____

3. How much would government spending and taxes both have to rise by under plan 3?

_____

_____

Self-Test

TRUE/FALSE QUESTIONS

_____1. An increase in d or x makes the *IS* curve flatter (less steep).

_____2. Autonomous consumption expenditure is positively related to income.

_____3. Planned investment spending includes purchases of stock by a corporation.

_____4. In contrast to fixed investment, which is always planned, some inventory investment is unplanned.

_____5. New residential housing construction is included in fixed investment.

_____6. The larger the *mpc*, the smaller the expenditure multiplier.

_____7. Keynes believed that changes in autonomous spending are dominated by unstable fluctuations in planned investment spending, which are influenced by "animal spirits."

_____8. The fiscal stimulus package of 2009 was not large enough to offset immediate declines in autonomous investment and consumption.

_____9. If unplanned inventory investment is positive, firms will increase production.

_____10. If foreigners suddenly get an urge to buy $100 billion more American goods, aggregate output will increase by $100 billion.

_____11. The *IS* curve shows the combinations of interest rates and aggregate output for which the goods market is in equilibrium.

_____12. If a company uses surplus funds instead of borrowed funds to undertake investment in physical capital, then the interest rate has no impact on investment spending.

_____13. A higher interest rate in the United States causes the dollar to depreciate, which leads to an increase in net exports and therefore aggregate output.

_____14. If unplanned inventory investment is zero, planned spending equals actual expenditure.

_____15. A decrease in financial frictions shifts the *IS* curve to the left.

MULTIPLE-CHOICE QUESTIONS

1. The four components of aggregate demand are
    a. consumption expenditure, planned investment spending, government spending, and net exports.
    b. consumption expenditure, unplanned inventory investment, government spending, and net exports.
    c. consumption expenditure, planned inventory investment, government spending, and exports.
    d. consumption expenditure, unplanned inventory investment, government spending, and imports.

2. A marginal propensity to consume of 0.50 means that
    a. people spend half of their income.
    b. the expenditure multiplier is 0.50.
    c. people spend half of their disposable income.
    d. people spend half of each additional dollar of disposable income.

3. If autonomous consumption expenditure is $100 billion, the marginal propensity to consume is 0.90, aggregate income is $1,000 billion, and taxes are $200 billion, consumption expenditures will equal
    a. $1,000 billion.
    b. $100 billion.
    c. $280 billion.
    d. $820 billion.

4. Suppose that Dell Computer Company starts the year with $20 million in inventory and ends the year with $14 million in inventory. Inventory investment for the year for Dell will be
    a. −$14 million.
    b. $14 million.
    c. −$6 million.
    d. $6 million.

5. If aggregate demand is $875 billion and actual expenditure is $900 billion, then
    a. unplanned inventory investment = −$25 billion, and firms will increase production.
    b. unplanned inventory investment = $25 billion, and firms will increase production.
    c. unplanned inventory investment = −$25 billion, and firms will decrease production.
    d. unplanned inventory investment = $25 billion, and firms will decrease production.

6. A decrease in the real interest rate will cause exports to _____ and imports to _____.
    a. increase; increase
    b. increase; decrease
    c. decrease; decrease
    d. not change; decrease

7. If the *mpc* is 0.80, then the expenditure multiplier is
   a. 5.
   b. 4.
   c. 3.
   d. 0.80.

8. If the marginal propensity to consume is 0.75 and autonomous spending increases by $25 billion, then aggregate output will increase by
   a. $25 billion.
   b. $75 billion.
   c. $100 billion.
   d. $125 billion.

9. If the government reduces taxes by $120 billion and the marginal propensity to consume is 0.50, then aggregate output will
   a. rise by $120 billion.
   b. rise by $240 billion.
   c. fall by $120 billion.
   d. fall by $240 billion.

10. If the government raises taxes and government spending by $20 billion and the marginal propensity to consume is 0.80, aggregate output will
    a. rise by $100 billion.
    b. rise by $20 billion.
    c. remain unchanged.
    d. fall by $20 billion.

11. An increase in the interest rate will cause
    a. investment spending to rise and net exports to fall.
    b. investment spending to fall and net exports to fall.
    c. investment spending to rise and net exports to rise.
    d. investment spending to fall and net exports to rise.

12. The *IS* curve slopes downward because the higher _____ lead to lower _____ and _____.
    a. government spending; consumption; investment spending
    b. interest rates; money demand; investment spending
    c. government spending; money demand; net exports
    d. interest rates; investment spending; net exports

13. During financial crises, financial frictions _____, leading to a _____ shift of the *IS* curve.
    a. increase; rightward
    b. increase; leftward
    c. decrease; rightward
    d. decrease; leftward

14. The *IS* curve shows combinations of interest rates and levels of income for which
    a. government spending equals taxes.
    b. the money market is in equilibrium.
    c. net exports and government spending both equal zero.
    d. the goods market is in equilibrium.

15. If both taxes and autonomous consumption expenditure increase, the *IS* curve
    a. will shift right.
    b. will shift left.
    c. will not shift.
    d. may shift right, left, or not shift at all.

16. Which of the following would NOT be considered part of planned investment spending?
    a. The purchase of new software and computers for a business.
    b. The building of a new residential subdivision.
    c. An increase in inventories from unanticipated weakness in demand for goods.
    d. Firms adding to inventories in anticipation of future increases in demand.

17. At points to the left of the *IS* curve,
    a. there is an excess demand for goods, which leads to an unplanned decrease in inventories.
    b. there is an excess supply of goods, which leads to an unplanned decrease in inventories.
    c. there is an excess demand for goods, which leads to an unplanned increase in inventories.
    d. there is an excess supply of goods, which leads to an unplanned increase in inventories.

18. When the real interest rate increases
    a. the *IS* curve shifts right.
    b. the *IS* curve shifts left.
    c. imports decrease.
    d. planned investment spending decreases.

19. During the 1960s, the real interest rate stayed constant, and fiscal policy was _____, leading to _____.
    a. not used; recession
    b. contractionary; inflation
    c. neutral; budget surpluses
    d. expansionary; decreased unemployment

20. A goods market equilibrium occurs when
    a. $Y = Y^{ad}$.
    b. unplanned inventory investment is zero.
    c. the economy is at a point on the *IS* curve.
    d. All of the above are correct.

Solutions

Terms and Definitions

 1 aggregate demand
11 "animal spirits"
15 autonomous consumption expenditure
16 autonomous investment
10 autonomous spending
 7 consumption expenditure
 3 consumption function
12 disposable income
14 exchange rate
18 exogenous

 4 fixed investment
 8 government purchases
 9 inventory investment
 6 IS curve
 5 marginal propensity to consume
 2 net exports
17 planned expenditure
13 planned investment spending

Practice Problems

1. a. $Y = 1500 - 10r$

   b.

r	Aggregate Output, Y	Consumption Expenditure, C	Planned Investment, I	Government Spending	Net Exports, NX
0	1,500	1,300	50	200	−50
2	1,480	1,284	49	200	−53
4	1,460	1,268	48	200	−56
6	1,440	1,252	47	200	−59
8	1,420	1,236	46	200	−62
10	1,400	1,220	45	200	−65

   c. As the real interest rate increases, this reduces planned investment and net exports, which reduces planned spending and hence the goods market equilibrium level of aggregate output and income. The lower equilibrium income means lower disposable income, and hence lower consumption.

   d.

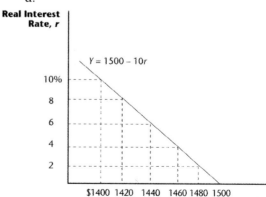

2. a. $Y^* = \$4{,}000$ billion.

    b. $Y^* = \$3{,}500$ billion.

    c. Expenditure multiplier $= 1/(1 - mpc) = 10$.

    d. $\Delta Y = [1/(1 - mpc)]\Delta G = \$1{,}000$ billion.

    e. $\Delta Y = -\$1{,}000$ billion.

3. a. $C = 3.3 + 0.75(Y - 4) = 0.3 + 0.75Y; I = 1 - 0.4r; NX = 0.5 - 0.1r$.

    b. $Y = 24 - 2r$.

    c. $Y = 20; C = 15.3; I = 0.2; NX = 0.3$.

    d. When $Y = \$21.5$ trillion, unplanned inventory investment is $\$21.5$ trillion $- \$20$ trillion $= \$1.5$ trillion. In this case, firms are producing too much goods relative to what the economy would like to buy, thus production is reduced until the goods market equilibrium level of production is achieved at $Y = \$20$ trillion. When $Y = \$19$ trillion, unplanned inventory investment is $\$19$ trillion $- \$20$ trillion $= -\$1$ trillion. In this case, firms are not producing enough goods relative to what the economy desires to buy; thus, firms will increase production until the goods market equilibrium level of production is achieved at $Y = \$20$ trillion.

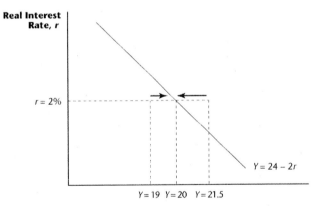

4. a. A recession in a foreign country would reduce domestic exports to that country, leading to a decrease in autonomous net exports and the *IS* curve shifting to the left.

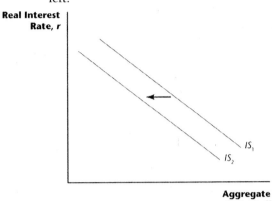

    b. An increase in taxes reduces disposable income, and hence consumption, causing the *IS* curve to shift to the left.

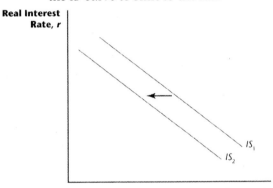

    c. Autonomous investment increases, causing the *IS* curve to shift to the right.

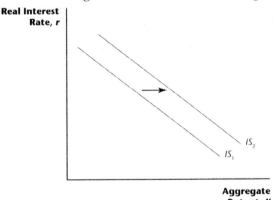

d. A stock market boom increases wealth, which increases autonomous consumption and overall consumption causing the *IS* curve to shift to the right.

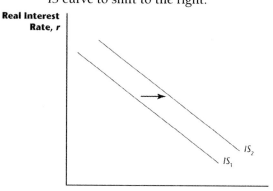

e. An increase in asymmetric information problems increases financial frictions, decreasing planned investment and shifting the *IS* curve to the left.

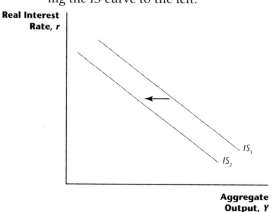

f. A decrease in the real interest rate increases both planned investment and net exports, is a movement along the *IS* curve, and does not shift the *IS* curve.

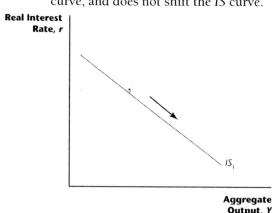

5. a. This will cause the *IS* curve to shift to the left. Fiscal policymakers can either reduce taxes, and/or increase government spending to shift the *IS* curve back to the right.

b. This will cause the *IS* curve to shift to the left. Fiscal policymakers can either reduce taxes and/or increase government spending to shift the *IS* curve back to the right.

c. This will cause the *IS* curve to shift to the right. Fiscal policymakers can either increase taxes and/or decrease government spending to shift the *IS* curve back to the left.

d. This will cause the *IS* curve to shift to the right. Fiscal policymakers can either increase taxes and/or decrease government spending to shift the *IS* curve back to the left.

e. This will cause the *IS* curve to shift to the left. Fiscal policymakers can either reduce taxes, and/or increase government spending to shift the *IS* curve back to the right.

Short-Answer Questions

1. Consumption expenditure, planned investment spending, government spending, net exports.

2. Autonomous consumption is 300, the *mpc* = 0.75, and taxes are 75.

3. Unplanned inventory investment is −50. Firms will respond by increasing production until the economy reaches equilibrium.

4. According to Keynes, changes in autonomous spending are dominated by unstable fluctuations in planned investment spending, which is influenced by "animal spirits."

5. $\Delta Y = [1/(1 - mpc)]\Delta NX = -\$100$ billion.

6. A change in taxes has a smaller impact on aggregate output than a change in government spending because when taxes are reduced, part of the increase in disposable income is saved. And when taxes are increased, part of the decrease in disposable income is paid out of saving.

7. Interest rates and aggregate output are negatively related along the *IS* curve because as interest rates rise, investment spending and net exports decline, which decreases planned spending and hence aggregate output.

8. When taxes increase, this reduces disposable income and consumption, which leads to a

decrease in planned spending and a shift to the left of the *IS* curve. An increase in government spending has the opposite effect of increasing planned spending and, hence, shifting the *IS* curve to the right.

9. If the economy is to the left of the *IS* curve, there is excess demand for goods, which results in an unplanned decrease in inventory. Firms will respond by increasing production until equilibrium in the goods market is restored, and the economy returns to the *IS* curve.

10. A decrease in asymmetric information results in lower financial frictions, which reduces the real cost of borrowing. This increases the amount of planned investment and shifts the *IS* curve to the right.

Critical Thinking

1. ΔG = $40 billion

2. ΔT = –$50 billion

3. $\Delta G = \Delta T$ = $200 billion

True/False Questions

1. T
2. F
3. F
4. T
5. T
6. F
7. T
8. T
9. F
10. F
11. T
12. F
13. F
14. T
15. F

Multiple-Choice Questions

1. a
2. d
3. d
4. c
5. d
6. b
7. a
8. c
9. a
10. b
11. b
12. d
13. b
14. d
15. d
16. c
17. a
18. d
19. d
20. d

21 The Monetary Policy and Aggregate Demand Curves*

Chapter Review

PREVIEW

In order to understand the role that monetary policy plays in helping to stabilize the economy, this chapter develops a model to explain changes in the real interest rate through the *monetary policy (MP) curve*. Using the *IS* curve developed in the last chapter, these two elements are used to derive the *aggregate demand curve* and provide a central role for understanding how monetary and fiscal policy can address short-run fluctuations.

THE FEDERAL RESERVE AND MONETARY POLICY

Most central banks around the world control monetary policy through adjustments in a short-term nominal interest rate. In the United States, the Federal Reserve conducts open market operations to affect bank reserves and influence the federal funds rate, the overnight borrowing rate between banks. However, it is the real interest rate that matters for economic activity and decision making, not the nominal rate.

Fortunately, the Federal Reserve can control the real interest rate with reasonable precision due to sticky prices. The real interest rate is equal to the nominal interest rate minus inflation expectations. Since prices are sticky in the short run, inflation expectations are essentially fixed in the short run as well. Thus, when the Fed makes changes to monetary policy to influence the nominal interest rate, it also affects the real interest rate, which is what matters for effectively managing economic activity. In particular, if the Fed lowers the federal funds rate, the real interest rate falls, and vice versa.

---

*This chapter is unique to the 10th ed.

THE MONETARY POLICY CURVE

The conduct of monetary policy is modeled through the *monetary policy (MP) curve*, in which the central bank adjusts the real interest rate (from changes in the nominal short-term interest rate) based on changes in the current inflation rate and changes in a target (autonomous) real interest rate. The MP curve is given as: $r = \overline{r} + \lambda\pi$, where λ is the parameter that dictates how strongly the central bank reacts to changes in the inflation rate, and $\overline{r}$ is the autonomous component of monetary policy in which policy changes are made independent of the current inflation rate. The component π is the part of monetary policy that automatically reacts to changes in inflation to ensure inflation stability. When the inflation rate rises, this signals the central bank to increase the real interest rate in order to choke off economic activity and lower inflation. Likewise, when the inflation rate falls (which is normally the case during recessions), this prompts the central bank to lower the real interest rate, thereby encouraging economic activity.

The parameter λ plays an important part in maintaining inflation stability. When λ is positive, this means that increases in the inflation rate will be met with an even greater increase in the nominal interest rate, thereby having an appropriate effect of raising the real interest rate to cool economic activity and, hence, lower inflation. It is for this reason that λ is set as a positive number and is what is described as the *Taylor principle*: Increases in expected inflation should be met with a more than one-for-one increase in the nominal interest rate in order to ensure inflation stability over the longer term. Since λ is positive, that makes the MP curve upward sloping.

It is important to note that when inflation rises, this does not change the monetary policy curve; it is a movement along a given monetary policy curve and is thought of as an "automatic policy adjustment." When the central bank changes its "policy stance" through $\overline{r}$, it will result in a shift of the MP curve. These are referred to as autonomous policy changes, as described below.

- **Autonomous tightening of monetary policy.** At any given current inflation rate, increasing the real interest rate by increasing $\overline{r}$ results in a shift upward of the MP curve. This may happen due to a worry about higher future inflation risk.

- **Autonomous easing of monetary policy.** At any given current inflation rate, decreasing the real interest rate by decreasing $\overline{r}$ results in a shift downward of the MP curve. This policy may occur due to the risk that a recession may happen.

The distinction between autonomous policy changes and interest rate effects due to inflation can be seen in the behavior of the federal funds rate in 2007 and 2008. Early on in this period, inflation was rising, suggesting interest rates should be increasing. However, due to the apparent weakness in the economy leading up to the global financial crisis, the Federal Reserve actually decreased interest rates, representing an autonomous policy easing.

THE AGGREGATE DEMAND CURVE

The aggregate demand curve can be derived from the MP curve described above, along with the IS curve described in the previous chapter. With a higher inflation rate, monetary policy responds by increasing the real interest rate moving up along the *MP* curve. The higher real interest rate will reduce output in a goods market equilibrium, moving up to the left along the *IS* curve. Thus, when inflation rises, the resulting goods market equilibrium implies a decrease in the amount of output demanded, hence, showing an inverse relationship between inflation and real output (which represents the aggregate demand curve).

To be seen another way, the *AD* curve can be derived algebraically from the equations for the *MP* curve, and the *IS* curve derived in the previous chapter. Substituting the *MP* curve into the *IS* curve gives a representation of the *AD* curve:

$$Y = [\overline{C} + \overline{I} - d\overline{f} + \overline{G} + \overline{NX} - mpc \times \overline{T}] \times \frac{1}{1 - mpc} - \frac{d + x}{1 - mpc} \times (\overline{r} + \lambda\pi)$$

Note that the equation above exhibits an inverse relationship between inflation and output because of the minus sign. Keep in mind also that anything that represents a movement along both the *IS* and *MP* curves (i.e. a change in inflation) will be a movement along the *AD* curve. Thus, any other factors besides changes in the inflation rate itself will result in a shift of the *AD* (and come from shifts of either the *IS* or *MP* curves). The *IS* curve shifts are summarized below.

- **Autonomous Consumption Expenditure.** An increase in $\overline{C}$ raises planned expenditure, shifting the *IS* curve and *AD* curve to the right.

- **Autonomous Investment Spending.** An increase in $\overline{I}$ raises planned expenditure, shifting the *IS* curve and *AD* curve to the right.

- **Government Purchases.** An increase in $\overline{G}$ raises planned expenditure, shifting the *IS* curve and *AD* curve to the right.

- **Taxes.** A decrease in $\overline{T}$ raises planned expenditure, shifting the *IS* curve and *AD* curve to the right.

- **Autonomous Net Exports.** An increase in $\overline{NX}$ raises planned expenditure, shifting the *IS* curve and *AD* curve to the right.

- **Financial Frictions.** A decrease in $\overline{f}$ raises planned expenditure, shifting the *IS* curve and *AD* curve to the right.

All of the above factors increase planned expenditure, which means output increases at any real interest rate. Along the *MP* curve, any given real interest rate is still associated with the same inflation rate, thus planned expenditure and output increase at any given real interest rate and inflation rate. This implies a rightward shift of the *IS* and *AD* curves. The opposite changes from the list above will result in the *IS* and *AD* curves shifting to the left.

The *MP* curve shifts are described below.

- **Autonomous tightening of monetary policy.** An increase in $\overline{r}$ will result in a higher real interest rate at any given inflation rate, shifting the *MP* curve up. When the real interest rate rises (at any given inflation rate), this represents a movement along the *IS* curve, resulting in lower output. Thus, at any given inflation rate, output will be lower, implying a leftward shift of the *AD* curve.

- **Autonomous easing of monetary policy.** A decrease in $\overline{r}$ will result in a lower real interest rate at any given inflation rate, shifting the *MP* curve down. When the real interest rate falls (at any given inflation rate), this represents a movement along the *IS* curve, resulting in higher output. Thus, at any given inflation rate, output will be higher, implying a rightward shift of the *AD* curve.

Helpful Hints

1. Note that in other economics courses, you may have used an aggregate demand framework in which output demanded depended on the price level rather than inflation, as presented here. Firms and households are affected by and concerned about the inflation rate, and make decisions based upon movements in inflation. Likewise, policymakers (particularly monetary policymakers) conduct policy as a direct response to changes in the inflation rate (rather than the price level).

2. Practice drawing the graphs of the *IS*, *MP*, and *AD* curves, particularly deriving the *AD* curve and showing the shifts that occur through policy changes or changes in autonomous spending. Understanding the distinctions between the different models and how they are tied together is crucial to mastering this material.

3. A change in the current inflation rate results in a movement along a given *MP* curve; however, a change in expected future inflation, holding current inflation constant, is likely to result in a change in the autonomous real interest rate and a shift of the *MP* curve.

4. A shift of the *IS* curve results in a similar shift of the *AD* curve, holding the *MP* curve constant. A shift of the *MP* curve shifts the *AD* curve, holding the *IS* curve constant.

Terms and Definitions

Choose a definition for each key term.

Key Terms:

_____ aggregate demand curve

_____ autonomous easing of monetary policy

_____ autonomous tightening of monetary policy

_____ monetary policy (MP) curve

_____ Taylor principle

Definitions:

1. The action of the central bank to increase the autonomous real interest rate so that real interest rates increase for any given inflation rate

2. The relationship between aggregate output demanded and the inflation rate when the goods market is in equilibrium

3. Where monetary policymakers increase nominal interest rates more than an increase in expected inflation so that real interest rates increase with inflation

4. The action of the central bank to decrease the autonomous real interest rate so that real interest rates decrease for any given inflation rate

5. The relationship between the real interest rate the central bank sets and the current inflation rate

Problems and Short-Answer Questions

PRACTICE PROBLEMS

1. Assume that the inflation rate is held constant at π^*. For each of the factors below, show the effects in the *IS*, *MP*, and *AD* graphs on the real interest rate and output.
   a. Taxes increase.

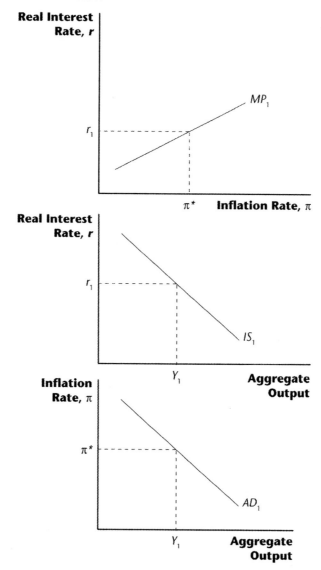

b. The central bank conducts an autonomous monetary policy tightening.

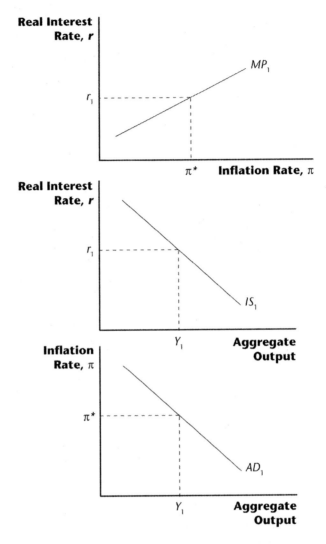

c. Financial frictions decrease.

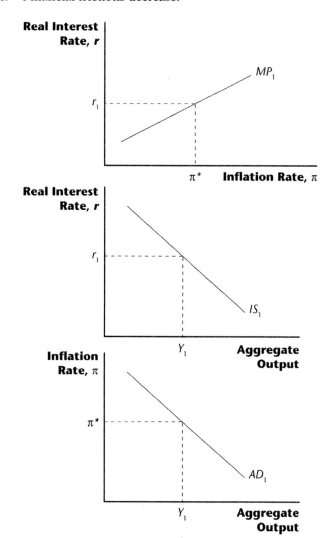

d. The autonomous real interest rate decreases.

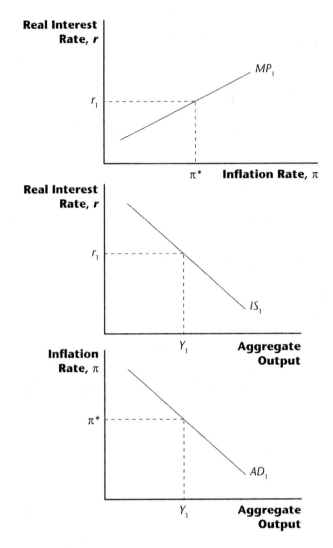

e. Business optimism declines, leading to a decrease in planned investment spending.

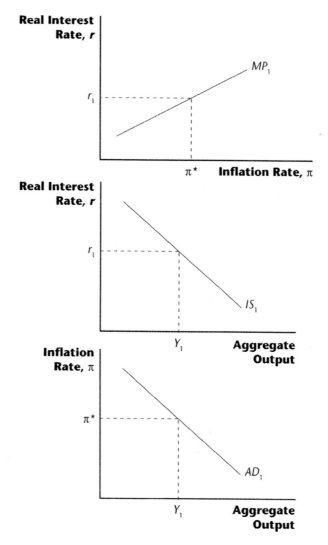

2. Complete the table by indicating whether each shift factor listed in the far left column shifts the *IS* or *MP* curve (right), (left), (up), (down) or not at all (no shift), and whether the resulting shift in the *IS* or *MP* curve causes interest rates and aggregate output to rise (+), fall (−), or remain unchanged (0). Assume the inflation rate is held constant.

Shift Factor	Direction of Change	IS Curve Shifts . . .	MP Curve Shifts . . .	Effect on Interest Rate	Effect on Aggregate Output
Autonomous Consumer Expenditure	+				
Autonomous Investment Spending	−				
Government Spending	+				
Taxes	+				
Autonomous Net Exports	−				
Autonomous Monetary Policy	Easing				
Financial Frictions	−				
Autonomous Monetary Policy	Tightening				

3. Assume the *IS* curve is given as $Y = 15 - 2r$, and the *MP* curve is given as $r = 0.75 + 0.5\pi$.
    a. Calculate an expression for the *AD* curve.

    _____

    b. Suppose inflation is $\pi = 1\%$. Calculate the real interest rate and output.

    _____

    c. If inflation increases to $\pi = 2\%$, what happens to the real interest rate and output? What are the effects on the *IS*, *MP*, and *AD* curves?

    _____

    _____

    d. Suppose an increase in autonomous spending changes the *IS* curve from $Y = 15 - 2r$ to $Y = 16 - 2r$. Calculate the new *AD* curve, and determine the real interest rate and output when inflation is $\pi = 1\%$.

    _____

    _____

    _____

4. Consider the economy described by the following equations:

$\overline{C}$ = $1.4 trillion

$\overline{I}$ = $0.9 trillion

$\overline{G}$ = $4.3 trillion

$\overline{NX}$ = $0.4 trillion

$\overline{T}$ = $4 trillion

$\overline{f}$ = 5

mpc = 0.75

d = 0.20

x = 0.05

$\overline{r}$ = 1.5

λ = 0.75

a. Calculate an expression for the *MP* curve.

_____

b. Calculate an expression for the *AD* curve.

_____

c. Suppose taxes are reduced to $3.6 trillion. Recalculate an expression for the *AD* curve, and show the effect on output in the graph below. Assume inflation is held constant at π = 2%.

_____

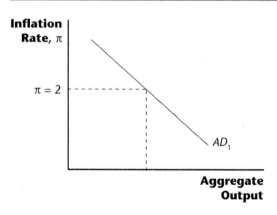

d. Suppose that the central bank is worried that any increase in aggregate demand could lead to a problem of higher inflation in the future. What could the central bank do to offset the fiscal policy change and keep the aggregate demand curve from shifting?

_____

_____

_____

SHORT-ANSWER QUESTIONS

1. How is it possible for the Federal Reserve to control the real interest rate if it can only adjust the nominal federal funds rate?

    _____

    _____

    _____

2. Why does the Taylor principle imply the *MP* curve is upward sloping?

    _____

    _____

3. What does it mean when the parameter λ increases?

    _____

    _____

4. Why did the Federal Reserve decrease interest rates in 2007 and 2008, even though inflation was increasing?

    _____

    _____

5. List the factors that shift the *MP* curve. How does this differ from a movement along the *MP* curve?

    _____

    _____

6. Under what conditions might the Federal Reserve conduct an autonomous easing of monetary policy? When would the Federal Reserve conduct an autonomous tightening of monetary policy?

    _____

    _____

7. List the factors that shift the *IS* curve. How does a movement along the *IS* curve occur?

    _____

    _____

8. Explain why the aggregate demand curve is downward sloping.

    _____

    _____

9. What monetary policy change will result in an increase in aggregate demand? What fiscal policy changes will result in an increase in aggregate demand?

    _____

    _____

10. If there is a decrease in autonomous consumption, how will that affect the *IS*, *MP*, and *AD* curves? What monetary policy can be used to keep the *AD* curve from shifting?

    _____

    _____

Critical Thinking

Most analysis of fiscal and monetary policy usually considers one type of policy at a time, holding the other type of policy constant. But in the real world, both monetary policy and fiscal policy are changing all of the time. Consider the combinations of monetary and fiscal policy listed in the table below. Fill in the missing columns in the table by indicating whether the given combination of monetary and fiscal policy has a positive (+), negative (–), or ambiguous (?) impact on aggregate output, and indicate which direction the *IS* and *MP* curves shift (right, left, up, or down).

Fiscal Policy	Monetary Policy	*IS* Curve	*MP* Curve	Aggregate Output
Expansionary	Autonomous Easing	_____	_____	_____
Contractionary	Autonomous Tightening	_____	_____	_____
Expansionary	Autonomous Tightening	_____	_____	_____
Contractionary	Autonomous Easing	_____	_____	_____

Self-Test

TRUE/FALSE QUESTIONS

_____1. Flexible prices in the short run allow the Federal Reserve to control the real interest rate.

_____2. The *MP* curve gives the relationship between the real interest rate and the goods market equilibrium level of output.

_____3. The *MP* curve is upward sloping due to the Taylor principle.

_____4. The Federal Reserve violated the Taylor principle in the 1970s.

_____5. An increase in expected future inflation has the same effect on the *MP* curve as an increase in the current inflation rate.

_____6. According to the *MP* curve, real interest rates increased in 2007 and 2008 since inflation was rising during that time.

_____7. Any factor that shifts the *IS* curve shifts the *AD* curve in the opposite direction.

_____8. The aggregate demand curve is the relationship between the inflation rate and quantity of aggregate output for which the goods market is in equilibrium.

_____9. If inflation decreases, the real interest rate decreases, and the goods market equilibrium level of output increases.

_____10. If financial frictions increase, this shifts the *MP* curve.

_____11. The *AD* curve is derived from the *AS* and *MP* curves.

_____12. If inflation increases, this shifts the *MP* curve, and hence shifts the *AD* curve.

_____13. If the economy were headed into a recession, the central bank would conduct an autonomous easing of policy.

_____14. Any factor that shifts the *IS* curve shifts the *MP* curve in the same direction.

_____15. According to the Taylor principle, central banks should increase the nominal interest rate more than one-for-one with an increase in expected inflation.

MULTIPLE-CHOICE QUESTIONS

1. Which of the following causes the *MP* curve to shift down?
    a. an increase in inflation
    b. a decrease in inflation
    c. an autonomous easing of monetary policy
    d. an autonomous tightening of monetary policy

2. The Taylor principle
    a. implies the *IS* curve is downward sloping.
    b. holds when $\lambda > 0$.
    c. leads to higher real interest rates when inflation decreases.
    d. All of the above are correct.

3. The Federal Reserve can control real short-term interest rates because
    a. prices are sticky.
    b. of the Taylor principle.
    c. nominal interest rates are fixed.
    d. expected inflation is perfectly flexible.

4. The Federal Reserve affects the short-term nominal interest rate
    a. by enforcing contracts.
    b. by changing the discount rate.
    c. through adjusting reserves in the banking system.
    d. through influencing fiscal policy.

5. A movement to the right along a given *MP* curve means
    a. inflation is increasing.
    b. an autonomous policy tightening has occurred.
    c. the federal funds rate is held constant.
    d. expected future inflation has increased.

6. When $\bar{r}$ decreases, this causes a movement along the _____ curve, and shifts the _____ curve.
    a. *MP; AD*
    b. *MP; IS*
    c. *AD; MP*
    d. *IS; AD*

7. When $\bar{f}$ increases, this causes a _____ the *IS* curve, and a _____ the *AD* curve.
    a. movement along; movement along
    b. movement along; shift of
    c. shift of; movement along
    d. shift of; shift of

8. The slope of the *AD* curve is given as
    a. $-\lambda$.
    b. $1/(1 - mpc)$.
    c. $-\lambda(d + x)/(1 - mpc)$.
    d. $1 - mpc$.

9. When the Federal Reserve decreased interest rates in 2007 and 2008, this demonstrated that
    a. it was violating the Taylor principle.
    b. potential increases in interest rates due to higher inflation were more than offset by an autonomous policy easing.
    c. the *MP* curve shifted upward.
    d. monetary policy was moving down along a fixed *MP* curve.

10. Suppose that taxes are decreased and the central bank conducts an autonomous easing of monetary policy. What will be the result?
    a. The *IS* curve shifts right, the *MP* curve shifts down, and the *AD* curve shifts right
    b. The *IS* curve shifts right, the *MP* curve shifts up, and there is an ambiguous effect on the *AD* curve
    c. The *IS* curve shifts left, the *MP* curve shifts down, and the *AD* curve shifts right
    d. The *IS* curve shifts left, the *MP* curve shifts up, and the *AD* curve shifts left

11. An autonomous monetary tightening results in
    a. $\bar{r}$ increasing.
    b. the *IS* and *AD* curves shifting left.
    c. a movement along the *IS* curve.
    d. Both (a) and (c) are correct.

12. Which of the following represents a movement along a given *AD* curve?
    a. Inflation increases, the real interest rate decreases, and aggregate output increases.
    b. Inflation decreases, the real interest rate decreases, and aggregate output decreases.
    c. Inflation decreases, the real interest rate decreases, and aggregate output increases.
    d. Inflation increases, the real interest rate increases, and aggregate output increases.

13. Any factor that shifts the _____ curve shifts the _____ curve in the _____ direction.
    a. *IS*; *AD*; same
    b. *IS*; *AD*; opposite
    c. *MP*; *IS*; same
    d. *MP*; *IS*; opposite

14. An autonomous _____ shifts the *AD* curve to the _____.
    a. consumption expenditure decrease; right
    b. tightening of monetary policy; left
    c. investment spending increase; left
    d. easing of monetary policy; left

15. If government purchases decrease and an autonomous monetary policy easing occurs simultaneously, what will be the effect?
    a. The *IS*, *MP*, and *AD* curves are unaffected.
    b. The *IS* curve shifts left, the *MP* curve shifts down, and the *AD* curve does not shift.
    c. The *IS* curve shifts left, the *MP* curve shifts down, and the *AD* curve has an ambiguous change.
    d. Inflation will increase, real interest rates will increase, and aggregate output will increase.

16. Why might the central bank choose to conduct an autonomous policy tightening?
    a. if the economy were entering a recession
    b. if inflation was increasing
    c. if inflation was decreasing
    d. if expected future inflation was increasing

17. A change in fiscal policy shifts the _____ curve, and an autonomous change in monetary policy shifts the _____ curve.
    a. *IS; MP*
    b. *IS; IS*
    c. *MP; MP*
    d. *MP; IS*

18. A leftward shift in the *AD* curve can be caused by
    a. an increase in inflation.
    b. an increase in financial frictions.
    c. an increase in government purchases.
    d. a decrease in the autonomous real interest rate.

For questions 19 and 20, assume that the *IS* curve is given as $Y = 20 - 2r$ and the *MP* curve is given as $r = 2 + 0.5\pi$.

19. Which of the following statements is true?
    a. The central bank is violating the Taylor principle.
    b. The *AD* curve is given as $Y = 16 - \pi$.
    c. When inflation is 3%, the nominal federal funds rate is 3.5%.
    d. When inflation is 3%, the goods market equilibrium level of output is $Y = 14$.

20. If the central bank changes the autonomous real interest rate to $\bar{r} = 3$, what will happen to output if inflation remains constant at 1%?
    a. Output will decrease from $Y = 15$ to $Y = 14$.
    b. Output will decrease from $Y = 15$ to $Y = 13$.
    c. Output will increase from $Y = 20$ to $Y = 22$.
    d. The effects on output cannot be determined.

Solutions

Terms and Definitions

<u>2</u> aggregate demand curve

<u>4</u> autonomous easing of monetary policy

<u>1</u> autonomous tightening of monetary policy

<u>5</u> monetary policy (MP) curve

<u>3</u> Taylor principle

Practice Problems

1. a.

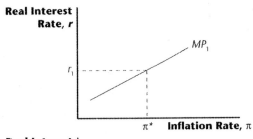

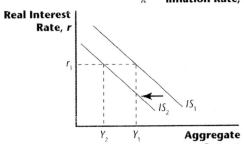

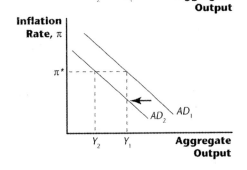

b.

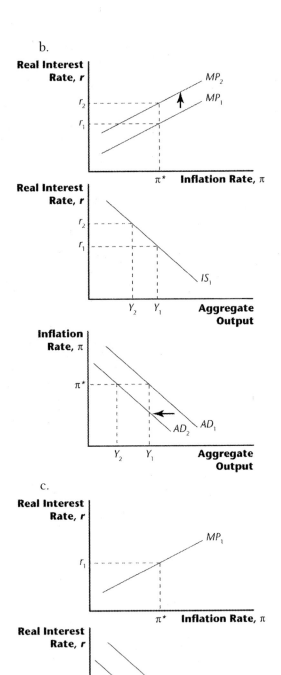

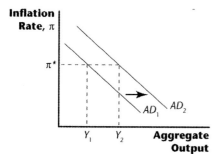

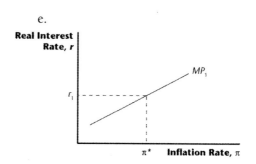

d.

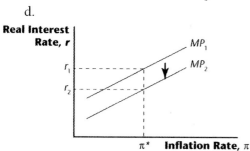

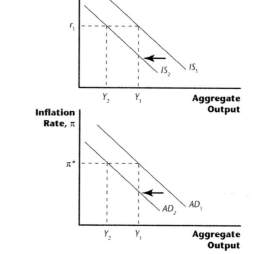

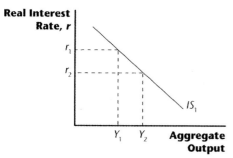

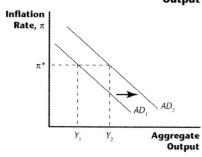

2.

Shift Factor	Direction of Change	IS Curve Shifts...	MP Curve Shifts...	Effect on Interest Rate	Effect on Aggregate Output
Autonomous Consumer Expenditure	+	Right	No Shift	0	+
Autonomous Investment Spending	–	Left	No Shift	0	–
Government Spending	+	Right	No Shift	0	+
Taxes	+	Left	No Shift	0	–
Autonomous Net Exports	–	Left	No Shift	0	–
Autonomous Monetary Policy	Easing	No Shift	Down	–	+
Financial Frictions	–	Right	No Shift	0	+
Autonomous Monetary Policy	Tightening	No Shift	Up	+	–

3. a. $Y = 13.5 - \pi$.

    b. $Y = 12.5$; $r = 1.25\%$.

    c. Output decreases to $Y = 11.5$; the real interest rate increases to $r = 1.75\%$. The *MP*, *IS*, and *AD* curves are unaffected because the change in inflation just represents a movement along the *MP*, *IS*, and *AD* curves, respectively.

    d. $Y = 14.5 - \pi$; $Y = 13.5$; $r = 1.25\%$.

4. a. $r = 1.5 + 0.75\pi$.

    b. $Y = 10.5 - 0.75\pi$.

    c. The new AD curve will be $Y = 11.7 - 0.75\pi$. At an inflation rate of $\pi = 2\%$, output was $Y = 9$ before, and after the tax change it increases to $Y = 10.2$.

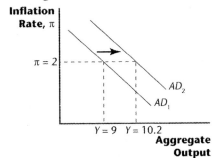

    d. The central bank can increase the autonomous real interest rate to $\bar{r} = 2.7$. This ensures that output will remain constant at $Y = 9$ when the inflation rate is $\pi = 2\%$.

Short-Answer Questions

1. Since prices are sticky in the short run and hence inflation expectations are essentially fixed, changing the nominal short-term interest rate has the effect of changing the real interest rate counterpart.

2. In order for monetary policy to be able to stabilize inflation, monetary policy must react by increasing the real interest rate whenever inflation increases, implying a positive slope of the *MP* curve. This requires a more than one-for-one change in nominal interest rates as expected inflation changes.

3. As λ becomes larger, it means that the central bank will react by changing real interest rates more in response to any given change in inflation. This can be interpreted as the central bank in some sense worrying more about inflation, and therefore acting more aggressively to keep it at a desired level.

4. With inflation increasing during this time, this would suggest a movement up along the *MP* curve and an increase in interest rates. However, due to the weakness in the economy due to the unfolding financial crisis, the Federal Reserve pursued an autonomous monetary policy easing, which actually resulted in interest rates decreasing, even though inflation was higher during this period.

5. An autonomous monetary policy easing shifts the *MP* curve down; an autonomous monetary policy tightening shifts the *MP* curve up. The economy moves along a given *MP* curve when the current inflation rate changes, which is viewed as an automatic policy response by the central bank.

6. The Federal Reserve might pursue an autonomous monetary policy easing if the economy is in danger of recession in the near future, or if expected future inflation decreases sharply. An autonomous policy tightening may occur if inflation is expected to increase in the future, or the economy is in danger of overheating.

7. Changes in autonomous consumption expenditure, autonomous investment, autonomous net exports, government spending, taxes, and financial frictions all shift the *IS* curve. A movement along a given *IS* curve occurs when the real interest rate changes, which could be due to a change in the current inflation rate, or a shift of the *MP* curve.

8. When inflation increases, this prompts an automatic response by the central bank to increase the real interest rate. When real interest rates rise, this reduces planned investment and net exports, which decreases the equilibrium level of output in a goods market equilibrium. The result is that when inflation increases, the quantity of output demanded in a goods market equilibrium decreases, leading to a downward-sloping relationship between inflation and aggregate output demanded.

9. An autonomous monetary policy easing shifts the *AD* curve to the right. An increase in government spending, or a decrease in taxes shifts the *AD* curve to the right.

10. A decrease in autonomous consumption will shift the *IS* and *AD* curves to the left; the *MP* curve is unaffected. To keep the *AD* curve from shifting, the central bank can conduct an autonomous monetary policy easing, which will shift the *AD* curve back to the right.

Critical Thinking

Fiscal Policy	Monetary Policy	*IS* Curve	*MP* Curve	Aggregate Output
Expansionary	Autonomous Easing	Right	Down	+
Contractionary	Autonomous Tightening	Left	Up	–
Expansionary	Autonomous Tightening	Right	Up	?
Contractionary	Autonomous Easing	Left	Down	?

True/False Questions

1. F
2. F
3. T
4. T
5. F
6. F
7. F
8. T
9. T
10. F
11. F
12. F
13. T
14. F
15. T

Multiple-Choice Questions

1. c
2. b
3. a
4. c
5. a
6. d
7. d
8. c
9. b
10. a
11. d
12. c
13. a
14. b
15. c
16. d
17. a
18. b
19. b
20. b

22 Aggregate Demand and Supply Analysis*

Chapter Review

PREVIEW

This chapter develops and applies the tools of aggregate demand and aggregate supply analysis. Those tools are used to illustrate the effects of changes in autonomous monetary policy, government purchases and taxes, financial frictions, autonomous spending, and supply shocks on output and the inflation rate.

AGGREGATE DEMAND

Aggregate demand is made up of four components: *consumption expenditure*, *planned investment spending*, *government purchases*, and *net exports*. The *aggregate demand curve* describes the inverse relationship between the quantity of aggregate output demanded and the inflation rate when all other variables are held constant. The aggregate demand curve slopes downward because as the inflation rate increases, the central bank will increase the real interest rate to keep inflation from spiraling out of control. The higher real interest rate causes planned investment spending and, therefore, the quantity of aggregate output demanded to decrease. Additionally, as the interest rate rises the domestic currency appreciates, which causes net exports and, therefore, aggregate output demanded to fall.

There are seven basic factors, often referred to as *demand shocks* that can shift the aggregate demand curve. The scenarios described below all shift the *AD* curve to the right, for any given inflation rate.

1. **Autonomous monetary policy.** A decrease in $\bar{r}$, the autonomous real interest rate controlled by the central bank, leads to higher planned investment spending and net exports and increases the quantity of aggregate output demanded.

---

*This is Chapter 23 in the 3rd ed.

2. **Government purchases.** An increase in government spending, $\overline{G}$, increases the quantity of aggregate output demanded.

3. **Taxes.** A decrease in taxes, $\overline{T}$, increases disposable income, increases consumption expenditure, and increases the quantity of aggregate output demanded.

4. **Autonomous net exports.** An increase in autonomous net exports, $\overline{\overline{NX}}$, increases the quantity of aggregate output demanded.

5. **Autonomous consumption expenditure.** An increase in autonomous consumption, $\overline{C}$, for instance due to increased consumer optimism or higher wealth increases overall consumption and the quantity of aggregate output demanded.

6. **Autonomous investment.** An increase in business optimism increases $\overline{I}$, which increases planned investment and the quantity of aggregate output demanded.

7. **Financial frictions.** A decrease in financial frictions, $\overline{f}$, decreases the real cost of borrowing, which increases planned investment at any given real interest rate and inflation rate. This increases the quantity of aggregate output demanded.

AGGREGATE SUPPLY

The *aggregate supply curve* describes the relationship between the inflation rate and the quantity of output supplied when all other variables are held constant. Because prices and wages take time to adjust fully to their long-run levels, there are two different aggregate supply curves: a long-run aggregate supply curve and a short-run aggregate supply curve. In the long run, output in the economy is determined by the amount of capital, labor, and technology, which means that the long-run aggregate supply curve is vertical at the *natural rate of output,* or *potential output.* The natural rate of output is the level of output produced when the unemployment rate is at the *natural rate of unemployment.* When the economy is at the natural rate level of output, it is also at full employment where the demand for labor equals the supply of labor.

The short-run aggregate supply curve is explained by three primary factors, which help explain the behavior of inflation in the short run.

- **Expected inflation.** When expected inflation increases, workers will demand higher wages to compensate for the higher cost of living, which will directly increase inflation.

- **Output gap.** When the *output gap,* the difference between output and potential output, increases, labor markets are tight, workers will demand higher wages as a result, and firms will opportunistically raise prices to compensate, all of which leads to higher inflation.

- **Price (supply) shocks.** When *price shocks* occur, they drive up inflation independent of the output gap or inflation expectations. This can come from energy price shocks or from *cost-push shocks* where workers demand wage increases higher than productivity gains.

Putting all three of these factors together gives the short-run *AS* curve as $\pi = \pi^e + (Y - Y^P) + \rho$, where π^e is inflation expectations, $(Y - Y^P)$ represents the effect of the output gap on inflation, and ρ captures the effect of *supply shocks* on inflation. When the parameter Y increases, this means prices and wages are more flexible, and the short-run *AS* curve becomes steeper.

SHIFTS IN AGGREGATE SUPPLY CURVES

Factors that affect the long-run aggregate supply curve, and hence potential output, include anything that affects the amount of capital, labor, or technology. These factors tend to change at a steady pace and so are viewed as relatively constant in the long run. Changes in the natural rate of unemployment over time can also affect potential output and hence shift the *LRAS* curve. Thus, an increase in capital, labor, or technology (productivity) or a decrease in the natural rate of unemployment all shift the *LRAS* curve to the right, and vice versa.

The three factors that affect inflation in the short run also can act to shift the *AS* curve. An increase in inflation expectations or an increase in price shocks increases inflation for any given level of output, thus shifting the *AS* curve upward and vice versa. In addition, persistent output gaps can shift the *AS* curve upward. An increase in output above potential output (representing a movement along a given *AS* curve) that lasts too long can have a spillover effect, with higher inflation fueling higher expected inflation, and eventually result in a shift upward in the *AS* curve. This process will continue as long as output remains above potential.

EQUILIBRIUM IN AGGREGATE DEMAND AND SUPPLY ANALYSIS

There are two types of (*general*) *equilibrium* in aggregate demand and supply analysis: short run and long run. A short-run equilibrium is at the intersection of the aggregate demand curve and the aggregate supply curve (point A in the figure below). A long-run equilibrium occurs when aggregate demand and supply intersect at the long-run aggregate supply curve (point B in the figure below).

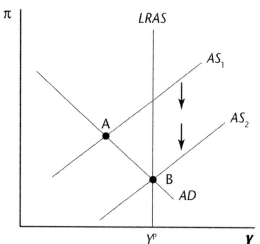

The economy has a *self-correcting mechanism,* which means that it returns to the natural rate of output in the long run. When aggregate demand and aggregate supply intersect below the natural rate level of output as shown at point A in the figure above, slack in the labor market causes wages to fall. As wages (a cost of production) fall, inflation and inflation expectations decline, and the aggregate supply curve shifts down until it intersects the long-run aggregate supply curve at the natural rate level of output (at point B in the figure above). When aggregate demand and aggregate supply intersect above the natural rate level of output, tightness in the labor market causes wages to rise. As wages rise, inflation and inflation expectations adjust upward, and the aggregate supply curve shifts up until it intersects the long-run aggregate supply curve at the long-run equilibrium.

CHANGES IN EQUIILIBRIUM: AGGREGATE DEMAND SHOCKS

Combining aggregate demand and supply with the long-run aggregate supply curve allows us to analyze the effects of various shifts on output and inflation. For example, starting from a long-run equilibrium, a positive *demand shock* such as an autonomous easing of monetary policy, a decrease in taxes, a decrease in financial frictions, or an increase in government purchases, net exports, autonomous consumption expenditure, or autonomous investment will all increase aggregate demand, shifting the *AD* curve to the right. This causes output and inflation to rise in the short run. Eventually, through the self-correcting mechanism, the economy adjusts back to the long-run equilibrium where output is at potential and the inflation rate is permanently higher.

One example of a negative demand shock is the Volcker disinflation. This was prompted by the Federal Reserve to conduct a sharp autonomous policy tightening in the early 1980s in an attempt to permanently reduce the long-run inflation rate. As our *AD/AS* analysis would predict, the policy was eventually successful at lowering the long-term inflation rate; however, it also produced a deep recession as the self-correcting mechanism operated. Another example is the period around 2000, when the "tech" bubble burst, among other adverse events. The negative shocks that occurred during the time acted to reduce autonomous consumption and planned investment, reducing aggregate demand. This produced a recession, which decreased inflation and increased unemployment in the short run.

CHANGES IN EQUIILIBRIUM: AGGREGATE SUPPLY (PRICE) SHOCKS

The effects of changes in aggregate supply ultimately depend on whether the shocks that occur are temporary or permanent. Shifts that affect only the aggregate supply curve tend to be temporary but still can be a source of fluctuations in aggregate output. Temporary negative supply shocks such as tightness in the labor market, a rise in the expected inflation rate, an increase in wages above productivity gains, or an increase in the price of raw material used for production all shift the aggregate supply curve up, which causes output to fall and the inflation rate to rise. Starting from a long-run equilibrium, an increase in the price of raw materials will cause the aggregate supply curve to shift up, which will cause output to fall and the inflation rate to rise. The combination of falling output and higher inflation is called *stagflation*. In this short-run equilibrium, the labor market is slack and so wages will decline, which will cause the aggregate supply curve to shift back to the right (the self-correcting mechanism) until the economy adjusts back to the long-run equilibrium. The ultimate long-run effect of negative supply shocks is that output and the inflation rate are unchanged. These types of shocks prevailed in the 1970s, in which there were two significant negative supply shocks due primarily to sharp increases in energy and oil prices. The effect was to sharply increase both inflation and the unemployment rate.

Positive or favorable supply shocks can be from improvements in technology that lower the cost of production and cause the aggregate supply curve to shift down. This causes output to rise and the inflation rate to fall in the short run; over time, the self-correcting mechanism will work to ensure that inflation and output return to their original long-run equilibrium.

The usual assumption in aggregate demand and supply analysis is that the natural rate level of output grows steadily over time, and shifts in aggregate demand and supply have no effect on the natural rate level of output. According to *real business cycle theory,* the natural rate level of output does not grow steadily over time. Instead, changes in tastes (worker's willingness to work, for example) and technology (productivity) cause the long-run aggregate supply curve to fluctuate and are therefore major sources of fluctuation in aggregate output. According to this theory, there is very little role for discretionary policy to reduce business cycle fluctuations.

One example of the effects of these types of permanent supply shocks is the period from 1995–1999. During this period, several demographic and productivity related factors led the *LRAS* curve to shift permanently to the right. The result is that in both the short run, and the long run, inflation decreased and output increased as predicted by *AD/AS* analysis.

An example of both negative demand and supply shocks occurring concurrently can be seen in the period from 2007–2009. In 2007, sharp increases in oil prices resulted in a negative supply shock; inflation increased and output began to decrease. By later into 2007, the global financial crisis began to cause a sharp increase in financial frictions, and by the fall of 2008 financial markets nearly collapsed. This lead to a deep, sharp drop in aggregate demand; inflation fell dramatically, and unemployment rose sharply to 10% by the end of 2009.

This leads to the following conclusions:

1. A shift in the *AD* curve affects output in the short-run but not the long-run. Inflation changes in both the short-run and long-run.

2. A temporary supply shock affects output and inflation only in the short-run. Holding all other factors constant, it will not have any effects on output or inflation in the long-run.

3. A permanent supply shock affects both output and inflation in both the short-run and long-run.

4. The economy's self-correcting mechanism ensures that output returns to potential over time.

AD/AS ANALYSIS OF FOREIGN BUSINESS CYCLE EPISODES

The United Kingdom and China fared much differently as a result of the global financial crisis that took hold in 2007–2009. The same negative supply shock from high oil prices that affected the United States had a similar effect in the United Kingdom, pushing the *AS* curve upward, raising inflation, and lowering output somewhat. It took a bit longer for the effects of the financial crisis to have an impact on aggregate demand in the United Kingdom, but eventually as demand contracted and the effects of the *AS* shock wore off, both inflation and output fell precipitously, with unemployment rising to 7.8% by the end of 2008.

The experience of China during the financial crisis is quite different from either the United States or the United Kingdom. For the most part, China was relatively unaffected by the rise in oil prices that affected so many other economies around the world, leaving the *AS* curve essentially unchanged. However, because China's economy is so dependent on exports to the rest of the world, the demand for goods worldwide, especially exports out of China decreased sharply following the crisis. As a result, the *AD* curve in China shifted sharply to the left, causing a significant recession. Rather than relying on the self-correcting mechanism, policymakers in China reacted quickly to prop up demand by creating a massive fiscal stimulus package, along with an autonomous monetary easing. These two measures shifted the *AD* curve quickly back to the right. Because of the swift and decisive policy measures, the Chinese economy weathered the crisis relatively well.

Helpful Hints

The key to understanding the aggregate demand and supply model is to understand that there are two types of equilibria. An equilibrium means a position of rest. The short-run equilibrium is a position of temporary rest. Short-run equilibrium is where the aggregate supply curve intersects the aggregate demand curve. This intersection can occur below, at, or above the long-run aggregate supply curve, which is the vertical line at the natural rate level of output. When this equilibrium occurs below (to the left of) the natural rate level of output, slack in the labor market will push wages down and cause the aggregate supply curve to shift downward until it intersects the long-run aggregate supply curve at the natural rate level of output. When the short-run equilibrium is above (to the right) of the natural rate level of output, tightness in the labor market will push wages up and cause the aggregate supply curve to shift upward until it intersects the long-run aggregate supply curve at the natural rate level of output. When the short-run aggregate supply curve intersects the aggregate demand curve at the long-run aggregate supply curve, the economy is in long-run equilibrium, and there is no tendency for the economy to move from that position unless some "shock" causes either the aggregate supply curve or the aggregate demand curve to shift.

Terms and Definitions

Choose a definition for each key term.

Key Terms:

_12_ aggregate demand curve

_13_ aggregate supply curve

_5_ cost-push shocks

_17_ consumption expenditure

_14_ demand shocks

_7_ government purchases

_16_ (general) equilibrium

_10_ natural rate of output

_11_ natural rate of unemployment

_6_ net exports

_4_ output gap

_18_ planned investment spending

_15_ potential output

_9_ price shocks

_2_ real business cycle theory

_1_ self-correcting mechanism

_8_ stagflation

_3_ supply shocks

Definitions:

1. A characteristic of the economy that causes output to return to the natural rate level of output regardless of where output is initially

2. A theory that views real shocks to tastes and technology as the major driving force behind short-run fluctuations in the business cycle

3. Changes in technology and the supply of raw materials that can shift the aggregate supply curve

4. The difference between aggregate output and potential output $Y - \bar{Y}$

5. Where workers push for wages higher than productivity gains, thereby driving up costs and inflation

6. Net foreign spending on domestic goods and services, equal to exports minus imports

7. Spending by all levels of government on goods and services

8. A situation when the inflation rate is rising and the level of aggregate output is falling

9. Shifts in inflation that are independent of the tightness in the labor markets or of expected inflation

10. The level of aggregate output produced at the natural rate of unemployment

11. The rate of unemployment consistent with full employment at which the demand for labor equals the supply of labor

12. The relationship between the quantity of aggregate output demanded and the inflation rate

13. The relationship between the quantity of aggregate output supplied in the short run and the inflation rate

14. The term used to describe the seven basic factors that shift aggregate demand

15. The natural rate of output; level of production that is sustainable in the long run

16. When all markets are simultaneously in equilibrium at the point where the quantity of aggregate output demanded equals the quantity of aggregate output supplied

17. Total spending on currently produced consumer goods and services

18. Total planned spending by businesses on new machines, factories, and other new physical capital, plus planned spending on new homes

Problems and Short-Answer Questions

PRACTICE PROBLEMS

1. Suppose the economy is initially in a long-run equilibrium at point A as shown in the figure below.

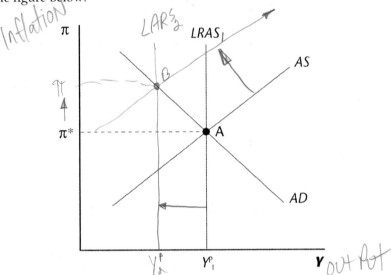

a. Use the graph above to illustrate the effect of an increase in the natural rate of unemployment on the inflation rate (π) and aggregate output (Y) in the short run.

b. Use the graph to illustrate the adjustment back to a long-run equilibrium starting from the short-run equilibrium you illustrated for part (a).

c. Describe the self-correcting mechanism that brings the economy back to a long-run equilibrium.

_____

_____

_____

2. Suppose the economy is initially in a long-run equilibrium at point A as shown in the figure below.

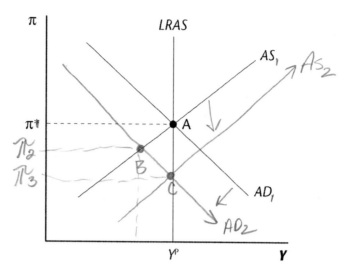

a. Use the graph above to illustrate the effect of an increase in the autonomous real interest rate on the inflation rate (π) and aggregate output (Y) in the short run. Label this point B.

b. Use the graph to illustrate the adjustment back to the long-run equilibrium starting from the short-run equilibrium you illustrated for part (a). Label this point C.

c. What is the effect of the change in monetary policy on aggregate output (Y) and the inflation rate (π) in the short run?

_____

_____

_____

d. Describe the self-correcting mechanism that brings the economy back to a long-run equilibrium. What is the effect of the change in monetary policy on aggregate output (Y) and the inflation rate (π) in the long run?

_____

_____

_____

_____

3. Suppose the economy is initially in long-run equilibrium at point A as shown in the figure below.

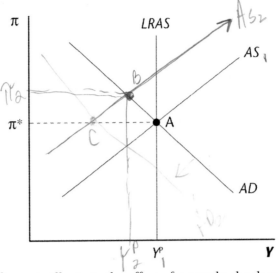

a. Use the figure to illustrate the effect of a supply shock such as a reduction in the availability of oil on the inflation rate (π) and aggregate output (Y) in the short run. Label this point B.

b. Use the figure to illustrate the adjustment back to the long-run equilibrium starting from the short-run equilibrium you illustrated for part (a). Describe the adjustment process back to the long-run equilibrium.

_____

_____

4. Suppose the economy is initially in long-run equilibrium at point A as shown in the figure below.

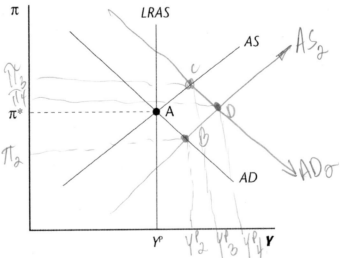

a. Use the figure to illustrate the effect of a temporary positive supply shock such as a temporary increase in agricultural production on the inflation rate (π) and aggregate output (Y) in the short run. Label this point B in the graph.

b. Use the same figure to illustrate the effect of just a positive demand shock such as an increase in autonomous consumption or investment spending on the inflation rate (π) and aggregate output (Y) in the short run, ignoring the shock occurring in part (a) described above. Label this point C in the graph.

c. If both the temporary positive supply shock and positive demand shock happen simultaneously, what will happen to inflation and output, based upon how you have drawn the graph? Label this point D.

_____

_____

d. More generally, can you say for sure what will happen to inflation and output in the short run in this case? Why or why not?

_____

_____

_____

SHORT-ANSWER QUESTIONS

1. Why does the aggregate demand curve slope downward?

_____

_____

2. What factors cause the aggregate demand curve to shift?

_____

_____

3. Explain why the aggregate supply curve slopes upward in the short run.

_____

_____

4. What factors would shift the aggregate supply curve up? What factors would shift the long-run aggregate supply curve to the left?

_____

_____

5. According to real business cycle theory, what is the major driving force behind short-run business cycle fluctuations?

    _____

    _____

6. How does the self-correcting mechanism operate to ensure that output will reach potential in the long run?

    _____

    _____

7. How did the Volcker disinflation affect the U.S. economy in the short run and long run?

    _____

    _____

8. What factors led to a brief period of stagflation, followed by a sharp decline in inflation and increase in unemployment during 2007–2009?

    _____

    _____

9. Describe the movements in aggregate demand and supply that resulted in the rise in inflation and the increase in unemployment during the periods of negative supply shocks during 1973–1975 and 1978–1980.

    _____

    _____

10. Describe the movements in aggregate demand and supply that resulted in the rise in aggregate output, the decrease in unemployment, and the decrease in inflation during the period of favorable supply shocks from 1995–1999.

    _____

    _____

Critical Thinking

You read in the newspaper that government spending is expected to rise by $30 billion this year and one of the Senators from your state is touting how this increase in spending will lead to an increase in employment and aggregate output. The economy is currently in long-run equilibrium at the natural rate of output.

1. Will the increase in government spending increase employment and aggregate output in the short run?

    _____

    _____

2. Will the increase in government spending increase employment and aggregate output in the long run?

    _____

    _____

3. What will happen to the inflation rate in the long run and the short run as a result of the increase in government spending?

    _____

    _____

4. Now assume that the economy is below the natural rate level of output and your Senator believes the self-correcting mechanism is slow. What policy action, if any, would your Senator likely favor? Why?

    _____

    _____

5. Now assume that unemployment increases and output decreases from its current long-run equilibrium and your Senator believes in real business cycle theory. What policy action, if any, would your Senator likely favor? Why?

    _____

    _____

Self-Test

TRUE/FALSE QUESTIONS

_____1. A decrease in the inflation rate causes the exchange rate to appreciate, which leads to a decline in the quantity of aggregate demand.

_____2. The four components of aggregate demand are consumption, planned investment, government spending, and exports.

_____3. An increase in financial frictions reduces the real cost of borrowing and shifts the aggregate demand curve to the right.

_____4. When the real interest rate changes due to a change in inflation, the aggregate demand curve shifts.

_____5. The aggregate demand curve would shift to the right if household wealth increased or businesses become more optimistic.

_____6. The self-correcting mechanism describes how the economy eventually returns to the natural rate level of output regardless of where output is initially.

_____7. The aggregate supply curve is downward sloping and the long-run aggregate supply curve is vertical.

_____8. Inflation expectations affect the short-run aggregate supply curve, but not the long-run supply curve.

_____9. A decrease in import prices shifts the aggregate supply curve down, increasing output and lowering inflation in the short run.

_____10. The natural rate of unemployment is the rate of unemployment that the economy gravitates to in the long run.

_____11. Inflation rises when the unemployment rate is equal to the natural rate of unemployment.

_____12. Starting from the natural rate level of output, an increase in autonomous consumption expenditure has no impact on the inflation rate in the long run.

_____13. When aggregate output is above the natural level of output, the aggregate supply curve shifts up; when aggregate output is below the natural rate level of output, the aggregate supply curve shifts down.

_____14. During the period of 2001–2004, the aggregate supply curve shifted right causing unemployment and inflation to fall.

_____15. China's economy fared better during the global financial crisis than did the economies of either the United States or United Kingdom.

MULTIPLE-CHOICE QUESTIONS

1. The aggregate demand curve describes the relationship between
   a. the inflation rate and the real interest rate.
   b. the real interest rate and the quantity of aggregate output demanded.
   c. the inflation rate and the quantity of aggregate output demanded.
   d. the inflation rate and the quantity of output produced.

2. The aggregate supply curve describes the relationship between
   a. the inflation rate and the real interest rate.
   b. the real interest rate and the quantity of aggregate output supplied.
   c. the inflation rate and the quantity of aggregate output supplied.
   d. the real interest rate and planned investment.

3. Which of the following shifts the aggregate demand curve?
   a. an increase in the autonomous real interest rate
   b. an increase in inflation
   c. an increase in expected inflation
   d. an increase in productivity

4. When financial frictions decrease, the real cost of borrowing _____, and the *AD* curve _____.
   a. decreases; shifts left
   b. decreases; shifts right
   c. increases; shifts right
   d. is unaffected; does not shift

5. A tightening of the labor market will cause
   a. the aggregate demand curve to shift left.
   b. the aggregate supply curve to shift up.
   c. the aggregate demand curve to shift right.
   d. the aggregate supply curve to shift down.

6. When inflation and inflation expectations adjust to move output to potential, this is an example of
   a. the self-correcting mechanism.
   b. the real business cycle theory.
   c. stabilization policy.
   d. autonomous monetary policy.

7. When the natural rate of unemployment increases,
   a. inflation is higher, and output is lower in the long run.
   b. inflation is higher, and output is the same in the long run.
   c. inflation and output are higher in the long run.
   d. inflation and output are lower in the long run.

8. When the labor market is tight,
   a. wages fall, and the aggregate supply curve shifts up.
   b. wages rise, and the aggregate supply curve shifts up.
   c. wages fall, and the aggregate supply curve shifts down.
   d. wages rise, and the aggregate supply curve shifts down.

9. If autonomous consumption declines, and there is a sharp increase in energy prices, you would expect
   a. inflation and output to decrease in the short run.
   b. inflation to have an ambiguous effect, but output to decrease.
   c. inflation to increase, and output to decrease in the short run.
   d. an ambiguous effect on both inflation and output in the short run.

10. Which of the following will not cause the aggregate demand curve to shift?
    a. a change in government spending
    b. a decrease in financial frictions
    c. a change in autonomous monetary policy
    d. tightness in the labor market

11. In the short run, a rightward shift in the aggregate demand curve will cause
    a. the inflation rate to rise and output to rise.
    b. the inflation rate to rise and output to fall.
    c. the inflation rate to fall and output to rise.
    d. the inflation rate to fall and output to fall.

12. In the long run, a rightward shift in aggregate demand will cause
    a. the inflation rate to fall and output to rise.
    b. the inflation rate to rise and output to rise.
    c. the inflation rate to rise and output to remain unchanged.
    d. the inflation rate to remain unchanged and output to rise.

13. An increase in the expected inflation rate will cause the
    a. aggregate supply curve to shift up.
    b. aggregate demand curve to shift left.
    c. aggregate supply curve to shift down.
    d. aggregate demand curve to shift right.

14. A successful cost-push shock by workers means
    a. wage increases are higher than productivity growth, and the aggregate supply curve will shift up.
    b. wage increases are equal to productivity growth, and the aggregate demand curve will shift left.
    c. wage increases are higher than productivity growth, and the aggregate supply curve will shift down.
    d. wage increases are less than productivity growth, and the aggregate demand curve will shift right.

15. A negative supply shock that raises production costs will cause the
    a. aggregate supply curve to shift up.
    b. aggregate demand curve to shift left.
    c. aggregate supply curve to shift down.
    c. aggregate demand curve to shift right.

16. An upward shift in aggregate supply *initially* causes
    a. the inflation rate to rise and output to rise.
    b. the inflation rate to rise and output to fall.
    c. the inflation rate to fall and output to rise.
    d. the inflation rate to fall and output to fall.

17. An upward shift in aggregate supply *ultimately* causes
    a. the inflation rate to fall and output to rise.
    b. the inflation rate to rise and output to rise.
    c. the inflation rate to rise and output to remain unchanged.
    d. the inflation rate to remain unchanged and output to remain unchanged.

18. According to real business cycle theory, short-run business cycle fluctuations are caused by
    a. changes in government spending and taxes.
    b. changes in autonomous monetary policy.
    c. changes in tastes and technology.
    d. changes in net exports.

19. The Volcker disinflation is an example of
    a. a negative demand shock.
    b. a negative supply shock.
    c. contractionary fiscal policy.
    d. expansionary monetary policy.

20. During the periods of negative supply shocks in 1973–1975 and 1978–1980,
    a. inflation increased, and unemployment decreased.
    b. inflation decreased, and unemployment increased.
    c. inflation increased, and unemployment increased.
    d. inflation decreased, and unemployment decreased.

Solutions

Definitions:

<u>12</u> aggregate demand curve

<u>13</u> aggregate supply curve

<u>5</u> cost-push shocks

<u>17</u> consumption expenditure

<u>14</u> demand shocks

<u>7</u> government purchases

<u>16</u> (general) equilibrium

<u>10</u> natural rate of output

<u>11</u> natural rate of unemployment

<u>6</u> net exports

<u>4</u> output gap

<u>18</u> planned investment spending

<u>15</u> potential output

<u>9</u> price shocks

<u>2</u> real business cycle theory

<u>1</u> self-correcting mechanism

<u>8</u> stagflation

<u>3</u> supply shocks

Practice Problems

1. a, b.

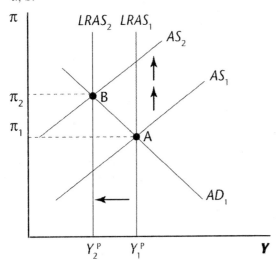

c. The increase in the natural rate of unemployment shifts the *LRAS* curve to the left. Once this happens, the short-run equilibrium at point A is at a level of output above the new potential level of output at Y_2^P. The self-correcting mechanism implies inflation and inflation expectations will increase, shifting the *AS* curve up over time, until the economy reaches the new long-run equilibrium at point B. Output is lower and inflation is higher in the new long-run equilibrium.

2. a, b.

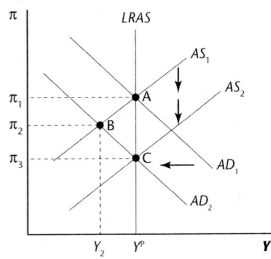

c. The autonomous policy tightening shifts the *AD* curve to AD_2. The new short-run equilibrium is shown in the graph at point B. Output and inflation both decrease in the new short-run equilibrium.

d. At point B, there is slack in the labor market and downward pressure on prices and wages. The self-correcting mechanism implies inflation and inflation expectations will decrease, shifting the *AS* curve down over time, until the economy reaches the new long-run equilibrium at point C. Output returns to potential output, and inflation is lower in the new long-run equilibrium.

3. a.

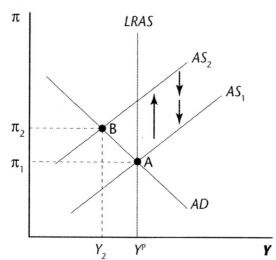

b. The negative supply shock shifts the *AS* curve up to AS_2. At the new short-run equilibrium at point B, inflation is higher, and output is lower. The self-correcting mechanism implies inflation and inflation expectations will eventually decrease as the supply shock wears off, shifting the *AS* curve back down over time until the economy reaches the original long-run equilibrium at point A. Output returns to potential output, and inflation returns to the original long-run equilibrium level.

4. a, b.

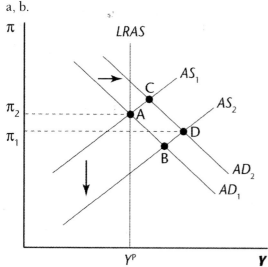

c. The temporary positive supply shock moves the *AS* curve down to AS_2, which would have the standalone effect of moving the economy to point B in the short run. The positive demand shock moves the *AD* curve to AD_2 and would have the standalone effect of moving the

economy to point C in the short run. Based on the way the graph is drawn above, with both the *AD* curve shifting right and the *AS* curve shifting down, inflation will decrease, and output will increase in the short run, moving the economy to point D.

d. You can say with certainty that output will increase in the short run because both shocks work in the same direction to increase output. However, you cannot say how inflation will be affected in the short run. This is because the aggregate demand effect works to increase inflation and the aggregate supply effect works to decrease inflation; without knowing the magnitudes of the shifts, it is impossible to say how inflation will be affected in the short run.

Short-Answer Questions

1. When the inflation rate increases, the central bank adjusts the real interest rate upward to stabilize inflation. As a result, when the real interest rate increases, planned investment spending decreases. In addition, the domestic currency appreciates, which decreases net exports. Both of these factors reduce the quantity of aggregate output demanded. Thus, when inflation increases, output demanded decreases and vice versa.

2. Changes in the autonomous real interest rate, government purchases, taxes, planned investment spending, consumption expenditures, net exports, and financial frictions shift the aggregate demand curve.

3. When production rises in the short run, the output gap gets larger, and there is very little slack in product and labor markets. As a result, it becomes more expensive to produce goods and services, so firms raise prices more readily. The result is that inflation rises in the short run as production increases.

4. An increase in inflation expectations, a persistently large output gap, or an adverse price shock such as a sharp increase in energy prices would all shift the *AS* curve up. Factors that would shift the *LRAS* curve to the left could be an increase in the natural rate of unemployment, a reduction in productivity (technology), or a decrease in the availability of capital or labor inputs in the long run.

5. According to real business cycle theory, shocks to tastes and technology are the major driving forces behind short-run fluctuations in the business cycle.

6. When the economy is producing at a level of output above the natural rate of output, labor markets are tight, and inflation starts to increase. The self-correcting mechanism implies that inflation expectations will increase, and this will shift the AS curve up, reducing output and closing the output gap until output reaches potential. Similarly, when the economy is producing at a level of output below the natural rate of output, labor markets are slack, and inflation starts to decrease. The self-correcting mechanism implies that inflation expectations will decrease, and this will shift the AS curve down, increasing output and closing the output gap until output reaches potential.

7. The Volcker disinflation was an attempt by the Federal Reserve to permanently decrease the long-run inflation rate from the high levels resulting from supply shocks and poor monetary policy in the 1970s. The Federal Reserve, under Chairman Paul Volcker, conducted a sharp autonomous monetary tightening in the early 1980s. The short-run effect was for the AD curve to shift significantly to the left, creating lower inflation and also a deep recession. In the long run, the self-correcting mechanism helped to push the AS curve down further, which closed the output gap and allowed inflation and inflation expectations to fall to a permanently lower level. By the middle part of the 1980s, unemployment was around 7%, and inflation had stabilized to below 4%.

8. Beginning around 2007, significant oil price increases led to a negative aggregate supply shock, which increased inflation to 5% and modestly increased unemployment to 5.5% by the middle of 2008. About this same time, financial frictions began to significantly increase as a consequence of the unfolding global financial crisis. In a matter of months, the negative aggregate supply shock disappeared and was replaced by a sharp contraction in autonomous consumption and planned investment. The result was a sharp decrease in aggregate demand, resulting in inflation falling to below zero into 2009, and unemployment increasing to 10% by the end of that year.

9. In 1973 the OPEC oil embargo caused oil prices to quadruple. In addition, crop failures caused food prices to rise, and removal of wage and price controls caused wages to rise. These three factors caused the aggregate supply curve to shift up, which led to a rise in both the inflation rate and the unemployment rate. Oil and food prices once again rose sharply in 1978, causing the aggregate supply curve to shift up. As a result, the inflation rate and unemployment rate again both shot upwards.

10. Over the period 1995–1999, medical costs fell, and productivity rose. These two factors caused the long-run aggregate supply curve to shift right. As a result, aggregate output increased over time, and unemployment and inflation both decreased to permanently lower long-run levels.

Critical Thinking

1. The increase in government spending will shift the aggregate demand curve to the right, which will cause employment and aggregate output to rise in the short run.

2. No. In the long run, aggregate output returns to the natural rate level of output (but at a higher inflation rate).

3. The increase in government spending shifts the aggregate demand curve right and leads to an increase in the inflation rate in the short run. In the long run, wages increase, and the aggregate supply curve shifts left, causing the inflation rate to rise further to a permanently higher level.

4. If your Senator believes the self-correcting mechanism is slow to work, the economy could be in a recession for a significant period of time. In this case, if the economy is below the natural rate level of output, he would probably advocate increasing government spending, reducing taxes, or an autonomous monetary easing in order to shift the aggregate demand curve back to the natural rate level of output.

5. If your Senator believes the real business cycle theory, he would likely favor no policy changes. This means that if the economy is below the natural rate level of output, he would advocate leaving government spending, taxes, and monetary policy unchanged. This is because he believes that the decline in output is due not to short-run factors that policy can offset, but rather

declines in the level of potential output. In this case, the implication is that policy should not play a role in trying to affect aggregate demand and the short-run equilibrium, since the economy is already in a long-run equilibrium.

True/False Questions

1. F
2. F
3. F
4. F
5. T
6. T
7. F
8. T
9. T
10. T
11. F
12. F
13. T
14. F
15. T

Multiple-Choice Questions

1. c
2. c
3. a
4. b
5. b
6. a
7. a
8. b
9. b
10. d
11. a
12. c
13. a
14. a
15. a
16. b
17. d
18. c
19. a
20. c

23 Monetary Policy Theory*

Chapter Review

PREVIEW

This chapter uses the aggregate demand and supply framework developed in the previous chapter to analyze the role of monetary policy to stabilize inflation and economic activity.

RESPONSE OF MONETARY POLICY TO SHOCKS

An important goal of central banks discussed in Chapter 16 (Chapter 19 in the 3rd ed.) is to achieve price stability, which can often be accomplished by implementing a formal *inflation target*. In practice, these central banks will then adjust monetary policy to minimize the *inflation gap*, or distance between the actual inflation rate and the target rate. Policymakers also care about stabilizing economic activity, which is generally thought of as keeping output close to potential output. In some cases, these sometimes competing objectives of policymakers can make difficult the decision of which type of policy response may be appropriate. As discussed below, depending on the type of shocks that hit the economy, a given policy response may be reinforcing to both objectives or can pose a tradeoff between price stability and stabilizing economic activity.

For instance, a negative demand shock such as a reduction in autonomous spending would shift *AD* to the left, reducing output and lowering inflation in the short run. There are several possible responses by policymakers. One possible approach is to do nothing. In this case, the self-correcting mechanism will lower inflation expectations and shift the *AS* curve down, bringing the economy back to potential output. The benefit of this approach is it requires no explicit action by policymakers. However, the self-correcting mechanism could take time to adjust

---

*This is Chapter 24 in the 3rd ed.

the economy to the long-run equilibrium, and in the short-run, neither inflation nor output is stabilized. In addition, the inflation rate ends up permanently lower in the long run, presumably below the desired inflation target.

Policymakers could instead respond to the shock to stabilize inflation and output. In this case, the central bank would conduct an autonomous monetary easing, which would shift the *AD* curve to the right and completely offset the shock. This approach is beneficial in that it does not rely on the timely adjustment of the self-correcting mechanism to take the economy back to potential output. In addition, both output and inflation are stabilized (at potential and the inflation target, respectively) in the short run and long run. Moreover, when policymakers acted to stabilize inflation, the same policy also stabilized output, so there was no trade-off in achieving the two objectives, resulting in the so-called *divine coincidence*.

A similar interpretation holds when the economy is faced with permanent supply shocks. For instance, with a negative supply shock, the *LRAS* curve shifts to the left. If no policy changes occur and the self-correcting mechanism is left to operate, inflation expectations will push the *AS* curve upward, eventually reaching a higher long-run inflation rate, with output falling to the new lower potential output. Note that in the long run this leaves inflation higher than the targeted inflation rate π^T, due to the rise in inflation.

If policymakers wished to instead stabilize the inflation rate, they would conduct an autonomous monetary policy tightening, which would shift the *AD* curve to the left, such that in the new long-run equilibrium with inflation stabilized at π^T, output would be at the new, lower potential output. Note that since the autonomous policy tightening also closed the output gap to zero, the policy that stabilizes inflation at target is the same policy that stabilizes output at the long-run level, thus there is no trade-off between inflation and output stabilization with permanent supply shocks.

The same is not true, however, when policymakers are faced with temporary supply shocks. Suppose that a temporary negative supply shock occurs that pushes the *AS* curve upwards. If policymakers do nothing, the economy will be stuck with higher inflation and lower output in the short run. Eventually, as the self-correcting mechanism takes hold and the temporary nature of the shock wears off, inflation expectations will fall and the *AS* curve will shift back down to its original position, and inflation and output will be unaffected in the long run. In this sense, the policy of doing nothing implies the divine coincidence holds in the long run (but as seen below, this importantly not the case in the short run). However, doing nothing can be costly, since the economy could be stuck in a recession (and with higher inflation) until the self-correcting mechanism takes hold.

Instead, policymakers may wish to stabilize inflation in the short run. This policy would require an autonomous monetary tightening, shifting the *AD* curve to the left. This keeps inflation at the target rate π^T in the short run, therefore stabilizing inflation. However inflation stability comes at the expense of output stability, since output decreases further away from potential output.

On the other hand, in order to stabilize output, the central bank would need to conduct an autonomous monetary easing, which would shift the *AD* curve up. This results in a different short-run equilibrium, where the output gap is closed. However, the inflation rate is permanently higher at the new long-run equilibrium, above the inflation target. Thus, output stabilization was achieved at the expense of inflation stability.

The analysis above leads to the following conclusions:

1. If most shocks to the economy are aggregate demand or permanent aggregate supply shocks, then policy that stabilizes inflation will also stabilize economic activity in both the short and long runs.

2. If temporary supply shocks are more common, then a central bank must choose between the two stabilization objectives in the short run.

3. In the long run, there is no conflict between stabilizing inflation and economic activity in response to shocks.

HOW ACTIVELY SHOULD POLICYMAKERS TRY TO STABILIZE ECONOMIC ACTIVITY?

There are two basic views on how policymakers should approach the issue of stabilization policy. Economists who are *activists* believe that price and wage adjustment is slow due to sticky prices; thus, the self-correcting mechanism does not work very quickly to move the economy to a long-run equilibrium when faced with shocks. As a consequence, like Keynesians, they advocate a greater role for government intervention to push the economy to a long-run equilibrium faster (particularly through expansionary policies to reduce high unemployment). Economists who are nonactivists believe that prices and wages are flexible enough to allow the self-correcting mechanism to move the economy quickly to the long-run equilibrium. Thus, efforts by policymakers to stabilize the economy are unnecessary, and possibly destabilizing.

Nonactivists point to several factors that make stabilization policy more difficult and weakens the case for activism. Specifically, due to various lags involved in the policy process, designing effective and timely policies can be challenging. These lags are:

- *Data lag:* delays in the availability of timely and relevant data to be able to identify a problem can slow a potential policy response.

- *Recognition lag:* even when data becomes available, it can take time to interpret what the data is signaling about the state of the economy.

- *Legislative lag:* once a problem is recognized to exist in the economy, policymakers must debate and decide what policy or policies would most effectively stabilize the economy.

- *Implementation lag:* after policymakers decide what policy approach is best, it may take even more time for the formal policy to actually be put into place (this is particularly true with fiscal policy changes).

- *Effectiveness lag:* even with policies in place, it can take time for the policies to actually have an impact on the economy. This can be particularly long (a year or longer) and can vary over time, particularly with monetary policy.

Ultimately, given the lags described above, nonactivists argue that by the time a policy is put into place and begins to have an impact, it may be too late to have any beneficial effect on the economy. Moreover, the economy's self-correcting mechanism may already have moved the economy close to a long-run equilibrium, causing any policies that are put in place to be destabilizing rather than stabilizing.

INFLATION: ALWAYS AND EVERYWHERE A MONETARY PHENOMENON

Milton Friedman's assertion that "inflation is always and everywhere a monetary phenomenon" is validated in the sense that monetary policymakers can target any inflation rate in the long run by expanding aggregate demand with autonomous monetary policy. Moreover, potential (long-run) output is independent of monetary policy.

CAUSES OF INFLATIONARY MONETARY POLICY

If monetary policymakers can control the inflation rate in the long run through changes in the target rate and high inflation is bad for the economy, then why would an economy suffer persistently high inflation? This question is examined in the context of two particular sources of inflation: *cost-push* and *demand-pull inflation.*

Cost-push inflation results from the *AS* curve pushing higher, either due to temporary negative supply shocks or from workers demanding higher wages (above productivity gains) that raise the costs of production for firms.

The effects of cost-push inflation are quite similar to what happens under a negative temporary supply shock when policymakers stabilize output. The only difference is that with cost-push inflation, the *AS* curve continues to shift upward, creating a spiraling upward of inflation. This spiraling effect could happen because workers may demand higher wages above productivity gains. The upward shift in the *AS* curve results in lower output (recession) and higher inflation. In an effort to stabilize output, activist policymakers may conduct an autonomous easing, which moves output back to potential with higher inflation. But because of the higher inflation eroding away workers' gains in real wages, they may again demand higher wages (above productivity gains), which further shifts the *AS* curve upward, and the cycle continues to push inflation ever higher.

Demand-pull inflation has a similar effect but is usually created through policy "mistakes." For example, policymakers (either monetary or fiscal) may try to achieve and sustain a level of output above potential output (or equivalently an unemployment rate below the natural rate) by continuously pushing the *AD* curve to the right. This temporarily raises output, but eventually the self-correcting mechanism will return output to potential. If policymakers see that the policy is not effective at maintaining output at the high output/low unemployment equilibrium, they may try to again shift the *AD* curve to the right, and inflationary pressures will continue to push the inflation rate ever higher. This process could work in reverse as well: continually pushing for an output target below potential output could result in a deflationary spiral.

Inflation caused by demand-pull and cost-push factors look similar but are distinguished by two key features: the inflation trigger and the behavior of unemployment. Typically in demand-pull inflation, the unemployment rate will be at or below the natural rate of unemployment for some time, whereas with cost-push inflation, unemployment will be at or above the natural rate for some time. In both cases, policy accommodation is required for the inflation episode to be sustained.

The period of the 1970s known as the "Great Inflation" included both cost-push and demand-pull inflation sources at times, which is why the economy experienced such high, sustained inflation during the period. Demand-pull inflation was caused beginning in the 1960s by an attempt to permanently lower the unemployment rate below the natural rate of unemployment, which fueled inflation later in the decade and into the 1970s. Further cost-push shocks from sharp oil price rises later in the 1970s raised inflation even higher. Since the public expected policymakers to maintain a low unemployment rate, this raised inflation expectations event further, contributing to the double-digit inflation rate by the end of the 1970s.

Helpful Hints

1. Aggregate demand and permanent aggregate supply shocks are easy to deal with by policymakers, since the policy that achieves price stability is also the same policy that moves output to potential.
2. Dealing with temporary supply shocks poses a significant dilemma for policymakers, since stabilizing inflation and output in the short run presents a trade-off of these two policy objectives. And even though the policy of "doing nothing" means the divine coincidence can be achieved in the long run when faced with temporary supply shocks, this is still a potentially costly option if the self-correcting mechanism is slow to adjust or the shock takes a while to wear off, since both inflation and unemployment can be potentially high for a prolonged period of time.
3. Activist stabilization policy is complicated by lags in the policy process that can create uncertainty about the effectiveness in stabilization policy. If these lags are long enough, the resulting greater policy uncertainty can imply that a nonactivist approach may be more appropriate.
4. Inflation can be triggered from a variety of sources but ultimately is sustained by activist policies.

Terms and Definitions

Choose a definition for each key term.

Key Terms:

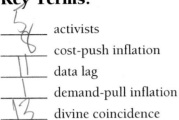

_____ activists

_____ cost-push inflation

_____ data lag

_____ demand-pull inflation

_____ divine coincidence

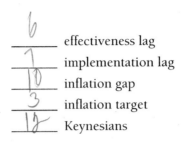

_____ effectiveness lag

_____ implementation lag

_____ inflation gap

_____ inflation target

_____ Keynesians

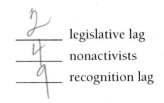

_____ legislative lag

_____ nonactivists

_____ recognition lag

Definitions:

1. Inflation caused by policymakers pursuing policies that increase aggregate demand

2. The time it takes to pass legislation to implement a particular policy

3. A desired rate of inflation that central banks attempt to maintain to achieve price stability

4. Group of economists who believe wages and prices are flexible, the self-correcting mechanism works quickly, and that government stabilization policies can do more harm than good

5. Group of economists who believe wages and prices are not very flexible, the self-correcting mechanism is slow, and advocate for government intervention

6. The time it takes for a policy to actually have an impact on the economy

7. The time it takes for policymakers to change policy instruments once they have decided on a new policy

8. Inflation caused by either temporary negative supply shocks, or by workers demanding wage increases above productivity growth

9. The time it takes for policymakers to interpret data regarding the state of the economy

10. The difference between inflation and the inflation target

11. The time it takes policymakers to obtain data regarding the state of the economy

12. Economists who are followers of Keynes, many of which are activists

13. A situation when in pursuing stabilization policy there is no conflict between the dual objectives of stabilizing inflation and economic activity

Problems and Short-Answer Questions

PRACTICE PROBLEMS

1. For each of the following shock scenarios, indicate in the table what monetary policy would be needed to achieve the stated short-run stabilization objective, an autonomous easing or tightening. Indicate which variables are stabilized with an "S," and which are not with an "NS." Finally, indicate whether the divine coincidence applies for that shock with a Yes or No.

Shock Type	Inflation Stabilization Policy			Output Stabilization Policy			Divine Coincidence?
	Policy	Inflation	Output	Policy	Inflation	Output	
Positive AD	_____	_____	_____	_____	_____	_____	_____
Negative AD	_____	_____	_____	_____	_____	_____	_____
Positive AS	_____	_____	_____	_____	_____	_____	_____
Negative AS	_____	_____	_____	_____	_____	_____	_____
Positive LRAS	_____	_____	_____	_____	_____	_____	_____
Negative LRAS	_____	_____	_____	_____	_____	_____	_____

2. For each of the following shock scenarios, describe what happens to inflation and the output gap by indicating a + (increase), – (decrease), or 0 (no change) as a result of the various types of shocks and stabilization policies. Indicate the effects in both the short run and long run under each scenario. A few have already been filled in.

Stabilization Type			Positive AD Shock	Negative AD Shock	Positive AS Shock	Negative AS Shock	Positive LRAS Shock	Negative LRAS Shock
Inflation Stabilization	Y Gap	SR	_____	_____	_____	_____	_____	_____
		LR	_____	_____	_____	_____	_____	_____
	π	SR	_____	_____	_____	_____	_____	_____
		LR	_____	_____	0	0	_____	_____
Output Stabilization	Y Gap	SR	_____	_____	_____	_____	_____	_____
		LR	_____	_____	_____	_____	_____	_____
	π	SR	_____	_____	_____	_____	_____	_____
		LR	_____	_____	–	+	_____	_____
No Policy Response	Y Gap	SR	_____	_____	_____	_____	_____	_____
		LR	_____	_____	_____	_____	_____	_____
	π	SR	_____	_____	_____	_____	_____	_____
		LR	_____	_____	_____	_____	_____	_____

3.   For each of the following, show the effect of the shock in the graphs, as well as the effect of the stabilization policy in the short run. Indicate below the graph the appropriate monetary policy to achieve the stabilization.
   a.   Autonomous investment spending suddenly increases.

Inflation Stabilization   **Output Stabilization**

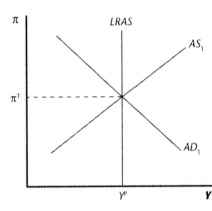   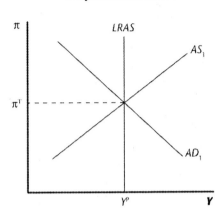

Policy: _____   **Policy:** _____

   b.   There is a temporary increase in productivity.

Inflation Stabilization   **Output Stabilization**

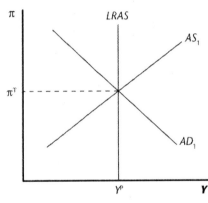   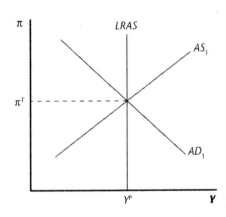

Policy: _____   **Policy:** _____

c. Households worry about a future recession, so autonomous consumption expenditures decline.

Inflation Stabilization

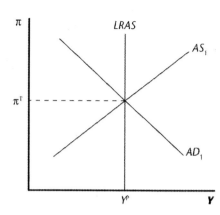

Policy: _____

Output Stabilization

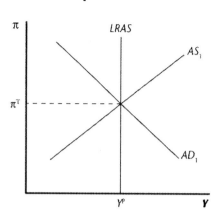

Policy: _____

d. A temporary oil shortage causes energy prices to increase.

Inflation Stabilization

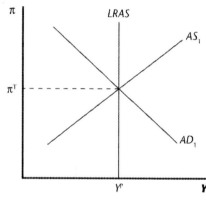

Policy: _____

Output Stabilization

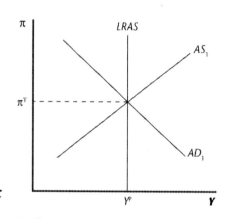

Policy: _____

4. For each of the cases below, indicate what type of activist policy would be implemented. Show in the graph the intended effect of the policy (label this AD_A), and also show and explain the effect of the policy that nonactivists argue would happen due to policy lags and the self-correcting mechanism working before the policy becomes effective (label this AD_{NA}).
    a. The economy is in recession.

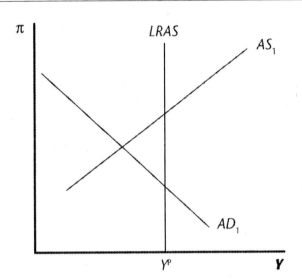

b. The output gap is positive.

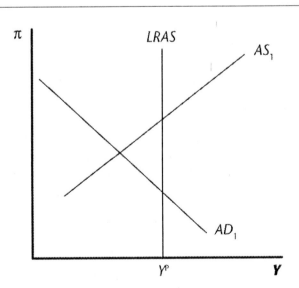

5. What is likely to happen if monetary policymakers mistakenly believe the natural rate of unemployment is higher than it actually is and pursue policy to stabilize output at potential?

_____

_____

_____

_____

SHORT-ANSWER QUESTIONS

1. What does it mean for the divine coincidence to hold?

_____

_____

2. What are the advantages and disadvantages in each of the three policy approaches under a temporary negative supply shock?

_____

_____

3. How are aggregate demand shocks similar to permanent supply shocks?

_____

_____

4. What are the main differences in views between activists and nonactivists?

_____

_____

5. What are the five types of lags associated with stabilization policy?

_____

_____

6. How do the legislative and implementation lags compare relative to the effectiveness lag when using monetary policy?

_____

_____

7. How might lags in policy produce undesirable outcomes?

_____

_____

8. What is the difference between cost-push and demand-pull inflation?

_____

_____

9. If policymakers attempt to achieve an unemployment rate lower than the natural rate of unemployment, what is likely to happen?

_____

_____

10. How is the behavior of inflation and unemployment consistent with both cost-push and demand-pull inflation between the mid 1960s to early 1980s?

_____

_____

Critical Thinking

Suppose you are hired as the economic adviser to the president. The president is trying to understand the long-term effects of various shocks to the economy, and asks you to help explain the circumstances. For each of the situations below, how would you explain what happened and the policy responses to the president?

1. During the decade of the 1990s, the economy grew steadily and inflation declined gradually. Productivity growth was significant and constant through much of the decade.

_____

_____

_____

_____

2. During the early 1970s, productivity unexpectedly decreased dramatically. Both unemployment and inflation increased.

_____

_____

_____

_____

3. During the middle part of the 2000s, household and business spending was strong, yet inflation was relatively stable and the unemployment rate was close to the natural rate of unemployment.

_____

_____

_____

_____

Self-Test

TRUE/FALSE QUESTIONS

_____1. The inflation gap is the difference between inflation and inflation potential.

_____2. The divine coincidence holds for negative aggregate demand shocks but not for positive aggregate demand shocks.

_____3. With no policy response, an aggregate demand shock results in a new long-run inflation rate.

_____4. The divine coincidence is when inflation and output move in the same direction in the long run.

_____5. With a positive aggregate demand shock, the central bank can stabilize both inflation and output with an autonomous monetary policy tightening.

_____6. Quantitative easing was used effectively to completely stabilize output and inflation as a response to the global financial crisis.

_____7. The divine coincidence holds for permanent, but not temporary supply shocks in the short run.

_____8. With an increase in potential output and no policy response, inflation will be below target in the long run.

_____9. The divine coincidence holds in the long run for a temporary supply shock with no policy response.

_____10. Under a permanent supply shock, there is a trade-off between inflation stabilization and output stabilization objectives.

_____11. Nonactivists are most closely associated with the Keynesian viewpoint.

_____12. The recognition lag is the time it takes for policymakers to interpret the data and determine if there is a problem in the economy.

_____13. There is a limit to how inflationary monetary policy can be.

_____14. Since the divine coincidence holds in the long run for temporary supply shocks with no policy response, it is the least costly policy solution in this situation.

_____15. When workers demand wages higher than productivity gains, this is an example of demand-pull inflation.

MULTIPLE-CHOICE QUESTIONS

1. A central banks main objective(s) typically are (is) to
   a. minimize the inflation gap and output gap.
   b. increase employment to as high a level as possible.
   c. set the inflation rate to zero.
   d. avoid temporary supply shocks.

2. When the inflation rate increases, the _____ increases.
   a. inflation target
   b. unemployment gap
   c. output gap
   d. inflation gap

3. The divine coincidence applies to
   a. positive aggregate demand shocks.
   b. negative aggregate demand shocks.
   c. permanent positive supply shocks.
   d. permanent negative supply shocks.
   e. all of the above.

4. When faced with shocks to the economy, central banks can choose to
   a. stabilize output.
   b. do nothing.
   c. stabilize inflation.
   d. All three are potential policy responses to a given shock.

5. If autonomous consumption suddenly increases, the best stabilization policy is
   a. autonomous monetary policy tightening.
   b. autonomous monetary policy easing.
   c. no policy response.
   d. to decrease taxes.

6. As a response to the global financial crisis, the Federal Reserve engaged in asset purchases and liquidity provision, which had the effect of
   a. increasing inflation.
   b. reducing financial frictions.
   c. fully stabilizing output at potential.
   d. shifting the *AS* curve down.

7. With a permanent negative supply shock and no policy response, inflation will eventually _____ and output will _____.
   a. stabilize at target; not change
   b. decrease; decrease
   c. increase; decrease
   d. increase; not change

8. When a temporary negative supply shock occurs and there is no policy response, in the long run
   a. the divine coincidence holds.
   b. inflation is stabilized.
   c. output is at potential.
   d. all of the above occur.

9. Stabilizing inflation at target as a result of a positive permanent supply shock results in
   a. recession.
   b. output stabilized at a higher level than before the shock.
   c. output permanently lower than before the shock.
   d. a higher natural rate of unemployment.

10. Which of the following statements is true?
   a. If shocks to the economy are aggregate demand shocks, then there will not be a trade-off in stabilization policy.
   b. In the long run, there is a conflict between stabilizing inflation and economic activity in response to shocks.
   c. If shocks to the economy are temporary supply shocks, the divine coincidence holds.
   d. All of the above are true.

11. Stabilizing economic activity as a result of a temporary negative supply shock results in
   a. higher inflation in the short run.
   b. inflation maintained at target in the short run.
   c. lower inflation in the short run.
   d. an ambiguous effect on inflation in the short run.

12. Keynesians believe
   a. the government should pursue policies to eliminate high unemployment.
   b. price and wage adjustment is slow.
   c. the self-correcting mechanism does not work quickly enough.
   d. all of the above.

13. Which of the following lags is longest for monetary policy?
   a. legislative lag
   b. implementation lag
   c. variable lag
   d. effectiveness lag

14. In 2009, activists in the United States argued for more expansionary fiscal policy because
    a. long implementation lags would stabilize the economy.
    b. monetary policy had already reached the zero-lower bound.
    c. the unemployment rate was below the natural rate of unemployment.
    d. the financial crisis was over and so inflation would not be a problem.

15. The Humphrey-Hawkins Act of 1978
    a. outlawed inflationary policies.
    b. repealed the Glass-Steagal Act.
    c. commits the U.S. government to pursue policies designed to produce high employment.
    d. eliminates the possibility of demand-pull inflation.

16. Which of the following is true regarding monetary policy?
    a. Monetary policy can achieve any inflation rate in the long run with autonomous policy changes.
    b. Potential output can be affected by monetary policy.
    c. Monetary policy can influence the natural rate of unemployment.
    d. Keynes believed that inflation was always and everywhere a monetary phenomenon.

17. Which of the following would directly result in demand-pull inflation?
    a. Workers demanding wage increases above productivity gains.
    b. Policymakers pursuing an unemployment rate target higher than the natural rate of unemployment.
    c. Monetary policymakers pursuing an autonomous easing policy when the economy is at potential output.
    d. Energy prices increasing sharply.

18. Which of the following would directly result in cost-push inflation?
    a. Unexpectedly large increases in productivity growth.
    b. Policymakers pursuing an unemployment rate target lower than the natural rate of unemployment.
    c. Monetary policymakers pursuing an autonomous easing policy when the economy is at potential output.
    d. A sharp increase in energy prices.

19. Cost-push inflation in the 1970s caused unemployment to be _____ the natural rate, and inflation to _____.
    a. below; increase
    b. below; decrease
    c. at; remain constant
    d. above; increase

20. During the mid-1960s, policymakers were committed to a target unemployment rate of _____, which was _____ price stability.
    a. 4%; not consistent with
    b. 5.5%; consistent with
    c. 6%; not consistent with
    d. 6.2%; consistent with

Solutions

Definitions:

_5_ activists

_8_ cost-push inflation

11 data lag

_1_ demand-pull inflation

13 divine coincidence

_6_ effectiveness lag

_7_ implementation lag

10 inflation gap

_3_ inflation target

12 Keynesians

_2_ legislative lag

_4_ nonactivists

_9_ recognition lag

Practice Problems

1.

Shock Type	Inflation Stabilization Policy			Output Stabilization Policy			Divine Coincidence?
	Policy	Inflation	Output	Policy	Inflation	Output	
Positive AD	Tightening	S	S	Tightening	S	S	Yes
Negative AD	Easing	S	S	Easing	S	S	Yes
Positive AS	Easing	S	NS	Tightening	NS	S	No
Negative AS	Tightening	S	NS	Easing	NS	S	No
Positive LRAS	Easing	S	S	Easing	S	S	Yes
Negative LRAS	Tightening	S	S	Tightening	S	S	Yes

2.

Stabilization Type			Positive AD Shock	Negative AD Shock	Positive AS Shock	Negative AS Shock	Positive LRAS Shock	Negative LRAS Shock
Inflation Stabilization	Y Gap	SR	0	0	+	–	0	0
		LR	0	0	0	0	0	0
	π	SR	0	0	0	0	0	0
		LR	0	0	0	0	0	0
Output Stabilization	Y Gap	SR	0	0	0	0	0	0
		LR	0	0	0	0	0	0
	π	SR	0	0	–	+	0	0
		LR	0	0	–	+	0	0
No Policy Response	Y Gap	SR	+	–	+	–	–	+
		LR	0	0	0	0	0	0
	π	SR	+	–	–	+	0	0
		LR	+	–	0	0	–	+

3. a.

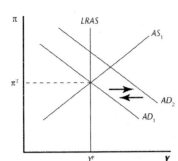

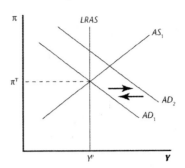

b.

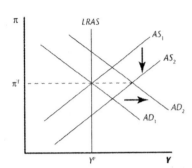

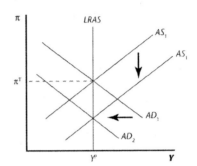

c.

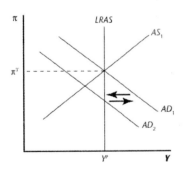

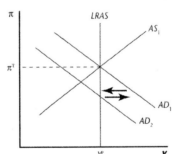

d.

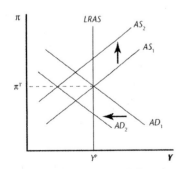

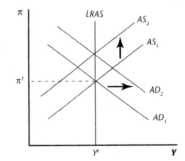

4. a. The activist policy is an autonomous monetary easing. Nonactivists would argue that aggregate demand would likely overshoot potential output on the upside, creating excessive inflationary pressure and destabilizing the economy.

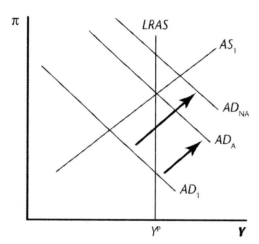

b. The activist policy is an autonomous monetary tightening. Nonactivists would argue that aggregate demand would likely overshoot potential output on the downside, creating a recessionary condition and destabilizing the economy.

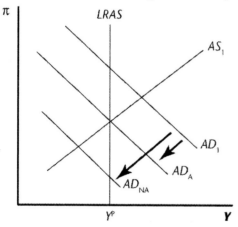

5. Monetary policymakers would mistakenly believe that the potential level of output is lower than it actually is and, if they were worried about stabilization policy, would want to constantly pursue an autonomous monetary tightening policy in order to stabilize output at the perceived lower potential level. In actuality, this would have the effect of continually pushing the economy into recession. As aggregate demand fell, inflation and inflation expectations would decline. The decrease in the *AS* curve would

help output increase, but policymakers would be worried that the economy was at risk of inflation and so would continue its contractionary policy stance. This has the opposite effect of a demand-pull inflation episode and would lead to inflation falling to zero and possibly result in a deflationary spiral.

Short-Answer Questions

1. The divine coincidence holds when the policy that is used to stabilize inflation at some desirable target is also the same policy that is consistent with stabilizing economic activity.

2. Under no policy response, the advantage of this approach is that in the long run, the divine coincidence holds, and both inflation and output return to target and potential, respectively. The disadvantage of this approach is that it relies on the self-correcting mechanism which can take time, meaning that inflation and the unemployment rate can remain high for some time and imply a lengthy recession.

    By stabilizing inflation in the short run, the advantage is that inflation remains at target and, therefore, keeps inflation expectations anchored at a low level. The disadvantage of this approach is that output falls further than it otherwise would since an autonomous tightening policy is required.

    By stabilizing output in the short run, the advantage is that output is stabilized at potential and the economy avoids a recession. The disadvantage of this approach is that inflation is permanently higher, above the targeted inflation rate.

3. They both are similar in that the divine coincidence holds under aggregate demand and permanent aggregate supply shocks.

4. The main differences between the two derive from the flexibility of prices and speed of the self-correcting mechanism. Nonactivists believe that prices and wages adjust quickly and that the self-correcting mechanism works rapidly. As a result, they believe that activist government intervention is unnecessary and can do more harm than good. Activists believe prices and wages are slow to adjust and the self-correcting mechanism is slow. Thus, activists believe there is a strong role for government to intervene to stabilize the economy.

5. Data lag, recognition lag, legislative lag, implementation lag, and effectiveness lag.

6. The legislative and implementation lags for monetary policy are relatively short since most central banks (including the Federal Reserve) can meet at short notice to decide and change policies. However, the effectiveness lag can be both long and variable for monetary policy, since interest rate changes can take a long time to have an effect on the real economy.

7. If policy lags are long, then by the time aggregate demand has shifted, the self-correcting mechanism may have already returned the economy to full employment, so when activist policy kicks in it may (in the case of expansionary policy, for instance) cause output to rise above potential and lead to an increase in inflation.

8. Cost-push inflation is caused by temporary negative supply shocks, or workers demanding wage increases above productivity gains. Demand-pull inflation is caused by policymakers pursuing overly expansionary policies which increase aggregate demand.

9. This would require policymakers to stimulate aggregate demand and achieve a level of output above potential output. The result is that demand-pull inflation will occur, in which policymakers expand aggregate demand, the self-correcting mechanism pushes inflation higher and output lower, and policymakers are prompted to continually increase aggregate demand to achieve the unemployment rate objective. Ultimately, it will result in spiraling inflation upward as long as activist policy is used to try and achieve the target.

10. During the 1960s, fiscal and monetary policy was highly expansionary in an effort to push the unemployment rate below the natural rate. As a consequence, through much of this period, the unemployment rate was below the natural rate, and inflation increased throughout the decade. During the 1970s, several cost-push inflation shocks shifted the AS curve upward. In an attempt to keep unemployment from increasing, policymakers tried to pursue expansionary policies, but it was ineffective since people just came to expect the higher inflation policies. As a result, inflation continued to rise, and the unemployment rate was near or above the natural rate of unemployment for much of the decade.

Critical Thinking

1. This is an example of a positive permanent aggregate supply shock. The strong productivity growth throughout the decade resulted in a rightward shift of the *LRAS* curve, and the behavior of output and inflation is consistent with no policy response. As a result, over time the *AS* curve shifted down, leading to higher output and lower inflation at the new long-run equilibrium. Considering that inflation was somewhat elevated at the beginning of the decade, letting inflation fall over the decade to a lower level more consistent with price stability is equivalent to resetting the inflation target to a lower level.

2. Having productivity decrease dramatically has effects on both aggregate demand and aggregate supply. On the aggregate demand side, with a sudden, unexpected decline in productivity policymakers will be trying to maintain and stabilize output at a level higher than is sustainable in the long run. In other words, policymakers will be targeting an unemployment rate that is lower than and inconsistent with the natural rate of unemployment as a result of the unexpected decline in productivity, which will lead to demand-pull inflation. On the supply side, the unexpected decline in productivity will mean that wage gains will be higher than productivity and will result in cost-push inflation. The fact that both unemployment and inflation increased concurrently indicates that the cost-push inflation effect was stronger, leading to higher upward shifts of the *AS* curve than the *AD* curve was shifting out. In other words, output was falling and inflation rising overall due to the stronger *AS* shift.

3. Strong household spending and business investment spending is consistent with expanding aggregate demand. If the *AD* curve was shifting out, you would expect to see the unemployment rate falling and inflation increasing. However, if inflation was stable and the unemployment rate stayed close to the natural rate, this would indicate that policymakers were able to successfully offset the demand shock to stabilize both inflation and output and achieve the divine

coincidence. Indeed, during this period the Federal Reserve increased interest rates to keep inflation and output stable (later in the decade however, the global financial crisis made stabilization policy extremely difficult to implement and achieve successfully).

True/False Questions

1. F
2. F
3. T
4. F
5. T
6. F
7. T
8. T
9. T
10. F
11. F
12. T
13. F
14. F
15. F

Multiple-Choice Questions

1. a
2. d
3. e
4. d
5. a
6. b
7. c
8. d
9. b
10. a
11. a
12. d
13. d
14. b
15. c
16. a
17. c
18. d
19. d
20. a

24 The Role of Expectations in Monetary Policy[*]

Chapter Review

PREVIEW

In previous chapters you learned how government policy could, in principle, be used to steer output toward full employment. But in practice (especially during the 1960s and 1970s), discretionary policies have not been successful. The theory of rational expectations was developed in the 1970s and 1980s to examine why discretionary policies performed so poorly. This chapter examines the analysis behind the rational expectations revolution. The existence of rational expectations makes discretionary policies less likely to be successful and raises the issue of credibility as an important element affecting policy outcomes.

LUCAS CRITIQUE OF POLICY EVALUATION

Macroeconometric models are models whose equations are estimated with statistical procedures and represent relationships among many economic variables. Those statistical procedures measure the relationship between variables that existed in the past. For example, suppose that in the past, increases in short-term interest rates were usually temporary and, therefore, had very little impact on long-term interest rates. The macroeconometric model will therefore show very little relationship between short- and long-term interest rates. Now suppose that policymakers wish to use that macroeconometric model to evaluate the effect of a permanent increase in short-term interest rates. The macroeconometric model will give a misleading result. It will show that an increase in short-term interest rates will have very little effect on long-term interest rates. But in reality, if the increase in interest rates is expected to be permanent rather than temporary, then the response of long-term interest rates will be greater than predicted by the model.

---

[*]This chapter is unique to the 10th ed.

The reason for this misleading prediction is that people will change the way in which they form expectations about a variable when the behavior of that variable changes. The past relationship between short-term and long-term interest rates was based on the expectation that increases in short-term interest rates are temporary. But if the behavior of short-term interest rates changes so that increases in short-term interest rates are permanent, then people will change their expectations and the relationship between short-term interest rates and long-term interest rates will change. This critique of macroeconometric models (called the Lucas critique after economist Robert Lucas) implies not only that conventional macroeconometric models cannot be used for policy evaluation, but also that the public's expectations about a policy will influence the response to that policy.

POLICY CONDUCT: RULES OR DISCRETION?

The Lucas Critique raises the broader issue of how beneficial it is to have policymakers conducting policies which they know may be flawed. In particular, is it wise for policymakers to be allowed to use judgment in the policy process? Should policymakers be bound by concrete guidelines when conducting policies?

Allowing *discretion* in the policymaking process can result in a *time-inconsistency problem* in which policymakers deviate from prudent long-run goals to pursue short-run objectives that can have adverse consequences in the long run. For example, in the short-run policymakers may be tempted to pursue expansionary policies that lower the unemployment rate but create higher inflation in the future. If households and firms are rational, they will expect that policymakers will have this incentive and adjust expectations accordingly. As a result, the policy may only result in higher inflation, and be ineffective at trying to reduce unemployment in the short run. Thus, tying the hands of policymakers can be beneficial in helping to avoid these less desirable outcomes due to the time-inconsistency problem.

For example, policymakers could be subject to a *constant-money-growth-rate rule* where the money supply grows at a constant rate regardless of the state of the economy (a nonactivist rule). A more activist approach would be for policymakers to follow a Taylor rule in which monetary policy is dictated by a specific rule dependent on the output gap and inflation gap, as discussed in Chapter 16.

These rules can be beneficial in that they don't allow policymakers, for instance, to exploit the short-run trade-off between inflation and unemployment, which eliminates the time-inconsistency problem. In addition, some would argue that policymakers and politicians cannot be trusted to make informed policy decisions, so rules may be necessary. Moreover, rules can preclude a *political business cycle* from occurring in which policymakers try to pursue expansionary policies during election periods to curry favor with voters.

However, conducting policy by rules rather than discretion does have drawbacks. First, policy rules may be too rigid to be able to effectively react to any and all economic shocks in the economy. Thus, during unusual or severe circumstances, policy by rule may be inadequate to address a problem in the economy. This implies a need for policymakers to use judgment in the policy process. In addition, nobody knows what the true structure of the economy is, so imposing rules based upon a flawed model will likely yield a flawed result. Finally, even if rules were in place, changes in the structure of the economy would likely lead to poor outcomes. Policymakers may be sluggish to update the rule in response to these structural changes, thus leading to flawed policies.

There is no clear answer to the rules versus discretion debate; however, there are beneficial aspects to both approaches. It is for this reason that policymakers such as current Federal Reserve chairman Ben Bernanke prefer a *constrained discretion* approach in which the policy regime is structured and disciplined enough to minimize the time-inconsistency problem, yet flexible enough to respond to adverse or unexpected economic shocks.

THE ROLE OF CREDIBILITY AND A NOMINAL ANCHOR

A regime of constrained discretion can be achieved by a central bank through the use of a nominal anchor. This implies that policymakers are credibly committed to maintaining a nominal variable such as the inflation rate, money supply, or exchange rate at a level that will enhance price stability. This is beneficial in that *credibility* by the central bank allows the public to believe policymakers and adjust expectations in a way that is reinforcing to the desired policies, making it easier for the central bank to achieve its goals. In particular, having a nominal anchor helps eliminate the time-inconsistency problem and keeps inflation expectations pinned down to a low and manageable level.

To see the benefits of a nominal anchor, consider policy when the economy is hit with demand shocks. In the case of positive aggregate demand shocks, a credible monetary policy will help stabilize inflation in the short run. With negative aggregate demand shocks, a credible monetary policy will help stabilize economic activity in the short run. This is because in both cases, weak credibility will lead to higher inflation expectations. The consequent upward shifts in the *AS* curve push inflation further away from target in the case of a positive aggregate demand shock and push output further from potential in the case of a negative aggregate demand shock. A similar result arises when the economy is faced with supply shocks. For example, under a negative supply shock the *AS* curve shifts up, leading to higher inflation in the short run. If price and wage setters do not believe the central bank is credibly committed to stabilizing inflation, expectations will increase, shifting the *AS* curve higher and leading to higher inflation than would otherwise occur under a credible policy regime.

The difference credibility makes in response to shocks can be seen in comparing the oil price shocks in the 1970s to a similar oil price shock in 2007–2008 in the United States. During the 1970s, the public had little faith that the Federal Reserve would take steps to contain inflation; the twin shocks that occurred lead to double-digit inflation and high unemployment. In contrast, inflation expectations remained fairly stable leading up to and during the shock in 2007–2008, implying a great deal of faith that the Federal Reserve would take steps to contain an outbreak of inflation. Indeed, inflation rose much less during this time than in the 1970s. Although the unemployment rate rose quickly in 2008 and 2009, this is attributed more to the financial crisis rather than the effects of the oil shock.

Credibility can also be crucially important in allowing the central bank to effectively pursue anti-inflation policies. In order to permanently reduce the inflation rate to a lower level, contractionary monetary policy must be implemented, resulting in a leftward shift of the *AD* curve. If the central bank has credibility, inflation expectations will also fall, leading to a downward shift in the *AS* curve and a lower inflation rate in the short run, as well as a smaller decline in output from potential.

Credibility is harder in practice to achieve than it may seem. In the United States, there have been several factors and instances in which credible commitment to a strong nominal anchor has been questionable, particularly during the period of the 1970s when the Federal Reserve frequently committed to tight monetary policy and lower inflation, only to revert to a lower real interest rate policy. In addition, sharp increases in budget deficits have periodically tested the ability of the Federal Reserve to maintain a low inflation policy.

APPROACHES TO ESTABLISHING CENTRAL BANK CREDIBILITY

The above discussion makes clear that credible policymaking can be extremely beneficial in facilitating economic stability. Thus, having an understanding of the factors that create and maintain a credible policy framework is important to anchoring inflation expectations and stabilizing the broader economy.

In addition to implementing formal inflation targeting frameworks or exchange rate pegs as discussed in Chapter 16, another way of establishing credibility is to appoint a "conservative" central banker. This implies appointing a central bank head who is known as a strong anti-inflation "hawk." This helps further solidify the central bank's commitment to low, stable inflation and thus sets favorable expectations by the public.

Paul Volcker, who was appointed as the chair of the Federal Reserve in the late 1970s, was viewed as a quintessential "conservative" central banker who had a firm resolve to lower inflation. This resolve was validated by the strong anti-inflation policies that were put into place to lower double digit inflation rates to below 4% by 1983. Although the policies induced a sharp recessionary period, the long-term benefits of permanently lower long-term inflation became apparent.

Helpful Hints

Rational expectations has important implications for the effectiveness of policy as it relates to credibility. If monetary policymakers lack credibility, both aggregate demand and aggregate supply shocks can be more destabilizing, implying strong benefits to maintaining credibility. Without a strong resolve to maintain credibility or formal mechanisms in place, policymakers can be tempted to give up long-term goals for short-term benefits.

Terms and Definitions

Choose a definition for each key term.

Key Terms:

_____5_____ constant-money-growth-rate rule

_____8_____ constrained discretion

_____7_____ credibility

_____4_____ discretion

_____2_____ macroeconometric models

_____6_____ monetarists

_____1_____ political business cycle

_____3_____ rules

Definitions:

1. Results when fiscal and monetary policy is expansionary right before elections to gain support of voters but results in inflation later on

2. Models whose equations are estimated using statistical procedures and that are used to forecast economic activity or evaluate policy options

3. Monetary policy based on binding plans that specify how monetary policy will react to particular situations

4. Making policy based on what is believed to be the right policy at the moment with no commitment to future actions

5. Rule in which the money supply grows at a constant rate independent of the state of the economy

6. Group of economists who believe that money is the sole source of fluctuations in demand and, therefore, believe that changing monetary policy can destabilize the economy

7. A policy framework that is believed by the public and reflects a strong commitment to a nominal anchor

8. An approach to policy that has the advantage of policy flexibility but also imposes some inherent discipline on policymakers

Problems and Short-Answer Questions

PRACTICE PROBLEMS

1. Suppose your roommate studies late in the library each night, returning to your room after you have gone to bed and turned out the light. In an effort not to disturb you, he leaves the light off but ends up bumping into things in the dark and making so much noise that you wake up anyway. Fortunately your roommate is fairly quick about it, and after five minutes or so he is usually in bed. In an effort to remedy this situation, you decide to leave the light on to reduce the noise. Your experiment fails. Not only does your roommate still make noise, but seeing that the light is on, he makes noise for ten minutes instead of five minutes.

a. How does your experiment with your dorm light relate to the Lucas Critique?

_____

_____

_____

b. How does your experiment with your dorm light relate to policymakers' ability to predict the effect of a change in policy on the economy?

_____

_____

_____

2. a. Under what conditions might implementing policy rules be advantageous?

_____

_____

_____

b. Why might allowing for policy discretion be best?

_____

_____

_____

c. How does constrained discretion have elements of both rules and discretion?

_____

_____

_____

3. In each of the following cases, use the AD/AS graph to show how credibility leads to a better inflation outcome in the short run than if the central bank has no credibility. In each graph, label the credible equilibrium with a "C," and the noncredibility equilibrium with a "NC."

    a. The economy experiences a positive aggregate demand shock.

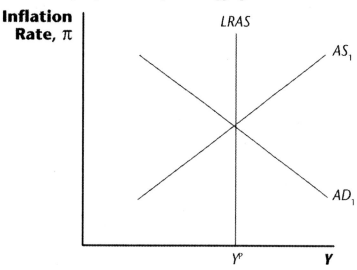

    b. The economy experiences a negative aggregate supply shock.

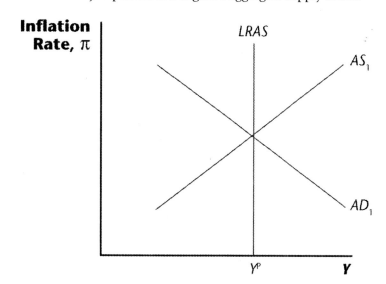

c. The Federal Reserve pursues an anti-inflation policy to permanently lower the inflation rate.

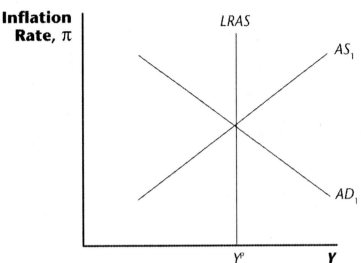

4. a. What are the three basic approaches to establishing credibility?

_____

_____

_____

b. What does it mean to appoint a "conservative" central banker?

_____

_____

_____

c. Are there any disadvantages to appointing a conservative central banker? Explain.

_____

_____

_____

SHORT-ANSWER QUESTIONS

1. Suppose that temporary increases in the budget deficit in the past have not caused interest rates to rise. Explain why it would be dangerous to infer that a permanent increase in the budget deficit will not cause interest rates to rise.

    _____

    _____

2. How can use of macroeconometric models that do not assume expectations are rational be problematic for policy analysis?

    _____

    _____

3. According to monetarists, what is the benefit of a constant-money-growth rule? What is the main disadvantage of such a rule?

    _____

    _____

4. What causes a political business cycle?

    _____

    _____

5. Why is judgment an important part of the monetary policymaking process?

    _____

    _____

6. Why did Switzerland abandon monetary targeting in the 1990s?

    _____

    _____

7. How does a credible central bank help stabilize output in the short run when faced with a negative demand shock?

    _____

    _____

8. Why is credibility important for the effectiveness of anti-inflation policy?

    _____

    _____

9. What might have been the outcome of the anti-inflation policy during the Reagan administration if the government had actively tried to reduce the budget deficit?

_____

_____

10. How does appointing a conservative central banker help to solve the time-inconsistency problem?

_____

_____

Critical Thinking

Suppose you are an economic advisor to the president. The inflation rate is currently 10%, budget deficits are high, and the central bank has a history of keeping inflation at undesirably high levels. The president asks you for recommendations to bring the inflation rate down to 5% without causing excessive unemployment.

1. What monetary policy changes, if any, could you recommend to lower inflation?

_____

_____

_____

2. What fiscal policy changes, if any, could you recommend to lower inflation?

_____

_____

_____

3. Is it realistic to be able to reduce inflation without adverse effects on the unemployment rate, as the president wants? Why or why not?

_____

_____

_____

Self-Test

TRUE/FALSE QUESTIONS

_____1. The Lucas Critique implies that macroeconometric models are not useful for evaluating the effects of alternative policies on the economy.

_____2. According to Lucas, when policy changes, the public's expectations stay the same.

_____3. Using discretion in policy eliminates the time-inconsistency problem.

_____4. Monetarists believe that fiscal policy is the sole source of fluctuations in aggregate demand.

_____5. The time-inconsistency problem implies policymakers may try to lower the unemployment rate in the short term.

_____6. The Taylor Rule is an activist rule, while a constant-money-growth-rate rule is a nonactivist rule.

_____7. The Federal Reserve has never made policy errors, so there is no need for a rules based approach on those grounds.

_____8. Monetary policy rules used in Switzerland led to high inflation due to structural changes in the economy over time.

_____9. Constrained discretion can help mitigate the time-inconsistency problem.

_____10. One way for a central bank to gain credibility is through a firm commitment to fixing its exchange rate to a sound currency.

_____11. Compared to a central bank with no credibility, when faced with a demand shock, inflation will be higher in the short run than if the central bank had credibility.

_____12. More credibility helps stabilize both output and inflation when faced with a negative aggregate supply shock.

_____13. A credible anti-inflation policy is less costly (in terms of lost output) than a policy that is not credible.

_____14. The conclusion that the Reagan budget deficits helped create a more severe recession in 1981–1982 is widely accepted by most economists.

_____15. The rational expectations revolution has caused a major rethinking about the way economic policy should be conducted.

MULTIPLE-CHOICE QUESTIONS

1. Which of the following statements is true?
    a. Lucas's policy critique suggests that macroeconometric models are useless for forecasting.
    b. Lucas's policy critique suggests that macroeconometric models are useful for forecasting.
    c. Lucas's policy critique suggests that macroeconometric models are useful for evaluating the impact of alternative policies on the economy.
    d. Lucas's policy critique says nothing about the usefulness of macroeconometric models as forecasting tools.

2. Which of the following examples is subject to the Lucas Critique?
    a. The central bank expects firm optimism to increase and so increases interest rates more in order to stabilize the economy.
    b. Policymakers adjust the coefficients in their macroeconometric model to take account of changes in expectations.
    c. The central bank reduces interest rates more than usual because of anticipated weakness in spending and declines in consumer confidence.
    d. Policymakers overestimate the effectiveness of a tax cut based on the effects of prior tax changes.

3. During a recession, monetarists such as Milton Friedman would prefer a policy of
    a. maintaining a constant rate of money growth.
    b. deficit spending.
    c. an autonomous easing of policy.
    d. an autonomous tightening of policy.

4. Which of the following would be considered an activist rule?
    a. a strict balanced budget rule
    b. a constant-money-growth-rate rule
    c. a Taylor rule where policy responds to the output gap
    d. policymakers deciding on a case-by-case basis which policies to implement

5. Which of the following supports the case for discretion?
    a. Political business cycles may occur.
    b. Policymakers frequently make mistakes.
    c. Nobody knows the true model of the economy.
    d. Judgment leads to poor policy outcomes.

6. Imposing a conceptual framework and inherent discipline on policymakers is referred to as
    a. strict inflation targeting.
    b. a rules based policy regime.
    c. constrained discretion.
    d. a monetarist rule.

7. Which of the following can provide a credible nominal anchor?
    a. pegged exchange rate
    b. inflation rate target
    c. conservative central banker
    d. all of the above

8. Under a positive demand shock with a fully credible monetary policy, the *AD* curve _____ and the *AS* curve _____ in the short run.
   a. shifts left; shifts up
   b. shifts left; shifts down
   c. shifts right; shifts up
   d. shifts right; does not shift

9. Under a negative supply shock with a fully credible monetary policy, the *AD* curve _____ and the *AS* curve _____ in the short run.
   a. shifts left; shifts up
   b. does not shift; shifts up, but by less than under a noncredible monetary policy
   c. does not shift; shifts down, but by more than under a noncredible monetary policy
   d. shifts right; does not shift

10. The difference between the 1970s oil price shocks and the 2007 oil price shock is that
   a. commitment to a nominal anchor was stronger in the 1970s.
   b. unemployment decreased after the 2007 shock, whereas unemployment increased with the 1970s shocks.
   c. inflation was lower in the 1970s period.
   d. monetary policy was more credible in dealing with the 2007 shock.

11. An inflation hawk
   a. prefers a zero inflation rate.
   b. describes a conservative central banker.
   c. leans toward higher inflation in order to stabilize output or unemployment.
   d. has a weak commitment to a nominal anchor.

12. Greater credibility of the central bank
   a. will lead to a slower decline in inflation under an anti-inflation policy.
   b. will lead to a more rapid decline in inflation under an anti-inflation policy.
   c. will have no effect on the speed of inflation adjustment under an anti-inflation policy.
   d. may increase or decrease the speed of inflation adjustment under an anti-inflation policy.

13. The reduction in the inflation rate that occurred in the United States between 1981 and 1984
   a. was costless.
   b. created one of the most severe recessions in the post-war period.
   c. decreased both inflation and unemployment.
   d. was credible.

14. Large government budget deficits
   a. do not affect central bank credibility.
   b. may reduce the credibility of the central bank as an inflation fighter.
   c. lead to a downward shift of the *AS* curve.
   d. can enhance a central bank's credibility and commitment to a nominal anchor.

15. An example of a country that has reduced high inflation rates without substantial cost in terms of lost output is
    a. the United States in the early 1980s.
    b. Bolivia in 1985.
    c. Zimbabwe in 2009.
    d. the United Kingdom in the early 1980s.

16. Switzerland abandoned its monetary targeting rule because
    a. political business cycles were no longer a possibility.
    b. it was ruled illegal.
    c. a structural change in the economy made the rule too inflationary.
    d. of the time-inconsistency problems that arose from its use.

17. In order to permanently reduce the inflation rate, Paul Volcker, former chairman of the Federal Reserve,
    a. raised the fed funds rate to nearly 20%.
    b. caused the unemployment rate to increase to near 10%.
    c. created one of the most severe recessions in the post-war period.
    d. did all of the above.

18. A credible reduction in aggregate demand designed to reduce inflation
    a. has the same costs in terms of lost output than if the central bank had no credibility.
    b. is costly in terms of lost output, but the cost is less than if the central bank had no credibility.
    c. is costly in terms of lost output, but the cost is greater than if the central bank had no credibility.
    d. increases output in the short run.

19. One possible drawback to appointing a conservative central banker is that
    a. inflation will be too high.
    b. the public's desire for a conservative central banker may change over time, but not be reflected in the actions of the conservative central banker.
    c. the unemployment rate will fall below desirable levels.
    d. inflation expectations may become unanchored.

20. When Richard Nixon was campaigning for re-election in 1972, he instituted price and wage controls and reduced taxes. This is an example of
    a. a political business cycle.
    b. fiscal inflation targeting.
    c. stabilization policy.
    d. why discretionary policy is desirable.

Solutions

Terms and Definitions

_5_ constant-money-growth-rate rule

_8_ constrained discretion

_7_ credibility

_4_ discretion

_2_ macroeconometric models

_6_ monetarists

_1_ political business cycle

_3_ rules

Practice Problems

1. a. Your prediction was based on your past observations of what happened when the light was out. You assumed that when you turned the light on, your roommate's behavior would not change—he would not make as much noise because he would not be bumping into things in the dark, but he also would not change the length of time he bumped around the room before going to bed. According to the Lucas Critique, econometric models assume this same type of unchanging behavior because they are based on past data. Your experiment failed because your roommate changed his behavior by staying awake for longer with the lights on.

   b. When policymakers use a macro-econometric model to predict the outcome of a change in policy, they fail to take account of the fact that by changing policy, people will change their behavior. The change in behavior (staying awake longer with the lights on) invalidates the prediction based on past data.

2. a. Having policy rules in place may be particularly advantageous under conditions when discretionary policy can lead to poor outcomes. In particular, policy rules can help solve the time-inconsistency problem that can arise with discretionary policy. Moreover, some argue that policy rules should be in place if policymakers or politicians cannot be trusted to make informed decisions or may be opportunistic and create a political business cycle.

   b. Discretion may be preferred because it is more flexible than a rules-based approach to policy. In particular, with a rules-based approach, it is impossible to specify a policy response for every contingency. In this sense, judgment is often times necessary and wouldn't be possible in a strict rules-based policy. Third, since we don't know what the actual model of the economy is, such a rules-based system would lead to flawed policies and outcomes. Moreover, it is likely that the structural model of the economy will evolve over time, and a rules-based approach would likely not evolve to reflect new changes in the economy. These factors imply discretion may be more preferable than a rules-based approach.

   c. Constrained discretion is like a rules-based framework in that it places some inherent discipline on the choices of policymakers, which helps reduce the time-inconsistency problem. However, it is also flexible enough to allow policymakers to use discretion when needed. This approach then has some of the advantages of both a rules-based and a discretionary policy approach.

3. a.

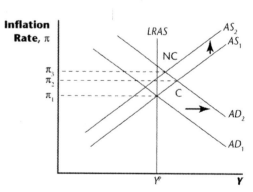

b.

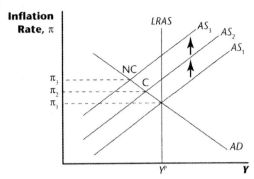

c.

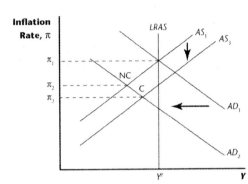

4. a. The three basic ways that a central bank can establish credibility all involve establishing and maintaining a credible nominal anchor. These can be achieved by adopting an inflation targeting framework, implementing an exchange rate peg, or by appointing a "conservative" central banker.

    b. By appointing a central banker who has an inherent aversion to high inflation, this imparts credibility to the public that the central bank, through the direction and actions of the conservative central banker, will go to great lengths to ensure that inflation will be maintained at a low, stable level. This ensures that inflation expectations will remain low, which reinforces the ability to keep inflation low.

    c. One potential problem with appointing a conservative central banker is that the views of the public may evolve over time in such a way that they are no longer aligned in such a way that reflect the actions of the central bank. In particular, the public may prefer a less conservative central bank over time, but this may not be possible and may be viewed as somewhat undemocratic.

Short-Answer Questions

1. The Lucas Critique implies that when the behavior of a variable changes, the expectation of that variable changes as well. Using past data on the relationship between budget deficits and interest rates will provide misleading predictions of the effect of a permanent increase in budget deficits on interest rates.

2. Using macroeconometric models that do not incorporate rational expectations ignore any effects of changing expectations and would be subject to the Lucas Critique and, thus, is unreliable for evaluating policy options.

3. Monetarists believe fluctuations in money growth are the main source of fluctuations in aggregate demand, and therefore, variation in monetary policy destabilizes the economy. Thus, keeping money growth constant presumably eliminates this source of destabilization. The disadvantage of such a policy is that even during recessions or other types of severe shocks, the central bank would be unable to adjust monetary policy to address the shock.

4. A political business cycle occurs when politicians, particularly incumbent politicians try to improve their chances of being re-elected by pursuing overly expansionary policies leading up to an election. This provides a short-term gain by increasing incomes and lowering unemployment, but has the side effect of increasing inflation later on.

5. Judgment is important because monetary policymakers may need to look at a wide range of information in order to decide on the appropriate monetary policy action, and some types of information is not easily quantifiable into a rules-based approach.

6. Switzerland targeted monetary aggregates as a nominal anchor from the 1980s through the early 1990s. Because of financial innovation and changes in the structure of the economy, less money was needed relative to what the monetary aggregate growth rule dictated, leading to higher inflation rates. This led to the abandonment of the monetary target, and demonstrates the perils of strict rules based policies.

7. A negative aggregate demand shock shifts the *AD* curve to the left, resulting in lower output. If the central bank is credible, it will

remain at that equilibrium for a period of time until policy can address the shock, or the demand shock itself reverses. However, if the central bank is not credible, people will expect expansionary policy to represent a lost commitment to the nominal anchor and expect inflation in the future. This will shift the AS curve upward in the short run, which increases inflation, but also reduces output further than if the central bank was credible.

8. When an anti-inflation policy is credible, people believe that policymakers will follow through with their commitment to decrease aggregate demand. As a result they will adjust their expectations to a lower inflation rate, which will shift the aggregate supply curve downward, which minimizes the decline in output resulting from the leftward shift in aggregate demand.

9. It is possible (but controversial) that the recession of 1981–1982 might have been less severe if the Reagan administration had raised taxes to reduce budget deficits. The failure of the Reagan administration to raise taxes lessened the credibility of policymakers to reduce inflation.

10. A conservative central banker is viewed as having a particular aversion to higher inflation. Even though the policymakers' hands may not be tied down with rules, because of the aversion to high inflation, the public has more faith that the policymaker will not be tempted to pursue overly inflationary policies to reduce unemployment. This helps to solve the time-inconsistency problem, without the need for formal oversight, rules, or accountability.

Critical Thinking

1. The central bank will need to pursue an autonomous tightening of policy, which will contract aggregate demand leading to lower inflation in the short run, and eventually the economy will adjust to the policy change and reach a permanently lower inflation rate. However, the speed of the adjustment, and hence the costliness of the policy, will depend on the credibility that the central bank has in committing to the lower inflation rate.

2. Large budget deficits can be perceived as leading to inflation since some people may believe that the central bank will be tempted or forced to use monetary policy in an inflationary way to finance future deficits or

pay off debt. Thus, reducing large budget deficits can have the effect of shifting aggregate demand downward, which has a direct effect of lowering inflation. However, lowering deficits can also reduce the possibility of inflationary monetary policy, and thus can shift the aggregate supply curve down by lowering inflation expectations. Both of these effects lead to lower inflation in the short and long runs.

3. In the current situation with fiscal and monetary policy, it seems unlikely that permanently lowering the inflation rate would be costless. Given the large budget deficits, it may be politically difficult to meaningfully lower the deficits to have an appreciable effect on lowering inflation expectations. Moreover, since the central bank has a history of high inflation policy, it is unlikely that the public, at least not initially, will view the anti-inflation policy as credible. In this case, it will take a highly contractionary policy over a potentially protracted period of time before the public is convinced that the central bank and the government are committed to a low inflation policy. In the meantime, this will mean a potentially deep recession with high unemployment will be necessary to permanently lower the inflation rate.

True/False Questions

1. T
2. F
3. F
4. F
5. T
6. T
7. F
8. T
9. T
10. T
11. T
12. T
13. T
14. F
15. T

Multiple-Choice Questions

1. d
2. d
3. a
4. c
5. c
6. c
7. d
8. d
9. b
10. d
11. b
12. b
13. b
14. b
15. b
16. c
17. d
18. b
19. b
20. a

25 Transmission Mechanisms of Monetary Policy[*]

Chapter Review

PREVIEW

Aggregate output, the unemployment rate, and inflation fluctuate constantly. Policymakers face the question of what policy or policies, if any, they should use to reduce those fluctuations. To answer that question, monetary policymakers must have an accurate assessment of the effect of their policies on the economy. This chapter looks at the link between monetary policy and its effects on the real economy, which is emphasized by the role of financial markets.

TRANSMISSION MECHANISMS OF MONETARY POLICY

The channels through which money affects the economy are called the *transmission mechanisms of monetary policy*. There are three primary categories of effects through which monetary policy impacts the economy: interest rate effects, (other) asset price effects, and credit effects. Since the main policy tool by most central banks is adjustment of short-term interest rates, the traditional interest rate channel plays an important role in the transmission mechanism. Through this channel, a decrease in real interest rates leads to higher investment spending and output. However, economists have identified additional channels through which lower interest rates lead to higher expenditures, for instance by stimulating *consumer durable expenditures* as well as net exports. Importantly, in periods when the economy is near the zero-lower bound on nominal interest rates, real interest rates can still be lowered through rising inflation expectations, meaning the interest rate channel can still be effective. Some economists believe the interest rate channel is very strong, while others believe credit effects and asset price effects are a more important mechanism through which monetary policy operates.

---

[*]This is also Chapter 25 in the 3rd ed.

With respect to asset price effects, a decrease in real interest rates leads to a depreciation of the domestic currency, which increases net exports and aggregate demand. In addition, expansionary monetary policy leads to higher stock, land, and housing prices. Higher stock prices boost investment spending by raising Tobin's q (the market value of a firm divided by the replacement cost of capital). Higher stock prices (as well as higher land and housing prices) boost consumer wealth and lead to higher *consumption,* which also increases output. In addition to these channels, which operate through interest rates, economists have identified a set of channels termed the *credit view.* According to the credit view, monetary policy operates by affecting bank lending as well as firm and household balance sheets. Recall from earlier in the text that banks are especially well suited to solve asymmetric information problems in credit markets. If banks provide lending services to firms that otherwise would not have access to credit markets (small firms for example), then expansionary monetary policy will lead to increased lending, increased investment spending, and increased aggregate output. The balance sheet channel also arises from the presence of asymmetric information problems in credit markets. Expansionary monetary policy improves firm and household balance sheets, as well as firm cash flows. As balance sheets improve and cash flows increase, asymmetric information and moral hazard problems are reduced and banks are more willing to lend to firms and households, which leads to increased spending. In addition, the increase in net worth of households reduces the likelihood of financial distress, leading to higher consumption and housing expenditure.

Credit channels are likely to be important, since financial frictions play an important role in employment and spending decisions. In addition, small firms that are more credit constrained are likely to be more affected than large firms during tight monetary policy episodes. Finally, asymmetric information as it relates to credit market imperfections is important to the functioning of financial markets and so is likely to be important in the effectiveness of monetary policy.

In response to the global financial crisis, the Fed eased monetary policy aggressively starting in September of 2007. Despite the Fed's rapid response, the economy continued to weaken. One reason was that adverse selection and moral hazard problems increased in credit markets, which in turn led to a slowdown in the economy. Another reason was that declines in stock market and housing prices lowered household wealth, which led to restrained consumer spending and weaker investment because of the resulting drop in Tobin's q.

LESSONS FOR MONETARY POLICY

The analysis of this chapter implies the following four basic policy lessons.

1. It is dangerous always to associate the easing or the tightening of monetary policy with a fall or a rise in short-term nominal interest rates.

2. Other asset prices besides those on short-term debt instruments contain important information about the stance of monetary policy because they are important elements in various monetary policy transmission mechanisms.

3. Monetary policy can be highly effective in reviving a weak economy even if short-term interest rates are already near zero.

4. Avoiding unanticipated fluctuations in the price level is an important objective of monetary policy, thus providing a rationale for price stability as the primary long-run goal for monetary policy.

Since 1990 the Japanese economy has suffered from deflation and low growth. The Bank of Japan (Japan's central bank) took the view that monetary policy was sufficiently expansionary when nominal interest rates fell to near zero levels. But Japan suffered from deflation, which means that real interest rates were actually high and monetary policy was tight. Another indication that Japanese monetary policy was not expansionary was that stock and real estate prices collapsed. Officials at the Bank of Japan claimed that monetary policy became ineffective when interest rates fell to near zero. According to the third lesson above, monetary policy can still be effective even when interest rates are near zero. Japan might have had far more success if it had heeded the advice from these four basic lessons.

Helpful Hints

Interest rate changes can be effective for monetary policymakers to influence the economy under typical circumstances, but other channels can be just as important if not more to impact the economy. Moreover, monetary policy can still be effective when nominal interest rates reach the zero-lower-bound, since monetary policy can increase inflation expectations and can operate through many different channels, which affect different sectors of the economy.

Terms and Definitions

Choose a definition for each key term.

Key Terms:

_____ consumer durable expenditure

_____ consumption

_____ credit view

_____ transmission mechanisms of monetary policy

Definitions:

1. Spending by consumers on durable items such as automobiles and household appliances

2. Monetary transmission operating through asymmetric information effects on credit markets

3. Spending by consumers on nondurable goods and services

4. The channel through which monetary policy affects economic activity

Problems and Short-Answer Questions

PRACTICE PROBLEMS

1. The traditional interest rate channel of monetary policy can be characterized by the following schematic

   $r\downarrow \rightarrow I\uparrow \rightarrow Y\uparrow$

   Match the names of the transmission mechanisms on the right with their schematic depictions on the left.

   _____1. $r\downarrow \rightarrow E\downarrow \rightarrow NX\uparrow \rightarrow Y\uparrow$

   _____2. $r\downarrow \rightarrow P_s\uparrow \rightarrow q\uparrow \rightarrow I\uparrow \rightarrow Y\uparrow$

   _____3. $r\downarrow \rightarrow P_s\uparrow \rightarrow$ wealth $\uparrow \rightarrow$ consumption $\uparrow \rightarrow$ $Y\uparrow$

   _____4. $r\downarrow \rightarrow$ bank deposits $\uparrow \rightarrow$ bank loans $\uparrow \rightarrow$ $I\uparrow \rightarrow Y\uparrow$

   _____5. $r\downarrow \rightarrow P_s\uparrow \rightarrow$ adverse selection$\downarrow \rightarrow$ moral hazard$\downarrow \rightarrow I\uparrow \rightarrow Y\uparrow$

   _____6. $i\downarrow \rightarrow$ cash flow$\uparrow \rightarrow$ adverse selection$\downarrow \rightarrow$ moral hazard$\downarrow \rightarrow$ lending$\uparrow \rightarrow I\uparrow \rightarrow Y\uparrow$

   _____7. $r\downarrow \rightarrow$ unanticipated $P\uparrow \rightarrow$ adverse selection$\downarrow \rightarrow$ moral hazard$\downarrow \rightarrow$ lending$\uparrow \rightarrow I\uparrow \rightarrow Y\uparrow$

   _____8. $r\downarrow \rightarrow P_s\uparrow \rightarrow$ value of financial assets $\uparrow \rightarrow$ likelihood of financial distress$\downarrow \rightarrow$ consumer durable and housing expenditure$\uparrow \rightarrow Y\uparrow$

   a. Tobin's q theory

   b. household liquidity effect channel

   c. cash flow channel

   d. unanticipated price level

   e. exchange rate effect

   f. balance sheet channel

   g. bank lending channel

   h. wealth effects channel

2. a. List the four basic lessons about monetary policy from this chapter.

   _____

   _____

   _____

   _____

b. Explain how heeding the advice from each of these four lessons might have led to a far more successful conduct of monetary policy in Japan in recent years.

_____

_____

_____

3. For each of the following, classify the channel as operating through the traditional interest rate channel (I), other asset prices (A), or credit effects (C).

a. Tobin's q theory ____

b. household liquidity effect channel ____

c. cash flow channel ____

d. $r\downarrow \rightarrow I\uparrow \rightarrow Y\uparrow$ ____

e. exchange rate effect ____

f. balance sheet channel ____

g. bank lending channel ____

h. wealth effects channel ____

i. unanticipated price level ____

j. $\pi^e\uparrow \rightarrow r\downarrow \rightarrow I\uparrow \rightarrow Y\uparrow$ ____

4. For each of the following, specify which sector(s) of the economy are affected by the monetary transmission channel listed.

a. Tobin's q theory _____

b. household liquidity effect channel _____

c. cash flow channel _____

d. traditional interest rate effects _____

e. exchange rate effect _____

f. balance sheet channel _____

g. bank lending channel _____

h. wealth effects channel _____

i. unanticipated price level _____

SHORT-ANSWER QUESTIONS

1. Why might changes in interest rates affect consumer durable expenditure?

   _____

   _____

2. If a housing market crash or stock market crash occurs, how is this likely to affect the wealth channel of monetary policy?

   _____

   _____

3. In what ways can monetary policy improve information problems in monetary policy?

   _____

   _____

4. Explain how monetary policy can stimulate the economy, even if nominal interest rates hit a floor of zero during a deflationary episode.

   _____

   _____

5. If expansionary monetary policy leads to a sharp increase in excess reserves, what would this say about the effectiveness of the bank lending channel?

   _____

   _____

6. How can a *decrease* in nominal interest rates actually be viewed as a tightening of monetary policy?

   _____

   _____

7. Why might the bank lending channel not be as powerful in the United States as it once was?

   _____

   _____

8. Which transmission mechanism suggests that the nominal interest rate matters for investment spending and aggregate output? Why?

_____

_____

9. Why are credit channels likely to be important?

_____

_____

10. Why did the economy continue to slow in 2008 despite the Fed's very aggressive easing starting in late 2007?

_____

_____

Critical Thinking

Suppose you are hired as an economic adviser to the Central Bank of Canardville (a fictitious country). Shortly after beginning your new position, the economy begins to slow rapidly.

1. Policymakers and economists within the central bank believe that lowering interest rates will not be effective since investment, housing, and durable goods spending will not be affected through the interest rate channel. What would you tell them to convince them that monetary policy can still be effective, even if that is true?

_____

_____

_____

_____

2. Despite successive rounds of lowering the interest rate based on your advice, the economy of Canardville falls into a deep recession in which the nominal interest rate is near zero and there is deflation. What policy would you recommend to bring the economy out of recession?

_____

_____

_____

_____

3. Suppose after implementing the policy you described in your answer to question 2, the economy experienced a financial crisis like the one that hit the U.S. economy beginning in the summer of 2007. Explain to the head of the central bank why the policy you recommended to bring the economy out of recession will likely result in a slow recovery.

_____

_____

_____

_____

Self-Test

TRUE/FALSE QUESTIONS

_____1. Ben Bernanke believes interest-rate effects operating through the cost of capital are strong.

_____2. The wealth effect is based on Modigliani's life cycle hypothesis of consumption.

_____3. The three main categories of monetary transmission effects are based on interest-rate effects, the effects on asset prices, and effects in financial and credit markets.

_____4. Tobin's q increased sharply during the Depression period of 1929–1933.

_____5. Interest rate changes can affect consumer durable expenditures.

_____6. During periods of deflation, the real interest rate is lower than the nominal interest rate.

_____7. Credit channel effects are likely important because large firms are more credit constrained than small firms.

_____8. From 1929–1933, consumer durable spending declined by more than 50%.

_____9. According to the interest rate channel, expansionary monetary policy reduces the real interest rate, which stimulates investment spending and leads to an increase in aggregate output.

_____10. Consumption is spending on all goods and services including durable goods.

_____11. An increase in housing prices, which raises the price of housing relative to the replacement cost, leads to a rise in Tobin's q for housing and an increase in the production of housing as well.

_____12. Since the mid-1980s, the bank lending channel in the United States has become more powerful.

_____13. When expansionary monetary policy lowers interest rates, high-risk borrowers make up a greater fraction of those demanding loans.

_____14. Asset prices besides those on short-term debt instruments contain no information about the stance of monetary policy.

_____15. Monetary policy is ineffective in economies with deflation and short-term interest rates near zero.

MULTIPLE-CHOICE QUESTIONS

1. With an autonomous tightening of policy, the cost of capital _____, and _____ decreases.
   a. is unaffected; the unemployment rate
   b. increases; the short-term interest rate
   c. decreases; imports
   d. increases; investment

2. If an expansionary monetary policy leads to a house price bubble that fuels strong consumer spending, this is an example of
   a. Tobin's q.
   b. the wealth effect.
   c. the unanticipated price level channel.
   d. the leverage channel.

3. A firm's net worth is _____ related to adverse selection and moral hazard and _____ related to investment.
   a. negatively; positively
   b. positively; negatively
   c. positively; positively
   d. negatively; negatively

4. Of the nine channels of monetary policy discussed in the chapter, how many have an impact on the investment component of GDP?
   a. 3
   b. 5
   c. 7
   d. 9

5. When nominal interest rates decrease but real interest rates increase,
   a. inflation is high.
   b. consumption and investment will increase.
   c. inflation expectations must have increased.
   d. monetary policy is tight.

6. Monetary policy can affect firms' balance sheets by affecting
   a. firm's cost of borrowing.
   b. exchange rates.
   c. a firm's stock and asset prices
   d. bank reserves.

7. When nominal interest rates hit a floor of zero during a deflationary episode,
   a. monetary policy can no longer stimulate the economy.
   b. monetary policy can stimulate the economy by pushing nominal interest rates below zero.
   c. monetary policy can stimulate the economy by raising the expected inflation rate.
   d. monetary policy can stimulate the economy by reducing the expected inflation rate.

8. According to the exchange rate effect, expansionary monetary policy will cause
   a. domestic interest rates to rise, the dollar to appreciate, and net exports to fall.
   b. domestic interest rates to fall, the dollar to depreciate, and net exports to fall.
   c. domestic interest rates to rise, the dollar to depreciate, and net exports to rise.
   d. domestic interest rates to fall, the dollar to depreciate, and net exports to rise.

9. According to Tobin's q theory, expansionary monetary policy will lead to an increase in investment spending because
   a. the market value of firms rises relative to the replacement cost of capital.
   b. the replacement cost of capital rises relative to the market value of firms.
   c. firms' balance sheets improve, which reduces adverse selection and moral hazard.
   d. the likelihood of financial distress falls, which leads to an increase in bank lending.

10. According to the bank lending channel, lending by banks rises when expansionary monetary policy occurs because
    a. the interest rate falls and the quantity of loans demanded rises.
    b. Tobin's q for banks rises.
    c. bank deposits increase, which leads to an increase in the quantity of bank loans available.
    d. stock prices rise, causing consumer wealth to rise, which increases the demand for bank loans.

11. Because of asymmetric information problems in credit markets, monetary policy may affect economic activity through the balance sheet channel, which holds that expansionary monetary policy
    a. raises equity prices, which lowers the cost of new capital relative to the market value of firms, thereby increasing investment spending.
    b. raises the net worth of firms, decreasing adverse selection and moral hazard problems, thereby increasing banks' willingness to lend to finance investment spending.
    c. raises the level of bank reserves, deposits, and the quantity of bank loans available, which raises the spending by those individuals who do not have access to credit markets.
    d. reduces the real interest rate, which leads to an increase in the quantity of bank loans demanded.

12. According to the cash flow channel, a 1 percentage point rise in both the nominal interest rate and expected inflation will
    a. leave the cash flow of firms unchanged.
    b. decrease the cash flow of firms, increasing the moral hazard and adverse selection problem, which makes banks less willing to lend to firms.
    c. decrease the cash flow of firms, decreasing the moral hazard and adverse selection problem, which makes banks less willing to lend to firms.
    d. increase the cash flow of firms, decreasing the moral hazard and adverse selection problem, which makes banks more willing to lend to firms.

13. When the price level rises unexpectedly, a firm's debt burdens _____, and net worth increases. The effect is to _____ adverse selection and moral hazard problems, which results in increased lending.
    a. increase; increase
    b. increase; decrease
    c. decrease; increase
    d. decrease; decrease

14. Because of asymmetric information about their quality, consumer durables and housing are _____ to sell compared to liquid assets and therefore _____ to hold in periods of financial distress.
    a. more difficult; less desirable
    b. less difficult; less desirable
    c. more difficult; more desirable
    d. less difficult; more desirable

15. Expansionary monetary policy _____ the likelihood of financial distress, which _____ consumer durable and housing expenditures.
    a. increases; increases
    b. increases; decreases
    c. decreases; increases
    d. decreases; decreases

16. Credit channels are likely to be important monetary transmission mechanisms because
    a. asymmetric information, which forms the core of credit channel theory, does a good job of explaining why financial institutions exist.
    b. credit market imperfections do appear to affect firm spending and employment decisions.
    c. small firms, which are more likely to be credit constrained, appear to be most affected by monetary policy.
    d. All of the above are true.

17. One reason the economy continued to weaken in 2008 was
    a. the Fed increased interest rates.
    b. adverse selection and moral hazard problems increased.
    c. credit spreads narrowed.
    d. stock prices fell, which led to an increase in Tobin's q.

18. It is dangerous to always associate the easing or tightening of monetary policy with a fall or a rise in short-term nominal interest rates because
    a. central banks often target the money supply rather than interest rates.
    b. stock prices are a better indicator of whether monetary policy is tight or easy.
    c. movements in nominal interest rates do not always correspond to movements in real interest rates.
    d. short-term interest rates have very little impact on borrowing and lending.

19. If short-term interest rates are low, stock prices and land prices are _____, and the value of the domestic currency is _____, then monetary policy is clearly _____.
    a. low; low; easy
    b. high; high; easy
    c. low; high; tight
    d. high; low; easy

20. In the late 1990s in Japan, short-term nominal interest rates _____ while short-term real interest rates _____, indicating that monetary policy was _____.
    a. increased; decreased; tight
    b. increased; decreased; easy
    c. decreased; increased; tight
    d. decreased; increased; easy

Solutions

Definitions:

_1_ consumer durable expenditure

_3_ consumption

_2_ credit view

_4_ transmission mechanisms of monetary policy

Practice Problems

1. _e_ 1.

    _a_ 2.

    _h_ 3.

    _g_ 4.

    _f_ 5.

    _c_ 6.

    _d_ 7.

    _b_ 8.

2. a. The four basic lessons about monetary policy from this chapter are: (1) It is dangerous to always associate the easing or the tightening of monetary policy with a fall or a rise in short-term nominal interest rates. (2) Other asset prices besides those on short-term debt instruments contain important information about the stance of monetary policy. (3) Monetary policy can be highly effective in reviving a weak economy even when short-term interest rates are already near zero. (4) Avoiding unanticipated fluctuation in the price level is an important objective of monetary policy, thus providing a rationale for price stability as the primary long-run goal for monetary policy.

    b. Japan thought monetary policy was expansionary because nominal interest rates were near zero, but in fact, real interest rates were quite high. The Bank of Japan claimed that it had no ability to stimulate the economy because interest rates were near zero, but it could have reduced real interest rates by raising expected inflation. The Bank of Japan could have seen that monetary policy was tight by looking at falling stock and real estate prices. The Bank of Japan would have been more successful if it had prevented deflation.

3. a. A

    b. C

    c. C

    d. I

    e. A

    f. C

    g. C

    h. A

    i. C

    j. I

4. a. Investment.

    b. Residential housing and consumer durables.

    c. Investment.

    d. Investment, residential housing, and consumer durables.

    e. Net exports.

    f. Investment.

    g. Investment and residential housing.

    h. Consumption

    i. Investment

Short-Answer Questions

1. A reduction in real interest rates can affect interest sensitive consumption goods, such as durable goods. Thus, lower borrowing costs can increase durable goods spending. In addition, lower interest rates can increase asset prices, and reduce the probability of financial distress. This can have the effect of allowing households to be more comfortable to make larger purchases such as consumer durables.

2. Most likely the wealth channel will not contribute to much of an expansionary impact on the economy. Monetary policy effects that would lead to higher consumption, *ceteris paribus,* would presumably be more than offset by the contractionary wealth effects of the stock or housing market crash. So even though expansionary policy may occur, consumption could actually decrease, but it would decrease less than if no policy change were to occur.

3. Through expansionary monetary policy, the central bank can reduce asymmetric information (reducing adverse selection and

moral hazard) by improving the net worth of firms (by increasing the value of firms' assets, or reducing the real debt burden of firms), or increasing firms' cash flows.

4. If nominal interest rates hit a floor of zero, the central bank can still reduce real interest rates by committing to increase the inflation rate.

5. With a sharp increase in excess reserves, this would imply that bank lending is not increasing very much, if at all. This would then not translate to higher investment and output, indicating that the bank lending channel would not be very effective when expansionary policy coincides with banks holding substantial excess reserves.

6. If inflation expectations decline more than the decrease in short-term interest rates, a seemingly expansionary reduction in nominal interest rates can actually result in an overall increase in real interest rates, implying a tightening of monetary policy.

7. The bank lending channel may not be as powerful in the United States as it once was because current U.S. regulation no longer imposes restrictions on banks' ability to raise funds.

8. The cash flow channel suggests that the nominal interest rate matters for investment spending. As nominal interest rates fall, firms' balance sheets improve, which makes it easier for lenders to assess whether the firm or household will be able to pay its bills. As a result, adverse selection and moral hazard decline and lending increases.

9. Credit channels are likely to be important monetary transmission mechanisms because (1) asymmetric information, which forms the core of credit channel theory, does a good job of explaining why financial institutions exist; (2) credit market imperfections do appear to affect firm spending and employment decisions; and (3) small firms, which are more likely to be credit-constrained, appear to be most affected by monetary policy.

10. One reason was that adverse selection and moral hazard problems increased in credit markets, leading to a slowdown in the economy. Another reason was that declines in stock market and housing prices lowered household wealth, which led to restrained consumer spending and weaker investment because of the resulting drop in Tobin's q.

Critical Thinking

1. You should tell the central bank officials that even if the traditional interest rate channel is not effective in increasing spending, lowering interest rates can still be effective by impacting the economy through asset prices, and improving the flow and availability of credit through the credit view. These other factors can still increase investment, consumption, and net exports, which will raise spending. In addition, there is some evidence that these channels may be much stronger than traditional interest rate effects anyway, implying interest rate policy could still be highly effective at keeping the economy from going into recession.

2. Even when nominal interest rates are near zero and there is deflation, the central bank can stimulate aggregate output by committing to raising inflationary expectations, which will reduce the real interest rate.

3. A financial crisis will make it more difficult for lenders to separate good credit risks from bad credit risks so the potential for adverse selection and moral hazard has increased. As a result, lending has slowed, which will slow the recovery from recession even if the real interest rate has declined because of an increase in expected inflation.

True/False Questions

1. F
2. T
3. T
4. F
5. T
6. F
7. F
8. T
9. T
10. F
11. T
12. F
13. F
14. F
15. F

Multiple-Choice Questions

1. d
2. b
3. a
4. c
5. d
6. c
7. c
8. d
9. a
10. c
11. b
12. d
13. d
14. a
15. c
16. d
17. b
18. c
19. d
20. c

Web Chapter

The *ISLM* Model[*]

Chapter Review

PREVIEW

This chapter develops the *ISLM* model, a widely used model for explaining output and interest rate fluctuations, and is an alternative to the *IS/MP* curve framework developed in the main text to understand the role of money and monetary policy in the economy. The *ISLM* model explains how interest rates and total output produced in the economy are determined given a fixed price level. It is sometimes called the Keynesian *ISLM* model because it is based on the work of John Maynard Keynes during the 1930s. In this chapter, we also use the *ISLM* model to evaluate the effects of monetary and fiscal policy.

KEYNES'S FIXED PRICE LEVEL ASSUMPTION AND THE *IS* CURVE

Keynes's analysis was developed during the Great Depression, when inflation was not viewed as a problem. One key assumption that comes as a result of this is that the price level is assumed to be fixed, and thus there is no distinction necessary between nominal and real interest rates. As a consequence, the *IS* curve as presented in Chapter 20 can then also be expressed as a goods market equilibrium relationship between aggregate output and the nominal interest rate.

THE *LM* CURVE

The *IS* curve tells us that equilibrium in the goods market depends on the interest rate so a natural question arises: What determines the interest rate? The interest rate is determined by equilibrium in the money market. The demand for money is

---

[*]This is the web chapter for the 10th ed.

described by the Keynesian liquidity preference theory, which tells us that the demand for money is positively related to income and negatively related to the interest rate. The intersection of the downward-sloping money demand function and the vertical money supply function determines the interest rate. As aggregate income rises, money demand shifts right, which moves the interest rate to a higher level along the vertical money supply curve. Therefore, higher levels of aggregate income are associated with higher interest rates along the *LM curve*, implying an upward sloping *LM* curve. Moreover, any point along the *LM* curve represents a money market equilibrium. If the economy is to the right of the *LM* curve, there is an excess demand for money. In this case, in an attempt to hold more money balances, people will sell bonds to "buy" money; this drives the price of bonds down and the interest rate up at any given level of output, until the money market comes into equilibrium.

ISLM APPROACH TO AGGREGATE OUTPUT AND INTEREST RATES

Both planned investment spending and net exports are negatively related to the interest rate and, hence, imply the interest rate affects the aggregate amount of output demanded. The inverse relationship between aggregate expenditures and the interest rate is called the *IS* curve, which is shown in the figure below.

At each point along the *IS* curve, the goods market is in equilibrium. Low interest rates are associated with equilibrium in the goods market in which aggregate expenditures are high. High interest rates are associated with equilibrium in the goods market in which aggregate expenditures are low. Likewise, at each point along the *LM* curve the money market is in equilibrium. Low interest rates are associated with low equilibrium output, and as output rises, a higher equilibrium interest rate occurs to ensure a goods market equilibrium. At point *E*, both the goods market and the money market are in equilibrium.

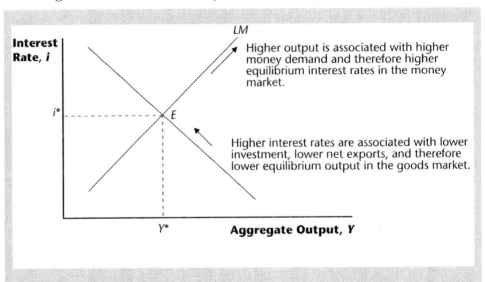

FACTORS THAT CAUSE
THE *LM* CURVE TO SHIFT

Two factors cause the *LM* curve to shift:

- Changes in the money supply

- Autonomous changes in money demand

An increase in the money supply shifts the *LM* curve right, since this decreases the equilibrium interest rate in the money market, for any given level of output. A decrease in the money supply similarly shifts the *LM* curve left. Autonomous changes in money demand are any changes that are not caused by a change in the price level, aggregate output or the interest rate. For example, if bonds suddenly become a riskier asset, the demand for money will rise. Because this increase in demand for money is independent of a change in the price level, aggregate output or interest rates, it causes a leftward shift in the *LM* curve. A decrease in autonomous money demand causes the *LM* curve to shift right.

CHANGES IN EQUILIBRIUM LEVEL
OF THE INTEREST RATE AND AGGREGATE OUTPUT

In the figure below, panel a shows the response of output and interest rates to an increase in the money supply. The increase in the money supply shifts the *LM* curve right, which causes the interest rate to fall and aggregate output to rise. A decrease in the money supply shifts the *LM* curve to the left, which causes the interest rate to rise and aggregate output to fall. Aggregate output is positively related to the money supply.

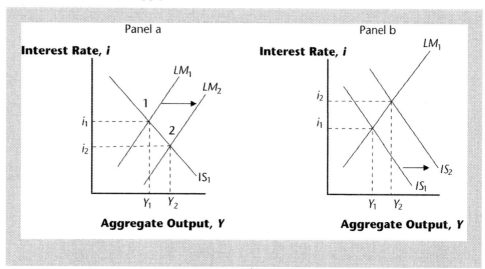

Panel b shows the response of output and interest rates to expansionary fiscal policy. Expansionary fiscal policy (either an increase in government spending or a reduction in taxes) shifts the *IS* curve to the right, which causes interest rates to rise and aggregate output to rise as well. Contractionary fiscal policy shifts the *IS*

curve to the left, which causes interest rates to fall and aggregate output to fall. Aggregate output is positively related to government spending and negatively related to taxes. More generally, the *IS* curve will shift right if any of the following occur:

- Autonomous consumption expenditure increases

- Autonomous investment increases

- Government spending increases

- Taxes decrease

- Autonomous net exports increases

EFFECTIVENESS OF MONETARY VERSUS FISCAL POLICY

When money demand is unaffected by the interest rate, the *LM* curve is vertical, and monetary policy affects output, but fiscal policy does not. Expansionary fiscal policy (either increasing government spending or decreasing taxes) shifts the *IS* curve to the right, but because the *LM* curve is vertical, the interest rate rises causing investment spending and net exports to decline enough to completely offset the effects of the expansionary fiscal policy. This special case, when expansionary fiscal policy has no effect on output, is called *complete crowding out*. Expansionary monetary policy does lead to an increase in aggregate output when the *LM* curve is vertical. In general, the less interest-sensitive money demand is, the more effective monetary policy is relative to fiscal policy.

APPLICATION: TARGETING MONEY SUPPLY VERSUS INTEREST RATES

In the real world, unanticipated changes in autonomous spending and money demand cause the *IS* and *LM* curves to shift. Because of these shifts, the positions of the *IS* and *LM* curves are uncertain. The central bank's choice of whether to target the interest rate or the money supply depends on which of these curves, the *IS* curve or the *LM* curve, is more unstable. If the *IS* curve is more unstable than the *LM* curve, a money supply target is preferred. If the *LM* curve is more unstable than the *IS* curve, an interest-rate target is preferred.

ISLM MODEL IN THE LONG RUN

So far in the *ISLM* model we have assumed that the price level is fixed. But in the long run, the price level does change, so when we use the *ISLM* model to analyze the effect of monetary or fiscal policy in the long run, we need to consider changes in the price level. Changes in the price level do not affect the *IS* curve. Recall that changes in the real money supply (M/P) shift the *LM* curve. So far we have only considered changes in the real money supply that arise from changes in the nominal money supply (M). Changes in the real money supply can arise from changes in the price level (P) as well.

Holding the nominal money supply constant, an increase in the price level reduces the real money supply and causes the *LM* curve to shift left. A decrease in the price level increases the real money supply and causes the *LM* curve to shift right. The *natural rate level of output* (Y^p) is the level of output at which the price level has no tendency to rise or fall. Suppose the economy begins at the natural rate level of output and expansionary monetary policy shifts the *LM* curve to the right. In the short run, aggregate output will rise above the natural rate level of output. In the long run, the price level will rise, the real money supply will fall back to its original level, the *LM* curve will shift back to its original position, aggregate output will return to the natural rate, and the interest rate will return to its original value as well. The fact that the increase in the money supply has left output and interest rates unchanged in the long run is referred to as *long-run monetary neutrality*. Expansionary fiscal policy also has no long-run effect on output, but it does leave the interest rate at a higher level.

Helpful Hints

1. Movements along the *IS* curve happen because an increase in the interest rate causes planned investment spending and net exports to decline, which leads to lower aggregate output (Y). Movements along the *LM* curve happen because higher aggregate output (Y) causes the demand for money to increase, which leads to higher interest rates. The equilibrium point is the point where both the goods market (described by the *IS* curve) and the money market (described by the *LM* curve) are in equilibrium at the same time.

2. Fiscal policy (changes in government spending and taxes) shifts the *IS* curve. Monetary policy (changes in the money supply) shifts the *LM* curve. In the long run, aggregate output returns to the natural rate level of output. If output is above the natural rate level, the price level rises, the real money supply declines, and the *LM* curve shifts left until aggregate output returns to the natural rate level of output. If output is below the natural rate level, the price level falls, the real money supply increases, and the *LM* curve shifts right until aggregate output returns to the natural rate level of output.

Terms and Definitions

Choose a definition for each key term.

Key Terms:

_____ complete crowding out

_____ LM curve

_____ long-run monetary neutrality

_____ natural rate level of output

Definitions:

1. When an increase in the money supply leaves output and interest rates unchanged in the long run

2. The long-run level of potential output

3. Combinations of aggregate output and interest rates for which the money market is in equilibrium

4. The situation in which expansionary fiscal policy does not lead to a rise in output because there is an exactly offsetting movement in private spending

Problems and Short-Answer Questions

PRACTICE PROBLEMS

1. Assume the economy is initially at the natural rate level of output (Y^P).
   a. Show what happens in the short run to the interest rate and aggregate output when the Fed increases the money supply.

b. On the same graph you used to illustrate your answer to part (a), show what will happen in the long run. Explain your result.

_____

_____

_____

c. Assume the economy is once again at the natural rate level of output (Y^p). Show what happens in the short run to the interest rate and aggregate output when government increases spending.

d. On the same graph you used to illustrate your answer to part (c), show what will happen in the long run. Explain your result.

_____

_____

_____

e. Now assume the economy is at the natural rate level of output (Y^p), but this time also assume that money demand is unaffected by the interest rate. Show what happens in the short run and the long run to the interest rate and aggregate output when government increases spending. Explain your result.

_____

_____

_____

2. Complete the table by indicating whether each shift factor listed in the far left column shifts the *IS* or *LM* curve right (right), left (left) or not at all (no shift), and whether the resulting shift in *IS* or *LM* causes interest rates and aggregate output to rise (+), fall (−) or remain unchanged (0).

Shift factor	Direction of change	*IS* curve shifts...	*LM* curve shifts...	Effect on Interest rate	Effect on Aggregate Output
Autonomous consumer expenditure	+				
Autonomous investment spending	−				
Government spending	+				
Taxes	+				
Net exports	−				
Money supply	−				
Autonomous money demand	−				

3. a. Suppose the *IS* curve is stable and the *LM* curve is unstable. In the graph below in panel a, illustrate the effect on aggregate output of following an interest rate target. In panel b, illustrate the effect on aggregate output of following a money supply target.

Interest Rate, *i*   Panel a   Interest Rate, *i*   Panel b

                      Aggregate Output, *Y*   Aggregate Output, *Y*

b. Based on your analysis in part (a), which type of policy would you recommend for an economy with a stable *IS* curve and an unstable *LM* curve? Why?

_____

_____

_____

c. Suppose the *IS* curve is unstable and the *LM* curve is stable. In panel a below, illustrate the effect on aggregate output of following an interest rate target. In panel b illustrate the effect on aggregate output of following a money supply target.

Interest Rate, *i*   Panel a   Interest Rate, *i*   Panel b

                      Aggregate Output, *Y*   Aggregate Output, *Y*

d. Based on your analysis in part (c), which type of policy would you recommend for an economy with an unstable *IS* curve and a stable *LM* curve? Why?

_____

_____

_____

4. Panel a in the figure below shows equilibriums in the money market corresponding to three different levels of aggregate income. Use the data from panel a to construct an *LM* curve in panel b.

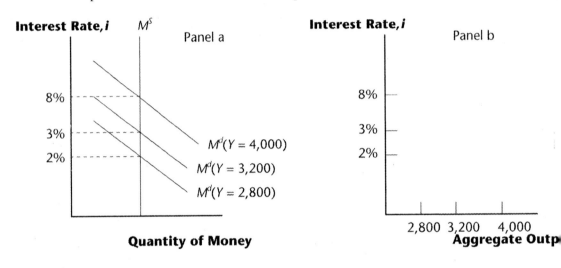

SHORT-ANSWER QUESTIONS

1. Why are interest rates and aggregate output negatively related along the *IS* curve?

_____

_____

2. Why are interest rates and aggregate output positively related along the *LM* curve?

_____

_____

3. Suppose the economy is to the left of the *LM* curve. Is there an excess supply or excess demand for money? Describe the adjustment of the economy back to the *LM* curve.

_____

_____

4. List the factors that shift the *LM* curve.

_____

_____

5. Give an example of a change in investment spending that would cause a shift in the *IS* curve. Give an example of a change in investment spending that would cause a movement along the *IS* curve.

_____

_____

6. Give an example of a change in net exports that would cause a shift in the *IS* curve. Give an example of a change in net exports that would cause a movement along the *IS* curve.

_____

_____

7. Give an example of change in money demand that would cause a shift in the *LM* curve. Give an example of a change in money demand that would cause a movement along the *LM* curve.

_____

_____

8. Suppose the economy is currently below the natural rate level of output and the demand for money is unaffected by the interest rate. What type of policy, monetary or fiscal, would you recommend to move the economy back to the natural rate level of output? Why?

_____

_____

9. Describe the adjustment of prices that will occur when the economy is above the natural rate level of output. Explain how the economy returns to the natural rate level of output as a result of the price adjustment you described.

_____

_____

10. Describe the adjustment of prices that will occur when the economy is below the natural rate level of output. Explain how the economy returns to the natural rate level of output as a result of the price adjustment you described.

_____

_____

Critical Thinking

Most of the analysis of fiscal and monetary policy in this chapter considers one type of policy at a time, holding the other type of policy constant. But in the real world, both monetary policy and fiscal policy are changing all of the time. Consider the combinations of monetary and fiscal policy listed in the table below. Fill in the missing columns in the table by indicating whether the given combination of monetary and fiscal policy has a positive (+), negative (–), or ambiguous (?) impact on interest rates and aggregate output.

Fiscal Policy	Monetary Policy	Interest Rates	Aggregate Output
Expansionary	Expansionary	_____	_____
Contractionary	Contractionary	_____	_____
Expansionary	Contractionary	_____	_____
Contractionary	Expansionary	_____	_____

Self-Test

TRUE/FALSE QUESTIONS

_____1. The *IS* curve shows the combinations of interest rates and aggregate output for which the goods market is in equilibrium.

_____2. Keynes's liquidity preference theory states that the demand for money in real terms depends only on the interest rate.

_____3. Equilibrium in the goods market produces a unique equilibrium level of aggregate output.

_____4. An increase in investment spending that is caused by a decrease in the interest rate is represented as a rightward shift in the *IS* curve.

_____5. An increase in net exports that is caused by a decrease in the interest rate, which leads to a depreciation of the dollar, is represented as a movement (down and to the right) along the *IS* curve.

_____6. If bonds become less risky, people will decrease their demand for money, which will cause the *LM* curve to shift right.

_____7. Complete crowding out occurs when the demand for money is ultrasensitive to changes in the interest rate.

_____8. An increase in the money supply caused by an open market purchase of bonds by the Federal Reserve causes the *LM* curve to shift right.

_____9. When the *LM* curve is more unstable than the *IS* curve, the Fed should target the interest rate to minimize fluctuations in aggregate output.

_____10. Although monetary and fiscal policy can affect output in the long run, neither affects output in the short run.

_____11. Fiscal policy affects the interest rate in the long run; monetary policy does not affect the interest rate in the long run.

_____12. When aggregate output is below the natural rate level of output, the price level rises.

_____13. When aggregate output is at the natural rate level of output, the price level remains unchanged.

_____14. Long-run monetary neutrality refers to the fact that in the long run, an increase in the money supply has no effect on the price level.

_____15. Any factor that shifts the *IS* curve shifts the *LM* curve in the same direction.

MULTIPLE-CHOICE QUESTIONS

1. An increase in the interest rate will cause
   a. investment spending to rise and net exports to fall.
   b. investment spending to fall and net exports to fall.
   c. investment spending to rise and net exports to rise.
   d. investment spending to fall and net exports to rise.

2. The *IS* curve slopes downward because the higher _____ lead to lower _____ and _____.
   a. government spending; consumption; investment spending
   b. interest rates; money demand; investment spending
   c. government spending; money demand; net exports
   d. interest rates; investment spending; net exports

3. In the money market, an increase in aggregate output leads to _____ in money demand and _____ in the interest rate.
   a. an increase; a decrease
   b. a decrease; an increase
   c. an increase; an increase
   d. a decrease; a decrease

4. The *IS* curve shows combinations of interest rates and levels of income for which
   a. government spending equals taxes.
   b. the money market is in equilibrium.
   c. net exports and government spending both equal zero.
   d. the goods market is in equilibrium.

5. The *LM* curve shows combinations of interest rates and levels of income for which
   a. government spending equals taxes.
   b. the money market is in equilibrium.
   c. net exports and government spending both equal zero.
   d. the goods market is in equilibrium.

6. When the supply of money is greater than the demand for money, people will
   a. spend the excess money, causing interest rates to rise.
   b. sell bonds, causing interest rates to fall.
   c. buy bonds, causing the interest rate to rise.
   d. buy bonds, causing the price of bonds to rise.

7. The difference between the long-run effect of an increase in the money supply and the long-run effect of an increase in government spending is that
   a. an increase in government spending results in a higher interest rate in the long run while an increase in the money supply does not.
   b. an increase in the money supply results in a higher interest rate in the long run while an increase in government spending does not.
   a. an increase in government spending results in a higher aggregate output in the long run while an increase in the money supply does not.
   b. an increase in the money supply results in a higher aggregate output in the long run while an increase in government spending does not.

8. At points to the right of the *LM* curve
   a. there is an excess supply of money, which will cause interest rates to fall.
   b. there is an excess supply of money, which will cause interest rates to rise.
   c. there is an excess demand for money, which will cause interest rates to fall.
   d. there is an excess demand for money, which will cause interest rates to rise.

9. The intersection of the *IS* and *LM* curves shows
   a. the only combination of interest rates and aggregate output for which the goods market is in equilibrium.
   b. the only combination of interest rates and aggregate output for which the money market is in equilibrium.
   c. one of many possible combinations of interest rates and aggregate output for which both the goods market and the money market are in equilibrium.
   d. the only combination of interest rates and aggregate output for which both the goods market and the money market are in equilibrium.

10. At point B in the figure below, there is excess
    a. demand for goods and excess supply of money.
    b. supply of goods and excess supply of money.
    c. demand for goods and excess demand for money.
    d. supply of goods and excess demand for money.

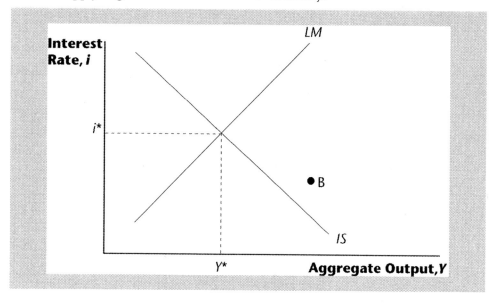

11. In the short run, an increase in taxes will lead to
    a. lower interest rates and lower aggregate output.
    b. higher interest rates and lower aggregate output.
    c. no change in interest rates and lower aggregate output.
    d. higher interest rates but no change in aggregate output.

12. In the short run, an increase in the money supply will lead to
    a. higher interest rates and higher aggregate output.
    b. lower interest rates and higher aggregate output.
    c. no change in interest rates and higher aggregate output.
    d. higher interest rates but no change in aggregate output.

13. Complete crowding out implies that
    a. an increase in the money supply has no long-run impact on aggregate output.
    b. an increase in government spending has no long-run impact on aggregate output.
    c. an increase in the money supply has no impact on output, even in the short run.
    d. an increase in government spending has no impact on output, even in the short run.

The figure below is for multiple choice questions 14–16.

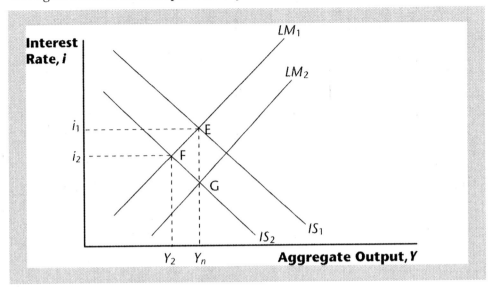

14. A possible reason that the economy moved from equilibrium point E to equilibrium point F in the figure is
    a. a decrease in the money supply.
    b. an increase in autonomous money demand.
    c. a decrease in autonomous consumption expenditure.
    d. an increase in autonomous consumption expenditure.

15. If policymakers are interested in moving the economy from point F back to the natural rate level of output at point E, they could
    a. increase in the money supply.
    b. decrease the money supply.
    c. increase government spending.
    d. decrease government spending.

16. If policymakers decided to do nothing in response to the economy moving to point F from point E, then in the long run the price level would
    a. fall, and the economy would return to point E.
    b. rise, and the economy would return to point E.
    c. fall, and the economy would move to point G.
    d. rise, and the economy would move to point G.

17. If the *IS* curve is relatively more unstable than the *LM* curve, then the optimal monetary policy is to target
    a. the money supply.
    b. the inflation rate.
    c. unemployment.
    d. the interest rate.

18. When the *LM* curve is completely stable, targeting the interest rate results in
    a. smaller fluctuations in aggregate output than would occur with a money supply target.
    b. larger fluctuations in aggregate output than would occur with a money supply target.
    c. no fluctuations in aggregate output.
    d. the same fluctuations in aggregate output as would occur with a money supply target.

19. Starting from the natural rate level of output, the long-run effect of an increase in the money supply is
    a. higher aggregate output and a higher interest rate.
    b. lower aggregate output and no change in the interest rate.
    c. no change in aggregate output and no change in the interest rate.
    d. no change in aggregate output but a higher interest rate.

20. An increase in the price level leads to
    a. a decrease in the real money supply and a rightward shift in the *LM* curve.
    b. an increase in the real money supply and a leftward shift in the *LM* curve.
    c. a decrease in the real money supply and a leftward shift in the *LM* curve.
    d. an increase in the real money supply and a rightward shift in the *LM* curve.

Solutions

Terms and Definitions

_4_ complete crowding out

_3_ LM curve

_1_ long-run monetary neutrality

_2_ natural rate level of output

Practice Problems

1. a. and b. The short-run (a) and long-run (b) effects of an increase in the money supply.

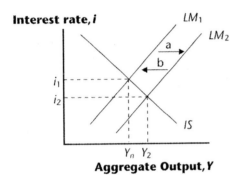

Aggregate Output, Y

An increase in the money supply shifts the *LM* curve to the right in the short run (a). In the long run, the price level rises because aggregate output is above the natural rate level. As the price level rises, the real money supply falls causing the *LM* curve to shift back to LM_1 (b). In the long run, aggregate output returns to the natural rate level Y_n.

c. and d. The short-run (c) and long-run (d) effects of an increase in government spending.

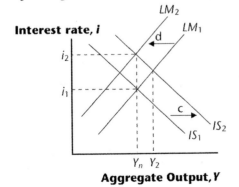

Aggregate Output, Y

An increase in government spending shifts the *IS* curve to the right in the short run (c). In the long run the price level rises because the aggregate output is above the natural rate level. As the price level rises, the real money supply falls causing the *LM* curve to shift left to LM_2 (d). In the long run, aggregate output returns to the natural rate level Y_n.

e. The short-run and long-run effects of an increase in government spending, when the demand for money is unaffected by the interest rate;

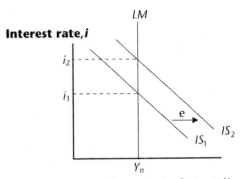

Aggregate Output, Y

In the short run, an increase in government spending shifts the *IS* curve to the right (e). Since the demand for money is unaffected by interest rates there is complete crowding out and aggregate output remains at Y_n. Since aggregate output remains at Y_n, the price level remains unchanged and the long-run response of interest rates and aggregate output is the same as the short-run response.

2.

Shift factor	Direction of change	IS curve shifts...	LM curve shifts...	Effect on Interest rate	Effect on Aggregate Output
Autonomous consumer expenditure	+	right	no shift	+	+
Autonomous investment spending	–	left	no shift	–	–
Government spending	+	right	no shift	+	+
Taxes	+	left	no shift	–	–
Net exports	–	left	no shift	–	–
Money supply	–	no shift	left	+	–
Autonomous money demand	–	no shift	right	–	+

3. a.

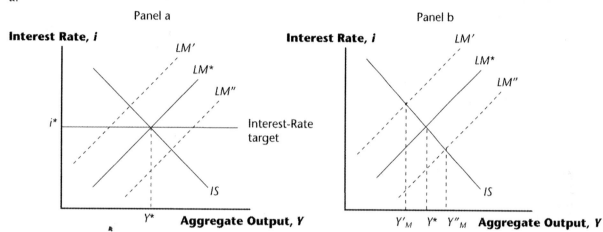

Panel a — Panel b

b. If the *LM* curve is unstable and the *IS* curve is stable (or more generally, if the *LM* curve is relatively more unstable than the *IS* curve), then a policy that targets the interest rate is preferred because it will keep aggregate output closer to Y* as shown in panel a.

c.

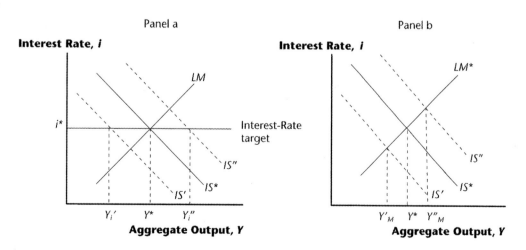

Panel a — Panel b

d. If the *IS* curve is unstable and the *LM* curve is stable (or more generally, if the *IS* curve is relatively more unstable than the *LM* curve), then a policy that targets the money supply is preferred because it will keep aggregate output closer to Y^* as shown in panel b.

4.

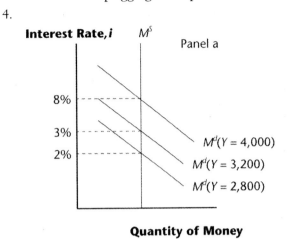

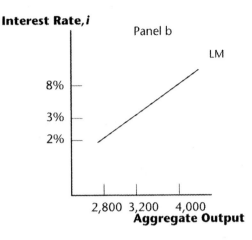

Short-Answer Questions

1. Interest rates and aggregate output are negatively related along the *IS* curve because as interest rates rise, investment spending and net exports decline, and as investment spending and net exports decline, so does aggregate output.

2. Interest rates and aggregate output are positively related along the *LM* curve because as aggregate income rises, the demand for money increases, which causes the interest rate to rise.

3. If the economy is to the left of the *LM* curve, there is an excess supply of money. People will purchase bonds with their excess money holdings. The increased demand for bonds will cause the price of bonds to rise, and the interest rate to fall until equilibrium is restored along the *LM* curve.

4. Two factors shift the *LM* curve: changes in the money supply and autonomous changes in money demand.

5. If firms become optimistic about the future of the economy and increase investment spending, then the *IS* curve will shift right. If the interest rate declines and firms increase investment spending because new investment projects are now profitable at the lower interest rate, then the economy moves along the *IS* curve.

6. If foreign buyers decide that U.S.-produced goods are fashionable, then exports will increase and the *IS* curve will shift right. If the interest rate declines, the dollar will depreciate relative to foreign currencies causing exports to rise and imports to fall, which will cause the economy to move along the *IS* curve.

7. If the rate of return on bonds becomes more volatile, and therefore riskier, people will increase their demand for money, which will cause the *LM* curve to shift left. If income rises, people will increase their demand for money, which will cause the economy to move along the *LM* curve.

8. Since money demand is unaffected by the interest rate, the *LM* curve is vertical and fiscal policy is ineffective because there is complete crowding out. The only type of policy that can be used to bring the economy back to the natural rate level of output is expansionary monetary policy.

9. When the economy is above the natural rate of output, the price level rises (in the long run). As the price level rises, the real money supply declines, which causes the *LM* curve to shift left until the economy returns to the natural rate level of output.

10. When the economy is below the natural rate of output, the price level falls (in the long run). As the price level falls, the real money supply increases, which causes the *LM* curve to shift right until the economy returns to the natural rate level of output.

Critical Thinking

Fiscal Policy	Monetary Policy	Interest Rates	Aggregate Output
Expansionary	Expansionary	?	+
Contractionary	Contractionary	?	–
Expansionary	Contractionary	+	?
Contractionary	Expansionary	–	?

True/False Questions

1. T
2. F
3. F
4. F
5. T
6. T
7. F
8. T
9. T
10. F
11. T
12. F
13. T
14. F
15. F

Multiple-Choice Questions

1. b
2. d
3. c
4. d
5. b
6. c
7. a
8. d
9. d
10. d
11. a
12. b
13. d
14. c
15. c
16. c
17. a
18. c
19. c
20. c

3rd edition Study Guide Material

Note: The previous pages of the Study Guide for this edition include the material for the 10th edition chapters and the chapters that are common between the 10th and 3rd editions. The following pages of the Study Guide include the material for the chapters that are unique to the 3rd edition.

13

Nonbank Finance[*]

Chapter Review

PREVIEW

The distinction between bank and nonbank financial institutions, such as insurance, pension funds, finance companies, and mutual funds, is blurring. This chapter addresses how nonbank financial institutions operate, how they are regulated, and recent trends in nonbank finance.

INSURANCE

Insurance companies sell policies and collect premiums in order to pay out benefits to policyholders after the occurrence of a catastrophic event. They are regulated by the states because they have never experienced widespread failures. The two main types of insurance companies are life insurance, and property and casualty insurance. Most life insurance companies (90%) are organized as stock companies while 10% are organized as mutuals. Since life insurance companies can predict their payouts, they hold long-term assets that are relatively illiquid: corporate bonds and commercial mortgages and some corporate stock. Life insurance companies offer permanent and term insurance. Property and casualty insurance companies are also organized as either stock or mutuals. Due to declining interest rates and large awards, property and casualty insurance companies may have moved into riskier activities to maintain profits. Since property and casualty insurance companies are subject to income taxes and because their payouts are less certain, they hold the largest portion of their assets in tax-exempt municipal bonds, and they hold much of their assets in U.S. government securities in order to be liquid. The rest of their assets are in corporate bonds and stock.

---

[*]This chapter is unique to the 3rd ed.

Banks are entering the insurance industry. Insurance companies have responded by supplying credit insurance with derivatives known as *credit default swaps (CDS)* and through *monoline insurance companies* that directly insure financial instruments.

To avoid adverse selection, insurance management principles suggest screening of prospective clients and application of risk-based premiums. To avoid moral hazard, insurance management principles require restrictive provisions that limit the insured's risky activities, prevention of fraud, cancellation of the insurance policy, *deductibles, coinsurance* (where the policy covers less than 100% of the loss), and limiting the amount of insurance.

PENSION FUNDS

Pension funds acquire contributions throughout a person's lifetime and then provide income payments upon retirement. Pension funds have grown rapidly because contributions tend to be tax deductible. Since the payouts are predictable, pension funds invest in long-term securities such as bonds, stocks, and mortgages. Two-thirds of their assets are now in stocks, which is about 10% of all outstanding shares of stock.

Defined-contribution plans generate payments that are determined by the contributions into the plan and their earnings. *Defined-benefit plans* produce payments that are set in advance based on years of service and income earned. Defined benefit plans can be *fully funded* or *underfunded,* depending on whether the contributions are sufficient to pay out the benefits when they come due. To be entitled to any benefits, a person often needs to work at a firm for five years in order to be vested. In private pension plans, the contributions are usually shared between the employer and employee.

Congress enacted the Employee Retirement Income Security Act (ERISA) in 1974 to protect employees from the abuses of private pension funds by setting rules for reporting information, vesting, the degree of underfunding, and investment practices. ERISA also created the Pension Benefit Guarantee Corporation, which insures pension benefits up to a limit. At present, its obligations exceed its assets, so there is fear that there may be a problem building that could be similar to the savings and loan bailout. Social Security is a public pension plan that operates on a "pay as you go" system. It is significantly underfunded, as are the public pensions in Europe and Japan. This has led to questions about whether Social Security and other public pension systems should be privatized. Proposals to privatize Social Security fall into three basic forms: (1) government investment of trust fund assets in corporate securities; (2) shifting trust fund assets to individual accounts that can be invested in private assets; and (3) having individual accounts in addition to the traditional accounts in the trust fund.

FINANCE COMPANIES

Finance companies raise funds by issuing commercial paper, stocks and bonds, or borrowing from banks, and they generally use the funds to make small consumer and business loans. Regulation of finance companies is much less restrictive than banks. States regulate the size of the maximum loan and the terms of the debt contract but do not restrict branching, their assets, or how they raise funds. There are three types of finance companies: Sales finance companies, which are owned by retailers or manufacturers to make loans to their customers; consumer finance companies, which are separate corporations that make consumer loans for things like furniture, home improvement, or debt consolidation; and business finance companies, which make loans to businesses or purchase their accounts receivable, called factoring.

SECURITIES MARKET OPERATIONS

Brokers and dealers, investment banks, and organized exchanges are not financial intermediaries, yet they may be considered "financial facilitators" because they help channel funds from savers to spenders.

- Investment banks assist in the sale of securities in the primary market. They advise on what the firm should issue, which is easy if it is a *seasoned issue* (more securities of a prior issue) but more difficult if it is an *initial public offering* (IPO). It then offers to *underwrite* the issue, which means that it guarantees the price for the issuing firm.

- Securities brokers and dealers conduct trading of securities in secondary markets. Brokers act as agents matching buyers with sellers and earn a commission. Dealers hold inventories of securities and sell them for more than they paid, which is a riskier business than brokers. *Brokerage firms* act as brokers, dealers, and investment banks. Due to cash management accounts (CMA), the line between banking and brokerage firms has blurred.

- Organized exchanges, such as the New York Stock Exchange, conduct trades in one central location, while over-the-counter markets use geographically diverse dealers. A dealer-broker called a *specialist* matches buy and sell orders and keeps the exchange orderly.

The Securities and Exchange Commission (SEC) regulates the financial institutions in the securities markets and ensures that adequate information reaches prospective investors.

MUTUAL FUNDS

Mutual funds sell shares and use the funds to buy securities. Their size allows them to reduce brokerage commissions and diversify the holdings for small investors, making them a relatively safe vehicle for saving. Because of this, mutual funds are mostly held by households. Funds can specialize in debt, equities, specific industries, maturities, or countries. Institutional investors (mutual funds and pension funds) hold over 50% of the outstanding stock in the United States.

Sovereign wealth funds (state-owned investment funds) have also become large institutional investors.

Mutual funds are structured in two ways. *Open-end funds* issue shares that can be redeemed at any time at a price tied to the asset value of the fund. *Closed-end funds* issue nonredeemable shares, which are traded like common stock. Money market mutual funds invest in short-term money market instruments such as U.S. Treasury bills, commercial paper, and bank certificates of deposit. These funds allow shareholders to redeem shares by writing checks, and the shareholders earn market interest rates, thus serving as checking with interest. All mutual funds are regulated by the Securities and Exchange Commission (SEC).

HEDGE FUNDS

Investors in a *hedge fund* provide funds to a managing partner. The managing partner receives a management fee and a percent of the profits. Hedge funds require an investment of between $100,000 and $20 million, a maximum of 99 investors, and usually require that investors commit their money for several years. They are largely unregulated, and despite their typically "market neutral" strategy, hedge funds do pose significant risk due to the highly leveraged nature of its investments. The near collapse of Long-Term Capital Management is a well-known example of this risk. Ultimately, the Federal Reserve helped organize a rescue of the company, which was controversial due to the belief that it increased moral hazard and weakened market discipline. Updated regulation of hedge funds by the SEC have been aimed at avoiding such a collapse in the future; however, most hedge funds have moved offshore, so enhanced regulation and oversight may be ineffective for the most part.

PRIVATE EQUITY AND VENTURE CAPITAL FUNDS

Private equity funds are similar to hedge funds, but they invest in companies that are not publicly traded. There are two types: *Venture capital funds* invest in start-up businesses while *capital buyout funds* invest in established businesses, often through a *leveraged buyout*.

Private equity funds have several advantages over investing in publicly traded companies. Private companies are not subject to costly regulations such as Sarbanes-Oxley. In addition, managers are under less pressure to show immediate profits and so can focus on long-term profitability. Managers are given a larger stake in the company and so have an incentive to maximize the value of the firm. And because private equity firms involve a small number of principles, monitoring and agency costs are minimal.

GOVERNMENT FINANCIAL INTERMEDIATION

The government gets involved in financial intermediation in two ways: It sets up federal credit agencies that directly engage in financial intermediation, and it guarantees private loans. The Farm Credit System issues securities and makes loans to farmers. Three other agencies issue bonds and use the proceeds to buy mortgages: the Government National Mortgage Association (GNMA or Ginnie Mae), the Federal National Mortgage Association (FNMA or Fannie Mae), and the Federal Home Loan Mortgage Corporation (FHLMC or Freddie Mac). Ginnie Mae is a government agency, while Fannie Mae and Freddie Mac are *government-sponsored enterprises (GSEs)*. The implicit government backing of GSE debt leads to moral hazard because the GSEs have incentive to take on excessive risk. These GSEs bought too many subprime mortgages, and when these mortgages went bad during the global financial crisis, the government had to use billions of dollars of taxpayer money to bail them out.

Helpful Hints

1. Three of the ways that insurance companies avoid moral hazard sound similar but are distinguishable. The insurance company offers insurance with a *deductible* (the insured pays the first $100 of the cost of the accident), the insurance company pays 80% of the remaining bill (*coinsurance*), and they are only willing to insure your loss up to say 90% of replacement value and no more (*limiting the amount of the insurance*).

2. Finance companies differ from banks in the following way. Banks usually collect small deposits and then make large loans. Finance companies borrow in large amounts by selling bonds or stock, or borrowing large amounts from banks, and lend small amounts. The lack of regulation of finance companies allows them to make small specialized loans tailored to the needs of their customers.

3. Money market mutual funds own liquid assets and are so large that they are able to spread low brokerage fees across many investors. As a result, they offer the ability to redeem funds by check, creating checking with market interest rates. To compete, banks offer money market deposit accounts, which are very similar.

Terms and Definitions

Choose a definition for each key term.

Key Terms:

_____ annuities

_____ brokerage firms

_____ capital buyout funds

_____ carried interest

_____ closed-end fund

_____ coinsurance

_____ credit default swap (CDS)

_____ deductible

_____ defined-benefit plan

_____ defined-contribution plan

_____ fully funded

_____ government-sponsored enterprises (GSEs)

_____ hedge fund

_____ initial public offering (IPO)

_____ leveraged buyout (LBO)

_____ load funds

_____ monoline insurance companies

_____ no-load funds

_____ open-end fund

_____ private equity fund

_____ reinsurance

_____ seasoned issues

_____ sovereign wealth funds

_____ specialist

_____ underfunded

_____ underwriters

_____ venture capital funds

Definitions:

1. The fixed amount by which the insured's loss is reduced when a claim is paid off

2. A stock issued for sale for which prior issues currently sell in the market

3. Firms that participate in securities markets as brokers, dealers, and investment bankers

4. A pension plan in which benefits are determined by the contribution into the plan and their earnings

5. Investment banks that guarantee prices on securities to corporations and then sell the securities to the public

6. A dealer-broker operating in an exchange who maintains orderly trading of the securities for which he or she is responsible

7. A mutual fund in which a fixed number of nonredeemable shares are sold at an initial offering, then traded in the over-the-counter market like common stock

8. A stock that is being issued for the first time

9. An allocation of the portion of the insurance risk to another company in exchange for a portion of the insurance premium

10. A situation in which only a portion of a loss is covered by insurance, so that the insured suffers a percentage of the loss along with the insurance company

11. A pension plan in which the contributions and their earnings are not sufficient to pay out the defined benefits when they come due

12. A pension plan in which benefits are set in advance

13. A mutual fund in which shares can be redeemed at any time at a price that is tied to the asset value of the fund

14. A pension plan in which the contributions to the plan and their earnings over the years are sufficient to pay out the defined benefits when they come due

15. A traded derivative in which the seller is required to make a payment to the holder if the underlying instrument is downgraded or goes bankrupt

16. Federally sponsored enterprises that function as private corporations with close ties to the government

17. Specializes only in credit insurance

18. Capital investment firms that make investments in established businesses

19. Fund that pools the resources from its partners and uses the funds to help entrepreneurs start up new businesses

20. A special type of mutual fund that engages in market neutral strategies and has a limited number of partners

21. Mutual funds sold directly to the public on which no sales commissions are charged

22. Insurance products that provide a fixed stream of payments

23. Process in which a publically traded company is purchased and made private by increasing leverage or debt.

24. State-owned investment funds that invest in foreign assets

25. Profits earned by venture capital or capital buyout funds through the sale of ownership stakes in firms

26. Investment fund similar to hedge fund which makes investments in nonpublically traded companies and has limited partners

27. Mutual funds that charge a fee when money is added or withdrawn from the fund

Problems and Short-Answer Questions

PRACTICE PROBLEMS

1. Insurance companies employ insurance management tools to help reduce adverse selection and moral hazard. From the following list of insurance management tools, choose the one that best describes the action taken by the insurance company described below. Then determine whether the action is intended to reduce adverse selection or moral hazard.

Screening	Cancellation of the policy
Risk-based premiums	Deductibles
Restrictive provisions	Coinsurance
Prevention of fraud	Limiting the amount of insurance offered

   a. An insurance company requires that the purchaser of an auto insurance policy pay the first $250 of the cost of an auto accident.

   _____

   b. An insurance company requires that the purchaser of a life insurance policy not engage in skydiving.

   _____

   c. An insurance company requires that a prospective purchaser of a health insurance policy get a physical examination.

   _____

d. An insurance company offers auto insurance policies that will pay no more than NADA book value of the car if the car is a total loss.

e. An insurance company offers health insurance policies that pay 80% of the cost of an illness.

f. An insurance company inspects the damages on a car after the insured files a claim for repairs from an auto accident.

g. An insurance company informs you that it will cancel your auto insurance if your driver's license is revoked.

h. An insurance company raises your auto insurance premiums after your second speeding ticket.

2. The following questions relate to pension funds.
   a. What is the difference between a defined-contribution plan and a defined-benefit plan?

   b. Which type of fund can be underfunded? Explain.

   c. Which type of pension fund is intended to place the greater risk on the employer? Explain.

   d. Which type of pension fund is guaranteed by the Pension Benefit Guarantee Corporation? Why?

e. Is there any moral hazard associated with government provision of pension insurance? Explain.

_____

_____

3. Genetic testing may allow people to gain greater knowledge about the probability that they will develop certain diseases. Although insurance companies may wish to require genetic testing in order to set risk-based premiums, government may restrict the use of genetic testing.

a. Suppose individuals are allowed to have genetic tests but insurance companies are not allowed to use this information. Explain the adverse selection problem generated by this regulation in the health insurance market.

_____

_____

_____

_____

b. How would allowing insurance companies to use genetic test results alleviate the adverse selection problem?

_____

_____

_____

_____

SHORT-ANSWER QUESTIONS

1. What is the difference between a stock insurance company and a mutual insurance company? Which is the dominant way to organize a life insurance company in the United States?

_____

_____

2. What is an annuity? Why have life insurance companies moved into that type of business?

_____

_____

_____

3. Which type of insurance companies needs to hold the more liquid assets, life insurance or property and casualty insurance companies? Why?

_____

_____

4. Why is Social Security considered a "pay-as-you-go" system? Is it fully funded or underfunded? Why?

_____

_____

_____

5. What types of assets do pension funds invest in? Why? What legislation sets the rules for the management of pension funds?

_____

_____

_____

6. What are the different types of finance companies? Which type are Sears Roebuck Acceptance Corporation and General Motors Acceptance Corporation?

_____

_____

7. Why do small savers tend to invest in mutual funds as opposed to directly investing in securities? What are the special properties of money market mutual funds? Do small savers invest in hedge funds? Why?

_____

_____

_____

8. What is the difference between a closed-end fund and an open-end fund? Which is more common?

_____

_____

_____

9. What do Ginnie Mae, Fannie Mae, and Freddie Mac do? Which one is truly a federal agency? Does that mean that securities issued by the others are less safe? Explain.

_____

_____

_____

10. What are the two main tasks of investment bankers?

_____

_____

_____

11. What are the four advantages that private equity funds have over investing in publicly traded companies?

_____

_____

_____

12. What is the inherent problem with government-sponsored enterprises?

_____

_____

_____

Critical Thinking

Social activists sometimes note that people who are in the greatest need of insurance are those who are sick and in need of medical care and those that have suffered great losses from floods and natural disasters and are in need of new housing. Suppose a friend argues, "These victims should be provided health insurance and household property insurance because of their obvious need. I can't believe that insurance companies are so heartless that they won't offer health insurance to sick people and property insurance to flood victims."

1. Can a private insurance company stay solvent if it insures people who are already sick and victims of past floods and natural disasters? Explain.

    _____

    _____

    _____

2. What do insurance companies do to avoid this adverse selection?

    _____

    _____

    _____

3. Even if these victims had tried to buy insurance prior to their catastrophic event, is it certain that an insurance company would have sold it to them? Why?

    _____

    _____

    _____

Self-Test

TRUE/FALSE QUESTIONS

_____1. Life insurance companies can predict their future payouts, so they hold long-term assets that are not particularly liquid, such as corporate bonds, commercial mortgages, and corporate stock.

_____2. Permanent life insurance policies are the fastest growth area for life insurance companies.

_____3. Most insurance companies are organized as mutuals.

_____4. Property and casualty insurance companies are more likely to hold tax-exempt municipal bonds than are life insurance companies.

_____5. "Coinsurance" is demonstrated when a policyholder is required to pay the first $250 of the cost of repairing a damaged auto.

_____6. Insurance companies charge risk-based premiums in order to avoid problems associated with adverse selection.

_____7. If a pension is a defined-contribution plan, it is considered to be underfunded if the contributions and their earning are not enough to pay the benefits when they come due.

_____8. Pension funds need to hold liquid assets, such as U.S. Treasury bills, because it is hard for them to predict their future payout obligations.

_____9. The Employee Retirement Income Security Act (ERISA) of 1974 created the Pension Benefit Guarantee Corporation ("Penny Benny") to insure private pension plans.

_____10. Social Security operates as a "pay-as-you-go" system, and it is currently underfunded because there are a growing number of retired people compared to working people.

_____11. Consumer finance companies are usually owned by large retailers and are utilized for making loans to the retailer's customers.

_____12. Mutual funds use their size to reduce brokerage commissions and diversify holdings for small savers.

_____13. Money market mutual funds are closed-end funds that invest largely in speculative high yield assets.

_____14. The Government National Mortgage Association (GNMA) is a federal agency that supervises, regulates, and examines savings and loans to make sure that there is sufficient funding for home mortgages.

_____15. Investment banks assist in the sale of securities in the primary market by advising firms on what securities to issue and then underwriting the issue.

MULTIPLE-CHOICE QUESTIONS

1. Which of the following institutions must hold a significant portion of its assets in liquid securities because it cannot easily predict its future payouts?
   a. life insurance companies
   b. property and casualty insurance companies
   c. pension funds
   d. hedge funds

2. Which of the following is the most heavily regulated?
    a. private equity funds
    b. finance companies
    c. commercial banks
    d. insurance companies

3. When John was without a job and health insurance, he did not play competitive softball for fear of an injury. Last week John landed a good job with excellent health insurance benefits. Today John joined a softball league. What problem faced by insurance companies was illustrated by this example?
    a. reinsurance
    b. coinsurance
    c. adverse selection
    d. moral hazard
    e. restrictive provisions

4. When a life insurance company requires prospective policyholders to take a physical examination and answer questionnaires about their health history, the insurance company is trying to
    a. reduce adverse selection by screening out poor insurance risks.
    b. reduce moral hazard by screening out poor insurance risks.
    c. reduce adverse selection by reducing risky behavior.
    d. reduce moral hazard by reducing risky behavior.

5. When a health insurance policy pays the policyholder 90% of the cost of an illness in order to reduce moral hazard, we have just witnessed the use of
    a. deductibles.
    b. underfunding.
    c. coinsurance.
    d. restrictive provisions.

6. When a small insurance company allocates a portion of the risk generated by a large or risky policy to another insurance company (such as Lloyd's of London) in exchange for a portion of the premium, we have observed what is known as
    a. mutual insurance.
    b. underfunding.
    c. coinsurance.
    d. reinsurance.

7. Which of the following is *not* an insurance management tool used to reduce an insurance company's exposure to *moral hazard?*
    a. requiring that the policyholder pay a deductible before the insurance companies pays for an insured event
    b. charging risk-based premium so that higher risk people pay more
    c. limiting the amount of insurance available for an insured event
    d. placing restrictive provisions in the insurance contract that limit the amount of risk undertaken by the insured

8. Which of the following has seen the greatest growth in their assets since 1970?
    a. insurance companies
    b. pension funds and mutual funds
    c. finance companies
    d. commercial banks

9. A pension plan that pays benefits that are determined by the contributions into the plan and their earnings is known as
   a. a credit default swap.
   b. a no-load plan.
   c. an open-end plan.
   d. a defined-contribution plan.
   e. a defined-benefit plan.

10. Social Security is
    a. a pay-as-you-go plan because the premiums of current workers pay the benefits of current retirees.
    b. fully funded.
    c. now completely privatized.
    d. All of the above are true.

11. Which of the following statements about private pension funds is correct?
    a. Private pension plans are required by the Employee Retirement Income Security Act (ERISA) of 1974 to be fully funded.
    b. Private pension funds have unpredictable future payouts, so they must hold assets that are very liquid.
    c. Private pension funds hold about two-thirds of their assets in stocks.
    d. Defined-contribution plans are sometimes underfunded.

12. Finance companies differ from commercial banks in that, unlike banks, finance companies
    a. borrow in large amounts and often lend in small amounts.
    b. are heavily regulated.
    c. only make consumer loans.
    d. All of the above are true.

13. General Motors Acceptance Corporation (GMAC) is an example of a
    a. consumer finance company.
    b. business finance company.
    c. sales finance company.
    d. public finance company.

14. Factoring occurs when
    a. an investment bank underwrites an initial public offering of stock.
    b. a finance company makes a loan to a business by buying some of its accounts receivable for a discount.
    c. a number of insurance companies join forces to insure against a very large risk.
    d. a mutual fund gains controlling stock in a publicly held company.

15. Mutual funds that charge a sales commission that is immediately deducted from the redemption value when the shares are purchased are called
    a. open-end funds.
    b. closed-end funds.
    c. no-load funds.
    d. load funds.

16. Which of the following statements regarding institutional investors is true?
    a. Hedge funds are extremely liquid.
    b. Money market mutual funds are an example of a closed-end fund.
    c. Mutual funds and pension funds together hold a dominant portion of the outstanding shares of stock in the United States.
    d. Mutual funds have relatively high brokerage commissions, but consumers are willing to pay it because mutual funds provide diversification for small savers.

17. When a corporation seeks advice and underwriting for its new issue of securities, it generally employs
    a. a takeover specialist.
    b. an investment bank.
    c. a specialist.
    d. a dealer.
    e. a finance company.

18. Which of the following organizations is a federal agency that issues bonds and uses the proceeds to purchase mortgages?
    a. Government National Mortgage Association
    b. Securities and Exchange Commission
    c. Pension Benefit Guarantee Association
    d. The Farm Credit System

19. Which of the following statements is true regarding brokers and dealers?
    a. Brokers do not hold inventories of securities while dealers do.
    b. Dealers are exposed to greater risk than brokers.
    c. Specialists on an organized exchange act as both brokers and dealers.
    d. All of the above are true.
    e. None of the above is true.

20. Which of the following is *not* a financial intermediary?
    a. commercial bank
    b. pension fund
    c. insurance company
    d. investment bank

Solutions

Terms and Definitions

_22_	annuities
_3_	brokerage firms
_18_	capital buyout funds
_25_	carried interest
_7_	closed-end fund
_10_	coinsurance
_15_	credit default swap (CDS)
_1_	deductible
_12_	defined-benefit plan
_4_	defined-contribution plan
_14_	fully funded
_16_	government-sponsored enterprises (GSEs)
_20_	hedge fund
_8_	initial public offering (IPO)
_23_	leveraged buyout (LBO)
_27_	load funds
_17_	monoline insurance companies
_21_	no-load funds
_13_	open-end fund
_26_	private equity fund
_9_	reinsurance
_2_	seasoned issues
_24_	sovereign wealth funds
_6_	specialist
_11_	underfunded
_5_	underwriters
_19_	venture capital funds

Practice Problems

1.
   a. deductibles, moral hazard
   b. restrictive provisions, moral hazard
   c. screening, adverse selection
   d. limiting the amount of insurance offered, moral hazard
   e. coinsurance, moral hazard
   f. prevention of fraud, moral hazard
   g. cancellation of the policy, moral hazard
   h. risk-based premiums, adverse selection

2.
   a. A defined-contribution plan generates payments based on the contributions into the plan and their earnings. A defined-benefit plan generates payments that are set in advance.
   b. Defined-benefit plans can be under-funded because the guarantee of benefits can be greater than the firm's accumulation toward that payment.
   c. In a defined-benefit plan, the firm bears the risk associated with generating the guaranteed future benefit, regardless of the contributions and their earnings.
   d. Defined-benefit plans require insurance because they may be underfunded, mismanaged, or suffer from fraud and other abuses.
   e. Yes. Firms are more likely to invest the employee's contributions in a risky manner, and employees are less likely to monitor the behavior of the firm managing the pension fund.

3.
   a. The insurance company will charge a premium that is the average for the healthy and unhealthy people. However, due to the information asymmetry, those people who are likely to stay healthy (and they know it) will be unlikely to buy health insurance because it is priced too high for them, leaving only the unhealthy people to buy insurance (adverse selection).
   b. If the insurance company can use the information, it can charge risk-based premiums and charge each group according to its probability of future poor health. With no information asymmetry, even the relatively healthy buy insurance because it is fairly priced.

Short-Answer Questions

1. Stock companies are owned by stockholders while mutuals are owned by policyholders. Over 90% of life insurance companies are organized as stock companies.

2. A customer pays an annual premium and receives annual payments at retirement until death. Weak returns on permanent life insurance in the 1960s and 1970s caused a reduction in life insurance sales and a movement of life insurance companies toward managing pension fund assets and selling annuities.

3. Property and casualty insurance companies need to hold the more liquid assets because their payouts are less certain.

4. Because benefits are paid out of current contributions. It is very underfunded because of the growth in the number of retired people relative to working people.

5. Pension funds invest in bonds, stocks, and long-term mortgages. Because the benefits paid out are highly predictable, pension funds need not be particularly liquid. The Employee Retirement Income Security Act (ERISA) of 1974 sets rules for managing pension funds.

6. The three different types are sales finance companies, consumer finance companies, and business finance companies. GMAC and SRAC are sales finance companies.

7. Because mutual funds have low brokerage fees and provide diversification, small savers invest in mutual funds. Because of the liquidity of the assets and the low transactions costs, MMMF are able to pay a market interest rate while offering checking services. Small savers do not because the minimum investment in a hedge fund is between $100,000 and $20 million.

8. Closed-end funds have a fixed number of nonredeemable shares that are traded like common stock. Open-end funds have shares that can be redeemed at any time at a price based on the asset value of the fund. Open-end funds are most common.

9. They provide liquidity to the mortgage market by issuing bonds and using the proceeds to purchase mortgages. Of the three, Ginnie Mae is the only true federal agency. As a practical matter, the federal government will not allow any of the agencies to default.

10. They *advise* on the type, maturity, and interest rate of issue the firm should sell. They *underwrite* the issue, which means they guarantee a price for the firm and then sell them to the public for slightly more.

11. They are not subject to the costs of Sarbanes-Oxley. They can have a longer-run goal for profitability. Since the managers of the fund own a big share of the fund, they tend to maximize the value of the firm. Since there are few owners, there is a greater incentive to monitor the firm and make sure it is run properly.

12. The implicit government backing of GSE debt issues leads to moral hazard on the part of the management of the GSE. As a result, GSEs (such as Fannie Mae and Freddie Mac) are able to take on excessive risk.

Critical Thinking

1. No. The premiums necessary to cover the cost of an event that has already occurred would equal or exceed the value of the loss, so no one would buy it. If the premiums were lower, the insurance company would become insolvent.

2. They screen prospective customers to separate good risks from poor risks by asking questions that provide information about a customer's risk exposure. They charge risk-based premiums so that higher risk people are charged more.

3. Not necessarily. If people smoke, are overweight, have a family history of bad health, and engage in risky activities such as racing or skydiving, they may be unable to purchase health insurance. If they live in a flood plain, they may be unable to buy household insurance.

True/False Questions

1. T
2. F
3. F
4. T
5. F
6. T
7. F
8. F
9. T
10. T
11. F
12. T
13. F
14. F
15. T

Multiple-Choice Questions

1. b
2. c
3. d
4. a
5. c
6. d
7. b
8. b
9. d
10. a
11. c
12. a
13. c
14. b
15. d
16. c
17. b
18. a
19. d
20. d

14 Financial Derivatives*

Chapter Review

PREVIEW

Due to the increase in interest rate volatility in the 1980s and 1990s, financial innovation has generated *financial derivatives* to reduce risks faced by financial institutions. Financial derivatives are instruments that have payoffs that are linked to previously issued securities, such as forward contracts, financial futures, options, and swaps.

HEDGING

To *hedge* is to engage in a financial transaction to reduce risk. Buying an asset is taking a *long position*. Selling an asset and agreeing to deliver it in the future is taking a *short position*. Hedging risk involves offsetting a long position by taking an additional short position, or offsetting a short position by taking an additional long position.

INTEREST-RATE FORWARD CONTRACTS

Interest-rate forward contracts are agreements to engage in a transaction on debt instruments at a future point in time, at a price determined today. For example, a bank holding $5 million worth of twenty-year bonds that it wishes to liquidate in one year may fear that the interest rate will rise during the year, causing a capital loss. An insurance company may be receiving $5 million in premiums one year from today and fears that interest rates will fall during the year, reducing its future returns. By agreeing to exchange the bonds in one year at a fixed price determined today, both parties have successfully hedged their interest-rate risk. The advantage of forward contracts is that they are flexible enough for parties to completely hedge

---

*This chapter is unique to the 3rd ed.

their interest-rate risk. The contracts also have disadvantages. First, the market is relatively illiquid because it is not easy to find a counterparty with whom to make a contract at a competitive price, and second, forward contracts are subject to default risk. Note that forward contracts can also be used to hedge foreign exchange risk.

FINANCIAL FUTURES CONTRACTS AND MARKETS

A *financial futures contract* specifies that a group of financial instruments are to be delivered by one party to another party on a specific future date. However, it does not suffer from the lack of liquidity and default problems of interest-rate forward contracts. In this market, each contract is for a bundle of bonds that has a face value totaling from $100,000 to $5 million, depending on the maturity of bonds and the market on which the contracts are traded. Due to arbitrage, at the time of expiration of the futures contract, the price of the contract and the price of the underlying asset to be delivered must converge. Prices are quoted in terms of points where one point equals $100,000.

For Treasury bonds on the Chicago Board of Trade, suppose a party sells a contract (takes a long position and agrees to deliver $100,000 of face value fifteen-year T-bonds) at 110 ($110,000), to be delivered six months in the future. If interest rates rise, so that on the expiration date of the contract the value of the bonds has fallen to $105,000 (105 points), the seller of the contract can buy the bonds for $5,000 less than the delivery price, and the seller has gained 5 points or $5,000. The buyer of the contract, who took a short position, could have purchased the bonds at expiration of the contract for $100,000 but had to accept delivery on the bonds for $105,000 (105) and has lost five points or $5,000. If interest-rate risk on larger amounts of assets needs to be hedged, parties can buy or sell a number of contracts. The number of contracts for the hedge is equal to the value of the asset divided by the value of each contract.

The total of *open interest* Treasury bond contracts (futures market contracts) is enormous and much larger than the volume of interest-rate forward contracts. Financial futures contracts are more liquid than forward contracts for the following reasons: (1) The quantities to be delivered and the delivery dates are standardized, making it easy for parties to match up; (2) the futures contract can be traded before the delivery date; and (3) more than one type of Treasury bond is deliverable on the expiration date.

Financial futures contracts reduce default risk because a clearinghouse sets up the transaction so the parties need not worry about the financial condition of the other party. The clearinghouse requires *margin requirements* to make sure each party can perform on the contract at the time of expiration. Margin requirements are adjusted daily as contracts are *marked to market*. Finally, the futures market is more efficient because futures contracts do not result in actual delivery of the asset. Instead, the seller may make an offsetting purchase of a futures contract, essentially canceling both contracts.

OPTIONS

Options give the purchaser of the contract the right to buy (*call option*) or sell (*put option*) a security at an *exercise price* or *strike price* during a specific period of time.

American options can be exercised any time up to the expiration date of the contract, whereas *European options* must be exercised on the expiration date. The right to buy or sell at a specific price has value so the purchaser is willing to pay for that right, called a *premium*. There are *stock options* and *financial futures options* (*futures options*). Suppose you buy a futures option contract on the same Treasury bond futures contract described above. For a $2,000 premium (2 points), you buy a call option on the $100,000 Treasury bond futures contract with a strike price of 110, to be exercised within three months. Suppose at the end of three months, the contract has a price of 105. Since you can buy the bonds for $105,000, you will not exercise the option to buy them at $110, but you do lose the $2,000 option price. If at the end of the three months, the contract price is 110, the option contract is "at the money" and you are indifferent about exercising the option. If the option contract is anything above 110, the contract is "in the money," and you will exercise the option.

The important difference between the futures contract and the option contract is that the option contract limits the buyer's losses to the amount of the premium, while the futures contract can generate enormous losses when the price moves in an adverse manner. In addition, the futures contract requires that the purchaser put funds in a margin account while the option contract requires a premium be paid for the contract, and the futures contract requires money to change hands daily as the contract is marked to market while the option contract requires money to change hands only when it is exercised.

Financial institutions use futures options to hedge interest-rate risk in a similar way as using financial futures and forward contracts. Futures options are preferred for *macro hedges* because they suffer from fewer accounting problems, and they allow for additional profit opportunities from movements in bond prices.

Other things equal, the following factors determine the premium on an options contract:

- The higher the strike price, the lower the premium on call options and the higher the premium on put options.

- The greater the term to expiration, the higher the premiums for both call and put options.

- The greater the volatility of prices of the underlying instrument, the higher the premiums for both call and put options.

SWAPS

Interest-rate swaps obligate one party to the contract to exchange a set of interest payments it owns for the interest payments owned by another party. Swaps can be used to hedge interest-rate risk in the following manner. Suppose a bank has borrowed short and loaned long, so it has too few rate-sensitive assets. Suppose a finance company has borrowed long and loaned short, so it has too many rate sensitive assets. These institutions could write a contract to swap interest receipts, so the bank pays the finance company a fixed rate return while the finance company pays the bank a variable rate based on the one-year T-bill rate. This allows each company to convert fixed-rate assets into variable-rate assets and vice versa without the transactions costs of rearranging their balance sheets and while maintaining their informational advantages of lending to their particular loan customers. These contracts can also be written for very long horizons, say twenty years, while other hedging contracts are usually for no longer than a year. However, swaps can suffer from lack of liquidity and default risk just like forward contracts, so large commercial banks and investment banks act as intermediaries and help match parties to a swap.

CREDIT DERIVATIVES

Credit options allow the holder of a credit instruments, say GMAC bonds, to be protected from a fall in the price of the bonds by buying an option to sell those bonds at a strike price equal to the current price. Another type of credit option ties profits to changes in interest-rate spreads, such as the difference between an average bond of a specific credit rating and U.S. Treasury bonds. This allows a holder of lower grade bonds to insure against that grade of bonds being viewed as less credit worthy and having their prices fall. *Credit swaps* are when risky payments on loans are swapped for each other in order to diversify the risk of lenders with specialized portfolios. *Credit default swaps* work like insurance against default of the downgrading of bond in that it pays off when triggered by a credit event such as a default. *Credit-linked notes* allow the issuer of the note to reduce their interest payment if some specified adverse event affects their company.

There are two major concerns about financial derivatives. First, financial derivatives allow financial institutions to increase their leverage, which allows them to place huge bets on movements in financial variables using little of their own money. Second, banks have holdings of huge notional amounts of interest-rate and currency swaps, exceeding their capital, so banks are exposed to risk of failure. The first risk is real, but the second risk is exaggerated.

Helpful Hints

1. Financial derivatives earn their name from the fact that the value of a derivative contract is *derived* from the value of some previously issued security. That is, a financial derivative *derives* its value from the underlying security.

Terms and Definitions

Choose a definition for each key term.

Key Terms:

_____ American option	_____ credit options	_____ financial derivatives
_____ arbitrage	_____ credit swap	_____ financial futures contract
_____ call option	_____ currency swaps	
_____ credit default swap	_____ European option	_____ financial futures option (futures option)
_____ credit derivatives	_____ exercise price (strike price)	
_____ credit-linked note		_____ forward contract

_____ hedge

_____ interest-rate forward contract

_____ interest-rate swaps

_____ long position

_____ macro hedge

_____ margin requirement

_____ marked to market

_____ micro hedge

_____ notional principal

_____ open interest

_____ option

_____ premium

_____ put option

_____ short position

_____ stock option

_____ swap

Definitions:

1. A hedge of interest-rate risk for a financial institutions entire portfolio

2. An agreement by two parties to engage in a financial transaction at a future point in time

3. The price at which the purchaser of an option has the right to buy or sell the underlying financial instrument

4. An option contract that provides the right to sell a security at a specified price

5. A futures contract in which the standardized commodity is a particular type of financial instrument

6. Elimination of a riskless profit opportunity in a market

7. A contractual obligation to take delivery of an underlying financial instrument

8. The amount paid for an option contract

9. A forward contract that is linked to a debt instrument

10. A financial contract that obligates one party to exchange a set of payments it owns for a set of payments owned by another party

11. An option contract that provides the right to buy a security at a specified price

12. To protect oneself from risk

13. Instruments that have payoffs that are linked to previously issued securities, used as risk-reduction tools

14. A contract that gives the purchaser the right to buy or sell the underlying financial instrument at a specified price within a specific period of time

15. A contractual obligation to deliver an underlying financial instrument

16. A sum of money that must be kept in an account at the brokerage firm

17. An option in which the underlying instrument is a futures contract

18. Repriced and settled in the margin account at the end of every trading day to reflect any change in the value of the futures contract

19. Option that gives the right to receive profits tied to an underlying security or to an interest rate

20. Options that can be exercised only on the expiration date of the contract

21. An option on an individual stock

22. A type of insurance in which one party can hedge credit risk and receive a contingent payment in the event of default or bankruptcy

23. The amount on which interest is being paid in a swap arrangement

24. Option that can be exercised at any time up to the expiration of the contract

25. A financial contract that allows one party to exchange a set of interest payments for another set of interest payments owned by another party

26. A swap that involves the exchange of a set of payments in another currency

27. Derivatives that provide payoffs on previously issued securities tied to credit risk

28. A hedge for a specific asset

29. A transaction in which risky payments on loans are swapped for each other

30. The number of contracts outstanding

31. A type of credit derivative that is a combination of a bond and a credit option

Problems and Short-Answer Questions

PRACTICE PROBLEMS

1. Suppose in January you purchase $100,000 face value of U.S. Treasury bonds for a price of $95,000. Suppose that the bonds mature in fifteen years and that you must sell them at the end of March.

	Price of Bonds at the End of March				
	$85,000	$90,000	$95,000	$100,000	$105,000
a. Selling Treasury bonds					
b. Selling futures contract					
c. Selling put option					

a. In row *a* in the table above, report the gain or loss that you would incur for selling the group of bonds for each of the listed potential end-of-March selling prices for the bonds.

b. In row *b* in the table above, report the gain or loss from selling a futures contract for $100,000 face value Treasury bonds for $95,000 (95 points) for end of March delivery for each of the potential end-of-March selling prices for the bonds.

c. In row *c* in the table above, report the gain or loss from purchasing a put option on $100,000 face value Treasury bond futures with a strike price of $95,000 (95 points) and a premium of $2,000 with an expiration date at the end of March for each of the potential end-of-March selling prices for the bonds. (Only exercise the option if it is profitable to do so.)

d. Suppose that you hedge the interest-rate risk of holding these long-term bonds from January through March by selling a futures contract. What is the net result of your hedge if the price of the bonds falls to $85,000 at the end of March? What is the net result of your hedge if the price of the bonds rises to $105,000? (Compare rows *a* and *b*.)

_____

_____

_____

e. Suppose that you hedge the interest-rate risk of holding these long-term bonds from January through March by purchasing a put option on Treasury bond futures. What is the net result of your hedge if the price of the bonds falls to $85,000 at the end of March? What is the net result of your hedge if the price of the bonds rises to $105,000? (Compare rows *a* and *c*.)

_____

_____

_____

f. Which method of hedging allows you to still profit from an increase in the price of bonds? Explain. What is the cost to you for this privilege?

_____

_____

_____

_____

2. Lend-long Bank, like most banks, lends long and borrows short. That is, it has more rate-sensitive liabilities than assets.

a. Suppose that Lend-long Bank has $100 million of long-term U.S. Treasury bonds that it must liquidate one year from today in order to make a $100 million loan to an established customer. It wishes to hedge the interest-rate risk it faces over the next year with a financial futures contract. Should it buy (take a long position) or sell (take a short position) in the financial futures market? Explain.

_____

_____

b. If Lend-long Bank makes the futures transaction on the Chicago Board of Trade and the contract size is $100,000, how many contracts should Lend-long Bank purchase or sell? (Assume that the futures contracts are selling at par.)

_____

_____

c. Suppose that Lend-long Bank holds $100 million in long-term mortgages that mature in fifteen years. It wishes to hold the mortgages to maturity because it knows the loan customers well and it feels that the mortgages have low default risk, but it would like to hedge the interest-rate risk. Which tool is most suitable for hedging this risk: interest-rate forward contract, financial futures, or interest-rate swap contracts? Why? How would the bank use this contract?

_____

_____

_____

_____

_____

SHORT-ANSWER QUESTIONS

1. One of the basic principles of hedging risk suggests that a party can offset a long position by taking an additional short position. What does this mean?

_____

_____

_____

2. One of the basic principles of hedging risk suggests that a party can offset a short position by taking an additional long position. What does this mean?

_____

_____

_____

3. Suppose the portfolio that you are managing holds $10 million of the 6s of 2026 Treasury bonds with a price of 105. What interest-rate forward contract should you engage in to eliminate your interest-rate risk over the next six months?

_____

_____

4. Suppose that one year from today you will receive a $1 million payout from a trust fund. You fear that interest rates will fall by next year so you wish to lock in current rates on twenty-year Treasury bonds. What interest-rate forward contract should you engage in to eliminate your interest-rate risk over the next year?

    _____

    _____

5. Suppose you sell a September futures contract for $100,000 face value Treasury bonds for 105. At the end of September, the value of the contract is 110. How many dollars have you gained or lost on the contract? Explain.

    _____

    _____

6. What characteristics of financial futures contracts make them more liquid than forward contracts?

    _____

    _____

    _____

7. What does it mean to say that a call option is "in the money"? What does it mean to say that a put option is "in the money"?

    _____

    _____

    _____

8. Why is it true that, other things equal, the greater the term to expiration, the higher the premiums for both call and put options?

    _____

    _____

    _____

9. Suppose the bank you manage has $75 million more rate sensitive liabilities than assets. Describe the interest-rate swap that would eliminate your bank's interest-rate risk.

_____

_____

_____

_____

10. How do credit swaps reduce credit risks for lenders with specialized portfolios?

_____

_____

Critical Thinking

Your friend is looking at the financial pages in the *Wall Street Journal*. He says, "Why are there so many different types of contracts used to hedge interest-rate risk? I think many of these markets and contracts are unnecessary and just intended to confuse people." You respond by telling him that each type of contract provides some advantages and disadvantages when compared to others.

1. What are the advantages and disadvantages of interest-rate forward contracts?

_____

_____

_____

2. What are the advantage and disadvantages of financial futures contracts?

_____

_____

_____

3. What are the advantage and disadvantages of futures options?

_____

_____

_____

4.   What are the advantage and disadvantages of interest-rate swaps?

_____

_____

_____

Self-Test

TRUE/FALSE QUESTIONS

_____1.   One of the basic principles of hedging is that financial market participants can reduce risk by offsetting a long position by taking an additional long position.

_____2.   An interest-rate forward contract can be tailored precisely to the needs of the participants so that the parties to the contract can completely hedge their interest-rate risk, but it suffers from lack of liquidity and default risk.

_____3.   When a financial market participant takes a "short position," that individual has agreed to sell a security at a future date at a price determined today.

_____4.   Due to arbitrage, at the expiration date of a financial futures contract, the price of the contract is the same as the price of the underlying asset to be delivered.

_____5.   If you sell a financial futures contract at 95, and the price of the contract is 105 on the expiration date, you have just made $10,000 on the contract.

_____6.   Owners of long-term U.S. Treasury bonds can hedge their interest-rate risk over the next year by buying financial futures contracts equal in size to their bond holdings.

_____7.   Unlike forward contracts, futures contracts can be traded prior to the delivery or expiration date.

_____8.   Other things equal, the greater the volatility of the prices of the underlying instrument, the lower the premiums for both call and put options.

_____9.   A call option gives the purchaser of the contract the right to buy a security at an exercise price during a specific period of time.

_____10. If you buy a put option on $100,000 face value long-term Treasury bonds for a 2-point premium and a strike price of 110 that expires at the end of September, and at the end of September the price of the contract is 109, then you will not exercise the option.

_____11. If you buy a call option on $100,000 face value long-term Treasury bonds for a 2-point premium and a strike price of 110 that expires at the end of September, and at the end of September the price of the contract is 114, then the contract is "in the money," you will exercise the option, and your profit is $2,000.

_____12. The buyer of a futures option contract can never lose more than the premium paid for the contract.

_____13. Other things the same, the higher the strike price, the lower the premiums on a put option.

_____14. If a bank has more rate-sensitive liabilities than assets, it can reduce its interest-rate risk by engaging in an interest-rate swap whereby it swaps some of its fixed interest payments with another party's variable-rate payments (say the T-bill rate plus some fixed percent).

_____15. One shortcoming of swaps is that swaps are usually written for very short periods of time when compared to contracts in futures and options markets.

MULTIPLE-CHOICE QUESTIONS

1. A basic principle of hedging risk is that one should engage in a transaction that offsets a
   a. micro hedge with a macro hedge.
   b. long position by taking an additional short position.
   c. swap with option.
   d. forward position by taking an additional futures position.

2. An advantage of an interest-rate forward contract is that it
   a. is standardized, thereby reducing the cost of finding a counter party.
   b. is default free because the contract is guaranteed by the either the exchange or the intermediary that matched the parties.
   c. can be tailored to the precise needs of the parties so that interest-rate risk can be completely eliminated.
   d. can be traded prior to the delivery date specified in the contract.
   e. All of the above are true.

3. At the expiration date of a financial futures contract, the price of the contract is
   a. equal to the price of the underlying asset to be delivered.
   b. equal to the face value of the underlying asset to be delivered.
   c. equal to the strike price.
   d. equal to the swap price.

4. When an investor agrees to buy a security at some point in the future at a price agreed to today, that investor is said to have
   a. engaged in arbitrage.
   b. engaged in a swap.
   c. taken a short position.
   d. taken a long position.

5. Suppose you purchase $100,000 face value long-term U.S. Treasury bonds at 110 and you wish to hedge your interest-rate risk over the next year. You sell a futures contract for $100,000 face value U.S. Treasury bonds for delivery in one year for 110. When one year has passed, interest rates have risen so that the price of $100,000 face value U.S. Treasury bonds is 105. Which of the following best describes your overall outcome of your hedge?
   a. You gained $5,000 on the bonds and lost $5,000 on the futures contract.
   b. You gained $5,000 on the bonds and gained $5,000 on the futures contract.
   c. You lost $5,000 on the bonds and lost $5,000 on the futures contract.
   d. You lost $5,000 on the bonds and gained $5,000 on the futures contract.

6. Referring to the previous question, which of the following statements is true?
   a. You successfully employed a call option.
   b. You successfully engaged in an interest-rate swap.
   c. You successfully hedged your interest-rate risk.
   d. You successfully employed a put option.
   e. You failed to reduce your interest-rate risk.

7. Which of the following is *not* true regarding the advantages of financial futures markets over interest-rate forward markets?
   a. Futures contracts are standardized making it easier to match parties.
   b. Futures contracts can be traded prior to the delivery date.
   c. Futures contracts don't require any funds to change hands until the delivery date of the contract.
   d. Futures contracts are set up through a clearinghouse, which reduces default risk.

8. If you take a short position in financial futures, you will profit if interest rates
   a. fall.
   b. rise.
   c. stay the same.
   d. are low.
   e. are high.

9. A contract that gives the purchaser the right to sell a security at an exercise price during some specific period of time is known as a
   a. put option.
   b. call option.
   c. sell option.
   d. hedge option.

10. Which of the following is true regarding the differences between a futures option contract and a futures contract?
   a. An option contract requires a margin account.
   b. An option contract is marked to market daily so it requires that money change hands daily.
   c. Futures contracts are preferred to options contracts for macro hedges.
   d. An option contract has a potential loss that is limited to the size of the premium paid for the contract.
   e. Futures contracts require delivery of the underlying asset.

11. A call option is "in the money" if the price of the option is
    a. less than the premium.
    b. greater than the premium.
    c. below the strike price.
    d. above the strike price.

12. If you buy a put option for $100,000 face value long-term Treasury bonds for a 2-point premium and a strike price of 110 that expires at the end of June, and at the end of June the price of the contract is 105, then you will
    a. not exercise the option.
    b. exercise the option and earn a profit of $3,000.
    c. exercise the option and earn a profit of $5,000.
    d. exercise the option and earn a profit of $7,000.
    e. exercise the option but earn no profit.

13. If you buy a call option for $100,000 face value long-term Treasury bonds for a 2-point premium and a strike price of 115 that expires at the end of June, and at the end of June the price of the contract is 113, then you will
    a. not exercise the option and lose $2,000.
    b. not exercise the option and break even.
    c. exercise the option and break even.
    d. exercise the option and earn a profit of $2,000.
    e. exercise the option and earn a profit of $4,000.

14. Which of the following is true regarding the premiums on futures options contracts? Other things the same,
    a. the shorter the term to expiration, the higher the premiums for call or put options.
    b. the less volatile the prices of the underlying instrument, the higher the premiums for call or put options.
    c. the higher the strike price, the higher the premium on put options.
    d. All of the above are true.

15. Which of the following terms is used to describe the type of hedge used by a financial institution that is hedging the interest-rate risk on a specific asset that it is holding?
    a. micro hedge
    b. macro hedge
    c. option hedge
    d. contract hedge

16. I you wish to hedge the interest-rate risk on $4 million worth of long-term Treasury bonds over the next year, and if the contract size is $100,000 per contract, which of the following transactions should you undertake?
    a. buy 4 million T-bond futures contracts with a delivery date in one year
    b. buy 40 T-bond futures contracts with a delivery date in one year
    c. sell 4 million T-bond futures contracts with a delivery date in one year
    d. sell 40 T-bond futures contracts with a delivery date in one year

17. Which of the following is used to diversify the default risk of lenders with specialized portfolios?
    a.   interest-rate swaps
    b.   credit swaps
    c.   options
    d.   credit-linked notes

18. A tool for managing interest-rate risk that requires a party to the contract to exchange a set of interest payments for the interest payments of another party is known as
    a.   a futures contract.
    b.   an options contract.
    c.   a forward contract.
    d.   an interest-rate swap.

19. Arbitrage is best described as
    a.   the right to buy or sell a security in the future at a price determined today.
    b.   the elimination of riskless profit opportunities in a market.
    c.   an important tool for managing default risk.
    d.   an important tool for managing interest-rate risk.

20. Which of the following is true regarding interest-rate swaps?
    a.   Swaps are intended to reduce interest-rate risk more cheaply than simply restructuring the balance sheet.
    b.   Swaps are quite liquid.
    c.   Swaps have little default risk.
    d.   Swaps are usually written for a term of one year or less.

Solutions

Terms and Definitions

24	American option	9	interest-rate forward contract
6	arbitrage	25	interest-rate swaps
11	call option	7	long position
22	credit default swap	1	macro hedge
27	credit derivatives	16	margin requirement
31	credit-linked note	18	marked to market
19	credit options	28	micro hedge
29	credit swap	23	notional principal
26	currency swaps	30	open interest
20	European option	14	option
3	exercise price (strike price)	8	premium
13	financial derivatives	4	put option
5	financial futures contract	15	short position
17	financial futures option (futures option)	21	stock option
2	forward contract	10	swap
12	hedge		

Practice Problems

1.

	Price of Bonds at the End of March				
	$85,000	$90,000	$95,000	$100,000	$105,000
a. Selling Treasury bonds	–$10,000	–$5,000	$0	$5,000	$10,000
b. Selling futures contract	$10,000	$5,000	$0	–$5,000	–$10,000
c. Selling put option	$8,000	$3,000	–$2,000	–$2,000	–$2,000

d. Lose $10,000 on the sale of the bonds, gain $10,000 on the sale of the futures contract so loss is completely offset. Gain $10,000 on the sale of the bonds, lose $10,000 on the sale of the futures contract so gain is completely offset.

e. Lose $10,000 on the sale of bonds, gain $8,000 on sale of put option, so loss was not completely offset. Gain $10,000 on the sale of bonds, lose $2,000 on the put option (the purchase price of the unexercised option), so a net gain of $8,000.

f. Selling a futures contract can completely hedge the interest-rate risk resulting in no gains or losses from variations in the price of the bonds, but a put option on a futures contract allows you to retain the ability to profit from an increase in the price of bonds. However, it costs you $2,000 (in this case) whether you exercise it or not.

2. a. Sell contracts in the financial futures market (take a short position), because the bank owns bonds (has a long position) so it must hedge this with an additional short position (agree to deliver

bonds in the future at a price decided today).

b. Sell $100 million/$100,000 = 1,000 contracts

c. Interest-rate forward contracts and financial futures contracts tend to be short term and involve the sale of the instrument. The bank wants to keep the instrument but hedge the risk, so an interest-rate swap contract is appropriate. The bank would swap fixed interest payments for variable interest payments that are tied to some short-term interest rate, thus turning non-rate-sensitive assets into rate-sensitive assets.

Short-Answer Questions

1. A party that owns an asset with an uncertain return (long position) can reduce risk by selling that asset for delivery in the future at a price decided today (taking an additional short position).

2. A party that is receiving cash at a date in the future (short position) can reduce risk by buying an asset today for delivery in the future at a price decided today (taking an additional long position).

3. You enter into a contract that specifies that you will sell the $10 million of 6s of 2026 at a price of 105 six months from today.

4. You should enter into a contract that specifies that you will purchase $1 million of twenty-year Treasury bonds one year from today at the current price of twenty-year Treasury bonds.

5. You have agreed to deliver the bonds for $105,000 at the end of September. The bonds cost $110,000 at the end of September, so you have lost $5,000. (105 − 110 = −5 points).

6. Financial futures contracts have standardized quantities and delivery dates so it is easier to match parties. Futures contracts can be traded before the expiration date. More than one type of Treasury bond is deliverable on the expiration date.

7. If a call option is in the money, it means that the price of the option is above the exercise or strike price, so it is profitable to exercise the option. If a put option is in the money, it means that the price of the option is below the exercise or strike price, so it is profitable to exercise the option.

8. The greater the time remaining until expiration, the greater the chance that the price of the underlying financial instrument will be very high or very low putting the option contract in the money. If the price of the underlying instrument moves in an adverse manner, the most that can be lost is the premium paid for the option.

9. The bank should swap the interest on $75 million of fixed-rate assets for the interest on $75 million of variable-rate assets (say an interest rate tied to the T-bill rate plus some fixed percent), so that if interest rates rise on the bank's liabilities, interest rates will also rise on their assets, for a term that coincides with the term of the fixed-rate assets.

10. It allows a lender that has specialized in loans to one industry to swap payments from those loans with another lender that has specialized in loans to another industry. Thus, both have diversified their credit risk.

Critical Thinking

1. Advantages: they are flexible enough for parties to completely hedge their interest-rate risk. Disadvantages: they are illiquid and they are subject to default risk.

2. Advantages: greater liquidity, reduced default risk, and efficient because futures contracts do not result in delivery of the asset. Disadvantages: losses from price movements are not limited as with an option so enormous losses are possible, a margin account must be maintained requiring money to change hands daily as the contract is "marked to market."

3. Advantages: limits the buyer's losses to the amount of the premium and provides gains if the value of the option rises, money only changes hands if the option is exercised. Disadvantages: a premium must be paid for the option.

4. Advantages: contracts can be written for very long horizons while others are usually not longer than one year, allows lenders to maintain their informational advantages of lending to their particular customers by just swapping interest payments and not the assets. Disadvantage: lack of liquidity and default risk requiring intermediaries to help match parties.

True/False Questions

1. F
2. T
3. T
4. T
5. F
6. F
7. T
8. F
9. T
10. F
11. T
12. T
13. F
14. T
15. F

Multiple-Choice Questions

1. b
2. c
3. a
4. d
5. d
6. c
7. c
8. b
9. a
10. d
11. d
12. b
13. a
14. c
15. a
16. d
17. b
18. d
19. b
20. a

15 Conflicts of Interest in the Financial Industry*

Chapter Review

PREVIEW

Conflicts of interest are a type of moral hazard problem that occurs when a person or institution has multiple objectives or interests and as a result has conflicts between them. Conflicts of interest help explain many recent corporate scandals and the global financial crisis.

WHAT ARE CONFLICTS OF INTEREST, AND WHY ARE THEY IMPORTANT?

Financial institutions can lower the cost of producing information for each service they provide by applying one information resource to many different services, thus capturing what is known as *economies of scope*. For example, a bank could use information developed about a firm's credit risk to help make decisions when making a loan to the corporation and use the same information to help sell bonds for this corporation. Conflicts of interest arise when financial firms or individuals misuse information, provide false information, or conceal information to serve their own interests rather than their customer's interests or to serve one client's interest at the expense of another client. This is most likely to occur when an institution provides multiple services to a given client or many clients. The resulting asymmetric information causes financial markets to become less efficient at channeling funds to those with productive opportunities.

---

*This chapter is unique to the 3rd ed.

ETHICS AND CONFLICTS OF INTEREST

The growing economies of scope in the financial industry have increased conflicts of interest and unethical behavior. To reduce unethical behavior, business schools are increasing awareness of ethical issues, and firms are establishing policies that make it harder for employees to exploit conflicts of interest.

TYPES OF CONFLICTS OF INTEREST

Four areas of financial service activities have the greatest potential for conflicts of interest. Each conflict reduces the amount of information available in financial markets.

- **Underwriting and research in investment banking:** An investment bank serves the firm for whom it is issuing the securities and the investors to whom it sells the securities. Issuers benefit from optimistic research while investors want unbiased research. If revenue from underwriting exceeds brokerage commissions, the information about the firm may be overly favorable. *Spinning* occurs when investment banks allocate profitable *initial public offerings* to executives of other companies to gain their investment banking business.

- **Auditing and consulting in accounting firms:** Accounting firms offer auditing services and *management advisory services*—advice on taxes, accounting or management information systems, and business strategies. There is pressure for auditors to make favorable reports to avoid losing management advisory services business, to avoid criticizing the management advice given to the client from the nonauditing portion of the accounting firm, and to retain the clients auditing business.

- **Credit assessment and consulting in credit-rating agencies:** Since firms pay to have their debt rated, there is incentive for credit-rating agencies to provide a favorable rating while investors and regulators want an impartial rating. Also, there is pressure for credit-rating agencies to provide favorable ratings because they wish to secure consulting contracts to advise firms on the structure of debt issues. This conflict of interest surfaced during the global financial crisis. In response, the SEC prohibited many of the past practices of credit rating agencies and required greater transparency in their rating activities.

- **Universal banking:** With the repeal of the Glass-Steagall Act in 1999, universal banking reappeared so that single firms offer commercial banking, investment banking, and insurance, causing many conflicts of interest. The underwriting department benefits from aggressive sales of debt issues to the customers of the bank while the bank's customers and trust accounts need unbiased advice. A bank may help a weak firm sell debt in order to help it repay its loans to the bank. A bank may make a generous loan to a firm in order to gain its underwriting business. A bank may force a borrowing customer to buy insurance.

CAN THE MARKET LIMIT EXPLOITATION OF CONFLICTS OF INTEREST?

When the exploitation of a conflict of interest is visible to the market, the market can punish the financial services firm by denying it business. Since reputation is important to a financial services firm, in many cases this threat reduces the incentive to exploit conflicts of interest in the long run. For example, credit-rating agencies usually don't provide overly favorable ratings because it would reduce the credibility of the ratings.

Before Glass-Steagall, the market reduced banks' incentives to exploit underwriting conflicts by reducing the value of securities underwritten by bond departments within banks. Thus banks created separate affiliates to do their underwriting. The market also values an analyst's buy recommendation more if it comes from an analyst whose firm didn't underwrite the issue. Clients of accounting firms ascribe less value to audit opinions from accounting firms with conflicts of interest. However, the market cannot completely restrain the incentive to exploit conflicts of interest because those exploiting the conflict may hide the information from the market, thus capturing the firm's *reputational rents*—profits that the firm earns because it is trusted by the marketplace.

WHAT HAS BEEN DONE TO REMEDY CONFLICTS OF INTEREST?

Three major policy measures deal with conflicts of interest. The Sarbanes-Oxley Act of 2002 was a result of major corporate and accounting scandals. The Global Legal Settlement of 2002 arose from the lawsuit by the New York Attorney General against the ten largest investment banks, and the Dodd-Frank bill of 2010 arose as a result of the global financial crisis.

The Sarbanes-Oxley Act had several key components, which (1) were designed to increase supervisory oversight to monitor and prevent conflicts of interest, (2) had provisions that helped directly reduce conflicts of interest by limiting some accounting firm behavior, (3) provided incentives for investment banks not to exploit conflicts of interest, and (4) took measures to improve the quality of information in financial markets.

The Global Legal Settlement had some similar provisions to Sarbanes-Oxley, but it focused on investment bank behavior. Specifically, it banned spinning and required investment banks to sever links between research and securities underwriting. In addition, it provided incentives for investment banks to not exploit conflicts of interest through fines, and took measures to improve the quality of information in financial markets.

Dodd-Frank provided various provisions that reduced conflict of interest with credit-rating agencies. These included a registration process with the SEC, providing reports on when employees leave for a company that they provide services to, prohibiting compliance officers from being involved in credit ratings, and restricting relationships of credit-rating agencies with issuers of asset-backed securities. Finally, it authorizes lawsuits against issuers of "bad" credit ratings.

A FRAMEWORK FOR EVALUATING POLICIES TO REMEDY CONFLICTS OF INTEREST

There are two propositions critical to evaluating what should be done about conflicts of interest.

- The existence of a conflict of interest does not mean that it will have serious adverse consequences because the marketplace may exert enough pressure on the reputation of the firm so that the firm does not exploit the conflict.

- Even if incentives to exploit conflicts of interest remain strong, eliminating the economies of scope that create the conflict may do more harm than good because the cure will reduce the flow of reliable information.

With this in mind, there are five remedies for addressing conflicts of interest listed below in the order of least intrusive to most intrusive.

- **Leave it to the market.** Markets penalize firms that exploit conflicts of interest, and markets create new organizations that don't suffer from conflicts of interest.

- **Regulate for transparency.** Due to the free-rider problem, there is an undersupply of information, so regulators can require that firms provide information.

- **Supervisory oversight.** In cases where transparency would harm a firm's profits, supervisors can observe proprietary information without revealing it. This is the approach taken in banking—regulators engage in onsite bank examinations.

- **Separation of functions.** Activities can be separated into different in-house departments, separately capitalized affiliates, or prohibited from having any organizational relationship.

- **Socialization of information production.** This has been done with the production of macroeconomic data.

There are strengths and weaknesses of each remedy listed above.

Sarbanes-Oxley, the Global Settlement, and Dodd-Frank can now be addressed in light of the criteria listed above. They all increase the flow of information in financial markets; for example, they require the CEO and CFO to certify financial statements, corporations to disclose off-balance-sheet transactions and entities, investment banks to make public their analyst's recommendations, and credit-ratings agencies to report on employees who leave for other companies. They have also increased disclosure of potential conflicts of interest. Importantly, Dodd-Frank still allows securities issuing companies to pay credit-rating agencies for ratings, indicating that markets can successfully constrain conflicts of interest.

Under Dodd-Frank, the Office of Credit Ratings was created, and Sarbanes-Oxley increases supervisory oversight by creating the Public Company Accounting Oversight Board (PCAOB) and by increasing resources for the SEC. The Act also makes the audit committee independent from management while the Global Settlement eliminates spinning. The $1.4 billion fine required by the Global Settlement and increased criminal penalties in Sarbanes-Oxley provide incentives for investment banks not to exploit conflicts of interest again. The required separation of functions in firms (research from underwriting, auditing from nonaudit consulting) and the socialization of research information may end up reducing information in financial markets.

Helpful Hints

1. Conflicts of interest are a particularly difficult issue to address because the conflicts themselves often arise from providing multiple services to multiple clients or a given client, yet the provision of these multiple services can increase efficiency due to economies of scope. The best solution to conflicts of interest is to employ the least intrusive solution necessary to resolve the conflict, thus retaining the greatest possible amount of efficiencies associated with economies of scope.

Terms and Definitions

Choose a definition for each key term.

Key Terms:

_____ conflicts of interest

_____ economies of scope

_____ initial public offerings (IPOs)

_____ management advisory services

_____ reputational rents

_____ spinning

Definitions:

1. Profits that a firm earns because it is trusted by the marketplace

2. A moral hazard problem that occurs when a person or institution has conflicts between multiple objectives or interests

3. A stock whose firm is issuing it for the first time

4. The allocation of profitable initial public offerings to executives of client companies by investment banks in order to gain their investment banking business

5. Advice on taxes, accounting or management information systems, and business strategies

6. The ability to use one resource to provide many different products and services

Problems and Short-Answer Questions

PRACTICE PROBLEMS

1. A number of financial services activities have potential for conflicts of interest.
    a. What are the two main conflicts of interest in investment banking? Explain.

    _____

    _____

    _____

    b. What event in the late 1990s increased the potential for conflicts of interest in universal banking? Explain.

    _____

    _____

    _____

    c. What are the conflicts of interest in universal banking? Explain.

    _____

    _____

    _____

    _____

    d. What is the downside when regulators force universal banks to separate these functions?

    _____

    _____

    _____

2. There are five remedies for addressing conflicts of interest. What are the advantages and disadvantages of each?

a. Leave it to the market

_____

_____

_____

_____

b. Regulate for transparency

_____

_____

_____

_____

c. Supervisory oversight

_____

_____

_____

_____

d. Separation of functions

_____

_____

_____

_____

e. Socialization of information production

_____

_____

_____

_____

SHORT-ANSWER QUESTIONS

1. How might a universal bank capture economies of scope in information production?

   _____

   _____

2. What conflicts of interest might arise in a universal bank when it utilizes information generated through economies of scope?

   _____

   _____

   _____

3. What general underlying conditions make conflicts of interest most likely to occur?

   _____

   _____

4. If an accounting firm offers both auditing and consulting services, why might the accounting firm make an overly favorable report on a client corporation?

   _____

   _____

   _____

5. Why would an investment bank engage in spinning?

   _____

   _____

6. Why might a credit-rating agency provide an overly favorable rating? Does the market limit this conflict of interest? Explain.

   _____

   _____

   _____

7. Can the market always eliminate conflicts of interest on its own? Explain.

_____

_____

_____

8. Are government remedies to conflicts of interest always an improvement over market solutions even if the market cannot eliminate the conflict on its own? Explain.

_____

_____

_____

9. What are the three main policy measures that deal with conflicts of interest since the year 2000? What general type of remedies do these policy measures promote?

_____

_____

_____

10. Referring to the question above, will all of the provisions in these three main policy measures increase information to the financial markets, thereby increasing efficiency? Explain.

_____

_____

_____

Critical Thinking

Suppose you have a friend who has just received a large payout from a trust fund. She must decide how to invest the funds. After talking with a number of brokers and financial advisors, she tells you, "I've decided to go with a very large conglomerate financial firm. It has different departments representing every area in the financial industry. My broker says that he usually suggests stocks and bonds underwritten by their own investment banking division because their in-house analysts know so much more about those corporations."

1. Are there conflicts of interest in underwriting, analysis, and brokerage services? Explain.

   _____

   _____

2. If financial firms such as this one were not regulated in any way, can you be certain that they would not exploit their conflicts of interest? Explain.

   _____

   _____

   _____

3. If financial firms such as this one were not regulated in any way, what might determine whether the financial firms choose to provide overly optimistic research on the firms for which they underwrite securities?

   _____

   _____

4. Why don't we just break up these financial companies into small pieces to avoid these conflicts of interest altogether?

   _____

   _____

   _____

Self-Test

TRUE/FALSE QUESTIONS

_____1. Financial services firms capture economies of scope by applying one information resource to the provision of many different services.

_____2. Conflicts of interest are most likely to occur in the financial services industry when financial firms specialize in the production of one service.

_____3. When a bank uses information developed about a firm's credit risk to help make a decision about making a loan, and then uses the same information to help that firm sell bonds, we have seen a demonstration of economies of scale.

_____4. When conflicts of interest cause an individual or firm in the financial industry to distort information to serve their own interests rather than the customer's interests, financial markets become less efficient at channeling funds to those with productive uses.

_____5. Due to its controversial nature, business schools are increasingly avoiding the discussion of ethical issues in business.

_____6. Investment banks have potential for conflicts of interest because they serve investors who want optimistic research about issuing corporations, and issuing corporations that want unbiased research.

_____7. When accounting firms offer both consulting advice and auditing, it is difficult for the auditors to criticize the advice given to the customer by the consulting side of the accounting firm.

_____8. Repeal of the Glass-Steagall Act in 1999 reduced the number of potential conflicts of interest faced by universal banks.

_____9. Even though firms pay to have their debt rated by credit-rating agencies and they clearly would like a favorable rating, credit-rating agencies usually don't provide overly favorable ratings because it would reduce the credibility of the credit-rating agency.

_____10. The market tends to value a security more highly if it received a "buy recommendation" from an analyst whose firm underwrote the security, because the analyst has access to superior information about the issuing corporation.

_____11. The market can often reduce the incentive to exploit conflicts of interest because reputation is very important to a financial services firm.

_____12. Regulations that eliminate the conflict of interest by separating a firm's functions, thus eliminating its economies of scope, may do more harm than good because it could actually reduce the flow of reliable information.

_____13. The least intrusive solution to conflicts of interest is to simply leave it to the market, but since the gathering of information is costly and since it will be undersupplied due to the free-rider problem, it is unlikely that the market alone can generate enough information to completely eliminate conflicts of interest.

_____14. The Sarbanes-Oxley Act of 2002 fined a number of investment banks a total of $1.4 billion dollars for past exploitation of conflicts of interest.

_____15. The Global Settlement of 2002 eliminated spinning.

MULTIPLE-CHOICE QUESTIONS

1. When an investment bank uses information it developed about a firm's credit risk to help market the firm's securities, and then its brokers use the same information to advise investors to whom it sells the securities, we have seen an example of an investment bank exploiting economies of
   a. scale.
   b. scope.
   c. finance.
   d. banking.

2. When a universal bank helps a weak firm sell debt so that the weak firm can repay its loans to the bank, we have seen an example of
   a. spinning.
   b. economies of scale.
   c. conflicts of interest.
   d. All of the above are correct.

3. A financial services firm captures economies of scope by
   a. growing very large so that the cost per unit of output falls.
   b. applying one information resource to the provision of many different services.
   c. allocating profitable initial public offerings to favored customers.
   d. None of the above is correct.

4. Which of the following statements about conflicts of interest is true?
   a. Conflicts of interest are a type of adverse selection problem.
   b. Due to recent legislation, conflicts of interest are no longer a problem.
   c. Firms always exploit their potential conflicts of interest.
   d. Conflicts of interest are most likely to occur when a firm provides multiple products or services.

5. Conflicts of interest make financial markets less efficient by
   a. reducing the quality of information to market participants and preventing financial markets from channeling funds to productive uses.
   b. causing firms to become smaller and thereby reducing their economies of scale.
   c. causing employees of financial firms to put their client's needs before their personal needs.
   d. All of the above are true.

6. As financial firms have increased the number of products they offer clients, there has been
   a. an increase in opportunities for unethical behavior.
   b. an increase in discussion of ethical issues in business schools.
   c. an increase in legislation dealing with conflicts of interest.
   d. All of the above are true.

7. Spinning occurs when
   a. a broker continuously buys and sells securities for a client in order to earn excessive sales commissions.
   b. when a bank helps a customer issue securities so that the customer can repay its debts to the bank.
   c. an investment bank allocates profitable initial public offerings to executives of a company to gain that firm's investment banking business
   d. an accounting firm provides a favorable audit for the financial news media in order to increase the firm's stock price.

8. Which of the following areas is *not* generally recognized to generate excessive conflicts of interest?
   a. commercial banking
   b. credit assessment and consulting in credit-rating agencies
   c. underwriting and research in investment banking
   d. auditing and consulting in accounting firms

9. Which of the following is *not* a reason why credit-rating agencies suffer from conflicts of interest?
   a. Firms pay to have their debt rated, and they want a favorable rating while investors want an impartial rating.
   b. Credit-rating agencies produce favorable ratings to attract consulting business to advise firms on the structure of their debt, while regulators want unbiased ratings.
   c. Credit-rating agencies own stock in the companies they rate, so they produce favorable ratings, while investors want honest ratings.
   d. Credit-rating agencies produce favorable ratings of companies they have advised so that they are not criticizing their own past advice, while regulators want unbiased ratings.

10. When an accounting firm provides auditing services and management advisory services, it feels pressure to provide favorable audits
    a. to avoid losing the client's consulting business.
    b. to avoid criticizing the accounting firm's past advice to the client.
    c. to retain the client's auditing business.
    d. All of the above are true.

11. The repeal of the Glass-Steagall Act in 1999 increased the conflicts of interest in
    a. accounting firms.
    b. universal banking.
    c. credit-rating firms.
    d. consulting firms.

12. Which of the following is an example of how markets limit the exploitation of conflicts of interest?
    a. "Buy" recommendations are of greater value if they come from an analyst from the same firm that underwrote the securities because the analyst has more information.
    b. Credit-ratings are more trusted if they come from a credit-rating agency that also consults with the firm it rated.
    c. Bonds underwritten by a separate affiliate of a bank are more highly valued than those underwritten by an underwriting department within the bank.
    d. All of the above are true.

13. A firm that provides commercial banking, investment banking, and insurance is known as a
    a. finance company.
    b. universal bank.
    c. global bank.
    d. conglomerate bank.

14. The main advantage of allowing the market to remedy conflicts of interest is that
    a. it tends to punish just the firms that exploit their conflicts of interest by reducing their profits.
    b. it can completely eliminate conflicts of interest.
    c. it does not suffer from the free-rider problem.
    d. All of the above are true.

15. Which of the following is *not* a policy measure that reduces conflicts of interest?
    a. Sarbanes-Oxley Act of 2002
    b. Global Legal Settlement of 2002
    c. The repeal of Glass-Steagall in 1999
    d. Dodd-Frank Bill of 2010

16. Which of the following is the least intrusive remedy for addressing conflicts of interest?
    a. require firms to provide information about their potential conflicts of interest
    b. separate the functions of a financial services business
    c. require regulatory supervision of businesses if transparency would reveal proprietary information
    d. let the market provide incentives to not exploit conflicts of interest

17. The main disadvantage of separating the functions of a financial firm in order to reduce conflicts of interest, such as separating commercial banking from investment banking, is that
    a. customers have to deal with two firms, or separate departments.
    b. economies of scope in information production are eliminated.
    c. economies of scale in information production are eliminated.
    d. financial firms will hide their conflicts of interest.

18. Which of the following is *not* a provision in Sarbanes-Oxley of 2002?
    a. imposition of a $1.4 billion fines on ten leading investment banks
    b. established the Public Company Accounting Oversight Board (PCAOB)
    c. requires corporation's CEO and CFO to certify that the firm's financial statements are accurate
    d. increased the SEC's budget to supervise securities markets

19. Which of the following statements about the Global Legal Settlement of 2002 is true?
    a. It requires investment banks to separate research and securities underwriting.
    b. It bans spinning.
    c. It requires investment banks to make their analyst's recommendations public.
    d. All of the above are true.

20. The Dodd-Frank Bill of 2010 created the _____ and prohibits _____.
    a. PCAOB; the auditing committee to be managers in the company
    b. Office of the Comptroller of the Currency; spinning
    c. Office of Credit Ratings at the SEC; compliance officers from involvement in credit ratings
    d. Management Advisory Board; reputational rents

Solutions

Terms and Definitions

_2_ conflicts of interest

_6_ economies of scope

_3_ initial public offerings (IPOs)

_5_ management advisory services

_1_ reputational rents

_4_ spinning

Practice Problems

1. a. Issuers of securities benefit from optimistic research about their firms while investors benefit from unbiased research. If underwriting revenues exceed brokerage commissions, investment banks may tend to produce overly favorable research about firms issuing securities. Underwriters may engage in spinning by allocating IPOs to executives of prospective underwriting clients.

    b. The repeal of the Glass-Steagall Act in 1999 re-established universal banking thus allowing firms to combine commercial banking, investment banking, and insurance. Provision of these services creates conflicts of interest.

    c. Underwriters benefit from aggressive sales of securities while the bank's customers and trust funds need impartial advice. The commercial banking side may pressure the underwriters to help weak firms issue debt in order to help the weak firm repay its loans to the bank. The underwriters may want the commercial banking department to make generous loans to a firm in order to gain its underwriting business. A bank might force loan customers to buy insurance.

    d. There are economies of scope in the provision of these services because departments can share the information that has been produced by the firm. Separating these functions reduces conflicts of interest, but it also reduces efficiency because of the lost economies of scope.

2. a. Advantages: market-based solutions use market forces to punish with pecuniary penalties just those firms that exploit their conflicts of interest, avoiding the regulatory overreaction that would punish all firms and reduce economies of scope. Disadvantages: it won't work if information is not available and if the public's memory is short. Information may be underproduced due to the free-rider problem.

    b. Advantages: it eliminates the free-rider problem in information production by requiring firms to report information on potential conflicts of interest. Disadvantages: it could reveal so much proprietary information that it makes the firm unprofitable; firms may avoid the reporting requirements; there is an additional free-rider problem of insufficient monitoring of the reporting; and costs of complying could exceed costs of the conflicts of interest.

    c. Advantages: in cases where transparency would harm a firm's profits, supervisors can observe proprietary information without revealing it. Standards of practice can be developed. Disadvantages: financial firms have incentives to hide their conflicts of interest, and supervisors have not always done their jobs well.

    d. Advantages: eliminates the source of the conflict of interest. Disadvantages: reduces efficiency by eliminating economies of scope in information production, which could reduce information production below the level associated with the original conflicts of interest.

    e. Advantages: causes production of untainted information when undersupplied by private firms. Disadvantages: few incentives and too few resources for the production of high quality information.

Short-Answer Questions

1. It could use information collected about the risk characteristics of a loan customer by its commercial loan department to help underwrite and market bonds for the same corporation from its investment banking division.

2. The underwriters want favorable research on the client corporation and aggressive sales pressure on the customers and trust accounts of the bank, while the bank's customers need unbiased information. The bank may market debt of a weak firm in order to help it repay loans to the bank and may give a corporation a generous loan to get its underwriting business.

3. Conflicts of interest occur when an institution provides multiple services to a given client or many clients.

4. To avoid losing the clients consulting business and auditing business and to avoid criticizing advice given to the client by the consulting division of the accounting firm.

5. To attract new underwriting business by allocating hot IPOs to executives of prospective clients.

6. The firm being rated pays for the rating, so high ratings attract credit-rating business, and high ratings attract consulting business. Yes, overly favorable ratings would reduce the credit-rating firm's credibility, reducing profits in the long run.

7. No. If the incentive to exploit the conflict of interest is great enough, those that would capture the firm's reputational rents will hide information from the market. Also, there is a free-rider problem in information production, and people in the market may suffer from a short memory of past exploitation of a conflict.

8. No. Some government solutions limit economies of scope, reducing information more than the conflict of information did, and thus reducing efficiency.

9. Sarbanes-Oxley Act, the Global Legal Settlement, both of 2002, and the Dodd-Frank Bill of 2010. They increase the flow of information, increase supervision, and separate functions of some financial institutions, all enforced by greater criminal penalties.

10. No. The separation of functions and the socialization of research may end up reducing information and the efficiency of financial markets.

Critical Thinking

1. Yes. Underwriters and analysts want optimistic research while investors want unbiased research.

2. No. The market punishes firms that exploit their conflicts of interest. The market ascribes less value to "buy recommendations" from analysts who are employed by the firm who underwrote the security.

3. It would depend on whether the revenue from underwriting exceeds the revenue from brokerage commissions.

4. Breaking up firms eliminates the efficiencies associated with economies of scope. Thus, firms would be unable to apply one information resource to the production of many different services.

True/False Questions

1. T
2. F
3. F
4. T
5. F
6. F
7. T
8. F
9. T
10. F
11. T
12. T
13. T
14. F
15. T

Multiple-Choice Questions

1. b
2. c
3. b
4. d
5. a

6. d
7. c
8. a
9. c
10. d
11. b
12. c
13. b
14. a
15. c
16. d
17. b
18. a
19. d
20. c